luxury fashion bran

luxury fashion branding

trends, tactics, techniques

Uche Okonkwo

First published 2007 by
PALGRAVE MACMILLAN
Houndmills, Basingstoke, Hampshire RG21 6XS and
175 Fifth Avenue, New York, N.Y. 10010
Companies and representatives throughout the world

PALGRAVE MACMILLAN is the global academic imprint of the Palgrave Macmillan division of St. Martin's Press, LLC and of Palgrave Macmillan Ltd. Macmillan® is a registered trademark in the United States, United Kingdom and other countries. Palgrave is a registered trademark in the European Union and other countries.

ISBN 978-1-349-35657-7   ISBN 978-0-230-59088-5 (eBook)
DOI 10.1057/9780230590885

A catalogue record for this book is available from the British Library.

A catalog record for this book is available from the Library of Congress

13   12   11   10   9   8   7   6   5   4
17   16   15   14   13   12   11   10   09   08

This book is for my mother Rhoda Ada Okonkwo, from whom I learnt that quality and substance are always better than quantity and size

Contents

List of tables and figures

Tables

Figures

Foreword

The luxury industry is relatively small in terms of the number of companies. The boundaries are hard to define, but consensus would probably indicate an 'industry' populated by no more than several hundred brands. However these businesses punch far above their weight, both in terms of sales – current estimates put the sale of luxury goods running at more than $100bn per annum – and perhaps more importantly, in terms of influence. This is the industry where you'll find the best design, the best materials, the best merchandizing and the best packaging, and hence luxury brands frequently lead the way for the rest of the world. In the process they drive both aspiration for the genuine article and the numerous mass-market imitators.

Whilst of course 'luxury' has changed little in an abstract sense, the word is now (mis)applied to all manner of products. The term 'masstige' has been coined to describe a place where 'mass' and 'prestige' meet and this democratization of luxury is probably the greatest change in the last decade. Almost all luxury brands now have products that start at low price points, whether it is a pair of socks from Polo Ralph Lauren, a Tiffany keyring, or even a 1-series BMW. This is both to secure aspirational sales and to lead customers into the high-ticket items.

The biggest challenge facing a luxury brand today is devising a strategy that can cope with the extremes of the modern luxury marketplace, with a product range that may extend from $20 socks to $20,000 couture pieces and which may be selling both to Shanghai secretaries and Park Avenue Princesses. This is where Uche Okonkwo's book comes in: a practical and essential resource for anyone involved in the business of selling luxury fashion. It will of course be useful well beyond the confines of the fashion industry: as we have learned over the years from our own subscriber base, there is an extraordinarily wide variety of individuals who watch the luxury fashion industry including those from all the other luxury sectors as well as advertising, design, public relations, management, finance, property, the academics and the wider business community. Every one of them will find something of value in this book.

I started *Luxury Briefing* just over a decade ago and it has been an exciting period for the industry. But during that time the 'landscape', especially in the world of luxury fashion, has become ever more complex. I have lost count of the number of times that we have been asked for guidance on all manner of aspects connected with luxury fashion so I am delighted that – at last – I have a resource to which I can refer people.

JAMES OGILVY
Publisher
Luxury Briefing

Author's note

I have a unique neutral position in not having a pedigree from any of the luxury key markets. This implies that my analysis in presentation of the luxury fashion sector is likely to be highly objective. Previous writers on the subject of fashion have often been accused of a biased point of view in favour of their countries or the brands that provide them with financial backing. So I hope these will be some of the criticisms I might escape. However, I apologise in advance if after reading this book, you feel that it has a French undertone. This is probably the effect of writing '*à côté de la Tour Eiffel!*'

The second advantage I can claim is that I live in Paris and writing this book from the fashion capital of the world provided me with access to major brands and a wealth of invaluable resources that I might not have found elsewhere. Also the central geographical positioning of Paris meant that I could easily access the rest of the fashion centres: Milan, London, New York, Florence and everywhere else that the business of fashion has resources.

The idea for this book came almost as an accident (every author probably says this to sound modest, even though they had been thinking about their books for ages, but believe me, it was truly an accident).

Towards the end of my MBA studies at Brunel University Business School, London, I chose to conduct the obligatory business management consultancy and dissertation project on the corporate strategy of the luxury fashion sector. The majority of my colleagues opted for 'serious' business sectors and topics relating to corporate finance, investment banking and global trade. While they had a field-day with abundant academic and practitioner research materials, I was shuttling between London, Paris and Milan and frantically emailing contacts all over the world, in search of the right people to interview to gain an insight into the management of luxury fashion brands. This was mainly because I couldn't find any reliable book that provided what I was looking for. There were numerous helpful published articles on different aspects of the fashion sector and a few texts (mostly in French), but although they were generally informative they lacked the in-depth business analysis I was looking for. At a point, practicality almost took over and I nearly changed my research area to a more accessible sector but my passion for fashion prodded me on. Finally, one day in Paris, while speaking to an executive of one of the largest luxury brands in the world (who by the way prefers to remain anonymous), I voiced my frustration and he entirely agreed with me but added, 'if you can't find the type of book you're looking for on the subject, why don't you write one? You surely have adequate expertise and experience to do this.' And so here we are!

The book you have in your hands is the result of more than two years of meticulous and extensive research and continuous practice in the luxury goods sector. The journey began at Brunel Business School, London, through to close collaboration with key luxury fashion brands, branding, marketing and strategy companies, specialists, institutions and consumers in France, Italy, the UK, the USA and several parts of Europe and Asia. It also includes constant consultation of highly insightful academic material from notable experts like Jean-Noel Kapferer, Kevin Keller, David Aaker, Rod McColl, Geraldine Cohen, Adrian Woods, Peter Doyle, Charles Dennis, Lisa Harris and Joseph Pine II.

The information provided in the following pages, including statistics, charts, web contents and company information were correct at the time of writing (November 2004 to August 2006). Also, the required translations from French and Italian were done by myself so I apologise in advance to anyone who feels my translations do not do him or her justice.

Writing this book was a challenge and a relish, similar to the creation of luxury products; and writing in Paris was an additional source of pleasure similar to the delight of shopping for luxury products. I hope that after reading this book you'll find it as enriching as luxury fashion goods. Only then would I have succeeded in my mission to bring some serious insight into the concept of luxury fashion.

UCHE OKONKWO

Acknowledgements

A few years ago, a professional contact granted me an enormous favour and when I asked how I could possibly repay him, he said, 'It's simple. Write a book and put down my name as the author!' If this formula works in business circles, then I owe all the people mentioned below 'books', if not in this lifetime, then maybe in the life to come.

First and foremost, I'm grateful to all the companies and brands that graciously granted me permission to reproduce their company images in this book. They are too numerous to mention individually but I am thankful for the confidence you had in me and in this text. A special thanks goes to the House of Worth for providing me with access to the archives of Charles Worth, the inventor of Haute Couture.

I am especially thankful to James Ogilvy, publisher of the foremost luxury industry journal, *Luxury Briefing*, for his special gift of a one-year subscription and also to Catherine McDonald-Kier for ensuring that it actually happened. Thanks James for fuelling my passion for fashion through your 'gold-mine' publication. I also thank Jean-Baptiste Danet, CEO of Interbrand, France, and Aaron Simpson, CEO of Quintessentially, two highly insightful business practitioners and great intellectuals, for sharing their knowledge and time with me. Thanks to James Lawson of Ledbury Research, London, for the meeting that practically opened the door to this project and to Stuart McKay of Ergo, London, for his insights. I'm also grateful to Philippe Schaus of Louis Vuitton, Paris for his time, insight and assistance; to Susie Rogers of Gucci London for being such a pleasant adviser; and to Alessandro Guarise of Gucci Milan for his support. My gratitude also goes to my academic mentors Adrian Woods, Geraldine Cohen and Steve Smith of Brunel Business School at Brunel University, London, and to Rod McColl and Michael Ward of Ecole Superieur de Commerce de Rennes, France, for their invaluable guidance and for believing in me and to Stephanie Morin for being so efficient.

I also received immeasurable support from people too numerous to mention including Denise Silber, CEO of Basil Strategies, Paris, from whom I constantly draw inspiration; Daniele de Winter, CEO of Daniele de Winter cosmetics, Monaco, for being a supporter from day one; Mark Tungate, author of *Fashion Brands, Branding Style from Armani to Zara* (buy his book, its great!); Brad Fox of Royal Elastics, California, for sharing my ideas; my 'sisters by choice' Mélinda Mercan, Vanessa Louis, Sophie-Ann Haberbusch, Véronique Dessout and Amalia Damesin; my 'second and third parents by choice' Jean-Guy and Colette Mercan and Alain and Bernadeatte Jougla. Thanks also to Alexandre Fabre and Jean-Laurent Louis of Adexen Paris for lending me your office so many times; to Neil for the illustration ideas and advice. And to talented fashion photographer, Sara White Wilson for making me presentable in the back-cover photo. Kisses to Jean-Pierre and Ambroise Evano, thank you for your enthusiasm and support. It made a big difference!

To Alexandra Dawe and the inspiring team at Palgrave Macmillan, this is saying 'Cheers' to all the hard work. Thanks for believing in this project and for taking a chance with me! I look forward to the future.

A big THANK YOU to my darling mother, to whom this book is dedicated and from whom I learnt all the fundamentals about fashion and business. And to my father and brothers and sisters for the incessant love and support especially my lovely sister Uju, my proof-reader (although she dozed off behind the scripts sometimes!) and ideas girl (if this book is boring, it's her fault!).

Finally but most importantly, I thank God, for giving me the foresight to begin writing this book and the energy to actually complete it.

UCHE OKONKWO

Introduction
Who said fashion is not serious business?

'The secret of successful fashion management is a complete blend of Creative Genius and Business Management acumen, skill and resourcefulness.'
Daniele de Winter, CEO, Daniele de Winter Cosmetics, Monaco

Anyone who thinks fashion is inconsequential and doesn't deserve serious attention must think again. Fashion is a strong force that has always played a significant role in the evolution of mankind's society. As far back as the Egyptian, Greek and Roman Empires, fashion was a key social element that reflected the society through apparel, accessories and cosmetics. Fashion also had an influence on decisions regarding politics, economy, education and art. In the ancient Roman Empire, the visual representation of fashion was so ingrained within the society that the ruling government decreed the models and colours of shoes worn by the members of each social class. Also during the early years of industrialization, wealthy Americans and Asians travelled to Europe to acquire luxury goods, boosting international trade and the expansion of the global economy. In addition, the Grand Nobles of the Renaissance period and the aristocrats of the past centuries all stamped their significance and contribution to society's evolution through fashion. The fashion tradition remains prevalent today, albeit in a modern way.

Luxury fashion played a prominent role in the social and economic order of previous centuries and continues to influence our modern societies, economies and governments. The global luxury fashion sector is estimated to be worth US$130 billion. The sector is one of the few industrial segments that have remained a constant world economy contributor with an annual growth rate of approximately 20 per cent. In addition, the industry has made noteworthy contributions to national economies. The luxury fashion sector is the fourth largest revenue generator in France; and one of the most prominent sectors in Italy, Spain, the USA and the emerging markets of China and India. The sector is currently one of the highest employers in France and Italy. In the USA, the fashion apparel industry is the fastest growing sector, while several Asian economies have witnessed a boom as a result of the entrance and expansion of luxury brands in the region. The clothing and accessories retail business is also among the fastest growing industries in several parts of the world. Fashion has become so influential in the current global economy and world affairs that the United Nations recently launched a program of fashion shows, called '*Catwalk the World*', as a platform for raising humanitarian aid. Fashion is now also directly linked with film, music, literature, arts, sports and lifestyle as never before. The contribution of fashion and its growing influence has also permeated into other aspects of the business sector as has never before been witnessed.

Despite the high influence of fashion in our society, its analysis from a business strategy viewpoint lacks consensus and structure. This is perhaps a result of the assumption that the intellectual analysis of fashion is an impossible challenge. Or because fashion creativity and business intellect have been viewed as two parallel lines with no meeting point. In luxury fashion, where there's a heavy emphasis on design and creativity, this perspective is more underlined. Well, the days of these assumptions are gone because, today, the business of fashion requires sophisticated management techniques in addition to a high level of creativity and innovation. The rapid development of the business strategy aspect of fashion management and its balancing act with the creative world are some of the factors that prompted the writing of this book on luxury branding.

The marketplace would be colourless without luxury brands. Luxury fashion brands are unique, intriguing and special. This is not a biased statement from someone who has an innate affinity for fashion branding. It is rather a statement of the fact that luxury fashion provides a means to a lifestyle that is triggered by deep psychological and emotional needs, which is expressed through ingenious products.

A respected writer and branding expert recently told me that he believes that luxury brands deceive customers by selling over-priced branded goods that are produced at a fraction of their price tags. I disagree with this view (excuse me, Mark). I subscribe to the apparent fact that luxury brands provide a complete package of significant benefits to consumers, the social environment and the global economy. When people purchase a luxury fashion item, they don't just buy the product but a complete parcel that comprises the product and a set of intangible benefits that appeal to the emotional, social and psychological levels of their being. It is quite challenging to find another sector apart from luxury goods, that can claim an emotional connection with their consumers to such an extent that the desire for a product increases as the price tag increases.

Our society thrives on fashion as a form of identity and expression and a source of progression. Fashion, especially luxury fashion, has seeped its way into the lives of consumers, whether they're wealthy or not. Luxury brands have affected the way consumers think, act and live, both directly and indirectly. Take a moment to reflect on this. When you make a choice of clothes, shoes or other products related to your appearance and grooming, you are making a statement choice based on how you want to appear to yourself and to others. These choices may comprise of what makes you comfortable or what provides you with a means to other forms of satisfaction like belonging to a specific social group. Your choices might be based on brands or not, but the underlying fact is that your choices are influenced by fashion. One thing is certain, and that is the undisputable reality that fashion has become a permanent part of our lives, including the lives of those that consciously decide to distance themselves from fashion in order to avoid falling into the 'victim' bracket.

So why write about luxury fashion branding?

The luxury fashion industry is a global multi-billion dollar sector comprising of a multitude of brands with high relevance. Among these are brands like Louis Vuitton, Hermès and Gucci. They are also among the most valuable and influential brands in the world. Despite the large size and income generation of the global luxury fashion industry, the sector has witnessed a slow growth in its strategic business direction. This is because for a long time luxury brands were managed through traditional business methods where decisions were made based on intuition and sometimes on a trial basis. These traditional methods also featured a strong focus on product development and publicity generation through conventional advertising methods. However, the rapid development and complexity of the global business environment currently requires modern and sophisticated business practices in luxury goods management.

In a bid to find a synergy between its origins in tradition and the requirements of modern business, the global luxury goods sector is currently undergoing an important evolution and several management shifts. These changes range from the use of business concepts such as brand equity and brand asset valuation, to e-business; and the development of consolidations and private equity financing. Also, several factors have contributed to the lowering of the sector's entry barrier, giving way to increased competition.

In addition to these, other aspects of the luxury market are also changing. These include the expansion of the luxury consumer market to include a broader mass market; competition from mass fashion brands; the reinterpretation of the luxury concept by the consumer society; the emergence of new luxury markets like China, Russia and India with new opportunities and outlook; and the increase in the number of the world's wealthy and changing attitudes in their spending patterns.

The different evolutionary stages of the luxury market in several parts of the world also create a challenge for luxury fashion brand management. For example, the European luxury scene is in its mature stage and consumers in this market approach luxury and fashion as concepts that can be adapted to their lifestyles. This contrasts with US consumers who view luxury as a means to a lifestyle because the US luxury market is still in its growth phase. In the Middle East, where luxury fashion is in its full-bloom growth phase, consumers acquire luxury goods to make a statement of their wealth and Western know-how. Japanese consumers also have a similar attitude to luxury fashion goods, albeit with a twist of affinity to specific French brands. In the rest of Asia, the luxury scene is in its introductory phase while in Africa the concept of luxury fashion is in its early introductory phase. Luxury brands face the challenge of finding a balance in the requirements of each of these markets through their products and service offerings and business strategies.

Changes in the luxury goods sector and the consumer market have also dispelled several old notions of luxury. The Internet has altered the way luxury products are accessed and contributes to the changing consumer psychology and perception of luxury. For example, the retail cliché that assumes that buyers buy and sellers sell, is no longer valid. Buyers now sell in addition to buying, through websites like ebay.com. Buyers can now also borrow luxury goods from several companies like bagborroworsteal.com and milaandeddie.com. These possibilities are creating new attitudes to luxury and more challenges to managing luxury brands.

Further changes in the luxury fashion industry include rapid market expansion and competition as a result of easier entry into the industry. Brands can now be launched and achieve global awareness and credibility within a short timeline of only five years. Also the increase in wealth and mobility of luxury consumers and the emergence of new luxury markets is fuelling the sector's expansion. This has led to a shift in the focus of the luxury market from 'products' to 'consumers' and the 'competition'. The rife competitive business environment calls for a strong concentration on developing cutting-edge strategies through relentless innovation. The time has come for new brands to act like old brands; for consumers to be reached through new media like Internet Shopping and Mobile Shopping; and for luxury brands to represent something substantial and valuable to customers through their brands' offerings.

The branding aspect of luxury goods management is integral to a luxury brand's sustainability. The brand is the reason that consumers associate themselves with a luxury company. It is what creates and sustains the attraction and desire for products. The strong attachment that luxury consumers have to brands, which often defies logic, is the result of branding. Brands are not products and should not be managed like products. Brands are a complete package that provides a source of identity for products. This identity becomes a springboard for the associations and perceptions eventually developed in the minds of consumers. This is what draws consumers to luxury brands and remains their source of satisfaction.

Although Brand Management is the most influential business aspect, the concept remains in its introductory phase in the luxury goods sector, despite the fact that the 'brand' is the core competence of the industry. Luxury fashion brands are yet to absorb the full implication of branding and its management systems. In most cases, the brand is managed through the view of product development and the brand portfolio is seen as the same as the product portfolio. The sequence is often to first develop products and then make branding decisions afterwards. This is a wrong approach. There's no easier way to say it. Branding decisions ought to be at the core of all the corporate decisions that a luxury brand makes, including product development.

The journey of branding begins from crafting a clear brand concept and brand identity and projecting it to the public through an equally clear brand personality and brand image. What the public sees and interprets through the brand image leads to a positioning of the brand in their minds through perceptions and associations. This further leads to the allocation of a space for that brand in their minds according to their sentiments towards the brand. This is called the brand share and influences future purchase decisions and subsequently brand loyalty.

The total branding concept (and not just the brand image) is the source of a luxury fashion brand's wealth. When the sum of all distinctive qualities of a brand results in the continuous demand and commitment to the brand by consumers, the brand is said to have high brand equity. The brand equity is what translates to brand value, which is the financial gain that a luxury company eventually accrues as a result of its brand strength. The brand equity ought to be painstakingly managed and nurtured to retain its value-creation ability. Brands are invaluable creators of wealth for companies and luxury brands that aim to attain competitive edge ought to be fanatic about their brand-strategy management. This is the most important tool the luxury fashion sector has.

Developing and effectively managing a luxury brand is a painstakingly long process. It requires a consistent integrated strategy, innovative techniques, rigorous management control and constant auditing. This is the reason that there are few existing brands that can claim true 'luxury' status. Although several brands aim towards attaining a 'luxury and prestige' rank and every talented designer aspires to creating their own luxury brand, only a few brands eventually succeed. The successful brands are those that understand the challenge of finding a balance between being timeless through a firm brand concept and heritage; being current and relevant for the moment through strong brand positioning; and being innovative in crafting a future, all at the same time.

The aim of this book is not to tell you what you already know about fashion branding and management, business strategy or the luxury goods market. It rather provides you with highly relevant analytical information about the luxury goods sector and, most importantly, a framework of business management techniques that can be applied to the sector and beyond. It also reviews strategies that can be used to interpret current and future market changes and ways that luxury brands can be alert to face competitive challenges. The information and business strategies presented in this book are the results of both sound research and confirmed practice. They are sources of new approaches towards the business of smartly bringing objects of desire into the marketplace.

Chapter 1
A question of luxury

'Luxury is a necessity that begins where necessity ends.'
Gabrielle Coco Chanel (1883–1971)

When you flip through the pages of a fashion magazine, what do you see? An array of luxury fashion advertisements, featuring colourful and alluring pictures of models displaying products that tease your eyes and sensitivity. When you switch on the television, you're constantly bombarded with celebrity news and reality shows that touch your natural human craving to feel beautiful, important and recognized. The gorgeous people in the magazines and on television unconsciously speak to you, telling you that their lifestyle and material possessions like their clothes and accessories can also make you beautiful and help you become a part of their world. All you need to do is to obtain the right fashion goods by the right designers. You then begin to crave the Gucci watch, the Louis Vuitton bag and the Chanel glasses, not to mention the Jimmy Choo shoes or the Bvlgari jewellery that beckon you every time you see a picture of a celebrity icon. Welcome to the luxury fashion land. You're not alone but a minute part of a world that constitutes of millions of people that have been hooked by the luxury fashion fever called brand loyalty. Don't worry, this is not a sickness and you're not a victim but it is a part of the definition of your personality and lifestyle. In this world, it is not easy to make an exit because it is quite challenging to be logical-thinking in the midst of luxury fashion goods.

When the fashion design icon Coco Chanel stated that 'luxury is a necessity that begins where necessity ends', she knew exactly what she was talking about. Also as far back as 1899, notable writer T.B. Veblen acknowledged in his celebrated text The Theory of the Leisure Class, that the consumption of luxury goods was a 'conspicuous waste'. The truth is that we don't need luxury goods to survive as human beings, but we need luxury goods to fuel the sensations that contribute to our overall appreciation of ourselves and our lives. It may sound uncanny but the appealing brand features that luxury fashion represents contribute to our general well-being.

Still in doubt? Then think about this. On a daily basis, we make most of life's decisions based on brands, beginning with the toothpaste we use in the morning to the cereal we have for breakfast, the car we drive, the phone we use, the restaurants we eat in and also the toilet paper we use. We make daily purchases based on the trust we have that the consistent promises of a brand will be delivered. Now take this trust for basic consumer goods to the higher level of luxury fashion and you'll find that you have even greater brand promises and more reinforcement that they will be delivered. This increases your level of trust. And when your expectations are met and exceeded, what do you think will be the result? Of course you'll be hooked. If you can place your trust in a toilet paper or detergent manufacturing company every time you spend two dollars on their product, then what level of trust do you think you'll have for a high fashion brand that contributes to shaping your lifestyle and defining your identity? It is likely to be enormous. And this is what luxury is all about.

Fashion is not only a matter of clothes and accessories but is also highly influential in structuring society's culture, identity and lifestyle. Luxury fashion even goes further to reinforce the evolution and voice of society. In this generation where image underlies every aspect of our lives, luxury brands have gained more prominence and are affecting the daily lives of both consumers and non-consumers on a greater level.

An intelligent, pragmatic and highly educated friend once told me that she would rather not wear sunglasses than wear ones that are not made by Gucci. She has been a loyal Gucci sunglasses devotee from the day she bought her first Gucci sunglasses many years ago. She also wears prescription glasses and the first time she went for her eyeglass fitting in London, the optician was out of stock of her desired Gucci frames. She didn't mind waiting for one month for the frames to arrive, in the meantime straining her eyes daily and risking her vision, such was her level of love and loyalty to Gucci. Of course she knew that she wouldn't become blind but she was ready to jeopardize her faltering vision for the love of a luxury brand. When I raised this point, she simply said that I might not understand the intense contentment she feels each time she wore her Gucci glasses. This emotional core that the Gucci brand touched in my friend is the impact luxury brands have on consumers on a daily basis all over the world. When a consumer wants a luxury brand, there is no substitute. Such is the mind-game that 'high branding' plays with consumers. Again, this is luxury.

So what is luxury fashion branding all about?

First, let's look at the concept of branding. Brands are powerful and symbolic elements that have the potential of influencing cultures, societies and generations. They play a daily role in our lives from the product decisions and choices we make to the people we choose to speak to or associate with. They are also wealth-creators and a source of a steady income stream for the companies that own them. These statements will become clearer as you read further.

The concept of branding has been in existence for hundreds of years. The origin of brands comes from the times when early cattle-rearing men stamped their ownership on their livestock by burning a mark of their name or identity on the cattle, to distinguish one cattle-farmer's stock from another's. Through this means of differentiation, the good quality cattle could be easily identified. This crude method has translated into the trademarks and logos of today, which forms a crucial part of the brand.

The current definition of a brand has however evolved from marks, names, logos and shapes to elaborate marketing development and strategies. The result is the creation of something powerful and consistent, which has the ability to produce emotional and psychological attachment with consumers and financial value for the brand owner.

A brand symbolizes a guarantee and credibility that assures the consumer that what they are about to purchase will deliver its promise. The instant recognition and definition of certain products is mainly as a result of the brand. However, a product is not a brand and neither is a service a brand nor a company a brand. If we were to go by the book definition of branding from the experts, we might summarize branding as the following:

> A brand is a name, term, sign, symbol, design or a combination of these that is intended to identify the product of a seller and to differentiate it from those of competitors. It is an identifiable entity of a company's total offerings that makes specific and consistent promises of value, which results in an overall experience for the consumer or anyone who comes in contact with the brand.

A product is a commodity that is made in a factory, which possesses attributes and features, making it tangible. A brand is the sum of all experiences and communications received by the consumer resulting in a distinctive image in their mind-set based on perceived functional and emotional benefits, which makes it intangible. This means that branding and all its associations reside in the mind of the consumer, therefore you and I (the consumers) are important players in the branding scenario. Products can be easily copied and become outdated, but brands are unique and timeless.

Branding has become very prominent in the last fifty years as a core aspect of marketing and business strategy. The concept has been stretched beyond the product or service application level to become one of the most important business categories. As a modern concept, branding can be applied to anything from products and services, to companies, countries and even individuals.

Every brand possesses the characteristics of identity, promise, value and differentiation. These are the features that create the relationship between the consumer and the brand. The fundamental benefit of a brand is value-creation both for the brand owner and the consumer. From the consumer perspective it is 'the promise and delivery of an experience', while from a business perspective it is 'a distinguishable piece of intellectual property and an intangible asset that secures future earnings.'

Having said this, let's now look at luxury goods and their interesting position in the whole branding set-up.

The luxury and prestige fashion goods sector utilizes fierce brand development strategies in its overall marketing strategy development, visibly in communications. Luxury brands recognize that the art of product design, innovation and aesthetic beauty can only be effectively portrayed through creating strong brands that appeal to the psychology of consumers. Branding is the lifeline of the luxury industry while design and creativity are its bedrocks. Without branding, there would be no luxury goods.

Luxury fashion brands strive for innovation, differentiation and appeal. This is because the fashion business is forward-thinking. Fashion always incorporates the past and the future and is hardly preoccupied with the present. It draws inspiration from the past in order to create the desire of the future. The present is only a temporary phase because if fashion is here today, it is already old-fashioned. This is where the role of branding is most prominent because it fuels the continuous desire of luxury products despite the constant changes of fashion.

Luxury brands set the fashion trends for every season during the fashion weeks held in Paris, Milan, New York, London and other prominent cities. In the past century, haute couture designers like Christian Dior and Valentino decreed the colour of every fashion season and the cut of every jacket through their designs. Presently, the scenario is gradually changing as a result of a wider choice and variety in brand and product offering fuelled by branding. However, luxury fashion designers are still considered like demi-gods in the fashion business. They tell the consumer public what to wear and not to wear, indirectly determining the tastes of the fashion society. If Marc Jacobs of Louis Vuitton showcases white as the colour of a fashion season; behold the world of fashion adopts white. If Karl Lagerfeld at Chanel decides that wedges should be the must-have accessories for a fashion season, then wedges it must be. If Jean-Paul Gaultier at Hermès rises in the morning and is suddenly inspired by a dream he had of an African safari trip, he can decide that zebra prints are the new season's fashion flag and so it will be. The consumer population awaits the judgements of these luxury fashion designers and the mass fashion brands take the dictation of these trends to the mass-production manufacturing factory.

But you may ask; who bestows the luxury fashion designers and their brands with such powers? How can we trust their opinions without question and how can the fashion population become like enthusiastic robots under their control? The answer is simple: luxury brands have the power of BRANDING! If you believe that brands like Dior or Gucci have the absolute prerogative to determine the appearance of the entire global fashion consumer population every season, then you've acceded to the absolutely powerful and commanding brand strengths of luxury brands.

Now, take a look at the following brand logos:

LOUIS VUITTON   PAUL & JOE®

                    BURBERRY

H&M   GIVENCHY   Dior

The brand symbols shown are a mixture of luxury and prestige, premium and mass fashion brands. When you looked at each of the logos, something happened in your mind. You had a thought about every one of the brands, no matter how fleeting. Now take another look at the logos, this time a little bit longer. What connotations do you have from your perceptions of each of the brands? If you make a note of them, you'll discover from your list that you already have an idea of their brand attributes, brand strengths and their level of influence. You can gauge the brands that are likely to have a high brand asset value, even without looking at their financial figures. If this is the case, then you already know exactly what I'm talking about!

We as consumers expect luxury brands to be innovative in designing products and in creating trends. We don't expect them to wait around to understand what we want before creating them. We desire for them to understand our psychology, changing tastes and way of thinking before even we do! We expect them to be ahead of the game. We want them to analyse the current trends, evaluate what needs to be changed, and to innovate and produce desirable products that will appeal to us. And this is what true luxury brands do. However, the magical offerings of luxury brands is reinforced through branding.

Luxury brands didn't happen by accident. There is no such thing. They have been uniquely crafted through consistent and diligent strategies in branding, marketing strategy. They enjoy a specific position in the global consumer world and branding spectrum as well as in the consumer's subconscious.

The core characteristics of luxury brands are: *brand strength, differentiation, exclusivity, innovation, product craftsmanship and precision, premium pricing and high-quality*. It is the *differentiated* quality of the materials, design and performance of a wristwatch from Chanel that separates it from a basic functional watch sold at a supermarket. As a result, Chanel can charge a premium price of $3,000 and the supermarket $30. It is also as a result of the foresight and innovation characteristics of Louis Vuitton that the brand introduced the canvas in the nineteenth century. It is the *craftsmanship* and *precision* qualities that result in an eighteen-hour manufacturing process of one Hermès Kelly bag by a single workman, from start to finish. It is the *high-quality* feature that has resulted in the high cost of the Hermès Birkin bag, which is equivalent to two first-class tickets from Paris to New York. It is the *strong brand image* of Gucci that results in several of the brand's products being back-ordered for up to two years. The end result of all these characteristics is of course the creation of brand value, which translates into billions of dollars in revenues and an indispensable intangible asset for the companies. The brand value is also related to consumers, who attain an immeasurable level of satisfaction from luxury fashion products.

The following chapters explore the deep and intriguing subject of branding and other business aspects related to luxury fashion goods. This is what this book is all about.

Chapter 2
What's in a name? The history of luxury fashion branding

> 'What is in a name? That which we call a rose, by any other name would smell as sweet.'
>
> William Shakespeare, English playwright (1564–1616)

In the quote above, legendary English playwright William Shakespeare raised an age-old question, 'What is in a name?' In the luxury fashion branding scene, the 'name', in other words the 'brand name', is everything. This is because it is the 'brand name' and the 'brand logo' that attracts consumers to a brand and launches the often enduring relationship between them and their chosen luxury brand.

Shakespeare indicated that if a rose were to be known by another name, it would still smell as sweet. Does the same principle apply to the luxury fashion sector? Would brands like Louis Vuitton and Giorgio Armani have the same associative elements and success if the names of their founders were different? The answers to these questions will become clear as we take a trip down the history lane to the origins of branding and the evolution of the global luxury fashion sector.

Branding evolution

The notion of branding as part of ancient trading can be traced to the Greek and Roman empires, before the modern industrial revolution. During this period, market awareness was created through carving out shop route signs and product descriptions, in stone along footpaths. This method progressed on to the early sixteenth century when whisky distillers began to ship their products in wooden barrels with the name of the producer burned into them. The sole purpose of this method was to differentiate the maker of each type of whisky from his competitors and to aid consumers in identifying the original products from cheaper substitutes.

Branding can also be traced back to pre-historic times when cattle-rearing men imprinted their names or a distinctive mark on their livestock to differentiate one farmer's livestock from the others. This system was also used to separate the good quality cattle from the low quality ones, and helped consumers to make better purchasing decisions by associating certain attributes to certain cattle farmers.

These elementary methods indicate that early traders understood the underlying principles of branding even without exposure to sophisticated business techniques.

The development of branding was further enhanced by the industrial revolution, urbanization, improvements in transportation and the social infrastructure, beginning from the late eighteenth century. This period brought about the introduction of city signs on products as a form of brand symbol. The method was adopted to indicate the origin of products, which often had certain 'associations' and 'perceptions' among consumers. Certain product manufacturers such as Twining of England introduced branded products as early as 1706. It was also in this century that Schweppes introduced its branded drinks in 1798. Branding methods, however, became more prominent towards the end of the industrial revolution in the latter part of the nineteenth century.

Branding, as we know it today, has advanced from crude methods of differentiation to a refined and indispensable business concept for any enterprise that desires long-term benefits. It plays a key role as the most important intangible asset generator for an organization. The luxury fashion sector in particular recognizes the crucial role of branding and therefore applies branding as a core competence and central factor of all business strategies.

Origins of luxury fashion

The history of luxury fashion is similar to that of branding in terms of development from ancient to modern times. Fashion's history has, however, been written about extensively by those more qualified than myself to do so; therefore its repetition is not the purpose of this chapter. However, there are key periods, events and circumstances that led to the evolution of modern luxury branding, which are worth recounting. For example, events following the industrial revolution brought about mass production techniques and led the way for the current prêt-a-porter fashion. Also, the dissolution of the world's monarchies, aristocracy and social class systems brought a change in luxury fashion, notably after the First World War. These factors show an important link between fashion and mankind's history and social evolution.

Fashion is a symbol of society and has continuously been influenced by historical, social, traditional, religious, political, economic, psychological and more recently technological changes. The luxury industry has also witnessed these aspects of evolution and like fine sculpture, the old luxury brands have become modified and enhanced with age; and the new brands have become highly appealing with the aid of effective modern techniques. Several of today's largest and most valuable luxury brands like Louis Vuitton, Guerlain and Gucci originated in France and Italy in the nineteenth and early twentieth centuries and therefore have a long history. These brands and their countries of origin have played a key role in the development of the global fashion industry. The twentieth century also produced several American brands like Ralph Lauren and Donna Karan; as well as Far Eastern brands like Yoji Yamamoto and Issey Miyake. In addition, other respectable global luxury brands such as Burberry of Britain have a strong historical legacy surrounding their creation.

A look at the very beginnings of luxury fashion will provide some direction to the analysis and understanding of the current luxury fashion scene.

Early civilization fashion (3200 BC to 80 BC)

The concept of beauty and its association with human beings can be traced to the Christian Bible, when Eve, the first woman created by God according to Christian beliefs, placed a flower over her ear to make herself more beautiful and attractive to Adam, the first man. The Bible also provides other historical accounts of the lavish consumption of luxury materials like gold, silver and myrrh during the times of King David, King Solomon and the Queen of Sheba, particularly between 1010 BC and beyond 100 BC. These give evidence of the early appreciation of the notion of luxury and beauty by man.

However, the concept of luxury and its association to appearance, beauty and fashion evidently became prominent during the ancient Egyptian civilization of this period. Early Egyptian art reveals the intricate detailing and prominence of clothes and accessories such as headgears, crowns and jewellery, made of fine materials like gold. Also, the Pharaoh exemplified luxury dressing and opulence through his total control of all aspects of society, including appearance. His perception as both a leader and a representation of God heightened fashion opulence in this era as his subjects related to his appearance. The royal Pharaohs dressed flamboyantly and engaged the services of the best artistes, jewellers, craftsmen and designers to fabricate their wardrobe. The finest materials were used to produce their fashion goods, including footwear, which were often made of pure gold.

In this society, tradition and religion were deep-seated and clothing and appearance played a key role during religious and social ceremonies. Also the Egyptian belief in life after death and the elaborate rituals that were performed during burial ceremonies of dead nobles (involving dressing and mummifying them), reinforced the role of luxury in clothing and beautifying corpses. For these ceremonies, the best and most talented designers and craftsmen were used.

The visual representation of fashion was a key aspect of early Egyptian society, and men and women both wore jewellery, and made-to-measure attires, mostly in linen. The colours and styles of jewellery were specifically selected to complement each type of clothing similar to the fashion pairings of today. Personal hygiene was also important in this society shown through a highly developed cosmetics sector. Men and women used make-up, notably on their eyes. Their product assortments also included pomades and moisturizers with ingredients ranging from honey, salt and milk. Perfumes and oils were used on skin and local tree formulas for tooth hygiene. The women also used strict beauty procedures and treatments like massages to stay slim and fresh. It can be concluded that members of this society were almost obsessed with perfecting their bodies, and may be compared to the fitness and well-being consciousness of our current society.

Evidence of this society's important attachment to luxury, beauty and fashion can also be seen in the paintings of the period, which clearly showed the social class system that ruled the society and the material opulence that was associated with the upper social class. Naturally, the luxuries of the day were reserved for members of the royal families and the upper social class and an individual's style of dressing indicated their position in society. Also, the house designs and tombs and pyramids constructed during this era reflected the society's social status consciousness. Several discoveries have ascertained the high level of luxury consumption in this era, including a recent discovery, a shirt made of luxury linen around 1360 BC, which was displayed at the Victoria & Albert Museum, London, in early 2006.

The ancient Egyptians can be considered purveyors of the current global taste in luxury fashion goods. The elaborate designs and luxurious style of ancient Egyptian fashion has been a source of inspiration for several luxury fashion designers of today, including Salvatore Ferragamo and John Galliano, in addition to the numerous Hollywood movies that have been produced to recapture this period. Although no evidence of this exists, it can be imagined that the talented craftsmen and designers of the day had distinctive styles, or what are currently known as 'signatures', which differentiated their work and possibly brand names.

From Egypt to Crete and Greece (700 BC to 1150 BC)

The Cretan period also known as the Bronze Age was the first real period of European civilization and the fore era that influenced European fashion and lifestyle. Crete was the centre of bronze and ceramics production and exports and its structured system and emphasis on development ultimately influenced the fashion of the time. As time progressed and the society developed, fashion also developed. Researchers have found indications of permissive half-male nudity, where people working in production sites could wear only shorts. For the women, who played traditional home-making roles, the story was a bit different. They showed their beauty through displaying elaborate belts on very slim waists that were acquired as a result of girdles worn around the waist from childhood. This can be related to the modern day fashionistas who sometimes starve themselves of food and undergo other forms of pain to appear thin and fashionable.

The Cretan era led to the early Greek civilization of the 4th and 5th centuries BC, whose society showed more attachment to luxury fashion. This period also witnessed the progress of politics, history, philosophy, maths, science, geometry and medicine. Its fashion representation was therefore a reflection of intellectual judgement and an indication of an individual's level of education and upbringing. It was also in this era that men and women's fashion gradually became separated. Women's dressing became feminine and elegant through style and fabric choice, while men's fashion became more structured and masculine. The luxury dimension of fashion was shown through the heavy use of jewellery to indicate the wealth of the wearer.

Appearance and grooming were important aspects of this society and the beauty sector was also well-developed. As early as the 4th century BC, make-up and cosmetics ranging from eye colours to foundation and lipstick were widely used by women. Also, make-up application techniques like the circular fingertips movement on the face, used by today's dermatologists, were introduced in this period. Moisturizers made from local ingredients were also used by day and masks were applied by night. Perfumes were also fabricated using the best scents and oils such as violet and myrrh. Each type of fragrance had a symbolic representation and was only applied to the appropriate and specific part of the body. Also, there was a special method for body-hair removal and hairstyles, especially for women, were also given great attention. Both men and women used massages and other therapeutic means for well-being and the men also exercised to stay in shape. These examples show that the society appreciated luxury living and beauty.

The Etruscan and Roman fashion influence (800 BC to AD 476)

The Etruscan Empire found in today's Tuscany region of Italy existed between Venice and Po and also included the present Rome. This empire was, however, eventually conquered by the Roman Empire.

This society was unique and maintained an independence from Greek and Asian cultural influences in its political, government and social development. The empire was rich in gold and its society portrayed luxury and beauty through the use of gold. Etruscan aristocratic women flaunted their status with heavy jewellery and somewhat introduced the modern bling-bling fashion style currently prominent in the United States. Make-up and cosmetics also played a key role in the fashion of this period.

The Roman Empire whose beginning has been traced to 1500 BC also played a key role in elevating fashion and incorporating it within the culture of society. The empire's high impact on world politics and trade led to the internationalization of fashion. This era is also considered as the true birth of the Italian fashion style.

Appearance was an important part of Roman culture and people went to great lengths to look good. Fashion was so much ingrained within this society that the ruling government decreed the models and colour of shoes of each social class because shoes represented a mark of distinction. This factor contributed to the influence of talented designers and shoe craftsmen who were sought after by the rich aristocrats and royal family members. The Italian shoe manufacturing industry which became prominent during this period continues to exist and is considered the most superior in the world.

Roman society also paved the way for several innovations in luxury fashion, still practised today. Notable among them are the following:

1 The concept of elevated fashion was introduced by the members of the royal family through elaborate dressing made with rare materials.
2 Seasonal fashion was invented to cater both for the changing weather conditions and the changing tastes of the fashion-conscious society.
3 Women's fashion was prominently separated from men's fashion, through the materials and colours used in the design and manufacture of clothes.
4 The legendary private thermal baths and saunas were invented as well as the rich ingredients that were used to nourish the body and improve the mind. This concept was also exported to the town of Bath in England, where the Roman Empire members owned private baths.
5 Exercise and balloon balls were invented to enhance appearance.

Cosmetics and grooming products were also important in Roman society and were directly linked to well-being. Although women's freedom and privileges were limited to attending to the needs of their husbands and children, they also played a key role in defining the style of the day through their clothes, make-up and jewellery.

The fashion sense of the Roman Empire was greatly influenced by British, German and Hispanic styles, the first signs of international influences in fashion.

From Rome to the Byzantine Empire and the Middle-Ages (AD~ 450~1500)

The Byzantine Empire, located between Europe and Asia, existed between the 5th and 12th centuries AD. The capital of Byzantine, Constantinople, was considered the richest and largest centre of commerce and fashion of the period which contributed to its influential role in the development of culture, fashion and history. The era witnessed an even higher level of taste and demand for luxury goods than the Roman Empire.

Emperor Justin I and his wife, Theodora, had a refined taste in luxury goods and can be considered as the precursors of the demand for celebrity-style high fashion goods. They emphasized the important role of clothes and appearance as a mark of distinction. Their enhanced taste for luxury and opulence was displayed through their dress style and the lavish nature of the several ceremonies they organized. Empress Theodora was exceptionally stylish and was the first woman to exploit fashion as a source of power. She had an impeccable style and a penchant for clothes made of the most expensive materials such as brocade and silk and adorned with embroideries made of gold and pearls. Her jewellery was also made by the best craftsmen using the rarest and finest gems.

Unlike during the Roman Empire, the Byzantine Emperor and Empress gave each individual the freedom to choose what to wear. This led to women imitating the dress patterns of Empress Theodora with cheaper materials. Dressing and appearance, however, continued to be used as an indicator of wealth and status. Since women's and men's clothes were made with similar materials such as silk and damask, individual style played an important role in differentiation and this encouraged women to be imaginative. Jewellery was also an important accessory and there are also indications of the use of toiletries for grooming in this era.

The Middle Ages between the 5th and 7th centuries, on the other hand, was not an influential period in the development of fashion. Although the fashion of the early period of this era was somewhat influenced by the Byzantine period, the style adopted was mostly hideous. The jewellery, for example, compared to the Byzantine period was pale. The events of the Middle Ages were focused more on the development of national monarchies and political systems than on fashion and society. Furthermore several conflicts between nations, notably between England and France, also distracted the society. This period witnessed the emergence of universities, the construction of cathedrals and churches and the formation of modern Europe which were viewed as sources of national pride.

As the European empires became more established, the distinctive dress styles of the national monarchies also emerged, leading to the creation of national fashion. Other notable developments of this era include the following:

1 England became known for its growing textiles industry.
2 The influence of professional tailoring in France soared to such an extent that by 1300, there were 700 active tailors in Paris.
3 Luxury materials such as silk were heavily imported from Asia whose textile industry was considered to be more advanced than Europe's.
4 The rise of the Italian influence in international fashion became more visible.

Although the fashion industry expanded in this era, the development of fashion style and sophistication remained static. For example, there was no distinction between summer and winter fashion unlike in the Roman Empire. Also men and women wore similar long and floating clothing, covering the whole body, all year round, until the fourteenth century. The social class, however, continued to determine the choice of materials for dressing.

On the other hand, better and meticulous personal hygiene emerged and more attention was paid to personal grooming. Sophisticated toilet and bathroom systems were built and the adoption of the bathing tradition of the Roman era was widespread. Public baths became available in most parts of Europe almost round the clock. The use of cosmetics and make-up also became important especially for women who had a strict code of honour but at the same time were expected to look beautiful for men's admiration. The English invented eye shadow in the 13th century and with it the fad for make-up. The mirror also emerged as an important accessory for both men and women.

National differences and attitudes to beauty and fashion were also visible during this period. For example, the Spanish use of red lipstick, the purple make-up preference of Germans, the adoption of white by the English, and the use of natural colours by Italians were all defined during this period.

The Renaissance, Italy and fashion (15th and 16th centuries)

The explosion of the Renaissance period changed the face of fashion and art forever. This was a period of cultural development in the whole of continental Europe. It was also an era of exchanges, inventions, discovery, communication and travel between the East and the West. The Asian world was discovered by the Portuguese during this period and Christopher Columbus also discovered America in 1492. There were also other discoveries notably in medicine as well as cultural progression.

The Renaissance also witnessed the rise of great Italian artists such as Leonardo Da Vinci and Sandro Botticelli and the birth of literature in Italy, France, Spain and England which influenced society's outlook on the arts and fashion.

Fashion was, therefore, an integral aspect of this era. Clothes and accessories were given an important role in the society as an indicator of social class and knowledge. As a result clothes became an investment. In England even tombstones bore the descriptions of the dressing of the deceased. Other European countries such as Germany and Spain also emerged as important influencers of fashion. For example, between the 16th and 17th centuries, the fashion trend called 'slashing' which featured cutting slits in garments through which linings were pulled, emerged in Germany and was adopted all over Europe, although it was later banned in France. Other styles like shoulder pads were also invented in this period.

However, the biggest influencers of fashion and culture in this era were the Italians. Italy's re-emergence as a strong force in fashion after the Roman Empire was heightened by the county's riches, particularly in Rome, Florence and Venice. Florence became a major centre of jewellery production and trade in this era. Also, Italy's textile industry which produced the best silk in Europe grew significantly and contributed to the development of the continent's fashion and lifestyle authority. In addition, the Italian government reinvested in fashion and culture using the revenues from textile mills to fund numerous projects.

This Renaissance period also witnessed the emergence of the Grande Aristocratic families who highly influenced fashion and society and can be likened to the celebrities of today. Notable of these are the Italian Gonzague de Montoue and Medici families who lived in splendour and majestic habits to the marvel of the society. The citizens emulated their fashion style and lifestyles in the same manner that the current consumer society follows the lifestyles of celebrities.

All over Europe, luxury and art were being fused and the notion of beauty became an obsession. Women were ready to do anything to be beautiful and their influence in both fashion and society began to develop. The demand for beauty was so high that as early as 1582, a beauty book was written by Jean Liebaut, a Parisian doctor, titled *L'Embellissement et Ornement de Corps Humaine* (The Improvement and Beautification of the Human Body). Also, high-society women had exclusive clubs where new fashion and beauty products were previewed. This can be likened to the current Trunk Shows and Pre-collection Shows organized by luxury brands like Fendi and Burberry.

Seventeenth-century baroque fashion

The Renaissance period was the age of Italian influence, while the Baroque era which existed between 1600 and 1750 was the century of France. This period witnessed the prominence of France and the French lifestyle in Europe and the rest of the world. The high influence was made possible by the King of France, Louis XIV, who is often referred to as, 'Le Roi Soleil' (The Sun King) or 'Louis Le Grand' (Louis the Great). He was an exceptional ruler who reigned for 72 years and had enormous political, economic and cultural strength that enabled him to position France as a major force of global politics, economy, lifestyle and fashion. He portrayed a sophisticated and refined taste, lifestyle and product choices, ranging from fashion, food, art, theatre and literature. The reign of Louis XIV from 1661 marked the return of opulence and exuberance and his tastes in luxury influenced the royal families and aristocrats of the entire continent.

Although the century began with a high influence of the exuberant tastes of the Italians and Spanish fashion evident from the magnificent opera houses and churches built in this period, the French fashion style fully emerged around the middle of the century.

Louis XIV loved fashion and luxury living and consequently supported the fashion industry through government reforms that provided incentives and financial aid to designers, artisans and craftsmen. As far back as 1665, he introduced policies to increase export of French fashion goods and reduce imports of foreign fashion goods. France therefore emerged as the biggest supplier of luxury fashion goods in the world. Louis XIV also ensured that France had a well-established textile industry, which generated wealth and influenced the culture of the nation and beyond.

In addition, French magazines and newspapers distributed all over Europe increased the influence of France in fashion. Paris' Rue Saint Honoré became established as the treasure land for renowned tailors such as Monsieur Regnault and Monsieur Gautier; similar to London's Savile Row of the 1960s and Jermyn Street of today. Talented women couturiers like Madame Villeneuve and Madame Charpentier also emerged and competed with the male tailors. Although the role of women in the general society remained minimal, the emergence of 'Les salons reunions des grands maison privees' (The meeting rooms of the grand private residences) increased the influence of women in lifestyle. Noblemen of the society were known to make secret visits for advice and opinion exchanges.

As lifestyle and education became linked with fashion and sophistication in France, the country became a reference point for stylishness. This gave way to the birth of the French 'Art e Vivre' and 'Savoir Faire', especially with inventions like the use of the fork and knife and the formal dance. Consequently, throughout Europe, high society either spoke French or had a French undertone. However, several religious frictions in Europe, mainly between the Protestant north and the Catholic south and the 30-year war between 1618 and 1648 stunted the growth of the French fashion influence for a short time.

The societal structure of the Baroque period also gave way to the detachment of clothing from the social class although this was a gradual process that would take centuries to manifest. Members of the middle social class began dressing similarly to the upper class as a result of increased apparel production no longer restricted to made-to-measure. Clothes also lost their stiffness and more emphasis was placed on comfort, movement and fluidity. The unexpected social liberty also materialized in the design of women's clothes through the emergence of the cleavage and clothes cut close to the body. It also brought about the introduction of the nightgown around 1670 and the skirt in 1680.

Simple, elegant and highly expensive jewellery such as diamonds and pearls were in high demand especially with Paris as a prominent supplier.

Pearls were heavily used by women all over the body to advertise their sophisticated tastes and status. The handbag also emerged as an important accessory preceded by the perfume bag. Perfumes and fragrance were also prominent in this period, especially for men who used it to conceal their bad odour as a result of lack of bathing as they paid less attention to personal grooming.

The eighteenth century, France and luxury fashion

The eighteenth century was a century of contrasts in wealth and status. The prominence of France as the centre of style, civilization, education, intellect, arts and culture continued to rise during this century. By the end of Louis XIV's reign in 1715, the supremacy of France in fashion and lifestyle was unarguable. The rise of France led to the fading of Italy's influence in fashion especially as Italian fashion became less unified and more regional.

Louis XIV established himself as the arbiter of fashion and also propelled the Palace of Versailles, where he lived, as a centre that dictated fashion and lifestyle all over Europe and beyond. The Versailles courts were known for their splendour, opulence and luxury tastes shown through the dress styles and fabrics made of very expensive material. Everyone who wanted to be recognized followed and adopted the style that emanated from Versailles. Versailles Palace fashion led to *haute mode* high-society fashion, which dictated the tastes of society. Dressing emerged as one of the most sensitive aspects of society and fashion became a unifying factor and a source of respect.

Although national styles already existed in this century, the authority of French fashion in defining global tastes was so high that the dress style adopted all over Europe, including the royal courts, was the French style. From Germany to Spain, Portugal, Scandinavia and even Russia, there was a French undertone in fashion, lifestyle and appearance. The influence of the French lifestyle on Germany was so high that under the rule of King Frederick I, a total French taste was mandated in everything from furniture to dressing. Anyone who wanted to be seen as cultivated, well-educated and well-groomed adopted the French taste and style. There was a universal acceptance that only France possessed the secrets of sophistication and charm. Even England, which had a long history of political and colonial rivalry with France and which had a preference for simple clothing, acknowledged the elegance and sophistication of French fashion.

By 1760, French standards of taste, fashion and life known as the *art de vivre* had been universally adopted, characterized by wit, elegance, style, civilized manners and relationships and cultivated tastes in politics, society and intellect. The French language also became the European *lingua franca* of the educated elite, replacing Latin. The French courts, which were main centres of discussions, were established and became hubs where intelligent people, opinion-seekers and the fashionable were found.

Paris became the centre of fashion and Rue Saint Honoré continued to reign as the Mecca for the supply of textiles to the fashion industry including French silk made in Lyon, which were the most highly priced textiles in the world. Parisian fashion stores were highly reputed for their tantalizing fashion goods notably at Palais Royal. A Russian visitor in awe of the luxury goods found in Paris commented that 'all the riches of the world are displayed to the astonished eye ... all the inventions of luxury to the embellished eye' (Ribeiro, 2002, *Dress in Eighteenth Century Europe*, 52). This status of Paris in luxury fashion was, however, boosted by the high demand for luxury goods especially by Europe's aristocrats and royal family members.

Fashion in this century continued to grow with the invention of prominent fashion magazines from the 1770s in France, England and Germany. The magazines provided a basis for the emergence of English tailors who first began their craft through adopting the French featured style. They later developed a highly stylish and original English men's fashion sector. A case in point is the men's coat, which was the focal point of men's fashion of the period. Particular attention was paid to the choice of fabric, trimmings, braiding and embroidery lace. Men's hats were also invented together with hat cocking during this period. The retailing of clothing in London also grew significantly in this century, especially at Covent Garden, the Royal Exchange and Oxford Street.

The eighteenth century also brought about fashion role models or what might be known today as fashion icons or 'fashionistas'. These women, who were mostly French, wielded high power and influence in European society and were emulated by most Parisians. Since the rest of the world copied Parisian women, everyone in the world indirectly copied these fashion role models. Notable among them was Madame Pompadour who promoted elegance and classic style and Marie-Antoinette who was the fashion icon of the day. They changed clothes and accessories frequently and caused several women to almost go bankrupt in the process of imitating their style. The influence of Marie-Antoinette was so high that when she became pregnant, women wore skirts stuffed with pillows to mimic the look of pregnancy.

One of the first prominent fashion merchants and designers, Rose Bertin, also emerged in this century. Born in 1747, she rose to prominence as the couturier and supplier of the best fashion to the aristocrats and royal family members of France and beyond. She is perhaps the first luxury fashion designer to own shops beyond her country's shores, with the opening of her London store in the 1780s. At the height of her fame, even royal family members felt honoured to be on her client list including the Grand Duchess of Russia who travelled to Paris to purchase her dresses. Although her fame in Paris diminished during the years of the revolution, her London store sustained her business until its eventual closure.

While the high influence of France in dictating fashion and lifestyle continued well into the next century, the political disturbances the country faced during and after the French revolution years (1788–90) had an impact on both French fashion and the world. However, France was yet again to restore its fashion leadership position in the following centuries, and further reinforce the position of Paris as the undisputable fashion capital of the world.

The nineteenth century and modern luxury fashion

The nineteenth century marked the beginning of the modern luxury goods sector and the launch of many of the highly valuable luxury brands that we know today. The rapid development of the fashion industry during this period was made possible by the bolstering of social and economic conditions and rising prosperity. The demand for luxury goods remained high and extremely talented and entrepreneurial designers emerged and grasped business opportunities made possible by their predecessors.

In following with the tradition of the previous historical periods, outward appearance remained an indicator of wealth and social status. In addition, fashion became more than a vocation for knowledgeable people, and was recognized as an important contributor of economic growth. The French and most of continental Europe saw fashion as an intricate part of their societies and a necessary subject of discussion alongside literature, arts and history among intellectuals. The French government reinforced its support for the textile and fashion sectors through creating incentives and favourable policies. In England, however, fashion and luxury were perceived as frivolous and irrelevant subjects, especially among scholars.

By the beginning of the nineteenth century, the fashion industry in Paris had become an established world leader and was mainly segmented into two parts: dressmaking which was mostly controlled by highly influential women, and textile merchandizing and professional tailoring which was mostly controlled by men.

The buoyancy of this period gave rise to the launch of some of the luxury brands still in existence, including Guerlain by Pierre-François Pascal Guerlain in 1828 and Cartier by Louis-François Cartier in 1847, both in Paris. Also a young and gifted Louis Vuitton created the Louis Vuitton brand in 1854 as a leather luggage goods company in Paris while in Hampshire, England, 21-year-old Thomas Burberry founded the Burberry brand in 1856.

One man, however, was to change the face of luxury fashion and its marketing and management style forever. He was the Englishman, Charles Frederick Worth, who invented *haute couture* in Paris in 1858. During this period, when dressmaking was the sole domain of women, he became the first prominent male couturier and the private designer of the wife of Napoleon, Empress Eugenie, and other high-society women. His talent didn't rest solely in the design and construction of garments, he was also a marketing genius. He changed the way fashion was retailed by introducing models and the '*defilé*' (private fashion shows), and publicizing his creations through the 'celebrities' and influential women of the day. He also cut the production time of dress-making by more than 50 per cent, taking only one fitting to make a dress instead of the usual six fittings. His fashion empire was so successful and vast that at the peak of his career he employed more than 1,000 seamstresses.

The rapid development and transformation of the fashion environment was boosted by Europe's fast industrialization and improvement of manufacturing techniques. As a result the following important changes took place and became visible towards the end of the century:

1 Fashion, both for men and women became simple, understated, unadorned and classic as a result of the mind progressiveness of the people.
2 The simple and functional English fashion style for women emerged as a complement to the French elaborate and elegant style. Men were also influenced by the English country style.
3 The French revolution acted as a catalyst for the move towards the adoption of simplicity and more democracy in fashion as a sign of modernity, especially in the 1780s.
4 The rise of the Victorian era from the 1820s to the middle of the century also heralded the commencement of ready-to-wear as sewing machines were introduced to everyday women.

At the same time, America, the New World, was on the rise in both economic and cultural influence. Although Americans widely adopted fashion from Europe, their own tastes began to emerge especially during and after the French revolution years, which led to less imports of French fashion into America. Fashion for the masses also developed rapidly in America during this period, especially after the emergence of the cowboys and their dress style towards the end of the century. At the same time Americans embraced jeans, introduced in 1850 by Levi Strauss, a Bulgarian immigrant. Although jeans were originally a coverall made for California gold-rush miners from sturdy tent material and were made popular a century later in the 1960s, their foundation was laid during this period. The casual dressing of Native American Indian women also influenced the fashion simplicity of this period. Thus by the late 1800s a new kind of fashion freedom had been ushered in, both in Europe and in America.

The rise of the yankees

The nineteenth century was the beginning of America's influence in global fashion. This was propelled by extensive industrial and economic growth as well as growing levels of literacy. Increased opportunities in different sectors, notably in New York, also contributed to American fashion progress. Although most of the fashion products retailed in New York at this time were imported from France and the rest of Europe, American fashion consumers developed sophisticated tastes from extensive travels and cultural influence. The introduction of fashion magazines such as Godey's *Lady's Book* in 1837 also significantly influenced the fashion development of America.

Additional influencing factors of fashion growth include the expansion of the American middle class and their increased wealth. Also, the invention of the sewing machine and the creation of paper dress patterns established a means of copying the styles of Parisian and London women. In addition, other machines that could create patterns, covered buttons and embroidery were invented and adopted by dressmakers, contributing to the rise of the ready-to-wear market. Further progress was made in mass production techniques making ready-to-wear goods widely adopted in New York between the 1860s and 1890s. The fashion public also embraced ready-to-wear fashion as a result of the simplicity of the American lifestyle, which was different from the prevalent European aristocratic opulence. However, European imports remained perceived as more superior and sought after throughout the century.

All through the nineteenth century, the American fashion public, however, continued to favour the French style. As a result, wealthy members of society imported their fashion goods from France while the rest of the population relied on New York to produce 'copies' of the French style. This factor also contributed to the rise of New York as the centre of business and fashion for those who could not travel to Paris. By the middle of the nineteenth century, New York stores like A.T. Stewart, founded around 1875, offered custom-made clothes and fitted ready-to-wear replicas of French fashion.

Several fashion retail innovations were also developed in America during the nineteenth century. Notable among these are the concept of 'Opening Days', which were special days when the designs of the next fashion season were shown. This can be likened to today's pre-collection shows. Another retail innovation of this period was the introduction of the decorative window display at retail stores, which remains a prevalent aspect of luxury fashion retailing.

The American fashion advancement of the nineteenth century also extended to the emergence of other luxury fashion departmental stores in New York, that continue to exist today. Notable among them are Lord & Taylor, which began in 1852; R.H. Macy, currently known as Macy's, which started in 1878; and Brooks Brothers and Hearn. The fashion retail industry and competitive levels in New York grew rapidly during this century. The concept of retail 'cathedrals' also materialized during this period with the introduction of A.T. Stewart's elaborately decorated $3 million New York store in 1862, which occupied five storeys and two basements. The store also had continuous organ music and its clients included the first lady at the time, Mary Todd Lincoln.

By the end of this decade, America's prestigious retail locations like New York's Fifth Avenue could be compared with Paris' Rue de la Paix and Rue Saint Honoré and London's Regent Street. The American luxury departmental stores retailed both imported and homemade fashion goods. The stores also contributed to the growth in acceptance of indigenous American dressmakers, milliners and fashion designers. Although this century did not produce an American designer who attained international recognition, it paved the way for the success of the designers of the next century. By the end of the nineteenth century, the American fashion scene had evolved to a level of international standing.

The twentieth-century fashion explosion

The expeditious growth of industrialization and trade at the beginning of the twentieth century relegated fashion to the background. In the first half of the century, fashion was generally perceived as frivolous and a non-crucial aspect of economic development. This notion was changed through the influence of France and later Italy in elevating fashion and putting it on the same par as other forms of art like literature and theatre. It is no surprise then that the foundation of modern luxury fashion was laid in France, notably in Paris, which is still considered as a city of style and the fashion capital of the world.

Throughout the twentieth century, fashion relentlessly evolved and influenced society and several luxury fashion designers whose brands remain in existence emerged during this period. The fashion product categories were also expanded to include accessories and cosmetics, encouraged by the craving for fashion change as a result of the end of the Victorian era with the death of Queen Victoria of England in 1901.

During the early part of the twentieth century, Charles Worth, the inventor of *haute couture*, remained the supreme fashion force and the most respected couturier in the world. However, the rapid development of the luxury fashion market and the rise of other talented designers led to fierce competition. A notable competitor was Gabrielle Coco Chanel who launched her business as a hat-maker for the French aristocracy in 1910 in Paris. Chanel quickly created a niche market for her business, which led to its rapid expansion. Other designers that posed as competitors to Worth were Jeanne Lanvin who started her couture house in 1889; Paul Poiret who opened his in 1904; Madeline Vionnet who launched her design house in 1912; and Elsa Schiaparelli who started in 1927.

The early twentieth century also witnessed an explosive growth of the beauty and cosmetics sector. After the World Fair held in Paris in 1900, François Coty launched his cosmetics company in Paris, known today as

Coty Inc. Elizabeth Arden opened a decade later in America in 1910. They both pioneered the modern make-up and cosmetics industry. One year later, in 1911, Paul Poiret launched the first branded perfume, Rosine, which marked the birth of the luxury fragrance sector. Other designers, like Chanel, followed with the launching of Chanel No. 5 perfume in 1922 and the 'La Maison Worth' branded perfume in 1925. Jean Patou also introduced his branded fragrance in this period and extended the fragrance experience by establishing the innovative presentation of scents like cocktails to be mixed and tested like drinks.

The First World War, however, dominated the 1910s and influenced society's attitudes towards luxury and fashion. By the end of the war, the tastes of women in fashion had changed dramatically as a result of the increased responsibilities and hardship they underwent during the war. Although women continued to desire luxury fashion goods, they sought simplicity rather than the pre-war extravagance. Coco Chanel was one of the few designers who understood this significant consumer change and responded by designing highly sought-after clothes including the classic black dress. The post-war era also ushered in Popular Youth Culture to replace the sorrow of the war years. This was the forerunner period of the fashion revival that would take place shortly in the 1960s through pop culture.

After the war, the cinema became the most established entertainment medium and gradually personalities from the world of film replaced aristocrats as fashion icons and influencers. The popularity of Hollywood film stars like Greta Garbo and Marlene Dietrich and their fashion style greatly influenced the development of fashion in the 1920s and 1930s. In Paris, Josephine Baker also became a fashion icon and the most influential and highest paid entertainer in Europe.

Coco Chanel, Jeanne Lanvin and Madeleine Vionnet rose to high prominence during this era. On the other hand, the fashion businesses of Charles Worth and Paul Poiret slowly fizzled out, ushering in a new era of designers who showed a better understanding of the fashion environment.

At the same time, in Italy, fashion was re-emerging as a prominent social feature and created a favourable environment for the launch of Prada by Mario Prada in 1913 and Gucci in 1921 by Guccio Gucci. In America, however, fashion also developed within retailing and distribution through departmental stores rather than Parisian style boutiques. This evolution made fashion more visible and accessible to the growing American middle class. The concept would later pave the way for the successful retailing of ready-to-wear fashion which began in New York.

During the early twentieth century, society's wealthy also dominated and influenced luxury fashion in a similar manner to the royalties of the previous eras. The strict social class system that characterized societal structure provided the major fashion designers with a clientele comprising royal family members in Europe and the world's wealthy. The products of accessories designers like leather goods and luggage designer Louis Vuitton were in high demand by aristocrats in Europe and beyond. Guccio Gucci was also highly successful in this period as a result of developing a clientele consisting of Europe's royals and international stars that later included Princess Grace Kelly of Monaco and US first lady Jackie Kennedy.

During the 1940s and 1950s, the Second World War changed the outlook of fashion once again. The war brought shortages in almost every category of goods including fashion. At the same time, fashion tastes were enhanced through the cinema, which provided a form of distraction from the war. This led to the increase of the style and fashion influences of Hollywood actresses like Marilyn Monroe, Liz Taylor, Audrey Hepburn and Brigitte Bardot.

It was also during this period that Christian Dior emerged as a major fashion designer. Dior was a highly talented *haute couturier* and the expertise and precision he applied to his designs quickly gained him high popularity. With general society being more influenced by the cinema, designers like Dior were sought to construe the fashion styles of the movies. Other designers such as Hubert de Givenchy, Pierre Cardin and Cristobal Balenciaga also gained world renown during this period.

The twentieth century was the century that established the modern luxury fashion industry. Several luxury brands that continue to exist today such as Cartier, Burberry, Louis Vuitton, Chanel and Prada were created between the late nineteenth and early twentieth centuries. These brands have not only survived for more than a century, but have also maintained their core tradition and heritage while adapting to the constantly changing fashion and business scenario. Although most of them have diversified their product and services offerings, they have all remained true to their historical values.

The founders of the early luxury brands also recognized the importance of several business concepts like trademarks and global branding, long before branding became a core business aspect. For example, the French brand Cartier opened its first international store in London as early as 1902 and its first American store in New York in 1909. Thomas Burberry also had the foresight to register his brand logo as a trademark in 1900 prior to his international expansion. Louis Vuitton created the famous LV logo as far back as 1896 and the GG logo was developed by Gucci in the 1960s. The creators of the historical luxury brands were considered the geniuses of their day. However, the designers and business managers currently overseeing the activities of these brands are the true innovators of modern luxury fashion.

The sixties

The success of designers like Christian Dior, Pierre Cardin and Hubert de Givenchy in the 1940s and 1950s paved the way for other young designers in the 1960s. Yves Saint Laurent who worked for Dior opened his design house in 1962 and his first boutique in 1966. Other notable designers that were influential in this decade are Emilio Pucci, Paco Rabanne, Mary Quant, Milo Schoen, Nina Ricci, Valentino and Franco Moschino. Each of these designers contributed a form of innovation to fashion development. For example, Yves Saint Laurent was one of the first designers to create a complete collection per season, and Emilio Pucci introduced the use of the print in luxury apparel. The 1960s also witnessed a rapid growth of the Italian influence in fashion and the expansion of the accessories market, including the Italian invention of the stiletto.

The social temperance of the 1960s highly favoured fashion. Society gravitated towards women's liberation and fashion became one of the most visible ways of portraying the new woman. The designs of Chanel, Yves Saint Laurent and Christian Dior all embodied the new woman's freedom. Women's independence also extended to the adoption of fashion as a trendy vocation, leading to the emergence of several fashion schools in Europe and America.

The 1960s was also the first decade of the popular and youth culture movements. People became non-conformist to fashion dictations and began to express their individual attitudes and mood through their clothing and accessories. British designer Mary Quant played a key role in this social order through her unconventional approach to fashion. Her eccentric style, introduced at a time when the fashion society craved a revolution, contributed to her success. The pop culture of the 1960s would later lead to other fashion culture spin-offs such as the punk culture of the 1980s.

Towards the end of the 1960s, designers also became bolder and more experimental, using materials such as metal, plastic and wires to design clothes. These generated great press coverage and became a tool for the later utilization of *haute couture* for publicity rather than for commercial gains.

This decade of great fashion moments also ushered in the era of the 'Designers as Celebrity', which is still prevalent. However, fashion designers were not the only popular group. Other celebrities especially Hollywood stars and international icons, notably America's first lady Jackie Kennedy, also contributed to the growth of fashion in the 1960s.

The seventies

The 1970s was the decade of the growth and prosperity of fashion manufacturers, notably the American ready-to-wear mass producers. The advancement in manufacturing technology and expertise led to rapid design and product turnover and increased ready-to-wear exports all over the world. Mass production also began to threaten the fashion leadership position of Paris for the first time. This was amplified by the decline of the demand for *haute couture*, which had its domain in Paris. However, the lack of a single city in dictating mass fashion trends ensured that Paris retained its fashion leadership position. Another aspect of fashion affected by mass production was boutique fashion retail, which became less favoured than departmental store fashion retail.

The interaction of fashion and music was an additional prevalent feature throughout the 1970s. Musicians replaced the Hollywood stars of the previous decade as fashion symbols. Rock bands such as the Rolling Stones and stars like Mick Jagger became fashion icons. They injected a nonconformist mood into society through their jet-set lifestyles. This attitude was aptly translated in fashion through the casual and individual look that was prevalent throughout this decade.

This music cultural influence on fashion was heightened by other changes in society. Significant among these is the disappearance of the social class system, which predominated fashion in the previous periods. The seventies also boosted the wealth accumulation of the former middle class and enhanced fashion independence, personal tastes and styles. Other factors such as the increase in international travel and cultural exchanges also became a source of inspiration for expressing fashion taste and style.

The 1970s also marked the beginning of the gradual disappearance of *haute couture*. Women became less interested in fashion fittings and consultations because fashion had become accessible and was being adopted as a lifestyle. The state of 1970s fashion also contributed to the success of Ralph Lauren and Calvin Klein who launched their businesses in 1967 and 1968 respectively but gained prominence in the 1970s. Their major consumers, who were Americans, demanded simplicity in fashion designs, and this inclination towards simplicity in fashion also spread to other cities including Paris and London. French designers like Yves Saint Laurent, who was known to express anti-status in his designs, embraced the American understated fashion style. He also adopted denim material, breaking from the convention of using expensive and luxurious material for luxury goods. This cemented the way for the current use of denim by other brands like Christian Dior and Louis Vuitton. British brand Mulberry, which was established in 1971, also became immediately successful as a result of its simple and contemporary style favoured by the fashion society of the seventies.

The eighties

The casual fashion attitude of the seventies created a backdrop for a mature modern fashion environment and numerous fashion evolutions in the 1980s. Several successful fashion designers like the Americans Donna Karan and Tommy Hilfiger and the Japanese Yoji Yamamoto, Issey Miyake and Kenzo Takada gained global prominence during this decade. At the same time, the casual style of Ralph Lauren became widely appealing in America. The rest of the world interpreted this look through the wide adoption of denim and jeans trousers. German designer Karl Lagerfeld also launched his fashion house in 1984, around the concept of a brave anti-status style and in line with the fashion society's demand for unfussiness.

The 1980s was also the decade that saw a major change in the global perception of beauty, with the rising status of highly paid black models like Iman, Naomi Campbell and Beverley Johnson. The ascent of fashion models also led the way to the advent of supermodels as celebrities. The promotion of supermodels was pioneered by Gianni Versace, who also enhanced the use of colours and prints in fashion design through his Miami Beach inspired collections. The stimulation of fashion through multiple sources also extended to ethnic influences from Africa, India, China and the Mexican peasant looks. At the same time, Britain's Princess Diana injected a much needed fresh style into the British fashion scene. The impacts of these influences were felt on a global level, with the increase in international travel and communications.

The 1980s was also the decade of Punk Culture and a radical fashion revolution, pioneered by designer Zandra Rhodes. It featured a rebellious attitude towards fashion that was prevalent throughout the decade. This culture was also propelled by musicians like Madonna and music groups and rock bands like the Sex Pistols.

The decade's revolutions also encouraged the association of fashion with modern art. In 1983, Yves Saint Laurent became the first living designer to have his clothes presented in the Metropolitan Museum of Modern Art in New York, to honour his 20 years of fashion contribution. Exhibitions featuring other talented designers have also been held in several museums in different cities.

Several major changes in luxury fashion management also took place in the 1980s. They include multiple mergers, acquisitions and alliances among companies, propelled by global business sophistication. These processes revealed the importance of the concept of branding as an intangible asset for companies. It also led several luxury brands to take steps to strengthen their brand assets. Examples of these steps include the appointment of Karl Lagerfeld (who was at Chloé for 20 years) by Chanel in 1983, to revive the iconic French brand.

However, the most notable fashion business phenomenon of the 1980s was the assumption of Bernard Arnault as the President of LVMH (Louis Vuitton Möet Hennessey) in 1989. Arnault would later turn LVMH into the world's largest luxury goods conglomerate and launch a new era of strategic management in the modern luxury fashion sector. His later assemblage of a portfolio of luxury brands would also spark attempts at consolidations in the luxury goods sector, leading to the creation of rival luxury conglomerates such as PPR (Pinault, Printemps, Redoute), which owns the Gucci Group; Richemont, which owns Cartier and Chloé among others; and the Prada Group, which owns Prada and Miu Miu among others.

The nineties

The 1990s was a decade of explosive global consumption of modern luxury fashion goods, spearheaded by the vast expenditure of Japanese and Middle Eastern consumers on luxury goods. As a result, the majority of the existing luxury brands launched international market operations, notably in Japan. Luxury brands also expanded their product portfolios and placed increased emphasis on accessories like leather goods and jewellery, in response to consumer demand.

The decade also witnessed rapid developments in the competitive structure of the luxury goods industry, which led to the adoption of advanced fashion management practices. The most noteworthy of these developments is the reinforcement of the luxury brand's equity as an intangible asset generator for luxury companies. This recognition of the important role of the 'branding' factor in the performance of luxury companies led to the revival of staid brands like British brands Burberry and Mulberry and the rise of other brands like the Italian brand Roberto Cavalli.

Also, for the first time in centuries, Britain, which is considered the global centre of business services rather than fashion, began to take fashion seriously with the recognition of the huge corporate potential of the luxury goods sector. Efforts in this regard include the establishment of The British Fashion Council in 1991, to protect and support the interests of the British fashion sector and to discourage talented British designers from leaving the country. British fashion schools like Central St Martin's College of Art and Design, London, were also highly promoted as a centre of learning and fashion excellence.

An additional change in the luxury competitive environment was the gradual lowering of the high entry barrier of the luxury goods sector. This was made possible partly as a result of the interest of external non-luxury companies in funding new brands and acquiring old ones. Consequently, brands like Ozwald Boateng, Alexander McQueen and Jimmy Choo were launched in 1990, 1992 and 1996, respectively. They also paved the way for the 2001 launch of the Stella McCartney brand.

The management methods of luxury fashion brands was also highly affected by the rapid growth and influence of LVMH, the first luxury goods conglomerate with a portfolio of more than 50 brands including Louis Vuitton and Christian Dior, among several others. LVMH's success led to the emergence of a new luxury goods sub-sector and other conglomerates and corporate brands like the Gucci Group, Richemont and the Prada Group.

In response to growing competition, luxury brands also focused on product retailing by adopting the strategy of colossal 'cathedral-type' retail stores, with great emphasis on architectural design. Several innovations were also made in selling strategies in addition to store design and atmosphere as tools for representing the brand image. These include the use of advanced information technology in inventory management and control and in tracking product stock and delivery. Technology also provided a new channel of retail and distribution through the Internet. However, the dotcom crash of the late 1990s highlighted by the failure of the first fashion e-retail start-up company, boo.com, discouraged the adoption of Internet retailing during this decade. The Internet, however, affected other aspects of fashion such as the influence of celebrities like Sharon Stone and Elizabeth Hurley on a global level.

The 1990s was also the decade that launched the luxury services sub-sector in response to the increasing business needs of luxury brands. The company that pioneered this sector was Atlantic Publishing Ltd London, owned by James Ogilvy, which publishes the pioneer luxury industry journal, *Luxury Briefing*. The journal was launched as a response to the market size expansion and competitive structure changes which called for specialized market information and analysis.

Another significant fashion market change of the 1990s was in the mass fashion division but with a direct impact on the luxury fashion sector. The mass fashion sector grew rapidly as a result of advanced manufacturing, designing and retailing techniques. Brands like Zara from Spain, H&M from Sweden and Top Shop from Britain began to produce catwalk-style fashion at low cost, offering consumers luxury fashion alternatives at significantly lower prices. Their fashion goods were instantly embraced by global fashion consumers, leading to swift success. Their presence in the fashion market also led to a dramatic change in luxury fashion consumption attitudes, as had never been witnessed in the history of fashion. These changes have been more prevalent in the noughties.

The noughties

The luxury fashion terrain has undergone significant developments so far in the noughties. The decade was ushered in with the negative impact of the dotcom crash of the late 1990s and early 2000s, which led luxury brands to develop an aversion to e-commerce at the beginning of the decade. LVMH, however, changed this stance with the launching of an e-retail company, eluxury.com, which sold products from its brands, Louis Vuitton, Christian Dior, Donna Karan and several other internal and external brands in the US market. The unexpected success of eluxury.com led to the 2005 launch of e-retail operations in France and the United Kingdom for LVMH brands like Louis Vuitton and Christian Dior. Eluxury.com also spurred competitor luxury brands like Gucci, Hermès and Giorgio Armani to adopt e-retail. However, there remains a continuous debate among several luxury brands over the adoption of e-retail. The main concern of the luxury brands that are reluctant to adopt e-retail such as Chanel, is the dilution of the 'exclusive' and 'prestige' attributes of their brands, on the Internet. The advancement of e-retail strategies, which includes tactics for enhancing a brand's image and replicating a prestigious atmosphere online, however, invalidates this viewpoint.

An additional development in the luxury fashion sector since the beginning of this decade is the adoption of several non-standard strategies in product development, branding and retailing. These strategies include product extension in traditionally non-luxury goods divisions like furniture, restaurants and hotels; co-branding exercises with both luxury and non-luxury brands; and product discounting and retail outlet shopping villages. These strategies arose as a result of the current rife competition among luxury brands and the changing needs of luxury consumers.

The most visible and dramatic change of the decade has, however, been with the luxury consumer. The consumer landscape has undergone such a sweeping transformation that the existence of a typical 'luxury consumer' has been brought into question. Consumers that currently purchase luxury goods are now well-informed, individualistic, demanding and above all no longer loyal to a single brand. The change in consumers was brought about by several factors like the Internet, globalization, the advent of mass luxury, immigration, global wealth creation opportunities, the prominence of mass fashion brands, the emergence of new markets, the influence of digital television and the extension of luxury to lifestyle brands. As I write, several luxury brands are currently in the process of understanding who their consumers currently are and how to satisfy their needs.

The noughties has so far also been the decade of celebrity worship. Celebrities have greatly influenced consumers in this decade. International stars like Madonna, Beyoncé and Sara Jessica Parker have become more influential role models for consumers than political figures like Tony Blair and George Bush. This phenomenon has been prodded once again by advanced information and communications technology, including the Internet and Digital television. Global cult television shows like *Sex & The City* and movies like *The Devil Wears Prada*, which have fashion undertones, have become reference points for fashion consumers. Also several Reality Television shows in different parts of the world have encouraged the elevation of the celebrity status and the desire of consumers to become stars themselves. The implication is that luxury consumers crave personal attention through products and services, from luxury brands and expect to be treated as stars. As a result, there has been a wide adoption of the celebrity endorsement strategy in luxury goods advertising and communications. Luxury brands, however, have yet to adopt personalized services as a core aspect of their offerings, to satisfy the desire that consumers have to be treated as stars themselves.

The mass fashion brands like Zara, H&M and Top Shop have also risen in eminence and influence this decade. They have devised effective strategies that enable them to compete with luxury brands for the same consumers. These mass brands have spurred fashion phenomena like fast fashion, throwaway fashion and the democratization of luxury presented extensively in Chapter 7. They have also contributed significantly to the attitude change of luxury consumers who have also become their own stylists.

The market environment of the noughties has also steered towards unprecedented development in the globalization of luxury brands. This has been spurred by the continuous influence of the Internet and the emergence of new markets like China, Russia and India. Consequently, several luxury brands have launched rapid global expansion plans and many luxury brands now have more stores in some particular foreign countries than in their home countries. For example, American brand Coach has more than 100 stores in Japan alone. Other brands like Louis Vuitton and Giorgio Armani have launched aggressive expansions plans in several new markets.

On the level of market competition, the noughties has also seen great advancement in the concept of branding strategy as a core business aspect. The development has been most visible in the process of creating and managing the brand value as a company's asset. Great emphasis has been placed on the financial returns that a company accrues through its brand's asset. As a result, several luxury brands have made brand management central to their corporate strategies. In other words, every strategy adopted is measured against its role in the protection of the brand. The prominence of the intangible brand asset was highlighted through the annual Global Brands Scoreboard, conducted by brand consultancy company Interbrand and published by *Businessweek* magazine. The luxury brands that have featured in the scoreboard include Louis Vuitton, Gucci, Chanel and Hermès, among others.

An additional noteworthy emerging occurrence of the noughties is the advancement of several British luxury brands and fashion designers. While the 1990s ushered in an era of luxury fashion branding adoption in Britain, the noughties has been a decade of visible success for the British luxury brands like Jimmy Choo, Burberry, Mulberry, Ozwald Boateng, Stella McCartney, Alexander McQueen, Matthew Williamson, John Galliano and Alice Temperley, among others.

Finally, the noughties has also witnessed growth in the luxury services sub-sector. In addition to *Luxury Briefing* journal, which was launched in 1996, several companies that cater to the needs of luxury companies and luxury consumers alike have emerged. These include companies specializing in trend tracking, consumer insights, style reporting, exclusive clubs and private concierge services and product loaning, exchanges and auctioning.

2007 and beyond

The rest of the noughties and the following decades will feature symbolic developments in the luxury goods sector. Information and communications technology will become more extensively adopted by innovative brands, which will be extended beyond the Internet and e-retail to include Mobile Shopping and possibly iPod Shopping. There will also be advancement in sophisticated consumer behaviour tracking techniques such as Neuro-marketing science, which utilizes the measurement of the reaction of brain waves to track consumer response to marketing messages.

Consumers will also continue to be more demanding and assertive. They will become more mature in their attitudes towards luxury, and satisfying them will become more challenging. Their expectations from luxury brands will include substance in addition to quality as a measurement of value. These will be manifested in intangible qualities that are related to ethics and moral consciousness. As a result, luxury brands will be expected to show more socially responsible practices. Consumers will expect to have wholesome experiences with every interaction with luxury brands. They will also expect personal attention and the option of customized products and services.

The luxury consumer market will expand significantly and the influence of new markets such as China, India and Russia will form the core direction of several luxury brands. In addition, mass immigration in several parts of the world will bring an exotic change to the luxury goods scene. At the same time, consumers in the mature European luxury market and the growing American and Japanese markets will have a different set of expectations. Luxury brands will therefore be required to manage the cyclical position of their consumers in different global regions.

The market environment will also evolve with additional new luxury brands entering the market and mass fashion brands encroaching into the luxury sphere. Other strategies like globalization and consolidation will also prevail. These will intensify competition among luxury brands and reinforce the importance of carving a clear brand positioning strategy in the market. Innovative brands will thrive, while brands with unclear messages will fizzle out.

Finally, the luxury services sub-sector will become a well-defined industry that caters to the needs of luxury brands and consumers. These services will include Brand Valuation, Luxury Intelligence, Market Research, Consumer Research, Trend Tracking, Style News and Advisory, Lifestyle Branding and Luxury Goods Exchanges. Most importantly, more books like this will be written!

The dolce vita style blast

Italy like France is a country known for fashion creativity and expertise. It has been a major fashion force for centuries, from the period of the Roman Empire until today. Italian fashion know-how and production expertise is widely accepted as the best in the world. Brands like Gucci, Prada, Salvatore Ferragamo and Bvlgari have contributed significantly to establishing an important position for Italy in the world of fashion. However, unlike France, which views fashion as a form of art, Italy's outlook on fashion is more as a traditional business developed through a lifetime and passed through generations. In France, fashion and creativity is an obsession and a soubriquet of expression embedded in the genes. In Italy, fashion is both a lifestyle and a means to a lifestyle and culture.

Italy had a prominent position in global fashion during the Roman Empire and the Renaissance era. However, this diminished after the fall of the Venetian Empire in 1797 and the subsequent political unsettlement, giving way for the rise of France and later England in fashion. As a result, several talented Italian designers left their country in search of fortune in France and later in America. By the eighteenth century, Italian women like the rest of the Europeans had begun to adopt French fashion while Italian men adopted English tailoring, further demoting Italian fashion. Consequently by the early nineteenth century, Italian fashion had almost disappeared and had been nearly completely replaced by French *haute couture*. It took almost a century before Italian fashion was to become world-renowned once more.

The brands that launched the Italian fashion revolution on Italian soil in the late nineteenth and early twentieth centuries are Prada, Ermenegildo Zegna, Gucci and Salvatore Ferragamo, while Giorgio Armani, Gianni Versace and Dolce & Gabanna carried it forward. The first internationally recognized Italian designer was, however, Elsa Schiaparelli (1890–1973) who became famous after opening her couture house in Paris. Later, in 1906, Guccio Gucci started his saddlery shop in Florence and expanded to fashion accessories in 1923. Ermenegildo Zegna followed Gucci's launch in 1912, with menswear fabrics in the small village of Trivero. Salvatore Ferragamo launched his business in 1927. He was born in Italy in 1898 and emigrated to the USA in 1914 where he studied shoe design and started a flourishing business in California before returning to Italy to set up a workshop in Florence.

The fashion businesses of these talented Italian designers quickly gained world fame. Italian accessories, especially shoes, became popular and synonymous with style, class and high quality all over the world. Although Italian accessories flourished, fashion remained predominated by the dress and this was mostly made in France. As a result, Italian designers focused their attention on exports to America, rather than on developing a home fashion sector. As early as the 1920s, Americans were getting exposed to Italian fashion and its appealing associations to European aristocracy. Italy was also an attractive tourist destination for Americans with its beautiful landscape and seductive lifestyle. This combination served as an important formula for the success of Italian fashion abroad.

The Italian government also recognized the important role of fashion in resuscitating its economy and engineered reforms to favour the growth of fashion. For example, Italian leader Benito Mussolini's government established a National Fashion Office in Turin to promote the Italian fashion industry. However, the fashion influence of Italy was not to rise to its Renaissance-era glory until the mid-1940s, although the country maintained its rich art and cultural heritage.

Before 1945, Italy's economic mainstay was primarily agriculture-based and this was a challenge to the country's economy. The adverse effects of the Second World War further worsened the economy, and as a result the industrial production of fashion goods and innovation in couture and dressmaking remained minimal. The climate of a thriving social and economic structure which fashion needs in order to flourish was lacking. While Paris boomed as the world's fashion destination, Italian cities like Rome, Florence and Milan remained largely unappealing.

An additional factor that contributed to the slow growth of Italian fashion influence is that Italy had no constant and representative fashion capital city like Paris in France and London in Britain. Although Florence, Rome and Milan were (and still remain) important fashion centres, each region of Italy has always specialized in a specific type of fashion production. Florence has long been associated with woollen clothing; Sicily was the centre of artistic weaving while Lucca and Venice were known for silk textile and Venice the centre of shoemakers and cobblers, leatherworks, silk and cotton weavers, wool spinners and dyers.

One major contributing factor to the growth of Italian fashion was the Nazi occupation of Paris during the Second World War which disrupted the leading position of French fashion. During this period, America was again to play an important role in the take-off of Italian fashion. The post-war mass migration from Italy to America meant an export of Italian fashion style and culture and later an import of American ready-to-wear business and technology back to Italy. The peculiar family-orientation nature of the Italian fashion industry meant that every skill and technology learnt was passed from generation to generation. The effective blending of this family-oriented Italian craftsmanship with America's commercial orientation towards fashion would later serve as a backdrop for the success of several brands including Versace and Tod's.

Although Gucci and Ferragamo were the forerunners of Italian fashion, the Italian look as we know it today was pioneered by Giorgio Armani and Gianni Versace in the 1970s. Their ease of style and elegance was the opposite of the French opulence and greatly appealed to fashion consumers worldwide. They also highlighted the important complementary role of accessories like shoes, jewellery and sunglasses. The rapidly rising Italian designers effectively drew on the fame of their heritage of precision and craftsmanship and the renown of their accessories. Americans completely embraced this style while the French admired and respected it. The fashion world had changed and Italy contributed to the way the new world looked.

Italy flourishes today as a country of not only beauty but of immense fashion style and influence. The majority of the world's most valuable luxury fashion brands are from Italy and numerous other Italian fashion brands continue to gain fashion authority globally. Although the Italian fashion model is different from the rest of the world in terms of its family business orientation, the majority of Italian brands have shown apt flexibility in adopting modern business practices in fashion management. Italy has always had the typecast of fashion manufacturing, while France was known for fashion branding and Britain for fashion retailing. However, in the current fashion environment, these stereotypes are no longer applicable as each of these countries, especially Italy, has shown the ability for appropriate adaptation to the fashion market's needs.

America, fashion and commerce

The mention of Italian, English or French fashion immediately conjures up an image of a particular style in the mind. When 'American fashion' is referred to, however, people usually become confused. This is because unlike European fashion, which had an early evolution and definition, the American fashion style was unclear and difficult to describe during its evolution between the twentieth and twenty-first centuries. The perception of American fashion has ranged from the casual look comprising of t-shirt, denim and sneakers, to the hip-hop style that adds bold and flashy jewellery to casual wear, and to the California-style shirt and beach shorts. A lot of people in other parts of the world would use the term 'sportswear' to describe American fashion. Others will make references to the collared t-shirt made popular by Ralph Lauren as the American fashion style while yet others will just assume that American fashion comprises of cheaper spin-offs of the fashion styles produced in Europe. The reality is that Americans have known and shown good fashion taste and creativity through a consistent fashion progression spanning centuries.

In the early part of the twentieth century, America depended on Europe, particularly on Paris, for its fashion products and style guidelines. Wealthy Americans made several annual trips across the Atlantic to Paris for dress fittings at notable couturiers such as La Maison Worth. This fashionable elite also purchased their accessories in Italy, especially in Florence. Back home, those that could not travel to Europe copied the styles of the wealthy. This trend continued until the Second World War and the result was a great European influence on the outlook and interpretation of American fashion. This reality also created a mistaken portrayal of the American fashion style as lacking in taste and originality.

The Second World War brought several changes to the American fashion scene. The most prominent of these was the blockage of the flow of fashion goods from Paris to America, as a result of the occupation of Paris by German troops. Americans were forced to seek alternatives in local fashion designers. This period marked the emergence of the modern American style through several talented designers like Harvey Berin and Tom Brigance. American fashion magazines such as *Vogue* and *Harper's Bazaar* promoted these local designers, which encouraged the fashion public to patronize them. The period also contributed to the ascent of New York as a fashion city since the majority of the designers were based in New York. However, after the war Paris rose once more as the global fashion capital. The emergence of French designers like Christian Dior in 1947, Pierre Cardin in 1950 and Hubert Givenchy in 1952 contributed to the return of Paris' prominence in global fashion. Although Americans once more sought fashion inspiration from Paris, the taste for local fashion had been definitely roused and the American fashion industry had been born.

The growth of American fashion was also influenced by the numerous transformations in the consumer society and industrial sector. For example, advanced manufacturing techniques of ready-to-wear fashion made apparel more accessible and affordable to a wider consumer group. The rise of departmental stores such as Macy's, Bergedorf Goodman and Henry Bendel also contributed to fashion accessibility. The accessible fashion goods sold in these stores were complemented by the tailored apparel produced with sewing machines, which was invented in the nineteenth century. American consumers also adopted the use of the sewing machine for homemade clothes.

The rapid growth of the American middle class both in size and in wealth also contributed to the American fashion development. As the century moved into its second half, a larger proportion of the consumer population could afford either New York ready-to-wear clothes and accessories or the more expensive European imported fashion goods. As a result, several consumer segments emerged, conspicuously the ready-to-wear consumer group and the consumers of European luxury fashion goods. This marked the start of luxury goods segments still prevalent in today's American consumer society. Despite the different consumer groups, the American fashion taste remained simple and unfussy as a result of the simplicity of the lifestyle.

The increasing role of women in American society also led to fashion advancement, boosted by the invention of such home equipment as the washing machine. This created more time for female consumers to devote to fashion and their appearance. Also, more American women entered the corporate sector, which increased their level of sophistication and fashion outlook. The fashion development of American consumers was also encouraged by the adoption of several cultural and entertainment forms like the theatre and the opera, notably in New York.

The prolific fashion environment of the 1950s led to the emergence of several American designers still active today such as Bill Blass and Anne Klein in the 1960s. These designers adapted their creations to fit American society's expectation of easy and stylish fashion, rather than copying the styles from Paris, Milan and London. The sophisticated corporate fashion style also maintained a consistent undertone of simplicity. The simple American fashion was later established definitely by Jackie Kennedy, who was the country's first lady between 1961 and 1963. Her style constituted a combination of classic apparel accentuated with elegant accessories. She became a fashion icon for Americans and her influence eventually extended to other parts of the world. She was also one of the most famous clients of Italian brand, Gucci. The adoration of her style by the American public was the beginning of celebrity fashion influence in America and the rebirth of this trend in the European modern fashion environment.

In addition to Jackie Kennedy, who projected American fashion to the world, the 1960s also witnessed the emergence of two iconic designers, Ralph Lauren and Calvin Klein, who would eventually make American fashion global. The factors that contributed to their immediate success were the establishment of a standard American fashion style by Jackie Kennedy and also the lack of well-known American designers. Ralph Lauren, who launched his business in 1967, adopted a reserved English country style with American non-traditional undertones while Calvin Klein who started in 1968 projected the casual look through experimenting with sportswear and coat dresses.

By the 1970s, both designers had become highly successful experts in ready-to-wear fashion. In 1974, Ralph Lauren designed the wardrobe of the cast of the film 'The Great Gatsby', and stamped a definite place for himself in American fashion history. Calvin Klein's success was boosted by the care-free attitude of the consumer public and the growing independence of women. At the same time, fashion magazines like *Vogue* and *Vanity Fair*, which had become reference points, promoted their designs and contributed immensely to their fame. The success of Ralph Lauren and Calvin Klein encouraged other designers like Diane von Fürstenberg and Perry Ellis to launch their fashion businesses in the 1970s.

By the 1980s, the American fashion scene was competing on a par with several aspects of European fashion. However the advent of globalization and the increase in international travel, digital media and intercultural influences had an impact on American consumer society. The high cultural awareness acquired by several Americans led to a desire for overstated fashion especially from Europe. As a result, the demand for luxury goods from European brands like Gucci, Giorgio Armani and Chanel increased. The t-shirt, denim and sportswear that highlighted the 1970s in American fashion were replaced by a modern chic and trendy style. American women also became more health and fitness conscious and used luxury fashion as a platform to display their looks.

This environment contributed to the swift success of designers like Donna Karan who launched her fashion business in 1984, and Isaac Mizrahi in 1987. The American taste for flamboyant luxury fashion in the 1980s also led to a significant rise in the demand for Italian luxury fashion accessories and apparel. This factor amplified the affinity of American consumers with Italian luxury designers like Giorgio Armani, Versace and Dolce & Gabbana, still prevalent today. The love of Italian fashion by Americans would also later contribute to the success of Italian brands like Tod's, Hogan and Diesel.

The American luxury consumer market continued to mature into the 1990s. American fashion consumers adopted a more global outlook as a result of digital media, information technology, globalization and fashion magazines.

These factors also contributed to the rise in status of American designers like Michael Kors and Marc Jacobs, and mass-market fashion brands such as Guess and supermarket fashion like Wal Mart and Target. This decade also saw the most dramatic rise in the American luxury consumer population.

The American fashion environment of the 2000s is highly developed and sophisticated. The luxury consumer market has witnessed unprecedented expansion as a result of several wealth-creation opportunities. The wealth index of Americans is on a steady upward slope and a large proportion of these wealthy consumers are young. Their profiles, characteristics and attitudes towards luxury goods are different from their predecessors and their expectations include a complete luxury experience in product and service offerings. In response to this, several luxury brands began the 2000s by extending their product ranges to include a total lifestyle offering for the consumer. Luxury brands that previously produced accessories, expanded into apparel and vice versa. American designers such as Ralph Lauren and Calvin Klein launched high-end accessories, children's wear and furniture collections. Luxury brands also diversified into other products and services categories like hotels and restaurants as a strategy to extend their brands from 'luxury fashion brands' to 'luxury lifestyle brands'. Also, the American consumer's desire for convenient luxury shopping has led to the increased adoption of the e-retail of luxury goods by luxury brands. In addition to these, the American fashion market continuously influences global fashion trends and management practices through several developments.

The evolution of American fashion and its influence on the global luxury fashion industry has undoubtedly been significant. As the largest retail market in the world, the American fashion market has a stronghold on the global luxury fashion industry. The competitive and consumer fashion environments of America significantly influence the current state and future direction of the global fashion industry. As the market continues to advance and mature, its consumers' level of influence will doubtlessly remain important.

So, having said all this, what is the American fashion style? The answer to this question can be found everywhere. From New York, Paris, Milan, London, Stockholm, Hong Kong, Tokyo, Bombay, to Sydney and beyond. When we look around us, on the streets, in buses, trains and elevators, what we see in people is a relaxed attitude to fashion, an individual fashion interpretation that is sometimes elegant, sometimes casual, sometimes sophisticated yet with a consistent undertone of ease. That is the modern fashion and it is the American style.

The luxury brand index

Table 2.1 lists most of the fashion designers and brands that have contributed to shaping the global luxury fashion market. Some of these brands have

Table 2.1 Luxury fashion brands index

	Brand name*	Year	Founder	Country
1	Guerlain	1828	Pierre Francois Pascal Guerlain	France
2	Hermès	1837	Thierry Hermès	France
3	Loewe	1846	Enrique Loewe Roessberg	Spain
4	Cartier	1847	Louis Francois Cartier	France
5	Bally	1851	Carl Franz Bally	Switzerland
6	Louis Vuitton	1854	Louis Vuitton	France
7	La Maison Worth	1858	Charles Frederick Worth	France
8	Burberry	1856	Thomas Burberry	England
9	Lancel	1876	Alphonse and Angele Lancel	France
10	Cerruti	1881	The Cerruti Brothers	Italy
11	Bvlgari	1884	Sotinos Voulgaris	Italy
12	Lanvin	1889	Jeanne Lanvin	France
13	Jeanne Paquin	1890	Jeanne Paquin	France
14	Berluti	1895	Alessandro Berluti	France
15	Fendi	1897	Adele Casagrande Fendi	Italy
16	Paul Poiret	1904	Paul Poiret	France
17	Trussardi	1910	Dante Trussardi	Italy
18	Ermenegildo Zegna	1910	Ermenegildo Zegna	Italy
19	Chanel	1910	Gabrielle Coco Chanel	France
20	Madeleine Vionnet	1912	Madeleine Vionnet	France
21	Jean Patou	1912	Jean Patou	France
22	Prada	1913	Mario Prada	Italy
23	Balenciaga	1919	Cristobal Balenciaga	Spain
24	Gucci	1921	Guccio Gucci	Italy
25	Hugo Boss	1923	Hugo Boss	Germany
26	Norman Hartnell	1923	Norman Hartnell	England
27	Rochas	1924	Marcel Rochas	France
28	Elsa Schiaparelli	1927	Elsa Schiaparelli	France
29	Salvatore Ferragamo	1927	Salvatore Ferragamo	Italy
30	Nina Ricci	1932	Nina Ricci	France
31	Roger Vivier	1937	Roger Vivier	France
32	Celine	1945	Celine Vipiana	France
33	Brioni	1945	Nazareno Fonticoli and Gaetano Savini	Italy
34	Christian Dior	1947	Christian Dior	France
35	Pucci	1948	Emilio Pucci	Italy
36	Louis Feraud	1949	Louis Feraud	France
37	Pierre Cardin	1950	Pierre Cardin	France
38	Max Mara	1951	Achille Maramotti	Italy
39	Hanae Mori	1951	Hanae Mori	Japan
40	Givenchy	1952	Hubert de Givenchy	France
41	Chloé	1952	Jacques Lenoir and Gaby Aghion	France
42	Mary Quant	1955	Mary Quant	England
43	Krizia	1957	Mariuccia Mandelli	Italy
44	Guy Laroche	1957	Guy Laroche	France
45	Missoni	1958	Rosita and Ottavio Missoni	Italy
46	Mila Schön	1958	Mila Schön	Italy
47	Sergio Rossi	1950s	Sergio Rossi	Italy
48	Valentino	1960	Valentino Garavani	Italy

luxury fashion branding

Table 2.1 *continued*

	Brand name*	Year	Founder	Country
49	Yves Saint Laurent	1962	Yves Saint Laurent	France
50	Azzaro	1962	Loris Azzaro	Italy
51	Cacharel	1962	Jean Bousquet	France
52	Jean-Louis Scherrer	1962	Jean-Louis Scherrer	France
53	Karl Lagerfeld	1963	Karl Lagerfeld	France
54	Judith Leiber	1963	Judith Leiber	USA
55	Richard Tyler	1964	Richard Tyler	Australia
56	Emmanuel Ungaro	1965	Emmanuel Ungaro	France
57	Roberto Cavalli	1965	Roberto Cavalli	Italy
58	Bottega Veneta	1966	Vicence Bottega Veneta	Italy
59	Paco Rabanne	1966	Paco Rabanne	Spain
60	Ralph Lauren	1967	Ralph Lauren	USA
61	Calvin Klein	1968	Calvin Klein	USA
62	Sonia Rykiel	1968	Sonia Rykiel	France
63	Anne Klein	1968	Anne Klein	USA
64	Jil Sander	1968	Jil Sander	Germany
65	Zhandra Rhodes	1969	Zhandra Rhodes	England
66	Come des Garcons	1969	Rei Kawakubo	Japan
67	Oscar de la Renta	1969	Oscar de la Renta	USA
68	Paul Smith	1970	Paul Smith	England
69	Kenzo	1970	Kenzo Takada	France
70	Bill Blass	1970	Bill Blass	USA
71	Issey Miyake	1970	Issey Miyake	Japan
72	Vivienne Westwood	1971	Vivienne Westwood	USA
73	Mulberry	1971	Roger Saul	England
74	Yohji Yamamoto	1972	Yohji Yamamoto	Japan
75	Diane Von Furstenberg	1972	Diane Von Fürstenbreg	USA
76	Manolo Blahnik	1972	Manolo Blahnik	England
77	Thierry Mugler	1973	Thierry Mugler	France
78	Alberta Ferretti	1974	Alberta Ferretti	Italy
79	Giorgio Armani	1974	Giorgio Armani	Italy
80	Perry Ellis	1975	Perry Ellis	USA
81	Jean Paul Gaultier	1976	Jean Paul Gaultier	France
82	Escada	1976	Wolfgang and Margaretha Ley	Germany
83	Helmut Lang	1977	Helmut Lang	Austria
84	John Rocha	1977	John Rocha	Ireland
85	Ana Molinari	1977	Ana Molinari	Italy
86	Gianni Versace	1978	Gianni Versace	Italy
87	Gianfranco Ferre	1978	Gianfranco Ferre	Italy
88	JP Tod's	1978	Diego Della Valle	Italy
89	Azzedine Alaia	1980	Azzedine Alaia	France
90	Marina Rinaldi	1980	Achille Maramotti	Italy
91	Michael Kors	1981	Michael Kors	USA
92	Carolina Herrera	1981	Carolina Herrera	USA
93	Anna Sui	1981	Anna Sui	USA
94	Kenneth Cole	1982	Kenneth Cole	USA
95	Elie Saab	1982	Elie Saab	Lebanon
96	Moschino	1983	Franco Moschino	Italy
97	Nicole Farhi	1983	Nicloe Farhi	England
98	Thomas Pink	1984	Thomas Pink	England

Table 2.1   *continued*

	Brand name*	Year	Founder	Country
99	Karl Lagerfeld	1984	Karl Lagerfeld	France
100	Tommy Hilfiger	1984	Tommy Hilfiger	USA
101	Donna Karan	1984	Donna Karan	USA
102	Marc Jacobs	1984	Marc Jacobs	USA
103	Dries Van Noten	1985	Dries Van Noten	Belgium
104	Dolce & Gabbana	1985	Domenico Dolce an Stefano Gabbana	Italy
105	Patrick Cox	1986	Patrick Cox	England
106	Hogan	1986	Diego Della Valle	Italy
107	Isaac Mizrahi	1987	Issac Mizrahi	USA
108	Christian Lacroix	1987	Christian Lacroix	France
109	Ted Baker	1988	Ted Baker	Scotland
110	John Galliano	1989	John Galliano	England
111	L.K. Bennett	1991	Linda Kristin Bennett	England
112	Christian Louboutin	1992	Christian Louboutin	France
113	Alexander McQueen	1994	Alexander McQueen	England
114	Anya Hindmarch	1994	Anya Hindmarch	England
115	Hussein Chalayan	1994	Hussein Chalayan	England
116	Marni	1994	Consuelo Castiglioni	Italy
117	Alessandro Dell'Acqua	1995	Alesandro Dell'Acqua	Italy
118	Viktor & Rolf	1995	Viktor Horsting and Rolf Snoeren	Nethrlands
119	Paul & Joe	1996	Sophie Albou	France
120	Jimmy Choo	1996	Tamara Mellon	England
121	Mathew Williamson	1996	Mathew Williamson	England
122	Julien McDonald	1997	Julien McDonald	England
123	Narciso Rodriguez	1997	Narciso Rodriguez	USA
124	Alice Temperley	1999	Alice Temperley	England
125	Zac Posen	1999	Zac Posen	USA
126	Luella	2000	Luella Bartley	England
127	Stella McCartney	2001	Stella McCartney	England
128	Andre Ross	2004	Andrew Ross Blencowe	France
129	Tom Ford	2006	Tom Ford	USA

* Some brands might have been omitted as a result of either the unavailability of data regarding their founding dates and origins or the reluctance of the brands to reveal these.

continued to grow in strength while others have faded from the luxury fashion scene. The countries marked against the brands are the places where the brands were launched, and in most cases the brands' countries of origin.

Charles Frederick Worth: Le Père de la haute couture (1826–95)

It is impossible to write about the origins of luxury fashion without paying tribute to Charles Frederick Worth, the man who began everything about

Figure 2.1 *Charles Frederick Worth, the man who invented* haute couture *and later became the first fashion entrepreneur*

Figure 2.2 *A design of Worth showing his elaborate style and attention to detail*

modern luxury fashion. He has been hailed as the architect of luxury fashion branding and remains one of the most talented fashion designers of all time. He invented *haute couture* as we know it today and other modern fashion practices like the creation of seasonal fashion styles and trends, the use of fashion models and the fashion brand name as a label.

Figure 2.3 *A current lingerie design from recently launched brand Courtworth, an attempt at reviving the Worth fashion house. The style is inspired by the original designs of Charles Worth*

Charles Worth, an Englishman who went to Paris to enter the world of fashion, made a name for himself in *haute couture* and an indelible mark in the world of fashion. His name still commands great respect in fashion circles and beyond, even in France where the English have been widely regarded as lacking aesthetic appreciation. His high creative talent and business sense set the scene for the current modern-day luxury goods industry. He created the first true luxury fashion brand and paved the way for the application of modern branding and marketing principles in the world of luxury fashion.

The early years

Charles Worth was born in England, at Wake House, North Street, in the small market town of Bourne in south Lincolnshire, on 13 October 1825. He came from a family of solicitors with no connections to dressmaking. He was the last child of five children, three of whom died in infancy, leaving his parents with Charles and an elder brother. His father had a respectable legal career and Worth lived in comfort during his early years in the social-class-conscious society. He expected his life to follow the tradition of the family in the legal profession just like his grandfather, father and brother. However, drastic events changed his destiny.

In 1836, when Worth was ten years old, his father became bankrupt as a result of heavy gambling, drinking and bad business decisions. He deserted his family and his town and was not to return for thirty years. His bankruptcy humiliated the family and Charles Worth never forgave his father, refusing to have any contact with him even after he became successful.

Worth's mother, Mary, fled the village with him out of shame as luckily her elder son and Worth's brother had already left home to begin his legal training. This period marked the start of Worth's struggle in life. At the age of 11, he began his life of menial jobs as a cleaner in a printer's shop but was extremely dissatisfied with it. His desire was to become an apprentice in a textiles and clothing shop, but this ambition proved difficult to fulfil as during this period dressmaking was considered mostly as women's domain in England. However, he felt that he could accomplish his dream in London but since he had no money to travel to London he began making ladies' Easter bonnets for sale to raise money. Eventually, in 1838, he and his mother managed to raise enough money for his train fare to London.

In 1838, at the age of 12, Worth started his apprenticeship with textile merchants Swan & Edgar of Regent Street, London. He worked there for seven years until the age of 19. During his apprenticeship, he diligently studied the different types of materials, their characteristics and functions. His role also entailed courteously welcoming customers at the store's entrance and attending to special requests, which is an equivalent of the present-day Customer Services. He was completely immersed in the world of textiles as he worked 12 hours per day and six days a week. He also lived in the store and slept under the counters at night. All he lived and breathed for seven years was fashion. This period laid the foundation that would eventually lead him to *haute couture* in Paris.

Charles Worth was continuously fascinated by the high level of knowledge and cultural exposure of his superiors and colleagues at Swan & Edgar. The tales of their extensive travels captivated him and he constantly listened and learned. He was determined to overcome the social downfall of his father and secretly longed to improve his education, which had been cut short at 11 years. He began reading literary books and visiting galleries frequently to improve his level of knowledge. The National Gallery Trafalgar Square, which he visited often became his treasure of information. Through the displayed paintings he observed the changes in the dress styles of women over the centuries. He was intrigued by the progression of fashion and how the past influenced the future of fashion, sparking ideas of clothing women in his mind. The knowledge he acquired during this period later became valuable in his career in Paris.

As he continued his apprenticeship and self-education, his appetite for designing women's clothes grew and he became restless to satisfy it. He learnt from magazines that the centre of female fashion was Paris, and he immediately realized that his dreams could only become reality in Paris. He decided that his time in London would soon be over and he set his sights on Paris.

At the age of 19, Worth ended his apprenticeship period at Swan & Edgar and joined the prestigious establishment of Lewis & Allenby on the same Regent Street, London. He had become a sophisticated textile salesman and finessed his skills while planning to leave for Paris. His ambition was realized within a year.

Welcome to Paris

In order to realize his dream of going to Paris, Worth once again turned to his mother for financial support. Between them, they raised enough money to cover his transport fare from London to Paris, with £5 extra for pocket money. He had no contacts in Paris, no aristocratic connections, no knowledge of the French language, little education and almost no savings. Yet in the winter of 1845, just after his twentieth birthday, Charles Frederick Worth took his own destiny in his hands and left London for Paris to pursue his ambitions.

His early years in Paris were difficult. His lack of money, verbal and written communication skills in the French language and Parisian fashion know-how forced him to take menial jobs to survive. His hopes of success in fashion were quickly dashed but he refused to concede to failure and return home. Even if he had wanted to, he didn't have enough money for his transport fare back to England.

After one year, he eventually found a menial job in a dry goods store, where he improved his French language skills and became comfortable with dealing with customers. He continued to visit galleries, especially the Louvre, where he observed scores of costumes in paintings. He also frequented the streets that housed the prestigious shops of silk and textile mercers of high fashion on Rue Richelieu. He nurtured his dream of becoming a dressmaker although this was also considered a woman's job in Paris. Worth was determined to become a dressmaker rather than a man's clothing tailor, because he knew where his talent lay.

He eventually got his first real job in the textile trade in 1847, two years after arriving in Paris. It was at the prestigious textile merchants, Maison Gagelin on Rue Richelieu in the current first district of Paris. He worked at Gagelin for a total of 11 years from late 1847 to 1858, doing a similar job as he had at Lewis & Allenby in London but in a more sophisticated environment and in a foreign language.

Charles Worth witnessed several changes in the French fashion style as the society evolved. At the beginning of his stay in Paris, French fashion was at the height of its majestic glory and influence, but became austere through the political and economic upheavals such as the ousting of King Louis Philippe, the death of the French monarchy, the new Republic and the Napoleonic Empire. Also, the French revolution of 1848 brought a decline in the flamboyance of women's clothes and a general demure in French fashion. Through all this mayhem, Worth often wondered if he was in the right place.

The eye-opener

As the political crisis gave way to a more stable environment, a positive fashion and social attitude emerged in Paris. The construction of eminent buildings such as the Opera together with state visits and official receptions that followed their openings, created an opportunity for luxury to flourish. The opulence that accompanied these grand ceremonies aroused a taste for luxury fashion in the upper social class, which greatly benefited designers, jewellers, dressmakers and textile traders.

Worth was awestruck by the magnificent events in the French world of royalty and aristocracy. His first direct involvement with this world of opulence was when Gagelin, the company he worked for, was asked to supply the materials for Empress Eugenie's trousseau during her wedding to Napoleon III in January 1853. This came through their connection with dressmakers because although Gagelin was a textile supplier, they were constantly consulted by dressmakers on the suitability of specific materials for certain styles. The association of Gagelin with the wedding of Napoleon and Empress Eugenie gained Gagelin immense publicity in fashion magazines and fashion society, leading to increased sales. This was Worth's first lesson of the important role of aristocratic and celebrity connection to the success of a fashion business. Empress Eugenie, who was known for her style and charm, would later play a key role in Worth's success.

Paris had at this time gained great influence and attracted global attention as the brightest city in Europe. The *nouveaux riches* such as bankers and industrialists contributed to the social expansion of the city. The world looked to Paris as a source of fashion, culture and the *art de vivre* and the ever-observant Worth spotted an opportunity in the newly wealthy Parisian society. He saw the changing mannerisms and attitudes of the wealthy towards fashion and also the influence this had on the rest of Europe and beyond. The consumer public were more influenced by the destructuring of the society and the progression brought by industrial advancement. Worth recognized a market gap that had been created, which no designer or dressmaker had identified. During this period, the most prominent dressmaker was the renowned Rose Bertin, who had dressed Marie-Antoinette and other royals and aristocrats. Her approach to dressmaking and serving her clients, however, remained structured to the strict aristocratic system, even as the society evolved.

Worth's creative mind buzzed with ideas and thoughts of the new societal trends and he became restless to create women's clothes to address society's needs. He endlessly questioned the dressmakers he was in contact with about the tastes and styles of the nobles, which provided him with a defined image of the current consumer needs. He also relentlessly sought opportunities to realize his ambition of dressing women.

During this period Worth met one of the young apprentices at Gagelin, Marie-Augustine Vernet, who he would later marry and who would become the catalyst for his future success. As their relationship grew, he began making dresses for her. The styles were according to the emerging tastes that he could decipher from observing the society. The customers of Gagelin took notice of Marie-Augustine's finely cut and stylish clothes, which were different from the fussy clothing of the day. They began to request the same designs. As the demand grew, Worth asked Gagelin to start a women's department, which Marie-Augustine could manage. This idea horrified the management of Gagelin as they were considered the most distinguished silk mercers in Paris and arguably in the world of fashion and couldn't be linked with mere dressmaking. Worth pointed out examples of the dressmakers who had expanded their businesses to include the sale of textile alongside dresses, creating more choices and making selection easier for customers. After several rounds of persuasion and continuous pressure from customers, Worth was finally allowed to open a small dressmaking department within the company premises. He became one of the first men in the woman's trade of dressmaking in Paris. His presence in a textile house gave him great advantage in the choice and variety of fabrics for customers and his contacts with the silk mills in Lyon was an additional plus.

Worth's style was simple but he was obsessed with the perfect cut, exact fit and refined finishing. He also remained flexible and experimented with new concepts and colours. He was an extremely meticulous man and the great attention to detail that he paid to his designs and clothes separated them from others. These attributes would later elevate his clothes from dressmaking to *haute couture*.

In 1851, Gagelin was selected as a member of the French delegation at 'The Great Exhibition of Works of Industry of All Nations' at London's Hyde

Park. Worth's dress designs were displayed and won a gold medal. This was an honour for Gagelin and the entire French delegation. After this event, Gagelin began advertising Worth's designs in fashion magazines. Four years later, in 1855, Worth's designs won another first-class medal at the 'Exposition Universelle' in Paris. He had become an established dressmaker and Gagelin eventually realized his great value.

Worth, also recognizing his worth to his employers, requested a job promotion, possible partnership with the company, better working condition for his then pregnant wife Marie-Augustine, and the opportunity to rent one of the spare rooms at the store premises. He was refused all his requests. He realized that his time was Gagelin was over and he decided to leave the company to start his own business.

Worth and Bobergh (1858–70)

Charles Worth partnered with another dissatisfied employee at Gagelin, the Swedish Otto Bobergh, and together they raised the capital to start their fashion business. Their first store, Worth & Bobergh was opened at no.7 rue de la Paix, close to the Jardin de Tuileries in Paris, in 1858. Their strategic location in the centre of Paris meant that they were close to other dressmakers but, more importantly, to luxury apartments and the potential wealthy customers who lived in them.

Worth continued to design and make clothes in his signature simple and perfect cut style, while going through the challenges of a new start-up business with Bobergh. Their big break came almost as an accident a year later through the wife of a prominent novelist Octave Feuillet. She was to attend an imperial reception hosted by Emperor Napoleon and Empress Eugenie and was disappointed with the dress made by her dressmaker. In desperation she went to Worth for a solution at the last minute. Worth not only created a perfect dress for her on the same day (which was unheard of) but also gave her make-up as a complementary product. During the reception, Empress Eugenie noticed the dress and asked for the name of the couturier. When told that he was an Englishman, she was appalled and even amused at the thought of a male dressmaker. Although she didn't immediately patronize him, she didn't forget the dress or its maker.

At the beginning of their business venture, little business came the way of Worth & Bobergh and they became desperate for exposure. Worth understood that one of the quickest and most effective ways to rise in prominence as a dressmaker was through celebrities. He searched for the right candidate who was both influential in the fashion society and a friend of Empress Eugenie. He found his answer in high society lady Princess Von Metternich, wife of Austria's Ambassador to France and a close friend of the Empress. Worth and Bobergh sent Marie Worth to her with an album of their designs. Von Metternich was impressed with the designs and ordered two dresses immediately. She was also amazed that Worth required only one fitting to make the dress instead of the standard six fittings and was even more astonished with the results. She wore one of Worth's dresses to a ball and Empress Eugenie took notice. When the Empress enquired about the couturier, she was once again told that it was Charles Worth, the Englishman. This time, she sent for Worth at once. Worth & Bobergh thus became the official dressmakers of the Empress in 1860, two years after starting their business.

Since Empress Eugenie was the most fashionable and influential woman in Europe, all the royalties and aristocrats copied her style and sought her dressmakers. Within one year, Worth & Bobergh had clients across Europe and as far away as New York. Their client list consisted of the 'who's who' of royalty, fashion and society, including Queen Victoria of England. Their influence escalated in such a short time that Worth in particular became a personal clothes consultant to the Empress while other royals and nobles across Europe scrambled to be on his client list.

In the second half of the nineteenth century, Worth's fashion credibility and authority became established and he rose to become the dominant figure in French and global fashion. His astute business sense and innovative spirit led him to revolutionize the fashion industry, changing the simple function of dressmaking to become the art of *haute couture*. He also introduced the use of human models to showcase his designs, instead of the standard wooden busts. He organized private shows of his designs to clients, shop buyers and textile manufacturers, establishing the practice of fashion shows and private shopping. He was also the first couturier to have a seasonal collection and eventually became the first fashion business tycoon. Instead of going to his wealthy clients for fittings, he compelled them to come to his store, with the exception of Empress Eugenie. No one was too important for him and he soon became the most expensive couturier in the world. By 1864, he had over 1,000 seamstresses working for him.

During the early years of success, Worth's wife played a key role as both the model of his creations and the public face of Worth & Bobergh. In the current luxury fashion environment, her title would have been 'Brand Ambassador'. She regularly attended high society events where she modelled her husband's creations and created awareness for his business. In the process, she also became a fashion force in her own right.

The business of Worth & Bobergh, however, experienced a set-back through the negative impact of the French political crisis and war that preceded the end of Napoleon's reign. The unstable social environment forced Worth & Bobergh's clients, who were mainly royals and aristocrats, to minimize their fashion consumption. Otto Bobergh, sensing gloomy years ahead, requested to dissolve the partnership and share their profits; he left the business and Worth found himself alone. Later, during the war, Worth was forced to close down his store.

La Maison Worth (1871–1952)

Charles Worth reopened his couture shop as 'La Maison Worth' in 1871, but since most of his prestigious clients had been exiled during the war he found himself starting afresh. He diversified into theatre costume while continuing to design women's dresses. During this period he also mastered the art of self-promotion and incorporated art in his design and image, which set him apart from rising competition. Worth critically studied the fashion society to innovate fashion styles and anticipate changes in women's tastes. This was one of his most important business tools and contributed to the success of La Maison Worth.

As the political climate stabilized towards the end of the nineteenth century, Worth's business grew once more. He regained his authority in fashion and ultimately became a fashion entrepreneur and somewhat the fashion world's ruler. He was the first couturier to set seasonal trends and impose his tastes on his customers. The fashion society revered him and the rich and famous sought his attention. At the height of his fame, La Maison Worth was the most prestigious couture house for design and apprenticeship training.

Charles Frederick Worth died of pneumonia on 10 March 1895 aged 70. The news of his death reverberated in the fashion world amid great homage for his work. After his death, his wife Marie-Augustine and sons Gaston and Jean-Philippe, who were already working at La Maison Worth, continued to run the business. Gaston managed the finances while Jean-Philippe was in charge of design and production. Although they applied the skills and competences they learnt from their father, Charles Worth, La Maison Worth was never the same.

La Maison Worth flourished well into the 1920s but the couture house had to deal with rife competition from rising couturiers like Jeane Lanvin who opened her design house in 1890 and Paul Poiret, who came along in 1903. Also Coco Chanel emerged in 1910 and Madeleine Vionnet in 1912. These designers understood their consumers and the fashion requirements of the changing society, as much as Charles Worth did during his lifetime. They continually innovated to meet customer needs while La Maison Worth remained inflexible and restrictive. As a result, the popularity of the competitors grew and loyalty to Worth's house diminished. In a bid to promote their design house, which had also become a fashion brand, Jean-Philippe Worth wrote a biography of his father in 1928. The book was a success and Worth's name soared once again in fashion circles. The glory was, however, short-lived as this venture wasn't backed by concrete offerings of desirable clothing. La Maison Worth continued designing for the woman of the previous century, while its competitors had moved forward with current social needs. Finally, in 1953, after several years of business depreciation, La Maison Worth was taken over by the House of Paquin.

Modern business principles

The story of Charles Worth hasn't been recounted simply for entertainment, it is rather an important illustration that draws out highly relevant business guidelines for practitioners in the luxury fashion sector and beyond.

Charles Worth applied two major principles that made his fashion business highly successful. The first was his utilization of influential people in society as a publicity tool. He had an early realization of the importance of attaching his name to the celebrities that could influence fashion, and this practice continues to be applied by current luxury brands, notably with Hollywood stars.

The second business principle that he applied was the use of insight into consumer behaviour as a guide to creating desirable clothes. Worth understood the important role that societal evolution played in fashion, and was able to anticipate change and remain flexible enough to innovate his designs and business approaches according to changing consumer tastes and attitudes at different times.

Other business lessons that can be drawn from the fashion innovator and genius, Charles Frederick Worth, are the following:

1 He never gave up his ambition to become a couturier.
2 He spotted opportunities quickly and moved swiftly to exploit them.
3 He was bold enough to enter an industry dominated by women and was ready to be a laughing-stock in the short term in order to achieve his long-term goals.
4 He understood his business thoroughly and gained an unparalled level of expertise in both textile merchandizing and dressmaking.
5 He knew his signature style and never compromised it.
6 He understood the concept of differentiation and innovation and knew when a product and a brand required extension.
7 He was a true trend-watcher and recognized the evolution of his market environment.
8 He knew that the rich and famous not only mattered in society but are an effective tool for brand promotion.
9 He was a skilled self-promoter and extended his personality to his brand image.
10 He trained himself to be the best in his field and he became the best.

Additional business lessons can be drawn from the factors that contributed to the demise of La Maison Worth. They are the following:

1 La Maison Worth became too comfortable in its market leadership position and relaxed its competitive edge, giving room for newcomers to encroach

into its market space. Like the famous ship, Titanic, the couture house believed that it couldn't sink.

2 After Charles Worth's death, La Maison Worth overlooked changing societal trends and evolving consumer tastes.

3 The couture house ignored their competitors and failed to recognize their potential.

4 After the death of Charles Worth, La Maison Worth focused on promoting the spirit of Charles Worth to a diminishing consumer group instead of re-inventing the brand to attract a new consumer group and retain the interest of the old consumers.

5 Charles Frederick Worth did not prepare his design house well enough for his demise.

If La Maison Worth were still in existence with a similar level of prominence and fame, the brand value would have been among the highest in the world of luxury fashion. Although La Maison Worth no longer exists, Charles Worth undoubtedly set the foundation of the modern luxury fashion sector as an important aspect of the global society and a strong global economic force.

Great moments in the history of fashion

The history and evolution of fashion is undoubtedly fascinating. The world of fashion has witnessed several important phenomena that have brought change to both its consumption patterns and management practices. Here are ten events that so far can be summed up as the greatest moments in the evolution of luxury fashion. They incorporate the facet of creative design, the influence of society and the management aspect of fashion:

1 The early Egyptian era of opulence.

2 The Italian Renaissance period of art and fashion.

3 The reign of France's King Louis XIV and the rise of French luxury fashion and lifestyle.

4 The century of Charles Frederick Worth and the invention of *haute couture*.

5 Coco Chanel, Christian Dior and the birth of modern luxury.

6 The rise of New York and American ready-to-wear.

7 The second Italian fashion revolution of the sixties and seventies.

8 Tom Ford, the revival of Gucci and commercial luxury fashion.

9 Bernard Arnault, LVMH and modern luxury fashion management.

10 The internet revolution and e-commerce.

The history of luxury fashion branding indicates the unquestionable role of society in laying a foundation for the sector and contributing to its development.

It also identifies important chronological events that have shaped the luxury brands that we know today. These, together with constant interaction with luxury brands, provide a framework for the current and future practices of the sector and the continuous relationship between consumers and luxury brands.

Chapter 3
A passion for fashion: the luxury fashion consumer

'Twenty years ago, youngsters wanted to look like their parents. Now parents want to look like their children.'

Jean-Baptiste Danet, CEO, Interbrand France

The consumer is king

Gabrielle Coco Chanel thoroughly understood the luxury consumers of her time. She also recognized the influence of the wider society on shaping consumer expectations and outlook. In the early twentieth century after the First World War, fashion designers continued to apply the pre-war styles characterized by extravagant and elaborate designs. Chanel however opted for classic and practical clothing such as trousers and the famed little black dress for women. This design approach was embraced by society because consumer needs had evolved after the war. Women who had been forced to work during the war and also cater for their families in the absence of their husbands had been exposed to a different lifestyle that required dressing in a different and more realistic way. After the war, they maintained the same attitude towards fashion. They were no longer attracted to extravagant dressing but desired more practical clothing like trousers. Chanel's designs offered the fashion solutions they sought. The approach to anticipating and meeting consumer expectations formed one of the key success factors of the Chanel brand. It also significantly contributed to the continuous existence of the brand unlike Coco Chanel's contemporaries like Paul Poiret, Madeleine Vionnet and Elsa Schiaparelli who have all closed shop.

In a similar manner, when Gucci's former Managing Director, Domenico de Sole and former Creative Director, Tom Ford, left the company in 2004, the seat of de Sole was filled by an industry outsider, the former head of Unilever's frozen foods division, Robert Polet. The unexpected choice of this man considered as a stranger to fashion was a surprise to several practitioners in the highly protective luxury fashion industry. Gucci's reason for choosing him was strategic. The company wanted a manager who had a deep insight and understanding of the customer and would effectively apply the concept of meeting consumer needs and exceeding their expectations to the brand. Polet was credited with the know-how of providing the desired products and managing effective relationships with customers. Several people predicted that his lack of luxury experience, industry relationships and creativity and press savvy would backfire on the Gucci brand. However, the approach of customer orientation applied by Gucci has been effective, as the brand has increased its brand equity, sales and profitability under Robert Polet's helm.

It is apparent that insight into consumer behaviour is imperative in the luxury fashion sector and beyond. Gone are the days when products were guaranteed to sell, provided that they were well-designed, expensive and branded as luxury. Today's luxury consumers are different. They have to be surprised, tantalized, captivated, courted, pampered and constantly pleased without end. The competitive environment of luxury goods is also increasingly rife, making the quest of attracting and retaining the consumer's interest and loyalty more challenging.

There are currently two major segments of the luxury consumer population. The first is the 'traditional luxury consumer' who still reveres established brands like Hermès and Christian Dior; and the second segment constitutes a larger proportion of luxury consumers known as the 'new luxury consumer' population. This new consumer group are no longer lured by only brand names but also cherish a complete package of products and services that offer solid value through innovation and an exceptional experience in every element of the brand. They know exactly what they want and are not fooled by pseudo-luxury offerings. The luxury consumer of today has different desires, expectations, outlook, influences and characteristics from those of as recently as 30 years ago.

To illustrate the advanced level of the current consumer progression, an advertising campaign of the software solutions company, Siebel, in the 24 October 2005 edition of *Businessweek*, had the caption 'The Benefits of Selling to Sheep'. It showed a graphic image of a sheep, divided into four portions each with the following labels:

Sheep want simple things
Sheep are predictable
Sheep aren't demanding
Sheep don't mind being treated like sheep

The advertisement then proceeded on a cautionary note to highlight that companies should desist from treating consumers like sheep because consumers have evolved beyond exhibiting the attributes of sheep. The lesson

Figure 3.1
Consumers have evolved from the previous tag of 'Sheep' to the current tag of 'Smart'!

of the advert is simply that consumers are not sheep and should not be treated as sheep by companies, including luxury brands. Consumers are, rather, among the major assets and leeway that companies have for increasing revenue. They should therefore be considered as such and treated accordingly. The days are long gone when luxury consumers exhibited the characteristics of sheep through unbending single-brand loyalty. Consumers used to be pleased to make purchases from their favourite brands without seeking alternatives, but today the luxury fashion consumer is everything that is the opposite of a sheep.

Having said this, we have to understand the relationship between consumers and luxury brands and the role of luxury brands in the lives of consumers. The reason for the purchase of goods, regardless of category, is to fulfil consumer needs. When people pay for products or services, they are actually looking for solutions to problems and needs, and luxury goods form a part of those solutions. They are objects of desire that consumers view as a means to solving multiple problems and fulfilling multiple needs. Some of these needs are related to the consumers' real or aspirational identity, personality and lifestyle. Luxury brands help consumers define and accentuate the type of person they are or who they would like to be and also assist in communicating this definition to others. This is one of the roles of brand association in the luxury sector.

As is highlighted throughout this book, the concept of branding begins and ends with the consumer. The relationship between consumers and a strong brand is a type of bond or pact that starts with a psychological process in the mind of the consumer and is manifested through product purchases. This relationship is highlighted even more between luxury brands and consumers because of the profound role of the branding factor in the development of luxury goods. The source of the attachment of consumers to luxury goods is the role of luxury brands as symbols of personal and social identity.

Consumers offer their trust and loyalty to luxury brands with the understanding that the brand will deliver its promises and exceed their expectations. These expectations include the fulfilment of both functional and symbolic needs. The functional needs are the tangible and practical benefits of a product such as the time-keeping function of a wristwatch. The symbolic needs involve intangible benefits linked with the emotional and psychological dimensions of the consumer. These include fulfilling ego and self-esteem needs, reinforcing social status and projecting a self-image. The self-image extends from the consumer's true-self, that is who they truly are; their ideal-self, that is who they would like to be and their social-self, that is who they would like others to think they are. Although both tangible and intangible benefits are derived from luxury brands, the principal value of luxury brands to consumers is the intangible benefit. The intangible level brings the branding aspect of luxury goods into prominence and is reflected in consumer preferences and the decision-making process. It is also on the intangible level that the relationship between consumers and luxury brands moves from logic and functionality to what has been interpreted as irrationality. Now let's take a look at the 'rational' consumer decision-making process and compare it with the decision-making process of the purchase of luxury goods.

The consumer purchase-decision process

In their 2004 book titled *Consumer Behaviour*, Leon Schiffman and Leslie Kanuk define the term as the behaviour that consumers display in searching for, purchasing, using, evaluating and disposing of products and services that they expect to satisfy their needs. This means, in other words, how consumers make decisions to spend their available resources (time, money and effort) on consumption-related items (products and services). Further scrutiny of this definition shows the following aspects of the behaviour of consumers, presented in their hierarchy of influence:

1 What they buy (Products and Services)
2 Why they buy (Needs, Wants, Desires)
3 When they buy (Convenience)
4 Where they buy (Location)
5 How they buy (Channel)
6 How often they buy (Frequency)
7 How often they use the products (Relevance)
8 How they evaluate the products (After-Purchase)
9 How they dispose of the products (Durability)
10 How they decide future purchase (Loyalty)

This analysis can be applied to any category of goods, but since this book is concerned with luxury fashion goods, it will be related to the luxury goods sector. Each of the points above are further expanded according to the requirements of luxury goods:

1   **What consumers buy**   Luxury consumers buy more than luxury products and services. They buy a complete package of experiences, feelings and identities made up of the product, the service and the brand's characteristics.

2   **When consumers buy**   Luxury consumers purchase luxury goods whenever the opportunity arises. Luxury goods purchases often don't result from convenience as they are constantly desired and often fall within the priority of luxury consumers.

3   **Why consumers buy**   Luxury consumers do not buy luxury fashion goods when they are required because the desire for luxury goods is not fuelled by basic needs. Luxury products are 'cravings' and sometimes 'wishes', rather than functional needs, therefore there is a continuous yearning to possess them. Luxury goods are objects of desire and desires exist on a continuous basis.

4   **Where consumers buy**   Luxury consumers buy their products mainly in major fashion centres of the world where luxury fashion is prominent in consumer lifestyles.

5   **How consumers buy**   The majority of luxury consumers prefer to shop in the physical stores in order to benefit from a complete product selection and also enjoy the luxury retail atmosphere. However, other shopping channels such as the Internet and Mobile shopping are gaining increasing influence in the luxury arena and consumers are continuously shopping through these channels.

6   **How often consumers buy**   Luxury consumers buy luxury goods as frequently as is practically and financially possible for them. They often do not evaluate the buying decision of luxury goods on a logical basis. As previously indicated, luxury goods are objects of desire, meaning that if consumers can help it, they would fulfil this desire on a continuous basis.

7   **How often consumers use the products**   Luxury goods are highly relevant to consumers as a stamp of their personalities and lifestyles. As a result, the products are used frequently.

8   **How consumers evaluate the products**   The post-purchase evaluation of luxury products is almost a non-representational occurrence. This is because the appreciation of luxury goods extends beyond the products' functional attributes to include abstract and symbolic benefits. As a result, the evaluation focus is on the role of the luxury product in the life of the consumer and the satisfaction that it provides. Since the symbolic role of luxury products is continuous, their post purchase evaluation remains immaterial.

9 **How consumers dispose of the products** Luxury goods traditionally last for a lifetime and are rarely disposed of. However, an interesting occurrence has developed in the luxury goods sector in the last five years that has made luxury goods disposable. This occurrence is called the 'fast-fashion' phenomenon later discussed in Chapter 7 of this book. Fast fashion means that the design turnover of luxury products has become higher and the product lifecycles have become shorter. As a result, the 'It' fashion items change every few weeks. Consumers in a bid to keep up have also become smart and savvy in their luxury goods purchase cycle. They now sell their 'used' or 'semi-used' products for substantial amounts (sometimes close to the original price tag) in order to purchase new ones. Several second-hand dealers who trade in these items are cropping up in different global markets. This factor, however, does not diminish the value of the products or their brands.

10 **How consumers decide on future purchases** The decision for the future purchase of luxury goods has already been made. The future is now!

To further illustrate the decision-making process of consumers, Schiffman and Kanuk identified three main levels of influence which is illustrated in Figure 3.2.

The Input stage is mainly influenced by the strategies behind the marketing mix such as the product, pricing, retail channels and promotions. Other influencing factors are branding elements like the brand personality, brand image and brand awareness; and social groups like family, friends and colleagues.

The Process stage operates on a more intangible level, characterized by psychological and emotional elements such as perception, personality, attitude, and motivation.

The Output stage involves the use, evaluation and disposal of the goods.

Figure 3.2 *The three influential levels of the consumer decision-making process*

Source: Adapted from Schiffman and Kanuk, 2004.

A close examination of the model indicates that consumer evaluation of luxury goods purchases and use takes place mainly on the Input and Process stages. This is because of the highly aesthetic and symbolic nature of luxury brands. This fact does not, however, mean that the Output stage is irrelevant, but the elements of the Output stage feature on a minimal level.

Who is the luxury fashion consumer?

Consumers drive the luxury fashion sector. Any luxury brand that aims to succeed in the increasingly competitive luxury market environment needs to understand everything about the luxury consumer. And there's a lot to understand!

When we say 'luxury consumer', we don't mean only female fashion victims whose purses are stashed with endless cash and unlimited credit cards. Although women are highly influential in luxury buying decisions and constitute a large proportion of the luxury consumer market, men and children are also important luxury consumers.

Today's luxury consumer is different from the wealthy consumer of the past. Unlike in the past when wealthy consumers were easy to understand and satisfy, it is difficult to place the current luxury consumers in a box of definite descriptive characteristics. As one luxury brand manager rightly said, today's luxury consumer cannot be segmented. This is because the luxury consumer has evolved beyond the 'head-to-toe designer-clad single-brand loyalist' to a smart and savvy discerning consumer.

The current luxury consumer is highly sophisticated and brand literate. They are fashionable and aware of their tastes and preferences. Their choices of luxury products are based more on an understanding of their own style needs and less on the 'brand-name' factor. They also have an attitude that is a personification of youth, assertion and adventure, irrespective of their age. This attitude is reflected in the fact that today's parents and their children dress alike. Also older consumers can now look years younger through advanced cosmetics, giving them the freedom to appear like youths. The consumer market has consequently become loosened and diluted. For example, consumers of all ages including those in their forties, fifties and sixties, can be found at the payment queue for roller blades at Decathlon in Paris. Also the fitness and well-being craze now means that grandmothers, mothers and daughters can be found wearing the same clothes and accessories, and shopping in the same stores. These factors make understanding today's luxury consumer imperative and is responsible for the current huge market of Trend Trackers and Analysts.

The following characteristics provide an overview of the current luxury consumer's personality. These attributes only give an inclination of what to expect from the current luxury consumers and is by no way a definitive list;

luxury consumers are continuously evolving and their monitoring should be a permanent activity.

- **The luxury consumer is smart and intelligent**. It is difficult to mislead the luxury consumer of today in terms of any aspect of a brand's offerings. Consumers can now interpret marketing and branding messages in a whim. They are knowledgeable about product materials and their sources; they have travelled extensively and are interculturally aware and competent. They know the difference between Zen and Yen. They are also more informed through product comparison, reviews, virtual communities and publicly accessible information about luxury brands. Today's consumer has a personal calculator that helps them understand the overall value package of a brand's offerings in terms of product design and quality, price and brand identity. They also know when to trade down in some categories of goods in order to trade up in luxury goods. If a luxury brand offers an empty box, today's consumer can smell it from miles!

- **The luxury consumer is powerful**. There has been a power-shift from luxury brands to luxury consumers. The authority in the luxury market now belongs to consumers and they know it. This is because consumers have more choices in products, shopping channels and pricing of luxury goods. There are more luxury brands today than thirty years ago, offering more product variety and shopping choices. Also the old luxury brands are extending their offerings to include lesser-priced sub-brands. Consumers also have easier access to viewing the product choices and lower switching costs to purchasing them, especially on the Internet. They can now exchange digital photos of luxury products taken with their cameras or phones and can also shop on their mobile phones in addition to the Internet. Consumers also have the increasing flexibility of purchase and payment methods through credit cards and store accounts. They can buy at will but they also know when to buy and, most importantly, what brands to buy from.

- **The luxury consumer is individualistic**. Today's luxury consumer is a fashionista but not a fashion victim. They know who they are, what they want and how they prefer to interpret their personal style. Irrespective of location, from America to Europe, Asia, Africa and the Middle East, luxury consumers are becoming their own individual stylists. The expansion of the fashion market environment has provided them with the tools to become fashion experts. Diffusion fashion brands like Zara and H&M have given them the confidence to be experimental and bold enough to mix high-street with luxury fashion in one outfit; something that their grandmothers would have considered taboo in the past. This means the empowerment to stamp their personality through an independent style rather than through a single brand. Today's luxury consumer uses fashion as a definition of their individual personality and identity, in their own way and according to their own terms.

- **The luxury consumer is highly demanding**. The luxury consumer has grown from novice to smart. Smart people are less accepting of anything sub-standard and when people become knowledgeable, they also become demanding. Today's consumer wants individual attention and instant satisfaction. They also want a personal shopper, style adviser and shopping assistant at their disposal. They crave customized products and services both offline and online. They expect luxury brands to understand their needs in advance and to satisfy them. They are also interested in the ethical practices of the brands they endorse and the sources of the labour and materials of the products they buy.

- **The luxury consumer has high expectations**. Luxury brands already offer alluring products and high-standard services, but consumers are asking for more. Consumers want originality and authenticity in luxury products. They want to understand their source, material components and how they were made. They want genuineness in a brand's promise and its delivery. Consumers also want to be shown respect, to be greeted by their names in the stores, to be given privileged information through one-to-one marketing, to be invited for limited-edition product previews and for private shopping. More importantly, they want to be constantly delighted and surprised.

- **The luxury consumer has a disposable attitude**. The disposable attitude of luxury consumers is fuelled by multiple product launches; the pressure to be current and trendy; the speed of evolution of the global market; and the increasing pace of technological advancement. As a point of comparison, in the electronics goods category, home entertainment media has moved from VHS to VCD to DVD and now to iPod and iPod Video, in a space of ten years. This rapid development fuels disposability of goods beyond electronics. Luxury fashion consumers, who also use electronic products, have transferred this behavioural trait to luxury fashion. Also, as indicated earlier, the introduction of fast fashion has also fuelled the disposable nature of luxury consumers. Luxury consumers are no longer content to use a single luxury item for five years, without acquiring more. In the same way, they are no longer loyal to a single brand and have become brand hoppers.

- **The luxury consumer has strong values and principles**. The high level of moral ethics seen in the wealthy consumer segment is as the result of a different source of wealth. Most of the world's new wealthy consumers accumulated their riches through genuine discipline, persistence and hard work. It is uncommon for consumers with these personality attributes to be frivolous in their spending. Also, luxury consumers are no longer content with being outsiders. They want to be in the know of the ethical management practices of luxury brands. While these consumers appreciate and frequently purchase luxury goods, they are more likely to be associated with the luxury brands that share their moral values. These are the brands that are capable of showing core ethical associations; and at the same time represent real value and relevance through their offerings.

The twenty-first century fashion consumption environment

The personality and expectations of the luxury consumer are being shaped by several factors in the consumer market and general society, and an understanding of these factors provides an insight into the current consumer behaviour. More importantly, these factors are also indicators of the likely future behaviour of luxury consumers. The following are the factors that currently influence their behaviour:

1 **The rapid growth of information, communications and mobile technology**. It is no longer news that the Internet has changed consumers forever. The Internet has also changed business practices significantly. Consumers now have uniform and instant information at their fingertips everywhere in the world. The offerings from luxury brands are now in the public domain and consumers can access choices and alternatives at will. This has led to a desire and expectation of immediate solutions in terms of products and services. It has also contributed considerably to the 'brand-hopping' attitude and 'shopping-on-the-go' expectation of consumers.

2 **The increase in individual consumer wealth and wealth-creation opportunities**. A mass class of wealthy people have emerged the world over. At the beginning of the century, luxury consumers were a small segment of the global population. In the last four decades, however, an immense amount of wealth has been accumulated by individuals due to several economic, social and technological breakthroughs. Consumers are making money at younger ages, and they are also spending their money in a different way. They continuously have a penchant for luxury goods because as people get richer, they tend to spend proportionately less on necessities and more on luxuries. These luxuries include fashion, travel and property. In Europe, for example, the buoyancy of the luxury market is being driven by a steady increase in household income and the value of the property market. These newly wealthy consumers have replaced the traditional aristocratic consumers of luxury goods.

3 **The increasing spending power of women**. Women have become the major consumers of luxury goods as a result of their possession of more money due to increased education, career orientation and decreased financial responsibilities. Also women are marrying later, divorcing more and having fewer children, which has led to an increase in their disposable income. Women spend significantly more than men on luxury products and

at the same time are influential in the luxury purchase decisions of men. Four out of every five luxury purchases are either made by women or are controlled by women. Since women are working and earning more money, their impact on the current and future luxury retail market is important.

4 **An increase in international travel, intercultural exposure and artistic exchanges**. Consumers are travelling a lot more than in the past and gaining insight and interest in new practices and ways of life. For example, groups of Chinese tourists can be spotted everywhere all over Europe and the rest of the world; Americans are leaving home more and the European Union has opened up its national borders. It is also important to note that tourists around the world are responsible for approximately 25 per cent of the world's luxury goods purchases. Increased travel and cultural interactions lead to more varied material cravings. Also, the mind education gained through travel has increased the expectation of originality and substance of consumers towards luxury brands.

5 **Media saturation and information overload in the marketplace**. The commercial environment is congested with information screaming for the attention of the same consumer. As a result, consumers have to process multiple advertising information channelled towards them on a daily basis. There seems to be an advertisement in every visible public space. Luxury brands have also begun advertising their products at bus stands and on street billboards in a bid to catch on with consumer goods advertisements. This has led to mental fatigue of consumers, who therefore choose the messages and brands that have some meaning to them. This factor emphasizes the importance of having a brand essence.

6 **The changing retail environment**. Luxury goods are now accessible to more consumers through what has been popularly termed 'The Democratization of Luxury'. This means that mass premium brands like Zara and other retail discounters such as Primark have made it possible for consumers to have replica luxury products like clothes and accessories, at lower costs. When consumers have the possibility of spending less on clothes from Zara, they are likely to be able to afford more luxury products in other categories such as leather goods and jewellery. Also, several luxury brands such as Armani have extended their product portfolios to include lower-priced ranges.

7 **The increase in consumer credit and payment options**. This includes credit cards, store cards, fidelity cards and affinity cards. The use of consumer credit for luxury purchases has increased significantly in the last decade, which not only buoys the retail market and economic environments but also provides consumers with independence and higher spending power.

8 **The effect of immigration and mass movement of consumers**. Across Europe, America and in other parts of the world, the increase of immigration has diversified the ethnic make-up of local populations. This is

especially evident in the United Kingdom, where immigrants from India, Pakistan and the Caribbean have helped shape the national culture and identity. Their influences have affected the fashion styles, tastes and product preferences of the entire country. Also in France, the effects of the dress culture and style of immigrants from North Africa and Asia is gradually being reflected in the French fashion style. The case is similar in other parts of Europe and America, notably the USA and Canada. This factor has created new expectations and success opportunities for new luxury brands, and has also led to globalization of fashion tastes.

9 **The lowering of the entry barrier to the luxury goods sector**. The highly protective luxury goods industry has opened up. New luxury brands such as Jimmy Choo, André Ross and Paul & Joe have emerged, creating more competition for brands and more choices and variety for consumers. These brands have also proved to up-and-coming designers the feasibility of launching a new luxury fashion brand in the twenty-first century.

10 **The increase in outsourcing of the manufacture of luxury products and services**. Several luxury brands manufacture their products in Asia, East Europe and South America where labour costs are substantially lower than in their home countries. This has created cost-saving opportunities for the brands but also a loophole for the manufacture of counterfeit luxury goods. Also luxury brands are increasingly outsourcing their customer services through independent call centres, which leads to cost-saving but might also result in sub-standard services and unmet consumer expectations.

Luxury consumer market indicators

Several luxury brand managers accede that the luxury goods sector doesn't require market segmentation like other categories of goods. While this viewpoint is credible in some areas, the luxury market environment has changed dramatically and consumer groups need to be monitored. Luxury brands need to understand who their customers are, where to find them and the key factors that drive their behaviour. This is an aspect of market segmentation. For example, trend-watchers from London-based company The Future Laboratory have identified two groups of young and wealthy consumers that make up the luxury consumer population. They are Young Urban Professionals (YUPs for short) and New Entrepreneurial Nomads (NENs for short). These consumer groups exhibit characteristics that make them appropriate targets by luxury brands. In addition, there is a consumer group that is found neither among the extremely wealthy consumers nor the newly wealthy youth, and which also makes up an important market segment for luxury brands. However, the affluent market has no single or defined target and no uniform retail strategy that matches them. The key is to understand consumers and what drives them.

In order to better understand the luxury consumer market, the following indicators have been identified as having a substantial effect on the market:

Global wealth   A changing global economic environment has created immense opportunities for personal wealth accumulation, and the size of the world's affluent is on a steady rise. The beginning of the noughties witnessed a significant upward movement on the global wealth index. Between 2001 and 2002, there was an 18 per cent increase in the number of millionaires worldwide, creating 514 additional billionaires with a collective holding of US$25.5 trillion in the process. This figure jumped to US$44.9 trillion by the end of 2004. Presently, the number of billionaires in the world is estimated to be more than 26 million with a collective holding of US$30.8 trillion in assets. The annual rate of increase of the world's millionaires is estimated to be 7 per cent. These categories of high net-worth individuals are defined as those with investable assets of over US$1m. This group of wealthy consumers includes a newly emerged youthful elite of millionaires who are a part of the 'new' luxury goods consumers.

Other indicators of the world's growing wealthy and their consumption patterns include the popularity and interest in art auctions running into billions of dollars and the upsurge in the demand for gemstones, such as tanzanite and diamonds. Also, the personal asset management portfolio of the global private banking industry is on a steady increase. It is also interesting to note that 80 per cent of the world's new wealthy elite acquired their wealth in the last 20 years.

European coming of age   Europe has an ageing population. From the United Kingdom to Italy, Spain, Germany, Portugal, France (to a lesser extent) and the rest of the continent, this phenomenon resounds in government decisions, as well as in economic and social policies. There are more seniors in Europe than in America and Asia. People aged 60 and over make up nearly 25 per cent of the European population, compared with 16 per cent in the US. This might be bad news for several aspects of socio-economic governance, but it is welcoming news for the luxury goods sector. In France for example, individuals aged 50 years and above account for more than 30 per cent of the population. They earn 45 per cent of net domestic income; hold 50 per cent of the population's net financial assets; and represent a market for goods and services estimated at €150 billion. In the United Kingdom, Germany and other European counties, the senior citizen pattern is being set and this is an important indicator for the marketing, branding and retail strategies design of luxury brands.

The European senior consumer group wields considerable influence in the retail market. They have a high disposable income and also an inclination to spend more on luxury goods. They also have more time to shop for luxury goods in relation to their younger luxury consumer counterparts.

American baby boomer surge   The United States is the biggest retail market in the world for both luxury and non-luxury goods. Retail is the second-largest industry in the United States in the number of retail establishments and employees. The US retail industry generates $3.8 trillion in retail sales annually and approximately $11,690 per capita. The affluent market is also on the increase. In 2000, the total personal wealth of Americans was more than $25 trillion, with more than 7 million households having a net worth of over $1 million, and approximately 600,000 households with a net worth of over $5 million. A substantial proportion of these consumers are the baby boomers.

The consumer segment referred to as the baby boomers are those born after the Second World War, between 1946 and 1964. They number approximately 74 million consumers and make up 2 per cent of the US population. They are the largest and most influential consumer age segment in the United States and also have the largest earning capacity and the greatest disposable income in America. With an estimated annual spending power of $2 trillion, they are a tremendously significant target group for the luxury market.

The baby boomers have moved into their prime earning years and are currently independent of children who have mostly left home. This gives them more purchasing and consumption freedom. Also the approaching retirement of most baby boomers will provide more free time to spend their money. They will also enjoy longer, more productive lives than any previous generation as a result of advanced medical care and well-being practices.

Baby boomers are driven by a different set of characteristics than the previous consumer generation of their age. First, they are more physically and mentally active, more flexible and willing to try new products and experiences, including experimenting with luxury brands. A baby boomer will likely not be locked into loyalty for Chanel or Hermès for the rest of their lives. They will likely be curious to check out the offering of John Galliano, Matthew Williamson or Vanessa Bruno. Secondly, they are not afraid of change and even crave change to fuel their energy. They are staying longer in the corporate world and several of them are even on the verge of starting new careers or acquiring new education diplomas upon 'official' retirement. Thirdly, the divorce rate among this consumer group is also on the rise. This common phenomenon also drives change. When people get divorced, they want to change a lot of things in their lives beginning from their looks to their luxury brand consumption. This factor is important for luxury brands, as Americans are known to spend substantially on beauty and image.

Japanese balance   Japan is the world's second-largest economy with a consumer population of approximately 100 million people. This holds great significance for the luxury and prestige goods sector. The Japanese also have a special affinity for luxury goods. Japan also accounts for a quarter of the world's luxury-goods consumption, and therefore the state of the Japanese economy and currency value is crucial to the annual performance of luxury goods companies.

Japanese luxury consumers are highly fashionable. They are also more label-conscious and brand loyal than their European counterparts. The level of the Japanese luxury consumer loyalty to several brands such as Louis Vuitton and Chanel is so high that books have been written about it. According to statistics from stock market analysis company, Seeking Alpha, 94 per cent of Tokyo women in their 20's own a Louis Vuitton product; 92 per cent a Gucci product; 58 per cent a Prada product; 52 per cent a Chanel product; and 44 per cent a Dior product. Although Japanese consumers are sophisticated, they also value simplicity, high quality, well-crafted goods and distinctive packaging. These qualities are found among the identified European luxury brands, which Japanese consumers have a special penchant for.

The Japanese consumer demographic is also an important luxury market factor. More than 40 per cent of the population, representing 50 million people, are over the age of 50. They also control much of Japan's wealth. These consumers are more willing and able to spend freely on luxury goods and services. Japan also has another interesting consumer group, known locally as the 'parasite singles'. This group is made up of 5 million young, single working women who mostly live at home. Their high disposable income makes them a major force in the consumer economy. They are the single largest spending segment in Japan, and their expenditure on luxury goods is up to 10 per cent of their annual earnings. They also play an influential role in their parent's buying decisions.

China's might   China is the largest emerging luxury goods market in the world and is also establishing itself as a superpower of the world's economy. The country currently represents 12 per cent of global luxury goods purchases and is forecast to grow 26 per cent per anum for the next four years. There are currently 300,000 millionaires in China, who make up a part of the Chinese luxury consumer population. Within the next five years, the number of people who can afford luxury goods is expected to reach 1.3 billion. This means that the Chinese consumer is important for luxury brands because of the potential that this market will have to make or break the luxury goods sector.

China has seen one of the most dramatic explosions of wealth creation in human history, notably from 1978 to date. Twenty years ago, there was no middle class in China but currently, the middle-class population is more than 100 million. Every aspect of the Chinese economy is witnessing a boom. For example, the year-on-year growth of China's economy in the first quarter of

2006 was 10.2 per cent. It has been estimated that by the end of 2007, China's retail trade will be above $2 trillion, nearly twice as high as Japan and two-thirds the size of the American market. China is also likely to overtake the European Union in purchasing power within a decade. The Chinese textile and retail industries are being fuelled by cheap labour and an endless flow of Western clients and is currently on the verge of dominating the world's textile production and exports.

Travel in and out of China is also on the rise. In 2002, China had 36 million visitors and this number is expected to rise to 100 million by 2020. This influx of visitors into China is also fuelling the dilution of cultures and the acquisition of an international level of fashion sophistication for the Chinese luxury consumer. Also between 2003 and 2004, Chinese outbound tourism rose from 20 million to 29 million and it is estimated that by 2015, more than 100 million Chinese will travel abroad annually. Chinese visitors to Europe are also expected to exceed American visitors within the next five years. About 80 per cent of luxury purchases by Chinese consumers are made while on a trip abroad, especially to Europe. Chinese consumers purchase luxury goods while abroad and return home with the products, the style and the class acquired from their travels.

The high growth rate of the Chinese economy is an enticing market for the luxury fashion goods industry. For example, China has currently surpassed Japan to become the world's largest market for luxury watches. The country takes fashion retailing seriously and plans to build Asia's largest shopping complex in Shanghai.

China also poses several challenges and contradictions for luxury brands. For example, the country has the potential of being the largest consumer market of genuine luxury goods in the world within the next decade. At the same time, China is reputed to be the largest manufacturer and supplier of counterfeit luxury goods in the world. The potential problem that this contra-diction creates for luxury brands is a clash of the genuine luxury consumer population and the counterfeit consumers who might dilute the image of the luxury brands to an extent that could drive the genuine luxury consumers to seek alternatives.

Also China has a host of upcoming designers that will likely play influen-tial roles in the world of fashion. As a country that has fashion as a part of its culture, both designers and consumers of the present and next generations are being groomed to recognize and support talented indigenous Chinese design-ers. The impact of the rising Chinese designers will be heightened in the next decades when the influence of Western luxury brands on Chinese consumers eventually declines. Presently, China is a retail paradise for most European and American luxury brands but the Western luxury fashion influence is likely to last less than it did in other parts of Asia such as Japan. This is because unlike Japan and Hong Kong, China did not experience colonization by a Western country, therefore the consumer aspirational element towards

Westernization is less powerful. Although Chinese consumers will continue to look towards Hong Kong, Japan, Europe and America for fashion inspiration, they will eventually recognize and embrace their own luxury fashion brands.

India's rise   India is one of the emerging luxury markets gaining momentum worldwide. Although this market has been slower than China in embracing Western luxury brands, several indicators show that it is as ready for luxury fashion as the Chinese market. India has a growing literate population with potentially brilliant careers and spending power. There are currently 70,000 millionaires in India, which make up the top end of the luxury consumer population. The country's current per-capita income is $460 and the rapid growth of its services industry has contributed to more internal wealth creation. The population structure is also favourable for the luxury industry as the working-age population is growing. By 2020, 47 per cent of the population will be between the ages of 15 and 59, compared with 35 per cent in 2003. The economy is also expected to sustain an annual growth rate of 8 per cent as from 2006.

The Indian luxury consumer is also highly fashionable and is likely to make more luxury purchases than their Western counterparts in the near future. India's long-term fondness for jewellery has created a base for the upsurge of luxury brands into the lives of Indian consumers. This market substantially influences the luxury jewellery market which is expected to grow by 40 per cent annually to reach US$2 billion by 2010.

Russia's influence   Russia is a current luxury retail gold mine. It is a country that provides both design inspiration and a ready luxury consumer market. Its rapid and vigorous economic growth has given rise to increased luxury consumption and expenditure, and Russian consumers currently have access to acquiring luxury goods, which were previously unattainable under the previous communist regime.

Russia's Gross Domestic Product is growing at a rate of 6 per cent per annum compared with 2 per cent in the USA. The consumer population is 145 million with Moscow and St. Petersburg representing 10 per cent of this population. Moscow's luxury market is currently worth more than US$2 billion, which makes it larger than the luxury market of New York. Moscow and St. Petersburg have joined the world capitals offering access to all international luxury brands. It is also estimated that more than one hundred thousand people of Moscow's population fall within the consumers that can afford luxury goods.

There are 88,000 millionaires in Russia and a large proportion of their wealth is channeled towards luxury fashion purchases. The Russian luxury fashion taste is also becoming more global and attuned to Western flavour. Today's wealthy Russian shoppers are among the best-informed, discerning and sophisticated luxury consumers in the world. They also purchase the most expensive products such as limited edition accessories and off-the-catwalk creations. Russian luxury consumers have a preference for products made with special materials such as pure gold and diamond encrusted hardware finishing in leather goods. They have been described as daring in their portrayal of their fashion tastes, with tendencies of being obsessed with luxury. Russian consumers are likely to replace Japanese consumers in luxury expenditure.

Several luxury brands are already present in Russian cities notably Moscow and St. Petersburg and more brands and luxury departmental stores including Britain's Harvey Nichols are planning expansion into Russia. The country is also nurturing home talent and held its first Russian Fashion Awards in 2005.

The future luxury fashion consumer

There is no doubt that the luxury consumer will continue to be highly sophisticated, stylish and informed. The current luxury consumer can comfortably navigate around the luxury terrain and expertly position luxury and mass-market brands in a hierarchical order according to their values and offerings. This clear frame of reference has not been witnessed in the luxury consumer landscape until now.

In the future, consumers' awareness of their self-worth will continue to increase, and they will know exactly what they want and where to find it. They will no longer look to luxury brands to define themselves but will themselves determine the scope of luxury brands that will fit into their self-image and lifestyles. They will recognize their ownership of the power to determine their choice of luxury brands, and will also become savvier through an increased global and open outlook.

In addition, new technologies will continue to influence luxury consumers, and in addition, new avenues of shopping such as the Internet, mobile phones and possibly the iPod will play a key role in the way consumers view luxury shopping. This will make them even more demanding of instant gratification and innovative offerings, and expecting to be marvelled by every product and service of a luxury brand.

Another important factor that will drive the future behaviour of the luxury consumer is the increasing influence of the temporary-ownership culture. Consumers will become more disposable in their attitude to general consumer goods and this will also transfer to luxury goods, albeit on a lower scale. Since luxury goods cost as much as 600 per cent more than the same goods in other categories, luxury consumers will not dispose of luxury goods but will rather exchange or resell them. They will also increasingly subscribe to services that loan luxury products for a fee.

Strategic implications for luxury brands

The analysis of the luxury consumer market has several strategic implications for luxury brands. It forms a basis for a clear direction in the formulation of branding and overall corporate strategy, and an understanding of luxury consumers also enables luxury brands to gain a competitive leverage in the marketplace. In order to achieve this, the following tips are imperative:

1 Luxury brands must remain innovative and forward-thinking.
2 Luxury brands must streamline production processes for fast fashion turnover.
3 Luxury brands must embrace mass fashion brands as complements rather than as competitors.
4 Luxury brands must have a clear brand and market positioning. A brand that is stuck in the middle in the current market environment is going nowhere.
5 Luxury brands must never compromise their 'luxury' and 'prestige' status.

Chapter 4
Luxury retail design and atmosphere

'Only ever make splendid or awful impressions. The rest are forgotten.'
Alison Mosshart, musician

Luxury retail location

The most popular slogan in retail is the following:

The three most important things in retail are: location, location, location.

This watchword is used to emphasize the indispensable nature of an appropriate location in retail. Retail location involves more than physical space but includes the choice of a place that is most suitable for the sale of the products or services in question. An inappropriate retail location is difficult to overcome, irrespective of the feasibility of the rest of a company's overall strategies. Poor retail positioning can also negatively affect a store's accessibility and attractiveness to shoppers, regardless of the brand's positioning. This factor is even more crucial for luxury brands because in addition to visibility and accessibility, luxury brands ought to be situated in the most elite and prestigious locations of the cities where they operate. Retail location is therefore of paramount importance to the luxury goods sector.

In general goods retailing, the choice of store location is determined through utilizing socio-economic pointers like population, geography and consumer disposable income. Other factors include human-traffic flow and in some cases, tourist-traffic flow. In addition, technical business models that aid the choice of store location have been developed by experts, including the 'Catchment Area' method and the 'Central Place Theory' method. The main aim of these techniques is to identify the most commercially viable store locations for optimal sales turnover. These models are, however, more appropriate for general goods retail, so they will not be discussed in this book.

Luxury brands have a central requirement for retail location choice. This is the 'Prestige' indicator. The main distinguishing factor between luxury retail location and that of mass-market retailers is the requisite need that luxury

luxury retail design and atmosphere

Figure 4.1   *Avenue des Champs Elysées, Paris, a luxury retail heaven*

brands have to position their stores in exclusive and high-status districts and cities, which are at the same time commercially feasible. The prestige store location reinforces the core brand values and the differentiated brand status of luxury brands. Prestigious retail locations also attract and retain a niche-customer base while satisfying their ego needs during shopping.

In Paris, prestigious luxury retail locations can be found at Avenue des Champs Elysées, shown in Figure 4.1, and its environs, including Avenue Montaigne and Avenue George V. This district is also known as the '*Triangle d' Or*' or the 'Golden Triangle'. Other locations are the historical Rue Saint Honoré, which is considered the global luxury fashion industry's foundation, and its extension on Rue du Faubourg Saint Honoré and their environs. These streets are lined with several luxury brands.

The same pattern follows in other cities such as London, where the Knightsbridge area, including Sloane Street and Bond Street, is considered the epitome of luxury store positioning. In Milan, the '*Quadrilatero d'Oro*' or 'The Golden Rectangle', which runs between Via Monte Napoleone and Via Della Spiga, is the luxury retail district. It features the stores of Gucci, Armani, Prada, Tiffany and Louis Vuitton, among others. New York's prestigious shopping streets include Madison Avenue and Fifth Avenue and their environs, while in Los Angeles, Beverly Hills is the location of luxury fashion brands. Tokyo's Omotesando district represents the equivalent of luxury store positioning in Japan, while other examples abound in several cities around the world.

In addition to being located in high-status districts, luxury brands need to be in the fashion cities of the world to ensure both brand visibility and commercial viability. The fashion cities are those that have the highest catchments of luxury consumers in terms of indigenous population and visitors. They include Paris, Milan, New York, London, Tokyo and increasingly Los

Angeles and Hong Kong. Luxury brands usually begin their global expansion in these cities irrespective of the brand's origin. In addition to these locations, other rising 'fashion cities', in terms of style and commercial returns, include Moscow, Shanghai, Bombay, Dubai and Johannesburg.

Strategic store location guarantees a brand's visibility, which reminds the consumer of the brand's existence and core attributes. The store location also acts as an extension of the brand's personality and is used as a tool to ensure the vitality of the brand. Although luxury brands ought to be at the right locations to reflect their 'prestige' status, careful attention should also be paid to hasty store expansion at the same location in order to avoid over-exposing the brand. For example, Japan is host to numerous luxury fashion stores which often have multiple stores within the country, like Coach, which has more than 100 stores in Japan. This strategy ensures high sales returns, but at the same time it is important for luxury brands to attain the right balance between commercial feasibility and brand over-exposure. This can be done through a continuous evaluation of the costs and benefits of extensive store openings against the long-term effect on the brand equity. The 'prestige' brand attribute of luxury brands should be maintained through the store location choice, while pursuing global growth and expansion.

In addition to exclusive stand-alone stores, luxury brand store locations are also found in high-end departmental stores, where they rent retail spaces. Such department stores include France's Galeries Lafayette, Printemps and Le Bon Marché; America's Bloomingdale's, Sak's Fifth Avenue and Macy's; the UK's Harrod's, Selfridge's and Harvey Nichols; and Italy's The Galleria Vittorio Emanuele in the Piazza del Duomo. Others are Japan's Mitsukoshi, Core, Matsuya, Seibu and Matsuzakaya in the Ginza district of Tokyo; and Hong Kong's Lane Crawford. Other parts of the world also have impressive high-end department stores, which are emerging so fast that the level of competition has more than doubled in the last five years. Notable examples are the world's tallest building, Taiwan 101, where brands like Chanel, Prada, Loewe and Yoji Yamamoto have stores; and the highly publicized Dubai Mall also known as the Burj Dubai building, still under construction, set to become the world's largest shopping centre on completion. Other retail monuments in the Middle East include Dubai's Mall of the Emirates, which houses almost every major luxury brand as well as a five-star hotel and a ski slope; and the Villa Moda store in Damascus.

In Russia, luxury department stores include the Grand Palace in St. Petersburg and the new 'Luxury Village' in Moscow. India is also not left out in prestigious department stores, with its opulent shopping area at Mumbai's Taj Mahal Palace & Towers and the Hotel Oberoi. Also, countries that are usually classified as the 'rest of the world' or 'other countries', by luxury brands, where luxury retailing is still in the introductory phase, are catching up with the construction of retail and entertainment malls. For example, British luxury departmental store Harvey Nichols recently opened a store in

Istanbul, Turkey, and plans a Russian expansion. Also South Africa's largest city Johannesburg has the Sandton City Shopping Centre, often described as a 'World of Splendour', where Louis Vuitton has a store. In addition, the Nigerian city of Lagos has just seen the completion of two high-end retail shopping centres, although luxury brands are yet to enter this market. At the South American end, Brazil has witnessed the growth of independent retailers of luxury brands like Daslu in São Paulo, in addition to other luxury departmental stores in Brasilia and Rio de Janeiro. In most cases the retail spaces in these departmental stores are leased by major international luxury fashion brands.

Retail location techniques can also be exploited in order to create a more viable niche for luxury brands. This can be done by creating 'special products stores', which retail specific goods not usually found in the brand's permanent collection range. These goods could include limited edition products, special order goods, bespoke products and co-branded goods. Several brands have adopted this strategy, in following with the current consumer needs of constant delight and individualism. A notable example is sportswear brand, Puma, which currently has a New York flagship store called the 'Puma Sports Fashion Lab', devoted to its collaborative product ranges with Alexander McQueen, Christy Turlington, Philippe Starck and Neil Barrett. Nike also has a concept store called the 'Nike-ID Lab', which retails only limited edition products. Although several luxury brands have stores which retail specific products from the permanent range, the luxury sector is yet to make the concept-store retail location technique an important aspect of its retail strategy.

Retailing is a core aspect of the luxury fashion business. However, retailing doesn't end when a brand has successfully found a location. There are several additional tactical factors that determine retail success, and which make up the retail strategy. The retail location choice is the first step to the retail strategy, followed by the store concept.

Store concept

The store is an integral aspect of luxury retailing and is crucial in representing the brand identity and meeting the expectations of visitors. The store is often the first point of real physical contact between consumers and brands. A brand's identity is mostly projected through the store concept, from where an image is either crafted or harmonized. This image leads on to a mind positioning and internal judgement of the brand by consumers. For example, if a consumer sees the advertisement of a luxury product in the print media and visits the store afterwards, they would expect synchronism between the image that they already have in their minds based on the advertisement and what they see and experience in the store. The advertisement is like the cover of a book and the store is the actual book contents. The story should be in accord with the cover.

The store concept comprises the design, the atmosphere, the size and impersonal selling techniques.

Design

The design function is one of the most visible fundamentals of retail store strategy. It refers to the store layout and elements of its aesthetics such as its colours, decorations and lighting, among others. The effective combination of these features often result in enticing and captivating consumers and, of course, higher purchase probability.

The layout of a store greatly contributes to its image and manipulates traffic flow. In the conventional retailing of consumer goods such as supermarket retailing, the store layout choice follows the most commercially realistic pattern, which is often an outline called the Grid-Flow Layout. This layout features long vertical and horizontal rows of display units of goods with a single entrance and a separate single exit. Another general retailing pattern is the Guided-Flow Layout, with a pre-determined long path from the store entrance to its exit, as found in several furniture stores. In mass fashion retail, the most common and most feasible store layout is called the Free-Flow Layout. This pattern features several entrances and exits to the store and allows free movement of customers. It also provides the store with a better image and enhances the consumer's mood and feeling. An additional advantage of this pattern is that shoppers are likely to stay in the store for a long time if the atmosphere is complementary. However, its disadvantage is that shoppers might fail to spot several products as a result of the lack of a main entrance and a central exit.

In addition to these essential layout considerations, there are other factors that are essential in the selection of the luxury store layout. The first factor is to ensure that the layout best reflects a prestigious image and complements a luxury atmosphere. The second factor is to ensure that the layout optimizes the surface area while providing the customer with adequate comfortable space and distance to appreciate the store and the brand. The third factor is that the retail layout choice ought to provide room for a form of in-store animation and entertainment which enhances the image of the brand. Although each brand has a unique store arrangement that best reflects its brand personality, the luxury attribute is best shown through variations of the Free-Flow Layout and the Boutique Layout represented in Figure 4.2.

In addition to the store layout, the colour scheme that a brand adopts in its store design is essential to its image and positioning. This ensures synchronization of the brand's identity with the store representations, and cannot be over-emphasized. For example, the dark colour tones found in the stores of Alexander McQueen evoke a smouldering sexiness which is associated with

(a) The boutique store layout

(b) The free-flow store layout

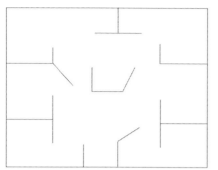

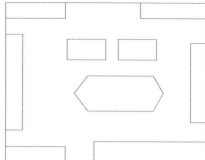

Figure 4.2 *Store layouts*
Note: Lines and boxes represent product shelves.

the brand. Also the gold and brown colour tones found in Louis Vuitton stores are in harmony with the brand's visual identity and luxurious brand appeal. The Chanel monochrome black and white, which evokes classic chic, is felt both in the stores and in the other aspects of the brand's communications.

Colour can also be used in retail stores to influence shoppers' moods and increase purchase probability. The appropriate management of colours through knowledge of colour functions often complements an effective store design. For example, the colour red is considered to be exciting and escalates the body's metabolism, and yellow is believed to be the colour of intellectual and mental stimulation. Blue is considered as the colour of calm and dignity while green fosters harmony and uplifts spirits. Brown is considered calming and wise; black is sexy and sophisticated; while white evokes purity, innocence and agelessness.

Another crucial aspect of retail store design is lighting. It is highly essential as a tool for the manipulation of space and enhancement of colour and visibility. Effective lighting can influence the size appearance of a store, making it appear large, small or long. Lighting can also affect the way a store's decorations are viewed, affecting the colour tones of both the store and the products displayed within the store. It is important to place strong lighting in the product display sections of the store, irrespective of the overall mood and atmosphere. Other design tools such as mirrors and glass are used to manipulate lighting to create an impression of a larger space. For example, large well-positioned mirrors can reflect lighting from one window, creating the appearance of two windows in a store with only one window.

Decorations within the retail store are also vital in luxury fashion retailing. The luxury store is more than a selling channel, it is also a means of artistic projections that present expertly crafted goods and an appealing brand image. The aesthetic appeal of a luxury fashion store is one of the major differentiating factors between a luxury store and a mass fashion store. Luxury store decorations may be in the form of the now commonly used wall-mounted plasma televisions featuring videos of the brand's fashion shows and product care guidance. Store decorations may also be thematic or seasonal. Luxury fashion stores are expected by consumers to have highly appealing store decorations that add to the brand's cachet. The messages of the store decorations should therefore go beyond the surface beauty and appeal of the products to the inner subconscious and psychological levels of the consumers' minds.

An example of an impressive store design concept is Louis Vuitton's flagship store located at Avenue des Champs Elysées, Paris. The store, which covers 1,800 square metres of retail space, embodies both high artistic and architectural design and has been described as '*Art à tous les étages*' or 'Art on all floors'. The concept of art and architecture has been transferred to every aspect of the store design and layout including the elevator. Unlike most retail stores where the elevator is a functional instrument that transports consumers from one floor to another, Louis Vuitton's store uses its elevator as a statement of creative imagination. The elevator, which is essential for the store's seven floors, is completely decorated in black and is empty of any signal, light and sound. As the lift transports visitors from one floor to another (with an escort), the total darkness and stillness that envelops the passengers is a powerful force of art and imagination. Its strategic purpose is to stimulate the loss of the senses of vision and sound. The effect of this sensory loss is the invigoration of the imagination of the person travelling in the lift because they find themselves in a space that is the opposite of the high visibility of the store. The intent is that when they eventually arrive at their desired floor, they will be likely to look at the products differently and appreciate them better. Although physically and sensually empty, the lift space is abundantly rich in the imagination, experience and psychological space of the customer riding the lift. Such is the level of interactivity expected between luxury stores and consumers.

Another example of a notable luxury store design is the Hong Kong boutique of Chanel. The store concept is an emulation of Coco Chanel's Parisian apartment, and its design displays include all the style elements associated with Coco Chanel during her lifetime, which have formed signature elements of the brand. These range from a 32-metre strand of pearls hanging down through three floors; tweed-replicating black and white lacquer panelling; chandeliers; and a diamond-dust portrait of Coco Chanel. The strategic reasoning behind this store design is to create a space where all the attributes associated with the brand's founder, Coco Chanel, are featured.

Mass brands such as Nike are also capitalizing on using the store concept to appeal to the lucrative upper-end market. The sportswear brand's Nike-ID store on New York's Elizabeth Street is designed to resemble an *atelier* where bespoke goods are manufactured. The store also retails only limited edition goods.

Figure 4.3   *Le Bon Marché departmental store, Paris, combines the free-flow and boutique store layout patterns (2005)*

Figure 4.4   *The André Ross store exterior, Hong Kong, harmonizes with the brand's personality and image (2006)*

Luxury fashion stores are required to have magic, energy and life in order to inspire consumers and also become embedded in the consumers' memories.

Atmosphere

In simple terms, atmosphere is the sum of the feelings that consumers experience within a store interpreted through their senses. It is a blend of sensory communications that exists on the subconscious and psychological levels of consumers, and is associated with terms like ambience, mood, impression, background, character and sensations. Atmosphere is connected with the five human senses: visual, aural, tactile, olfactory, and taste; and an additional sixth sense, 'emotion'. Appealing to consumers' visual and aural senses is essential in creating the appropriate atmosphere, but it is not sufficient in the current luxury marketplace. A complete sensory package comprising all the senses is required in luxury retailing.

Luxury goods are categorized as sensory in nature, which means that they rely heavily on intangible factors to ensure sales and to promote the brand.

Since sensory elements such as the visuals, touch and smell are intangible in nature, they ought to be manipulated to complement the intangible qualities of the brand like the brand personality and image. This will ensure that the atmosphere of the selling space harmonizes with the brand and reduces the risk of the brand losing its cachet.

Consumers mostly remember their experiences in a luxury store based on the feelings they had during and after the store visit. These feelings are shaped by their perceptions, which are influenced by the store's atmosphere through visual and other sensory elements. The visual aspect of a store is affected by its colour, lighting, size, shapes, packaging and so on, and visuals play a key role in defining the mood that a store evokes in consumers and has the highest level of impact on consumers' interpretation of a store's atmosphere.

The aural sensory element connected with sound (or in some cases noise) in a store also contributes significantly to the mood and ambience of the store. Sound considerations include music, volume, pitch, jingles and noise distractions. For example, in conventional fashion retail fast music such as pop is used during peak shopping hours to encourage high expenditure and impulse purchases while at the same time unconsciously promoting quick exits in order to accommodate more shoppers. Slow music on the other hand is used during low shopping hours to encourage shoppers to linger in the store, thereby increasing their purchase probability. Luxury brands could replicate these features through a higher level of application. For example, the choice of sound should not only focus on sales returns, but must complement the brand personality. In addition, luxury stores ought to avoid every possible noise distraction and retail gaffe that could disturb shoppers, including telephone exchanges of sales assistants.

The sense of touch or tactile sense is highly important in the luxury fashion store atmosphere. Luxury consumers have a strong need to touch and feel luxury goods before purchase. As indicated earlier, luxury goods are sensory in nature and consumer responsiveness to retail and product design is particularly connected with the sense of physical touch. The tactile sense is also described by the words 'emotion' and 'feeling'. This indicates that the sense of touch is linked with the emotional response that luxury brands strive to arouse in their consumers.

The olfactory sense or the sense of smell is also an important influential factor in luxury goods retailing. The sense of smell has become more crucial in luxury goods retailing because several luxury brands have extended their product range to include fragrances and cosmetics, which rely heavily on the sense of smell. Often these products are sold in the same stores as apparel, leather goods and other products manufactured by the brand, which emphasizes the importance of the sense of smell in luxury goods retailing.

Also, every brand has an associated scent and this should be perceived in the store. Consumers do not expect to visit a Hermès store and find that it smells of Chanel No. 5; or to visit the cosmetics section of a luxury brand's store to find that it smells of leather. The minimum olfactory requirement for luxury stores should be to smell fresh, clean and distinct.

The sense of taste is also increasingly being featured in the luxury fashion arena. Luxury brands like Giorgio Armani, Roberto Cavalli and Pierre Cardin have extended their offerings to include products that require the use of the sense of taste, such as sweets, chocolates, wine, champagne, vodka and coffee. Although these products highlight the increasing relevance of the sense of taste in luxury retailing, taste remains the least relevant of the senses in the overall retail of luxury fashion goods. Also, products that require taste are often distributed through other more appropriate channels like restaurants and food halls of major luxury departmental stores.

The additional sensory element of 'emotion' is also critical in luxury goods retailing. As indicated earlier, luxury brands present and retail their products through reinforcing the brand's aura and appeal, which produce emotional responses from consumers. This emotion stems from the consumers' overall feelings in the store and encompasses all the elements of the retail space, the products and the services. The feelings are then transformed into longing and are stored in the consumer's 'memory bank'. They are pulled out when decisions regarding the brand are required, which is often.

The store size

Store size is an important consideration in the store concept of luxury brands. In choosing the luxury fashion store size, the unspoken rule of thumb among luxury brands seems to be 'the bigger the better'. Luxury brands currently vie to outdo each other in the development of colossal stores mostly within flagship retail centres. For example, Louis Vuitton's flagship store in Paris covers 1,800 square meters over seven stories, while its New York store is set in a 20-storey building. Chanel has a 10-storey size store as its Asian flagship in Tokyo. Armani's planned Tokyo store opening in 2007 will cover 86,000 square feet over multiple floors. Also, Chloe's flagship on Paris' Avenue Montaigne is 2,000 square feet, while Fendi's largest store is located in a seven-story palazzo in Rome. Pucci's flagship store in the brand's hometown of Capri is 324 square feet. And the list goes on. In some cases, the store sizes of luxury brands are even larger than those of department stores, where space is a crucial determinant of retail prowess.

Adequate store space is crucial in luxury goods retailing and the large-sized stores have the additional role of making a bold statement of the brand's strength, austerity and personality. These factors are essential in the image development and preservation that makes luxury brands appealing to customers. Accordingly, although a giant store serves commercial purposes (because more goods can be displayed), large retail spaces also have underlying importance in luxury goods retailing. So, large retail space is a positive selling point and should be implemented wherever possible. However, the strategic question related to luxury store size is whether 'bigger' automatically translates to 'better' and whether the size of luxury stores influences luxury consumers.

Impersonal selling

This is the art of product display and store layout manipulation that promotes the customer's independence during shopping. Impersonal selling encourages the customer to move freely within the store and to spend as much individual time as possible without relying on the assistance of sales staff. It is a tactic that aims at providing a total brand experience and encourages impulse purchases.

Impersonal selling is the opposite of personal selling. It enables customers to request personal selling services when they actually need them, without feeling that sales assistants are crowding them. In several cases, unsolicited personal selling services come off as hard selling, which is often a put-off for consumers. Impersonal selling on the other hand empowers customers and in most instances is also more convenient for customers.

In addition, impersonal selling can be used to dispel misconceptions and put consumers at ease. Some luxury consumers feel intimidated by luxury stores because of the notion that such stores and staff have a cold and superior disposition. Impersonal selling is a way to counter this perception. Although the luxury store should have adequate sales staff on hand to assist shoppers, personal service is most effective when it is granted on request.

The additional benefits of impersonal selling include lower labour costs for the companies that own the brands and, in some cases, less floor space utilization. Impersonal selling techniques include product grouping, product spread, space liberty and hot-spots for bestsellers or new products, among others.

In designing the store concept, luxury brands are required to maintain the attributes of creating a desire and an aspiration, while ensuring sales feasibility. These will ensure that the consumer benefits from both the functional and socio-psychological gains of using luxury products.

Retail extension

The retailing scene has undergone dramatic development in the last three decades and continues to evolve. The current consumer culture has embraced shopping as more than an act of necessity. Shopping is now a leisure, cultural and entertainment activity in several parts of the world. For example, '*Mall Shopping*' is currently a major pastime in Dubai, London and most American cities, and has become a strong competitor for other forms of arts and cultural activities. The phrases 'Meet me at the mall' or 'Let's do the mall' is becoming as common as 'I need a glass of water'.

Retailers are also responding accordingly through providing consumers with what has been dubbed in marketing circles as 'Retailment', a combination of the words 'Retail + Entertainment'. This concept involves the combination of retail, leisure and entertainment services in a commercial location. Most retail establishments such as shopping centres now also have leisure centres, restaurants and cafés used as relaxation, refuelling and meeting points. Retailment has also been adopted in the luxury goods retail sector. For example, British luxury retailer Harvey Nichols is known for both luxury goods retail and gastronomic expertise. Also, The Mall of the Emirates shopping centre in Dubai has a ski slope although the mall is located in the middle of a desert. Other luxury departmental stores like Printemps in Paris also provide in-store entertainment for shoppers and spectators alike.

The use of retailment as a retail extension tactic is necessary to enhance the status of luxury brands. The method has been used by the luxury sector in the nineteenth and twentieth centuries through associating luxury fashion with different leisure aspects of society like arts and culture. As far back as the early part of the twentieth century, *haute couture* designer Elsa Schiaparelli collaborated with artists Jean Cocteau and Dali in fashion design. This blending of artistic and fashion talent is currently being adopted by several luxury brands and extended to other aspects to form an integrated luxury retailment offering. Luxury brands are placing a strong emphasis on the fusion of luxury retail with retailment forms like art, literature, music, film, sports and gastronomy. The association of luxury brands with an appealing form of entertainment has become a necessity in the current challenging luxury market because consumers increasingly seek substance from brands in the form of background stories, fulfilled through retailment collaborations. Providing consumer satisfaction through retailment links ought to feature as a prominent aspect of the luxury retail strategy.

Retailment is also an effective means of generating positive publicity for a brand through showing the brand's commitment and interest in its community. This also forms a part of corporate social responsibility, which improves the brand's public image in the long term. Retailment also offers a powerful means of linking the world of fashion with intellect through literature. An additional benefit of luxury retailment through art initiatives and sponsorships is the chance to project the brand as not merely 'profit-driven' but also able to share its financial gains with the wider society.

Several examples of art sponsorships and other related retailment initiatives abound in the luxury fashion sector. They provide evidence that luxury brands have recognized the importance of extended retail practices to include several forms of entertainment. An example is Louis Vuitton, which launched an Art Exhibition Centre named 'L'Espace Louis Vuitton' within its flagship store on Paris' Avenue des Champs Elysées in 2005. The centre is a means of artistic and cultural expression and showcases the works of avant-garde artists such as Vanessa Beecroft. Pierre Cardin also has a private museum at his Maxim's

Paris restaurant, which showcases artistic furniture and paintings from the eighteenth and nineteenth centuries. Also Italian high-end brand Furla supports art through an annual young artists award called '*Furla per l'Arte*', which it set up in collaboration with the Italian foundation for art and culture, *Querini Stampalia*. Another notable example is the Bally Museum owned by the Swiss brand, where visitors can find shoe displays from the early twentieth century. Other brands such as Bvlgari, Cartier, Rolex and Ermenegildo Zegna are all connected with several art initiatives, providing a link to retailment.

The fusion of art and fashion can also be extended to product development and often leads to success when effectively managed. For example, the 2005 collaboration between fashion designer Lulu Guinness and British sculptor Ann Carrington to create a limited edition collection of handbags was highly successful. Also, the famous Louis Vuitton monogram multicolour range is a result of the collaboration between the brand's Creative Director Marc Jacobs and Japanese artist Takashi Murakami. Several other examples can be found in the works of other luxury brands.

The combination of fashion and art, however, requires strategic direction. The strategic challenge lies in incorporating the brand's collaborations within the brand story and effectively communicating them to the public, rather than treating them as part of the periodic 'News & Highlights' of the brand.

In the literary entertainment sphere, British accessories brand Jimmy Choo provided a link with the art of photography and writing through its Coffee Table photography book, titled *Four Inches*. Other publications that are aimed at both informing and entertaining the public are the 20-years chronicle book of Dolce and Gabbana titled *20 Years: Dolce & Gabbana* published in 2005; the 150 years anniversary publication of Louis Vuitton in 2005; and the book that chronicles the history of fashion brand Diesel, titled *Fifty*, which was published in 2005 to coincide with the 50th birthday anniversary of Diesel founder Renzo Russo. Louis Vuitton has also incorporated a bookshop at its Avenue des Champs Elysées Paris store, where Louis Vuitton travel guides are sold.

Figure 4.5 *Vanessa Beecroft exhibition poster at L'Espace Louis Vuitton, Paris, January to March 2006*

Figure 4.6 *Brazilian carnival in-store entertainment at Printemps luxury departmental store, Paris, April 2005*

The blending of sports and fashion is another means of retail extension through providing luxury retailment. Examples include the collaborative design ranges between sportswear brand Adidas and Yoji Yamamoto and Stella McCartney respectively. Other collaborations have been between Puma and fashion designer Alexander McQueen and model Christy Turlington. While the fusion of luxury fashion with sports is unconventional, the synergy of tradition and technology that the two sectors offer often results in a highly creative collection. However, this strategy should be meticulously managed in order not to lead to the depreciation of the luxury brand's value.

Product merchandizing design

Merchandizing means the process of managing the methods used to push products into the market. It utilizes several methods to make the offerings of a brand attractive to consumers and increase purchase probability, and is therefore a push-marketing medium as it pushes consumers to make purchases. Merchandizing involves selling goods at the point of sale, which in most cases is the physical store. It utilizes visual representation, which is of paramount importance in luxury fashion retailing and is a constituent part of branding.

Effective merchandizing techniques are important in luxury fashion retail especially with the more demanding nature of consumers and the increasing level of competition among luxury brands. The merchandizing techniques and product offerings of luxury brands should be realistic, delightful and relevant to the lives of consumers, since luxury consumers now have multiple product choices and a multitude of fashion trends every season from a growing number of designers. As a result they can compare products and trends and make more informed choices. They also have information and choice overload, which sometimes leads to confusion and conflict. The result of these factors is that consumers are likely to lose trust for brands that have only surface-level offerings. This means that luxury brands need to differentiate themselves through creating desirable products and selling them with effective techniques.

Merchandizing involves product display and layout, pricing and ticketing display, product packaging, point-of-sale advertising, product zoning, traffic-generation techniques, product hot-spots and inventory control.

Product and price-ticketing display is driven by imagination. A large number of luxury brands often fall into the trap of sameness through lack of creativity in product presentation. For example, the product packaging of several luxury brands such as shopping bags and product boxes have a uniform look in style and concept and little differentiating features. Also the point-of-sale product display in the stores of numerous luxury fashion brands is often bland and uninspiring. On the other hand, the point-of-sale could be used as an advertising medium to introduce new products, showcase best sellers or display 'take-away' complementary goods such as small leather goods. However, when customers find these goods unappealingly displayed or encounter employees that show a lack of enthusiasm in promoting these goods, then the target of purchase probability will be lost.

Additional merchandizing techniques include 'Product Zoning', which involves the placement of complementary products side by side; and 'Traffic Generation', which features the positioning of high-demand products towards the centre or rear of the store thereby obliging customers to walk through the store to reach them. For example, leather goods such as bags and shoes are logically placed close to apparel, which are positioned close to other accessories such as belts and scarves. Jewellery and timepieces go together while cosmetics and fragrances complement one another. Eyewear and other high touch-based products are often grouped together. Other merchandizing techniques include 'Product Hot-Spots', which display new products or interactive products like fragrances, cosmetics and promotional goods. These products are usually presented in groups or categories as well as in rankings of importance, demand, relationship or interaction.

Window display is another important consideration in product merchandizing, as both a sales medium and a communicative medium. It is an important brand image projection tool because it addresses the public, which includes luxury consumers, potential luxury consumers and non-luxury consumers.

Window display merchandizing techniques currently require strong differentiation. This is a result of the visible convergence of retailing tactics of luxury brands with those of mass fashion brands, as a result of continuous evolution of the fashion industry. For example, fashion brands that do not advertise in the mass media, such as Zara, use their window displays as a communicative tool and therefore place great emphasis on its design and message. This is similar to luxury department stores such as Macy's or

Figure 4.7 *The store window display of luxury department store, Harrod's, Knightsbridge, London, April, 2006*

Figure 4.8 *The store window display of mass fashion brand H&M at Knightsbridge, London, April 2006*

Harrod's. The result is a greater level of creativity and imagination in window displays among luxury fashion brands, departmental stores and mass fashion brands. This factor has contributed to increased expectations of consumers from luxury brands, which therefore need to show greater creativity and imagination in window displays at all times. For example, there is little difference between the window displays of the two stores, Harrod's and H & M, Knightsbridge, London, shown in Figure 4.7 and 4.8.

Another crucial element of store image projection through merchandizing is the synergy between a store's interior and its exterior in terms of display, design and aesthetics. A store that habitually changes its exterior design motif should also routinely change the interior to maintain a consistent message. An example of a luxury store that has maintained interior and exterior design consistency over its long history is French department store Galeries Lafayette (Figure 4.9). The store often uses a thematic concept both indoors and outdoors to enhance its appeal.

Figure 4.9 *Luxury department store, Galeries Lafayette, Paris, maintains consistency between its interior and exterior designs*

Figure 4.10 *Louis Vuitton's creative giant monogram trunk façade covering the renovation work at its Paris Champs Elysées flagship store, 2004*

Figure 4.11 *Cartier's giant replica of its packaging box, covering the reconstruction work at its Paris Rue de la Paix store, 2005*

Finally, the exterior design of a store can also be a creative tool in all circumstances irrespective of condition. For example, during the renovation period of the Cartier and Louis Vuitton flagship stores in Paris, the stores' exteriors were covered with giant-sized reproductions of the brands' products and packaging. This is a creative communications tool that reminds the public of the presence of the brand and also a landmark and in some cases a tourist attraction (Figures 4.10 and 4.11).

New selling techniques

In order to gain competitive leverage in a more demanding retail climate and satisfy a more impatient consumer group, new and creative forms of luxury retailing are required. Luxury consumers have increasingly busy lifestyles and their shopping for luxury goods has become more challenging as a result of a crowded luxury market and the unavailability of online luxury shopping. This means that they are restricted to shopping in stores in most cases. However, several consumers no longer desire to go to stores but they want the store to come to them. As a result, several additional techniques have either emerged or are being revived to complement existing retail store practices. Among the new selling techniques are:

1 Trunk shows
2 Pre-season shows
3 Post-season sales
4 Personal stylist shopping
5 Shopping lunching

Trunk shows originated in America's mid-west as a shopping means where individual retailers took goods in their car trunks to wealthy housewives in the suburbs of major cities. Presently, several luxury brands like Burberry, Chanel, Celine, Alexander McQueen and Yves Saint Laurent have adopted the concept of trunk shows and modified it to suit a sophisticated clientele by giving it a prestigious aura.

In the luxury context, trunk shows are privately held fashion shows where the new season's collections are previewed to a select clientele prior to being displayed in stores for the public. Trunk shows offer customers the opportunity to shop privately in an uncluttered environment. They also provide access to products that are only available by pre-order, helping the clients to avoid being on long waiting lists. Another important benefit is the availability of expert advice and individual attention through style advisers and fashion consultants, which are often lacking in the stores. This personalized service leads to a higher purchase probability and increased customer satisfaction. Customers who attend trunk shows are generally likely to spend substantially higher amounts of money than they would during conventional shopping. This leads to higher sales turnover for the brands and a stronger attachment between the customer and the brand. Trunk shows are often held in the luxury store on a specific day, usually after the runway fashion shows and are mostly attended by appointment. However, brands like Ralph Lauren and Burberry are making trunk shows more available to a mass consumer public by providing information and access to them through their websites.

Pre-season shows are an extended form of trunk shows. The distinguishing factor is that pre-season shows are mostly by invitation and attendance is exclusive to the clients the luxury brands select. Also, pre-season shows focus on the sub-collections that are launched just prior to the main season's collections, while trunk shows are held as a preview of the next season's complete collection. The sub-collections are called Cruise Collections by some brands like Gucci and Jimmy Choo, while Dior refers to theirs as the Capsule Collection. Pre-season shows also provide the same benefits that trunk shows provide to both luxury brands and luxury consumers.

Post-season sales is the equivalent of price discount sales normally held by mass fashion brands or brands in other product categories. However, in luxury fashion, post-season sales are private and are mostly by invitation. They involve the sale of a luxury brand's previous season's collection at discounted prices, often up to 50 per cent of the original retail prices. Since luxury brands need to remain exclusive in order to maintain their brand equity, post-season sales have not been widely adopted by several luxury brands. The brands that practice post-season sales retailing do so exclusively for selected customers and on a restricted number of shopping days.

Personal stylist shopping is a selling technique that has been in existence in both luxury goods and conventional goods retailing for decades. However, shopping with a personal stylist was restricted to VIP clients but is now being required by a broader consumer base. Personal stylists are currently found at luxury brands, luxury departmental stores and also at major fashion magazines. Some of them also work independently such as the New York-based company, Paris Personal Shopper, which caters to the needs of clients intending to make shopping trips to Paris.

Personal stylists provide shoppers with invaluable advice on the season's trends and also how they can combine products in the store with the complementary products the clients already own. They also help less fashion-savvy clients define their tastes and choose the right goods to balance their looks. The ultimate goal of personal stylist shopping is to satisfy the customer, enhance their experience with the brand and develop a deeper relationship that often leads to brand loyalty. Personal stylist shopping is an important aspect of client relations, which also provides an opportunity for one-to-one marketing.

Previously, the luxury fashion sector had the reputation of poor customer services provided by cold and aloof sales staff. However, several luxury brands have realized the importance of client relations and are investing in smart and stylish sales staff with dispositions to be responsive to customer needs, with the right personality to embody the aura of the brand.

The shopping lunch is a relatively new retailing technique in luxury fashion retail, pioneered by innovative luxury brands such as Fendi. This method mixes the art of entertaining and socializing with shopping in a private setting. Shopping lunches take place when luxury brands invite a specific number of clients to an afternoon of eating, socializing and shopping, at a private venue. Fendi currently hosts four shopping lunches annually in the UK, each time in the home of a different Fendi client handpicked by the brand. The guest list is a chain of invited guests who are asked to invite other guests until all available slots are taken. The invited guests are shown a collection of products that include pre-order-only goods as well as collections that are yet to be displayed in the stores. The benefits of shopping lunches are similar to those of trunk shows, personal stylist shopping and pre-season shopping. These include the comfort of exclusive private shopping in a relaxed environment; expert and individual style advice; high customer satisfaction; high purchase probability; enhanced brand relationship; convenience for the shoppers; and increased sales turnover for the brand.

The case of designer outlet shopping villages

Discount shopping is a major retail feature that attracts consumers to brands. In pursuit of the best value for their money, consumers are ready and willing to go an extra mile for certain types of products including fashion goods. It was on this premise that the concept of discount outlet centres was developed for fashion goods. In the early days of this phenomenon, discount outlets were found mainly in North America, and were often warehouse-style retail centres on the outskirts of major cities where mass fashion brands often went to 'dump' their old stock that was no longer desirable in the main stores. These goods were sold at exceptionally low prices to attract consumers and to clear the stock. This concept was highly successful as consumers were often willing to travel the extra kilometres for a good bargain. However, discount or outlet shopping was for a long time the domain of mass-market retailers. Today, this concept has encroached into the luxury fashion scene.

It began when Prada purchased a mass piece of land in the small town of Montevarchi, Tuscany, located between Milan and Florence in Italy, and began developing a shopping mall that would later serve as a discount village for the brand. Today, the outlet mall officially named 'The Space' retails Prada and Mui Mui products, including apparel and leather goods, at prices that are sometimes up to 60 per cent below the main store prices. Gucci caught on shortly after this and purchased an equally massive piece of land in nearby Leccio Reggello, Florence in 1999. There, the company developed a shopping outlet named 'The Mall' where the products of 20 exclusive luxury brands including Gucci and all the Gucci Group-owned brands are retailed at discounted prices, sometimes up to 50 per cent lower than the original prices. Unlike the Prada-owned mall, which retails Prada and Mui Mui goods, the Gucci outlet mall retails a wide range of 'outside' luxury brands like Burberry. The Mall, however, focuses exclusively on luxury brands that desire to sell their end-of-season stock at discounted prices and doesn't retail the goods of non-luxury brands. Giorgio Armani also has a factory outlet store in Vertemate, near Como, while Jill Sander's outlet store is located in nearby Cirimido.

The common factor these discount outlet shopping centres have is that they do not advertise themselves as Prada-owned or Gucci-owned or Armani-owned spaces. This is because the strategy of discount shopping centres is in contrast with the brand attributes that form part of the desire for luxury goods, like 'exclusivity' and 'enhanced image'. Also, luxury brands do not include the addresses of their discount stores as a retail location in their media advertisements, for the same reason.

Luxury fashion discount shopping has, however, been made more popular by the founders of the Value Retail Chain, which owns designer outlet shopping villages on the outskirts of 11 cities around Europe. The shopping villages include Bicester Village, located between London and Oxford (Figure 4.12), La Vallée Village close to Disneyland Paris (Figure 4.13), La Roca Village in the outskirts of Barcelona, and other shopping outlets on the outskirts of Milan, Bologna, Brussels, Dusseldorf, Munich, Frankfurt, Dublin and Madrid. The group currently has a portfolio of 300 fashion brands and more than 600 stores across its network of villages. The target consumer group is the upper-income fashionable consumer set aged between 25 and 55.

The Value Retail discount shopping villages are built to resemble small towns, but instead of housing they feature only shops and restaurants. More than 60 per cent of the brands that occupy the stores are international brands such as Versace, Kenzo, Max Mara and Givenchy, although exclusive domestic brands are also promoted. The discount outlet villages focus mainly on retailing fashion goods although cosmetics, house wares and interior decoration brands are also well-represented. The goods are usually end-of-season products marked down at prices ranging from 30–70 per cent of the original store prices. Although discount luxury fashion retail dominates the activities of the Value Retail villages, there is also the presence of mass fashion brands such as Mexx, Puma and Reebok. This raises the following question:

Do designer outlet shopping villages dilute the luxury brand image? Is this a luxury brand killer?

Figure 4.12   *Discount shopping outlet, Bicester Village, near London, 2004*

Figure 4.13   *La Vallée Village discount outlet village, near Paris, 2006*

The sale of luxury goods at discounted prices is not a new practice, although it is not widely publicized, and is a practice that has amplified in the last decade. The adoption of the mass discounting strategy for luxury goods is a result of several factors in the changing environment of luxury fashion retailing. These factors have placed an emphasis on sales returns and commercial results, driving luxury brands to adopt discount selling strategies. Notable among these factors are the following:

1 Consumers have become wise to the variety of choices they have in terms of luxury and mass fashion goods. They increasingly know where to go to find what they want and are ready to reject the brand that doesn't meet their expectations in terms of value for money and product design.
2 The luxury market is expanding rapidly and the competition level has more than doubled in the last decade. This has put a lot of pressure on luxury brands.

3 The ownership structure of luxury brands is changing as several non-luxury companies have acquired luxury brands. This has increased the performance pressure on luxury brands with more emphasis on sales turnover, return on investment and shareholder value.

The answer to the question: 'Do designer outlet shopping villages dilute the luxury brand image?', is yes, placing luxury brands in discount outlet shopping villages undoubtedly affects the 'exclusivity' attribute associated with luxury brands. This is even more enhanced at the discount centres that mix luxury goods discounting with mass fashion discounting.

The answer to the question: 'Is this a luxury brand killer?', is no, the presence of a luxury brand in a discount outlet centre is not a brand killer. However, this strategy needs to be meticulously managed by luxury brands to ensure that the long-term benefits outweigh the costs in relation to the brand equity.

So how should this delicate strategy be handled? The following points act as guidelines for luxury brand retail positioning in discount shopping centres:

- Select the discount outlet centres that only retail goods from luxury brands. This factor retains the exclusive location attribute associated with luxury brands even though the prices of the goods have been lowered. It also minimizes the shoppers' impression of shopping among 'junk' goods.
- Provide only end-of-season goods at the discount shopping villages and avoid goods that are in the current collection in the main stores. This way, when consumers travel the several kilometres to the discount villages, they know that they are getting the previous season's goods at reduced prices only because the goods are 'last season' and no longer available in the stores, and not because the brand is a 'discount brand'.
- Provide expert and unparalleled in-store customer service at the discount store. This will give shoppers the impression of being in a special place and among highly crafted goods although they're being sold at reduced prices.
- Provide in-store animation and entertainment. The main stores of several luxury brands such as Roberto Cavalli and Chanel have plasma TV screens that showcase the fashion show of the latest collection. These features will enhance the atmosphere of the discount store even more.
- Maintain the brand personality and aura. Discounting is not an excuse for luxury brands to forget who they are and what they represent to the public. Consumers that visit outlet centres also shop in the main stores so the same attributes that are found in the main stores should be extended to the outlet stores.

In conclusion, store location, store merchandizing and atmosphere are intricate aspects of luxury fashion retailing that contribute to the public image

projection of the brand. These aspects of retail need to be constantly innovated in the rapidly changing luxury market. Also, several aspects of fashion
retail strategies like the convergence of both luxury and mass fashion brands
need to be meticulously monitored and managed. For example, Avenue des
Champs Elysées, Paris, which is considered as the epitome of luxury location,
currently has stores of non-luxury brands Zara and Naf Naf, among others, in
addition to Louis Vuitton and Cartier. In the same manner, London's
Knightsbridge is the location of Burberry and Harrod's as well as H&M, Zara
and several other mass fashion brands. The Sloane Street area which was
previously exclusive to luxury brands has also seen the encroachment of non-
luxury brands like Zadig & Voltaire, which recently opened a 1,300 square
foot store on the street.

The implication of these changes is that luxury brands need highly refined
retailing techniques more than ever before. Luxury brands are expected to
develop creative and innovative retail techniques to add to a more meaningful relationship with consumers. The strategic goal of luxury retailing should
not only be to reach sales targets, but also to satisfy customers through implementing strategies that enhance brand value. This means that it will take
much more than the brand name and product designs to maintain the long
queues in front of luxury fashion stores.

Chapter 5
The art of creating and managing luxury fashion brands

'Branding is not about getting your consumer to choose you over the competition. It's about getting them to see you as the only solution.'
L. Aldisert, cited in Dennis and Harris (2002)

What is branding, really?

'Brands' and 'branding' are among the most abused and misunderstood terms in the business vocabulary. If you ask the average consumer of luxury goods to define a brand, they'd probably relate it to a 'brand name' like Versace or Dior, or to a product like the famous Hermès Kelly bag. But if you prod deeper, you'll discover that consumers have different perceptions, feelings and attitudes towards different brands, simply because each brand is unique and customers understand the different messages that brands emit. This shows that consumers understand the branding concept.

Even more surprising is the range of responses from business professionals when asked the meaning of brands and branding. Some refer to branding as a corporate logo or identity, others believe that it is a company's trademark and yet others associate branding with the name of a company or its products and services, including the processes of new product launches and re-launches. These features do not define a brand but form parts of the associative elements of branding.

A brand, as mentioned earlier in this book, is an identifiable entity that makes specific and consistent promises of value and results in an overall experience for the consumer or anyone who comes in contact with the brand. This entity includes names, terms, signs, symbols, designs, shapes, colours or a combination of these elements. Their purpose includes identifying the products or services of a seller, differentiating them from those of competitors and providing value to consumers.

In brief, we can simply define a brand as the following:

A brand is the sum of all the feelings, perceptions and experiences a person has as a result of contact with a company and its products and services.

This means that a company's brand resides in the mind of consumers and that the success and failure of a brand depends on its position in the consumer's mind. It also means that contrary to popular belief, a product (which is something manufactured in a factory) is not a brand. However, the product becomes a part of the brand (the total experience), when it has been stamped with the brand logo and transported to the store and displayed within the unique store environment. It is this total package that consumers buy. Products are easily outdated and can be copied by competitors and counterfeiters but a brand is unique and timeless making it impossible to be imitated. Also, a company's corporate identity is not a brand but forms a part of the brand.

The luxury goods industry uses branding as a core competence and recognizes the important position of branding among consumers. For this reason, the sector places an emphasis on branding and marketing strategy development. These strategies are targeted at increasing the share of the brand in the consumer's mind through appealing to human emotions and psychology, which are of course controlled by the mind!

Branding sustains attraction and influences consumers. A well-developed brand is like vintage wine that increases in value with age and care and yields long-term benefits. The rewards of branding are overwhelming but the process of building a successful brand is a long, tedious and expensive exercise that requires dedication and scrupulous management. However, the benefits are sustainable and if carefully managed generate continuous returns. This chapter provides insights into branding as a long-term investment therefore it would be irrelevant for those seeking short-term branding benefits, which cannot be found in this book.

Branding benefits

Before we go further into the interesting subject of branding, let's take a look at the benefits that branding brings to companies and their implications for luxury brands.

Brands are assets to the companies that own them. This asset comes in an intangible form and results in added financial and social benefits for businesses. To get a clear picture of the asset worth of brands for companies, let's take a look at the following illustration.

In 2006, Interbrand placed a brand value of US$17.6 billion on Louis Vuitton, making it the most valuable brand in the luxury goods industry and the seventeenth most valuable brand in any product category in the world. This figure is exclusively attributable to the brand and excludes the company's assets, earnings and revenues. This means that if Louis Vuitton ever decides to sell its brand (which is highly unlikely, by the way), its brand name and associations alone could fetch the company more than its book price (its balance sheet worth). The case is similar with other 'highly valued' luxury fashion brands like Gucci, Armani and Rolex. In some cases, companies with strong brands are sold at up to 600 per cent of their balance sheet worth.

The average company is valued by the stock-market at twice its net assets, but companies with strong brands are valued at from 4–20 times their actual physical assets. This additional valuation is often a result of recognition of the intangible value assets of the brand and confidence in the long-term future earning potential of the companies due to their brands. The large amount of money companies with strong brands amass during mergers and acquisitions is also evidence of the importance of branding as an asset. For example, in March 2006 French cosmetics company L'Oréal offered to buy British brand Body Shop for a price 34 per cent higher than its worth, as a result of its brand value. Also, American high-end sportswear brand Tommy Hilfiger was recently acquired by British investment company Apax for $1.6 billion, a figure several times more than the company's physical worth. In the non-luxury fashion category, Nike bought sportswear company Converse for $305 million, a figure that far exceeded its book value. These indicators show the importance of branding to any company that wants to make substantial long-term financial returns.

A quick look at Table 5.1, which represents the most valuable luxury brands in the world, according to Interbrand, previews the significance of the business of branding. The values shown are solely attributable to the brands and exclude the company's assets and earnings.

Table 5.1 The Global Luxury Brand Value Scoreboard (2004–06)

Brand name	Ranking	Brand value, 2006 (US$ billion)	Brand value, 2005 (US$ billion)	Brand value, 2004 (US$ billion)	Country of origin
Louis Vuitton	1	17,606	16,077	6,60	France
Gucci	2	7,158	6,619	4,70	Italy
Chanel	3	5,156	4,778	4,416	France
Rolex	4	4,237	3,906	3,720	Switzerland
Hermès	5	3,854	3,540	3,376	France
Tiffany & Co.	6	3,819	3,618	3,638	USA
Cartier	7	3,360	3,050	2,749	France
Bvlgari	8	2,875	2,715	—	Italy
Prada	9	2,874	2,760	2,568	Italy
Armani	10	2,783	2,677	2,613	Italy
Burberry	11	2,783	—	—	Britain

Source: www.interbrand.com

You might wonder how branding has gained so much prominence in the luxury fashion business and for how long the concept of branding has been around. The answer to this can be found in Chapter 2 of this book.

In addition to being an asset to owners, brands also have invaluable benefits for consumers. Branding helps consumers identify the source of a product and reassures them that their purchase decision is the right one, making their buying process easier. A brand is also a symbolic device that signals quality, precision, craftsmanship and several other associations that make it unique. As a result of this, consumers are reassured that what they're buying is the most suitable for their needs. This results in a relationship of trust between the consumer and the brand. For strong brands that maintain their promise of value, the relationship is often sustained through brand loyalty. Luxury brands are also highly beneficial to consumers through the fulfilment of functional and emotional needs. These needs are identified through brand promises and brand perceptions. Branding also reduces the risk of disappointment with products and services for consumers.

Luxury fashion branding strategy development

This chapter doesn't provide a magic formula or a definite model for developing or managing a luxury fashion brand that would guarantee instant success and perpetual steady income. However it provides a guide to aid in strategic thinking through a critical analysis of brand development and brand management issues related to luxury fashion. As we all know, fashion and its industry is ever-changing, but what remains constant are branding principles and strategies that can be applied in luxury fashion and beyond.

We've already seen the importance of branding to the luxury fashion sector, and will now evaluate how luxury brands are developed and how they can be managed successfully. First, let's take a look at the attributes of luxury brands. A true luxury brand exhibits 10 core characteristics as indicated below:

1 innovative, creative, unique and appealing products;
2 consistent delivery of premium quality;
3 exclusivity in goods production;
4 tightly controlled distribution;
5 a heritage of craftsmanship;
6 a distinct brand identity;
7 a global reputation;
8 emotional appeal;
9 premium pricing;
10 high visibility.

Other important elements of a luxury brand are an indelible impression, a recognizable style, fast and high fashion design turnover, a strong country-of-origin link, especially a country with a strong reputation as a source of excellence in luxury fashion (such as France and Italy).

The key tools of luxury fashion branding are *differentiation* and *emotional appeal*. For example, when you see a woven luxury leather bag or shoe, you'll likely think of Bottega Veneta. In the same manner, tweed or pearls on a product is likely to evoke a Chanel image. This is because these brands have differentiated themselves through these specific product attributes that also serve as a signature for the brands. However, product differentiation forms a part of the tangible aspect of branding which is a complement to the intangible aspects of branding as explained further in the chapter. The intangible aspects of luxury branding include the psychological responses that consumers exhibit towards luxury fashion that leads to an emotional attachment to specific brands and their products and services. Emotional appeal connects with the consumer's sub-conscious, sensitivity, intelligence and personality. This implies an intimate relationship and a special bond between brands and their consumers.

In the current rife fashion market where the consumer is overwhelmed with product variety and choices, purchase decisions are mostly based on brand choices. This means that the brand that consistently reinforces its appeal to consumers through its differentiated offerings will draw the most loyal customers.

How can a brand differentiate itself from its competitors? The first step is through finding the answers to the following three questions:

1 What feature does my brand have that will appeal to customers?
2 What makes my brand unique, which competitors cannot copy?
3 What element do I need to make my brand a better choice than others that offer similar products?

After establishing the answers to these questions to ascertain a clear indication of the differentiation and emotional appeal features, the process of brand creation and development is set into motion.

In order to create a luxury fashion brand, four factors should be ingrained in the subconscious of every participant of the brand-creation process. These points include the following:

- **Strategic thinking** the ability to have a defined brand vision, foresight and orientation towards long-term brand benefits.
- **Creativity** the ability to use imagination, resourcefulness and innovation in creating and designing brand elements.
- **Clarity** a clear idea of everything the brand stands for, both for the company and for the target customers.

* **Consistency**   a uniform approach in designing every aspect of the brand and in delivering every communication regarding the brand.

The role of these points will become clearer in the following sections. The process of brand strategy development is stimulating and the results can be positively overwhelming. This step-by-step procedure, which I prefer to call an adventure, is explained in detail in the following sections.

The brand concept

This answers the question: *'What is your name?'*
The brand concept is simply the birth of a brand, in other words, the overall idea behind the creation of a brand. The core concept of the brand must be compelling and appealing to anyone that comes in contact with the brand. It should be both relevant for its moment of creation but, more importantly, it should have a lifetime potential. Prominent branding specialist Jean-Noel Kapferer perfectly sums up the approach to the Brand Concept in the following statement:

> The best way for a new brand to succeed is to act like an old brand!

In other words, the new brand should develop new products but conceive its strategies like an established brand. If you're wondering how this can be done, then keep reading.

The brand concept is reflected through the name of the brand, its country of origin, its history and story, its visual image, its logo, its colours, its shapes, its language and its total offerings. Luxury fashion brands each have a distinct brand concept that differentiates them from others although they generally share the similar characteristic of 'prestige'. For example, the horse carriage, which is part of the Hermès logo, represents the brand's beginnings in horse saddlery production. The colour orange is also unique to the brand and the taglines in the brand's print advertisements are often in French, reinforcing the brand's foundation and country of origin. Also, Louis Vuitton products are packaged in brown and this has become the colour attributed to the brand. It is also difficult to think about Tiffany without thinking of the colour turquoise, which is the brand's concept colour. These are all components of the brand concept.

The most visible aspect of a luxury fashion brand's concept, however, is the brand name. Traditionally, the brand names adopted are those of the founders or major designers of luxury brands. The names naturally depict the country of origin of the brands as exemplified by the following brands:

Salvatore Ferragamo	Italian
Yves Saint Laurent	French
Donna Karan	American
Yoji Yamamoto	Japanese

However, luxury brands also feature brand names that evoke a specific country of origin and sometimes do not typically represent the countries of the brands' founders. These brand names have been adopted for strategic associations with particular countries or for other reasons. They include the following:

Jimmy Choo	British
Comme des Garcons	Japanese
JP Tod's	Italian
Samantha Thavasa	Japanese
Paul & Joe	French

The adoption of a brand name for a luxury goods company increasingly requires careful handling. Since the brand name is the first point of contact between the consumer and the brand, the name should evoke all the associations that make up the brand. Consumers should easily be able to decipher a brand's connotations from its name without being in contact with its products or advertisements. This is quite challenging to achieve especially since the traditional practice in luxury fashion has been for fashion designers to lend their names, personalities, origins and beliefs to their brands.

The genesis of this practice can be traced to the French and Italian fashion designers of the eighteenth, nineteenth and twentieth centuries such as Pascal Guerlain, Thierry Hermès and Guccio Gucci. During their time, the notion of branding was less sophisticated and focused more on differentiation through brand name and product design. This meant that the business development aspects of the brands often came after the name choice, indicating that the brand concept was not the determinant of the brand name. This approach has been successful for more than two centuries. However, the twenty-first century branding context requires the application of a defined strategy in every aspect of brand development, including brand naming. This factor has led to an emerging trend of brand name adoption that reflects a specific message and appeal to consumers. A classic example is the brand, 'Comme des Garcons', launched by Japanese designer, Rei Kawakubo, which doesn't have its origin in France or the French language. The brand creators realized that as a country, France is recognized as having a strong luxury fashion heritage. They therefore used *French fashion appeal* in the brand name concept to reach consumers who might not ordinarily associate a Japanese brand name to luxury fashion. Also when Diego Della Valle created the Tod's brand in 1978, he chose the name JP Tod's from the Boston telephone directory because this was the only name he found that sounded good in all languages and also had ease of pronunciation. More importantly, the Tod's brand concept was developed to translate the American casual weekend style through Italian know-how of luxury product development and to introduce luxury weekend fashion style to the world. The brand name was therefore suitable for the brand concept.

Another often cited example of strategic brand naming in the non-luxury fashion category is the Baileys Irish Cream liqueur brand. The brand is named after a supposed 'R.A. Bailey', who also has his signature on the liqueur's bottle packaging, although he doesn't exist. This fictitious character has been used as a banding tool to sell the appeal of Irish beverage alcohol to consumers. The benefit of this conceptual approach is an acceleration of the understanding of the brand concept and the spread of brand awareness among consumers.

In addition to recognizing the symbolic role of the brand name, several traditional old luxury brands currently modify their brand names to reflect a modern look and increase their appeal to the changing tastes of consumers. For example, Christian Dior has erased the forename 'Christian' from its packaging, advertisements and communications. The brand is now simply known as Dior by consumers, although the company name remains 'Christian Dior Couture'. This name adaptation is a variation of the strategy of adopting the brand's initials like Louis Vuitton has done with the 'LV' logo; Yves Saint Laurent with the 'YSL' logo and Dolce & Gabbana with 'D&G'. The adoption of a brand's name initials aids consumer memory recall of the brand name but could also backfire on the brand if mishandled. For example, the adoption of the initials 'CD' could have several meanings for consumers, including 'Compact Disc'. The choice of the brand initials as a logo should only be made by a brand after achieving extensive global awareness and appeal. This would ensure that the brand's perception remains undiminished among consumers.

The brand name choice should also have elements of universality because luxury fashion brands are increasingly global in nature. Consumers of luxury goods appreciate exotic brand names associated with the brand's history and origin. At the same time, the disposable nature of today's consumer means that if the total brand package lacks appeal, then the name of the brand will count for little. There are thousands of brands launched annually but most of them fail and become forgotten as a result of unfeasible tactics. Only the few brands that have well-defined brand concepts and brand strategies are successful.

The brand concept is also reflected in the brand logo. Most luxury brands are built on a foundation of history and heritage. However the evolving luxury market requires an adaptation of the traditional outlook of luxury brands to a modern stance. This has resulted in the tweaking of the logos and the brand names of several luxury companies. As noted earlier, Christian

Figure 5.1 *The Dior logo has evolved from Christian Dior to simply 'Dior', depicting a modern outlook*

Dior's logo is now represented simply as 'Dior' (Figure 5.1). Also Diesel, which aspires towards the luxury sphere, has included a tagline *'For successful living'*, to its logo that interprets its status as a premium brand that helps its consumers show their success. Other brands like Hermès and Lacoste have maintained their traditional logos using their heritage as their symbol, while Prada's logo can be classified as 'hybrid'.

The logo plays a key role in both the brand and product recognition. For example the famous LV monogram of Louis Vuitton and GG of Gucci provide instant recognition of the products of these brands. Other brands like Bottega Veneta minimize the logos on their products and rely on their signature style as a recognition tool.

The strategic objective of accurate representation of the brand concept is to align all its features to show the idea behind the brand in the way that the public can understand. It is also essential for all other elements of the brand to complement the brand concept. These elements are discussed in subsequent sections. The brand concept is the root from which the brand grows and therefore should be solid because some aspects of the branding strategy might change with time but the brand concept remains constant.

The brand identity

This answers the question: *'Who are you?'*
The brand identity is the next branding element that is developed after the brand concept has been established. The identity of a brand is who the brand truly is and how consumers perceive the brand. In other words, the attributes and identifiable elements that make up the brand and how these are perceived and interpreted by the people that come in contact with the brand. This is the essence of the brand.

The brand identity comprises of the *brand personality* and the *brand image*. The brand personality is the core personality traits and characteristics that have been consciously chosen for the brand. It is who the brand has decided to be, how the brand views itself and how it wants to be viewed by others. It is the 'true self' of the brand.

The brand image on the other hand is the way the brand is seen by the people that it is exposed to. The brand image is developed in the mind of the public through their perception of the way the brand projects itself. The image is the consumer's interpretation of the brand personality. Sometimes the image of a brand that consumers see is different from the personality that the brand has adopted or desires to adopt. This means that the internal understanding of the brand (by its employees) is different from the external understanding of the brand (by its consumers). In this case, there is a miscommunication that requires the brand to re-align its communications.

To further highlight the difference between the brand personality and the brand image, let's use an illustration. When you think about a friend or colleague, certain qualities or 'associations' run through your mind regarding that person. These qualities, which would normally be different for each person you think of, is the image you project of them in your mind through your understanding of their personality. Sometimes this image is correct and at other times it could be wrong through your misjudgement of their personality. The same principle applies in branding.

The personality of a luxury brand is crucial for accurate positioning in the consumers' minds. It should be clear and consistent in order to project the right image to consumers. The brand personality should be memorable and affirmative and also distinguish the brand from its competitors. Brands often lose out on market share when their personality is not defined because consumers are left confused and guessing, which often drives them to seek alternatives. This is amplified among the current clever and demanding luxury consumer group who lack the patience for additional tasks such as 'guesswork' related to a brand's identity. An unclear brand personality often leads to one reaction: '*next, please*'.

The brand personality of a luxury brand could be checked against one of the most widely applied models in both business and academic circles, The Brand Personality Model by notable Marketing and Branding scholar, Jennifer Aaker (Figure 5.2). This model uses five dimensions to classify the personalities that brands could adopt. These are further given a set of descriptive traits, against which the personality is tested. The measurement attributes five points to traits that are extremely descriptive of the brand and one point to the least descriptive. Although several additional personality traits exist, this model is useful as a guide in the development of a set of attributes that could contribute to the meaning a brand has for consumers. The traits are shown in the following diagram.

Luxury fashion brands have a unique advantage in the brand personality and image development process because their consumers already perceive them as 'luxury'. This is the reason that luxury brands hardly need slogans or characters commonly found in other goods categories to accompany their brand symbols. The term '*luxury*' makes a lot of difference between luxury brands and conventional brands. Luxury is associated with denotative words like opulence, superiority, exclusivity and wealth. This means that no matter what peculiar personality attributes a luxury fashion brand adopts, they also ought to possess a strong element and projection of the 'luxury' and 'prestige' qualities. This implies that selecting the additional personality traits to complement the core 'luxury' attributes should be a straightforward task.

On one level, luxury brands generally share certain brand personality traits

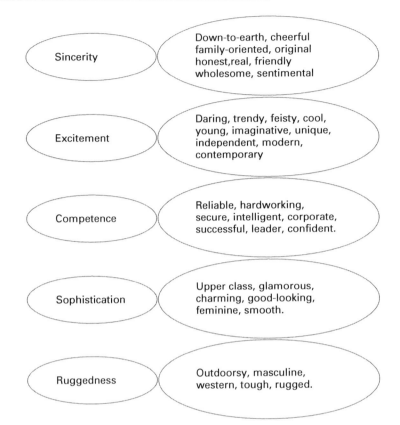

Figure 5.2 *The Brand Personality Model of Jennifer Aaker*
Source: Modified from valuebasedmanagement.net

such as glamour, reliance, originality and sophistication. On another level, different brands exhibit distinct qualities that make each brand unique. For example, American brand Michael Kors depicts modernity; Gucci has positioned itself with a mix of sophistication and lustre while D&G arouses a sense of excitement and adventure. Burberry on the other hand portrays the English lifestyle much more than Dior portrays the French lifestyle, and so on.

As a further guide, there are three critical features of brand personality and brand image development:

1 A clear and consistent theme in visual and verbal brand communications.
2 Uniformity between the core brand personality developed by the company and the brand image received and understood by the public.
3 A direct co-relation with other elements of the branding strategy, like the brand concept and the brand positioning.

Successful brand personality development does not automatically translate into the desired brand image, however. Brand image as mentioned earlier is based on the abstract form that people attach to a brand. It is the consumer's interpretation of the brand personality. This is achieved mainly through the brand message communications (pictures, images, colours, symbols and so on) or through direct contact with the brand (products, customer services and so on). Consumers sometimes misunderstand or misinterpret brand personalities as a result of an unclear message portrayal on the part of the luxury brand. Luxury brands ought to avoid this common error at all costs.

The brand personality and brand image must be reflected in all the elements of the overall corporate strategy such as product development and product naming as a part of its differentiating strategy. To sustain a brand identity that is unique and resistant to change, a brand must determine its core attributes that make it different from others and promote these as the tools that will enhance its ability to be recognized by its target market.

Finally, the golden rules of brand identity creation are:

1 Clarity in personality choice and image projection to the public.
2 Consistency in maintaining the chosen personality and image.
3 Constancy and relevance in the marketplace over time.

Brand awareness

This answers the question: '*Who knows you?*'

Brand awareness is when the brand goes public. Awareness constitutes a high level of knowledge and consciousness of a brand in its market to the extent of recognition and recollection among consumers. This means that the brand is in the subconscious of the consumers and easily remembered whenever they come across products or communications of the same category. In other words, the target audience are able to pull the brand name and its associations from their memory unconsciously.

Brand awareness comprises of two elements: *brand recognition* and *brand recall*. Recognizing a brand involves remembering the brand and its associations when exposed to that brand or a similar brand (for example, through print advertisement). This is usually less challenging to achieve as recognition could be developed in the early stages of the brand awareness creation through publicity and advertisements.

Recalling a brand from memory occurs when consumers relate a brand directly to its goods category without prior exposure to or direct interaction with the brand. This means that the brand has attained a powerful level of visibility and it has been imprinted in the memories of consumers as the most recallable brand in its category. For example, the luxury brand Gucci has high brand awareness among both male and female luxury consumers and Gucci might be the first brand that comes to consumers' minds in association to luxury fashion. This level of brand awareness is challenging and requires time and effort to attain. It is the desirable level of brand awareness for luxury brands.

As an illustration, take a moment to reflect on the first three brands that jump to your mind when you think of luxury fashion. These are the brands that have attained a high *recall* level within your mind. Now think of the numerous luxury fashion brand advertisements you see in the print media. How many of them do you instantly recognize? How many do you have to look at several times or study closely before recognizing or establishing their associations? The brands that you were able to recognize instantly are those that have high *recognition* while the others could have medium or low recognition levels.

Luxury brands generally have the advantage of attaining a higher level of global brand awareness than mass fashion brands. This is because luxury fashion brands, as the name denotes, fall within the category of 'luxury goods' and this offers an aspirational and unique quality that distinguishes them from an overcrowded fashion market. As a result, consumers remember them because they crave for products from within luxury brands. Also, the luxury sector is smaller than the mass fashion sector in size and focuses on a global market, making it easier for the brands to stand out. However, the task of creating brand awareness for luxury brands is becoming more challenging especially with the lowering of the sector's entry cost and subsequent expansion.

How can brand awareness be achieved?

The major tool of brand awareness creation is visibility, visibility and visibility. This means achieving a high level of exposure for the brand among its target consumer audience. Luxury brands should however attain high visibility without over-exposure. In other words, placing the brand to be seen, heard and thought about by the right people with the aim of registering the brand in their memory.

The effectiveness of brand awareness tactics varies between industries but communications tools like advertising, sales promotions and sponsorships can be used to increase familiarity with the brand and attain high brand awareness. The luxury sector also has the additional advantage of the global reach of the Internet, the increase in international travel and the globalization of the marketplace to enhance rapid brand awareness.

In creating brand awareness, luxury brands face an additional challenge of staying visible while retaining exclusivity. Luxury brands are elite by nature and are required to maintain this quality and the status of prestige. This means that they must be seen only in the appropriate communications media that enhance the 'luxury' quality. Consequently, the process of creating brand awareness for luxury brands is a carefully managed process that applies the most effective communications channels. For example, British luxury accessories brand Jimmy Choo attained rapid global awareness through celebrity connections, notably in Hollywood. The brand features celebrities in its print advertisements and associates itself with major 'Red Carpet' events like the famous American Oscar awards. The brand was also frequently featured in episodes of the world-famous American TV series, *Sex and the City*. An additional celebrity-linked promotional tactic by Jimmy Choo is the production of the book titled *Four Inches*, in 2005, which features photographs of Hollywood stars wearing nothing but Jimmy Choo shoes. Proceeds of the book sales were donated towards cancer research but the publicity generated from this venture was enormous. Similarly, shoe designer Manolo Blahnik attained a global consumer following through celebrity connections despite having only two stores. By adopting the celebrity promotional tactic, these two relatively new brands have succeeded in creating a link between their brand and the luxury goods category.

An additional brand awareness creation tactic is 'Word-of-mouth', which is often underestimated. Creating awareness for a luxury brand through word of mouth is both tricky and challenging. It is not something that is achieved on the street but is rather most effective when implemented through opinion leaders and experts in the luxury field and the fashion world. Examples abound in fashion magazine product reviews and features. Other effective methods of word-of-mouth promotion include the endorsement of experts in the luxury sector such as those that have authority in the global luxury fashion field. Think of who made Christian Louboutin famous.

Branding expert Kevin Keller asserts in his text, *Strategic Brand Management: Building, Measuring and Managing Brand Equity*, that if a brand desires a high brand recall level, then its name should be short, simple and easy to spell and pronounce. This opinion makes logical sense for conventional consumer goods such as FMCGs but it is unsuitable for luxury brands. Luxury brand names are more attractive when they are unique, symbolic and original. This is because the luxury consumer expects a high level of sophistication, exoticness and a degree of complexity in luxury brand names. For example, the brand names 'Comptoir Des Cotonniers', 'Marithe Francois Girbaud', 'Comme des Garçons' and 'Jaeger Le Coultre' are all difficult to pronounce for non-French speakers. The brand name 'Abercrombie & Fitch' on the other hand is a nightmare for the French to pronounce. However, the exoticness and originality of these brands' names atone for the difficulty in pronunciation and make them more appealing.

The brand awareness goal of every luxury brand is to attain a high level of familiarity with consumers, leading to affiliation with the brand. This will ensure that when consumers think of luxury goods, they would be likely to think of the brand. This can be achieved through repeated exposure and associations in the appropriate media.

Brand positioning

This answers the question: *'Where are you in the consumer's mind?'*
Brand positioning like all the branding elements resides in the mind of the consumer. It may be developed on an elaborate brand strategy chart and might be discussed extensively in boardrooms, but the final destination and home of brand positioning is in the consumer's mind. Brand positioning is the point where the relationship between a brand and consumers become apparent. It is also at this point that the value creation that a company obtains from its brand begins. The brand value is discussed extensively further in the chapter.

Brand positioning is often confused with market positioning although the two concepts are significantly different. Brand positioning involves the placement of a brand and all its associations (characteristics, attributes, personality, image) in a distinct place in the mind of the consumer. Market positioning on the other hand refers to the competitive position of a company in terms of size and market share, in a particular sector. Brand positioning emphasizes the connection between a brand and the consumer's mind and emotions.

Positioning begins with brand associations, which are defined by the brand identity, personality and image discussed earlier in this chapter. These associations include the company's brand communications interpreted through words, images, mediums, products and services that are channelled towards the emotions and subconscious of the consumer. Once the brand associations have been clarified, then the consumer uses this as a guide to place the brand in a distinct platform in his mind. For example, when consumers think about Cartier, certain associations are formed in their minds which are likely to be different when they think of Donna Karan. This shows that the positioning of the two brands are at different locations in the consumer's mind. Another example is luxury watch brand Ebel which recently featured the Brazilian model Gisele Bundchen in its print advertising with the goal to re-position its brand as modern, glamorous and more appealing to a younger fashion-conscious luxury consumer group. As a result, the previous position of the brand in consumers' minds might be altered by the new associations brought about by the advertisements.

Brand positioning occurs on two levels:

1 The Broad level of positioning.
2 The Narrow level of positioning.

Luxury brands clearly desire to occupy a position characterized by 'high-end, expensive and well-crafted products', in the consumer's mind. This level of positioning features the characteristics common to all luxury brands and is supported by the luxury concept. It is the broad sector positioning and is often easily and effectively achieved by most luxury brands. For example, there is no doubt that Versace, Fendi and Hermès are all positioned as luxury brands because they all share the broad attributes of luxury and prestige.

Narrow level positioning involves specific brand positioning that is attributed to each brand. Although luxury brands share the 'luxury' attribute as a broad positioning tool, each brand has its own unique positioning supported by its identity. This is where the battle for the consumer's mind begins and is often more challenging to attain than broad-level positioning. The positioning of different luxury brands varies and they highly influence the brand choices that luxury consumers make. For example, if you take a moment to think about John Galliano, Escada, Roberto Cavalli, Chloe and Jean Paul Gaultier, you'll discover that although these brands have the 'luxury' factor in common, they do not have the same brand positioning. They also do not send the same specific brand messages, neither do they address the same tastes.

Brand positioning is what drives consumer choices through comparisons. If consumers have a clear understanding and perception of a brand, then they're likely to place the brand in the right position in their minds and this will form a part of their selection process. This involvement in the selection process means that the brand has become part of the group of brands that have a place in the consumer's mind and the consumer recognizes the contribution the brand would make in their lives.

The task of brand positioning becomes even more challenging for luxury companies that own multiple brands such as LVMH and Richemont Group. On a group level, these companies are corporate brands that address the needs of their investors, employees and other stakeholders. This requires the development of a corporate brand strategy and positioning that has little to do with consumers. On another level, the brands that these companies control hold great significance to consumers and their positioning is associated with consumers. For example, the brands in the LVMH portfolio include Louis Vuitton, Fendi, Loewe, Givenchy and Dior; while Richemont owns Chloé, Cartier and Lancel; and the Gucci Group owns Gucci, Alexander McQueen and Yves Saint Laurent among others. These individual brands have different positioning points in consumers' minds. They are also different in their internal positioning levels and influence the holding companies' positioning as corporate brands. These varying brand positioning points create a challenge for the groups. Also there is a risk of developing brand positioning overlaps that could confuse consumers and internal competition that could affect the performance of the brands. To overcome the challenges posed by these factors, each brand ought to remain clearly distinct and original, while maintaining the luxury quality.

The following points are important in the evaluation of a luxury brand's positioning.

- The products and services must be in alignment with the desired positioning.
- The positioning must be credible, i.e. the brand must have a *raison d'être* and be deserving of it.

luxury fashion branding

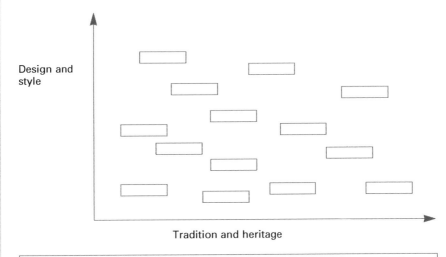

Design and style

Tradition and heritage

Prada, Louis Vuitton, Donna Karan, Versace, Gucci, Hermes, Ferragamo, Sonia Rykiel, Armani, Miu Miu, Chanel, Anna Sui, Max Mara, Coach, Ralph Lauren, Dior

Figure 5.3   *The luxury fashion brand positioning map*

- The positioning must be distinctive and cannot be shared by competitors.
- The positioning must justify a luxury association.
- The positioning must be relevant for the moment but also have the capacity to be extended with time.
- The positioning must have a contingency positioning plan.

The following exercise provides an illustration of the elements of brand positioning. The two-axis positioning map of Figure 5.3 shows two labels, several empty boxes and a list of luxury brands. You can take a few minutes to fill the empty boxes, according to the axis label indicators, with the brand names provided. If you succeed in filling all the boxes, then you understand the message of this section. The axis attributes can also be changed with varying positioning factors.

Brand loyalty

This answers the question: '*Who wants you?*'

Brand loyalty is simply a consumer's preference for a brand in a product category. It is often both a conscious and unconscious decision, expressed through an intention to purchase or the actual repurchase of the products of a brand continually and habitually.

Brand loyalty is clear evidence of the success and relevance of branding to both consumers and companies. For consumers, it reduces the search costs, and for companies it is the cornerstone of long-term profitability and competitive leverage. Brand loyalty also leads to lower costs for companies in acquiring and servicing customers because loyal consumers purchase more frequently and in higher quantities and also show less sensitivity to prices. Brand loyalty can also enable luxury brands to save the costs of attracting new customers, which is often four to six times more than retaining an old one.

When consumers become loyal to a brand, it is a demonstration of a high level of trust in the promises of the brand. Brand loyalty is the height of consumer affinity with a brand. In some cases, loyal consumers see the brand as the only solution to their consumption problems and needs fulfilment.

Luxury fashion consumers often show an apparent high level of loyalty and emotional attachment to luxury brands that is sometimes irrational to outside observers. Some consumers that are truly attached to specific brands offer their loyalty to their trusted brands to such an extent that the relationship with the brand departs from functionality to symbolism. This is because luxury brands help consumers project a self-image as a result of the 'prestige' and 'high-status' features with which the brands are associated. This implies that luxury goods serve as a communication tool that consumers use to speak to others and even to themselves of the type of person they are or would like to be. This connection that the brand has forged with the psychology and subconscious of consumers often results from brand loyalty.

Brand loyalty is attained progressively from brand positioning. As highlighted earlier, brand positioning occurs as a result of consumer's awareness of a brand and its image. When consumers have the right perception of a brand, they position the brand in their minds and are likely to involve that brand in their brand choices. If the brand is repeatedly favoured, its share in the mind of the consumer will increase. This is called *Brand Share* and a high brand share ensures the continuous choice of the products of that brand. This then leads to the manifestation of brand loyalty through repeat purchases or the intention to purchase.

However, repeat purchases of products from the same brand do not automatically have their source in brand loyalty. Several factors like product availability and high awareness could also be contributors to repeat purchases. This does not necessarily mean that brands with high awareness and large sales turnover benefit from more brand loyalty than their smaller contemporaries. Conversely, the high level of brand affinity that luxury consumers demonstrate towards their favoured brands indicates that product unavailability is not a deterrent to luxury consumers' loyalty levels. For example, Hermès customers often have a waiting period of up to eight months to purchase a Birkin bag, in addition to the high price tag of the product. Despite this, the waiting list of this product is always extensive and in some cases customers could wait for up to six months to get on the waiting list! Yet the Hermès Birkin bag has one of the highest loyalty levels in the luxury sector. The same can be said for the loyalty level of several limited-edition products from different luxury brands.

Consumers that are loyal to luxury brands are assets to luxury companies. They offer a lower service cost for the company because they show a high level of commitment to the brand and are often willing to pay a higher price for the products in addition to recommending the brand to others. They are also habitually keen to follow their favoured brands to new destinations and search for these brands everywhere they go. Brand loyalists are also open to new and different distribution channels. For example, luxury consumers are more willing and confident about buying products of their favoured brands on the Internet, provided that the website is authorized and genuine. This is another manifestation of brand loyalty.

Brand loyalty can be achieved by luxury brands through continuously appealing to consumer tastes. The current rapidly changing fashion consumer scene requires that the products offered must be appealing to consumers before loyalty can be attained. Also, consumers must like a brand's service package as well as the brand personality in order to become loyal to the brand. This means that luxury brands must continuously remind their consumers of the value of their products and the worth of loyalty to their brands. This can be done through reinforcement of the brand presence, essence and appeal in advertising and brand message communications. This is what forms the attitudes and beliefs of consumers regarding a brand and leads to brand loyalty.

Another important brand loyalty indicator is related to customer satisfaction. Luxury consumers are becoming more demanding and more individualistic, reducing the chances of single brand loyalty. This indicates that brand loyalty is no longer assured through offering appealing products with a brand symbol, a deluxe shopping environment and excellent customer services. Consumers are demanding a lot more, including a total and lasting brand experience. The previous magic formula of satisfied customer equals loyal customer is no longer valid. Today, a completely satisfied customer of a brand is also bombarded with the advertising messages and offerings of numerous other brands. This makes retaining the attention and loyalty of luxury consumers more tasking.

The most important lesson for luxury brands regarding brand loyalty is to treat all customers like royalty and to remember the 80/20 rule through recognizing the trophy customers and treating them accordingly.

Brand equity

This answers the question: '*Who likes you?*'
Brand equity is a term that has been much used and confused and has attracted endless questions and debates. In simple terms, it is the sum of all

distinctive qualities of a brand that result in the continuous demand and commitment to the brand. It is a set of attributes, elements and liabilities linked to a brand that add to or subtract from the value placed on the brand by consumers or companies. Brand equity is a means to an end, the end being the creation of brand value. It is what gives consumers a reason to prefer certain brands and their products to the alternatives offered by other brands of which they are aware. Brand Equity refers to the inherent worth that is attached to a well-recognized brand through the consumer's perception of the brand's superiority. This is the significant difference between brand equity and brand loyalty.

Brand equity is therefore the accountability and justification given for the existence and preference for a brand and is measured through the value placed on the brand. This value is expressed in two forms, which are directly related. The first form is based on the total positive or negative associations that consumers hold regarding a brand. If these associations are favourable, it leads to high consumer-based brand equity while low consumer-based brand equity is a result of negative brand associations.

The second form is approached from the point of view of the company. It is when the total sum of the consumer-based brand equity is translated into an intangible asset represented on a company's balance sheet. This is then called the corporate-based brand equity or what is commonly known in corporate circles as the brand value. It forms a part of a company's corporate assets and is often shown as the incremental cash flows that accrue to a company due to its investments in its brand. It is the sum of all the power that a brand has and exhibits. However, brand equity and brand value are different in the sense that brand equity is measured from the consumer viewpoint while brand value is financial-based.

Consumers are crucial to the development of brand equity in the same manner as they are to the other elements of branding. The power of a brand lies within the experiences that consumers have had with the brand and their attachment to the brand. This influences the consumer perception of the brand, made up of the feelings, thoughts, images, opinions, beliefs, emotions and associations. The implication is that brands generate positive consumer-based brand equity when they're favourably viewed by consumers and vice versa.

As previously mentioned, luxury brands utilize the branding concept as their core competence and major corporate strategy tool. This means that without branding, luxury brands would not be as appealing and might not exist. However, the question of brand equity is something that remains vague and often unanswered within the offices of several luxury brands. There are several reasons for this. The first reason is that in luxury fashion management circles the concept of brand equity is not completely understood and applied. Luxury brands place much emphasis on creating high brand awareness and the appropriate brand image with the objective of attaining a high level of brand loyalty and subsequently a steady income stream. What several luxury brands have exhibited is a lack of appreciation of the corporate asset that the branding elements lead to, especially brand equity.

Several luxury brands have the notion that brand equity and brand value come into play when a company needs to be valued for a merger, an acquisition or financial reporting. This is, however, only a surface-level approach to brand equity. Brand equity is a profound concept that should be sustained and grown in order to result in increased value for luxury brands. It is something that involves relentless long-term management and if left static, often takes a downward slope. Attaining a high level of brand equity requires nurturing all the previously discussed brand elements. In other words, what consumers see, hear, feel and know about a brand that results in their overall experience with the brand, over time should be sustained. Since these elements reside in the mind of consumers, the brand equity sustainability takes place through the enhancement of the brand associations in the consumers' minds.

In the luxury fashion sector, brand-equity measurement is done on two levels, depending on the corporate ownership structure of the brand. For luxury brands that are under the ownership of a conglomerate, their equity affects that of the individual brand and the equity of the holding company. For example, Louis Vuitton has a high brand equity but is owned by LVMH, a group with a portfolio of more than 50 brands, including Fendi, Emilio Pucci, and Thomas Pink. The high equity of Louis Vuitton is, however, transferred to the holding company, LVMH, since all the earnings of Vuitton are reflected on the balance sheet of LVMH. Each of the other brands owned by LVMH also has distinctive personalities, associations and positioning and therefore different levels of brand equity, which they contribute to LVMH. Although the brands are individual luxury brands and are independent of one another, they are ultimately linked because collectively, their equity affects the value of LVMH, its status as a corporate brand and its worth on the stock market, since it is a publicly traded company. The direct implication is that the higher the brand equity, the more intangible assets the company will acquire and the higher its stock market value. However, the challenge for conglomerates like LVMH is that each of the brands in its portfolio needs to be meticulously nurtured to ensure continuous growth.

The second approach to brand-equity measurement for a luxury brand is the simpler single-brand approach. This is where a particular brand is monitored and developed to generate a high value for its owner. It often occurs among brands that are privately owned such as Chanel, Hermès and Armani.

Table 5.2 shows the ownership portfolios of four of the largest luxury goods conglomerates.

An understanding of the brand equity measurement indicators is essential in assessing the financial value of brands, which we shall discuss in the following section. These indicators include image attributes, level of awareness and familiarity, loyalty, satisfaction and recommendation, among others. These are factors that measure consumer's perceptions of brands and how they influence brand choices and buying behaviour.

Table 5.2 The major luxury fashion conglomerates

LVMH* France	RICHEMONT Switzerland	GUCCI GROUP Italy	PRADA Italy
Louis Vuitton	Cartier	Gucci	Prada
Loewe	Van Cleef & Arpels	Yves Saint	Miu Miu
Celine	Piaget	Laurent\YSL	Azzedine Alaia
Berluti	Baume & Mercier	Beaute	Car Shoe
Kenzo	IWC	Sergio Rossi	
Givenchy	Jaeger – Le	Boucheron	
Marc Jacobs	Couture	Bédat & Co.	
Fendi	A. Lange & Söhne	Bottega Veneta	
Stefano Bi	Vacheron	Alexander	
Emilio Pucci	Constantin	McQueen	
Thomas Pink	Dunhill	Stella McCartney	
Donna Karan	Lancel	Balenciaga	
eLuxury	Montblanc		
Parfums Christian	Montegrappa		
Dior	Purdey		
Guerlain	Chloé		
Parfums Givenchy	Shanghai Tang		
Kenzo Parfums			
Laflachère			
Benefit Cosmetics			
Fresh			
Make-up Forever			
Acqua di Parma			
Parfums Loewe			
Tag Heuer			
Zenith			
Dior Watches			
FRED			
Chaumet			
OMAS			
DFS			
Sephora			
Sephora.com			
Le Bon Marché			
Samaritaine			

Notes: Some brands might have been omitted due to unavailability of data at the time of writing.
* LVMH brands shown are those in the luxury fashion goods division. Wines and spirits brands and brands in other activities have been excluded from this list.

Brand value

This answers the question: '*What have you gained?*'
Brand value is the bottom line of the business of branding. It is the final result of the success or failure of a brand. As indicated earlier, brand value is the end that all the branding elements discussed earlier, including brand equity, aim to reach. While brand equity is based on consumer psychological indicators,

brand value occurs when this equity translates into financial gains for the company that owns the brand.

Brand value in the simplest of terms is the financial benefit that a company receives as a result of the strength of its brand. This financial benefit is represented in the company's financial report or balance sheet as a part of its assets, specifically as an intangible asset. It oftentimes contributes substantially to the worth of a company. A high brand value is sometimes the sole reason that some companies are valued at more than ten times their net worth assets. Also it explains why certain companies sometimes generate up to five hundred percent of their actual book price, when they are sold.

The brand value is often represented on a company's balance sheet as a part of its 'goodwill'. The goodwill is the difference between a company's tangible assets and its actual worth, and goodwill often represents a statement of the confidence in the company's current strength and of assured forecast earnings and growth. It is this goodwill that translates into an intangible asset for the company. A major source of goodwill is the brand value. Goodwill could also comprise of other elements such as technology and patents. Consequently, companies with powerful brands have a high intangible asset base, which becomes the brand value when translated into financial worth. The intangible asset is arguably the most important asset for luxury fashion brands because a large proportion of the business value of luxury brands originates from the brand value.

For a long time, the concept of brand valuation as a business aspect has been controversial. This is because a company's asset source was viewed as tangibles such as land, machinery, capital and human resources. Although there was a general awareness that intangible aspects existed in business, there were no methods to measure or quantify these and to directly link them with the benefits that they provided. This was until the wave of mergers and acquisitions of the 1980s and 1990s led to the questions that has been continuously asked in the stock market valuation of companies:

What role do intangibles play in company valuations and how can these be measured?

For example, when Daewoo made a bid to purchase the electronics company, Thomson, it offered to pay an astonishing €1 because, according to Daewoo, the brand Thomson had no value. This extreme view was perhaps because, as a brand, Thomson had little branding weight to substantially contribute profitability to Daewoo. In the luxury fashion scene, Pierre Cardin, one of the pioneers of *haute couture* and *prêt-à-porter* put his brand on the market for sale at a price of approximately $500 million but industry sources indicate that buyers were not forthcoming. This could again be because the market believed that this asking price is an over-estimate of the true value of the brand. As a matter of fact, excessive licensing and questionable minimal quality and distribution control have devalued the brand in the luxury market. Although this business strategy has made Pierre Cardin one of the wealthiest men in fashion, it has severely damaged his brand image, brand equity and brand value. These examples provide a clear rationale behind brand valuation.

The process of calculating and determining the intangible asset worth of brands is called brand valuation. This valuation incorporates several business aspects such as branding, marketing, finance and production as well as features of the law of taxation and economics. This gives brand valuation a multi-subject dimension by bringing a synergy between the different business disciplines. It shows a direct co-relation between branding, marketing and finance and how the result of one directly impacts on the other. It also shows that the figures recorded on the balance sheet of companies with strong brands have their origin in marketing and branding. Since a company's brand value is recorded in its financial report as an asset, it is worth asking how this intangible asset is accurately calculated.

The methodology for brand valuation has been in debate ever since the importance of branding rose to the forefront of business strategy and management in the mid-1980s. Brand valuation is linked with accounting methodologies, standards and principles. This is because in financial reporting, a company's worth must be recorded against the specific source(s) of its value, which includes brands. Since accounting standards vary from country to country, it is quite difficult to pinpoint a standard brand valuation methodology that has been accepted internationally. In addition, unlike the measurement of other company assets such as stocks and bonds, which have comparable values, brand valuation lacks a market base from which to draw benchmarks. This makes the exercise of brand valuation both challenging and accuracy-focused.

So how can the value of luxury brands be reliably assessed? When should brand valuation feature in the balance sheet? How often should brands be evaluated? What about depreciated brands? Are they also featured on the balance sheet as lost revenue? The questions regarding brand valuation are endless and have led to intense debate in Western economies.

As much as accounting is complicated and is not the subject of this book, its discussion cannot be avoided in this section because of the major inter-relationship between accounting and brand valuation. Accounting principles work on the premise that brands acquire their value through the market. In other words, the true worth of a brand is not known until it is either sold or purchased. This is when the payment that has either been made or received as a result of a company's goodwill is explicitly represented on the balance sheet of the acquiring company. This viewpoint also supports the notion that as long as a brand has not been bought or sold, its brand value cannot be accurately estimated or represented. Therefore, only past and recorded transactions regarding brands are the reference points for the brand value. If this principle is right, then the implication is that several luxury brands that are believed to be of high value such as Louis Vuitton and Gucci can have only an estimated brand value until they're involved in a merger, acquisition or buy-out. It also means that brands that have been acquired by conglomerates and grown internally such as Van Cleef & Arpels of the Richemont Group cannot be accurately evaluated.

How realistic and applicable is this viewpoint in the current business scene and is it relevant for the global luxury goods industry? The answer is simple. Brands must be evaluated, whether grown internally or acquired externally. This especially provides a thorough perspective of the success and failure of the branding efforts made by a company. This is imperative for luxury brands that desire to remain competitive. It might seem contrary to the accounting system, which is based on the reliability of data, as the subjective nature of brand valuation creates a problem in accounting rules. However, this prudence is losing its bearing in certain business aspects including branding.

All brands are grown internally until they are sold and then they become external brands for the owners. As a result, all brands have internal value or the potential of attaining value without external transactions. For example, in 2001 private equity firm Equinox bought 51 per cent of Jimmy Choo. Equinox later sold this stake in 2004 to venture capital firm Hicks Muse now known as Lion Capital, in a transaction that valued the company at £101 million, although Jimmy Choo's annual sales at the time were about £40 million. This sum was justifiable because of the efforts made by the owners of Jimmy Choo to develop the brand strength internally before external transactions.

On another level there are brands like Armani, which remains a privately held company under the ownership of Giorgio Armani and hasn't yet been involved in acquisitions and buy-outs. How can such a brand that has been meticulously nurtured since its launch in 1974 be accurately evaluated based on its brand value if the principle of accounting were to be followed? Also since brand value does not remain static but either appreciates or depreciates, it is quite impossible to wait for a transaction to determine the result of a company's branding efforts. What if there is no transaction? Will the value of the brand never be evaluated?

Accounting and finance serve as a structure for accountability in terms of income, expenses, investments and taxation. When costs are accrued by a company with respect to brand promotion, for example print advertising, they are recorded as expenses and are often tax deductible. This was until accounting standards authorities realized that these expenses are rather investments, which yield enormous results in terms of assets for the companies in question. Thus these expenses began to be treated as investments and their returns as assets. This led to the identification that the same system that uses the value of a company's assets generated by investments to estimate the future earning potential could be applied to brands. So brands began to be evaluated through a method using forecast earnings projections.

The major problem with this method was that the objective of forecasting was different from the objective of brand valuation. Forecasting methods were used to evaluate the market value of fixed assets, while brand valuation represented the market value of intangible assets. Above all, the role of brand valuation in mergers or acquisitions is significantly different from the role of brand valuation for a company's internal use in strategy development. These factors have contributed to the ongoing debate of the brand valuation of companies, particularly luxury brands.

The exercise of brand valuation is necessary for brand-auditing purposes, that is to carry out a health-check for the brand. Another function of brand valuation is to aid in the creation, revision and implementation of effective marketing and corporate strategies. In addition, brand valuation when carried out frequently, helps to assess the short-term results and long-term impact of current strategies. However, this frequent evaluation shouldn't undermine the long-term nature and benefits of the brand. For example, luxury brands such as Prada have seen a significant rise in their brand value in recent years, compared to twenty years ago, as a result of efforts made towards brand value creation. However the high brand equity and long-term brand growth potential of Prada shouldn't hamper frequent brand valuation.

Several brand valuation methods have been devised by different companies and groups specializing in brand management strategy, as a result of the inconsistencies created by accounting methods and the need for constant brand valuation. These groups have differing approaches but have all recognized three important facts that accounting fails to reflect:

1 The importance of understanding how brands work, how they can be grown and how they can increase or decrease in value in the short and long terms.
2 The importance of creating synergy between all the departments involved in creating and sustaining brands within a company such as finance, marketing, operations, product development, e-commerce and audit.
3 The significant role of brand valuation in marketing, branding and corporate strategy formulation.

The methodologies created for brand valuation include the technique developed by brand consulting company, Interbrand Corp. This method recognizes brands as assets that have value through a projection of their future earning potential using current sales turnover and historical financial data. This projected figure is then discounted to a present value, creating what accountants call a Net Present Value (NPV). The NPV is arrived at after deducting operating costs, capital, taxes and other intangibles. Other factors such as the management capability, market position, global scale of operations and stability are considered in calculating the net present value.

Another brand valuation method is that of brand consultancy company

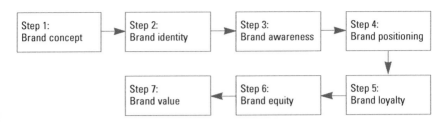

Figure 5.4   *The luxury fashion branding process*

Ogilvy. This method views brands as a means to an end, the end being higher earnings, revenues, cash-flows and profits. The significant difference between this method and that of Interbrand is that the latter puts an absolute value on brands as intangible assets and represents them on the balance sheet, while the former indicates that brands cannot be absolutely valuated and should only feature on the Profit and Loss accounts because their contribution to a company are clearly represented there. The method use by Ogilvy uses the regressed Compound Annual Growth Rate (CAGR) to measure strength through its growth potential and the Capital Asset Pricing Model (CAPM) to calculate the discount rate of companies with strong brands.

In addition to these methods, several branding experts such as Jean-Noel Kapferer also propose that different methodologies can be utilized according to the specific objective of the brand valuation. For example, if a brand is being valuated in order to generate capital funding from a financial institution, then it is worthwhile to use a brand valuation method that places an emphasis on the future earning potential of the brand.

Although the brand valuation methods that have been discussed can be applied to companies in various sectors, the method that is most relevant for the luxury sector is that which emphasizes the brand as an asset to companies. This is because the luxury sector does not only have branding as one of its core competences but also draws a high percentage of its value from the power in the concept of branding. The complete branding process, which has been discussed extensively in this chapter, is represented in Figure 5.4.

The luxury fashion marketing strategy

The process of branding begins from the marketing strategy, where the products and services are created and strategies for their pricing, distribution, promotion and positioning are devised for the target market(s). Branding and marketing have a mutually beneficial relationship. Branding is a core aspect of marketing and also depends on the marketing strategy for its existence because without products and services (which marketing devises), the branding process cannot exist. Marketing on the other hand benefits from branding because a strong brand enhances the marketing strategy while a weak brand suppresses it.

The luxury fashion marketing strategy comprises of the branding mix as its main component which will be tagged here as 'The Six Ps of Luxury Branding'. The branding mix are recognized marketing elements that drive the branding process forward. Like the famous Four Ps of the marketing mix, the Six Ps is a tool that propels the marketing and branding strategies of luxury brands in the direction of market success. The Six Ps are the following:

1 **The Product**
2 **The Pricing**
3 **The Place of Distribution**
4 **The Promotion**
5 **The People**
6 **The Positioning**

The product

A product is everything a consumer receives from a company in exchange for a cost. These include physical goods and services. A product has two dimensions: the tangible features that we can see, touch, smell, hear or taste; and the intangible features that we feel and experience. Using this brief definition, it is clear that the luxury goods sector is highly product specific. The meticulously crafted luxury goods that consumers purchase are tangible objects to treasure, while the intangible benefits constitute of the brand dimensions, the retail atmosphere, the customer services and the guarantees.

Products are designed to satisfy consumer needs. These needs could be functional such as the need for a pair of glasses to aid eyesight; or the needs could have intangible dimensions such as the need to wear a pair of glasses with the Prada logo, in order to make a statement of status to oneself and to others. The first level of need satisfaction can be found among the categories of goods that serve purely practical purposes such as consumer goods; while the second level of need satisfaction is found among products that have very strong branding concepts such as luxury goods. This is because luxury products provide much more than functional benefits to consumers. They are products that consumers use to project an image of themselves to the public as an expression of their true selves or their ideal selves. They are status symbol tools that show prestige, good taste and affluence. These factors indicate a symbolic role linked to the emotional, social and psychological benefits that are derived from purchasing and using luxury products. As a consequence, strategies behind the development of luxury products place a strong emphasis on branding elements. This is because luxury goods are evaluated by consumers on an abstract level with a focus on non-product-related associations, unlike non-luxury goods, which are evaluated on a concrete, product-related and functional level.

In the product development of conventional consumer goods such as basic toiletries, several factors are taken into consideration. They consist of the ease of product use and customer requirements. In the development of luxury products, however, there are certain features that cannot be compromised. They comprise the following:

1 Innovative, creative and appealing product designs and packaging.
2 Classic and timeless products.
3 Extremely high-quality materials.
4 Meticulous craftsmanship.
5 Manufacturing precision.
6 Rapid design turnover.

Other luxury industry-specific product features include: creative and emotion-evoking product names such as Christian Dior's '*J'adore*' and '*Dior Addict*' fragrances; Gucci's 'Envy Me' perfume; André Ross' '*Champs Elyseés*' bag and Chanel's '*La Ligne Cambon*' product range. Creativity also extends to packaging design such as the bottle designs of Givenchy's 'Organza' perfume, Jean-Paul Gaultier's 'Male' and 'Female' signature fragrances, Nina Ricci's '*Eau de Temps*' and Paco Robanne's 'Ultra Voilet' perfumes.

The luxury goods product division has five major traditional dimensions. These include Apparel, Leather Goods, Perfumes & Cosmetics, Eyewear and Watches & Jewellery. However, this traditional product range has been expanded through the recent trend of product and brand extension. Luxury goods now include completely new categories like restaurants, hotels and spas, and multi-category required products like iPod cases. Figure 5.5 shows the main luxury fashion product groups.

Several marketing experts have identified the conventional product as having four concentric levels represented through what is known as *The Anatomy of the Product*. This model can be applied in the development of luxury products with the four levels as follows:

1 The **Core Product**, which constitutes the major features and benefits of the product. This comprises the tools that are used to differentiate the core product, such as design specifications and packaging. For example, the Dior Saddle bag and the Vuitton Speedy bag both have distinctive signature designs. The André Ross bag comes with 23k gold-plated hardware and Hermès has a characteristic packaging in orange. These are all aspects of the core product.
2 The **Basic Product** is the functional attributes of the product from which consumers derive their tangible benefits. These include the time-keeping

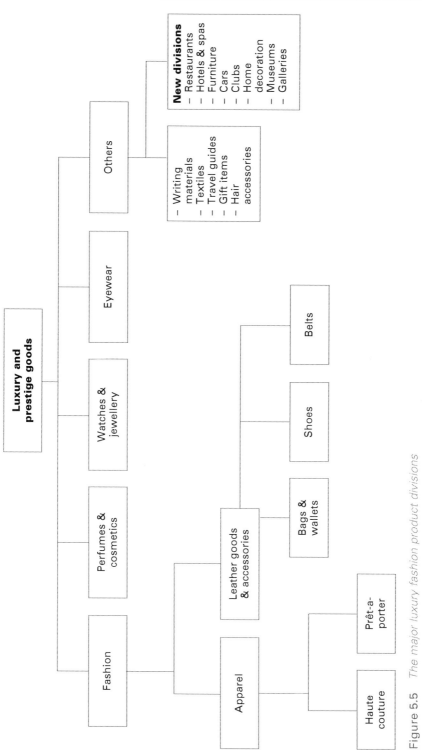

Figure 5.5   *The major luxury fashion product divisions*

function of a wristwatch and the ability of a business portfolio to contain folders, a laptop computer and other business tools.

3 The **Augmented Product**, which comprises the unexpected extra features that improve the attractiveness of the product. These include extra services, guarantees and, in the case of luxury goods, free repairs, exchanges and lifetime warranties.

4 The **Potential Product** is what the product should and could be in future. It gives an indication of how many different directions the product could be stretched to in order to give it leverage and attractiveness.

New product development (NPD)

Luxury brands are constantly faced with market pressure to launch new and desirable products in short life cycles. This means that as a product is launched, new products are already in the design process. This factor calls for a clear strategic direction in product development. In order to achieve an articulate direction, the following steps are necessary:

1 Generation of new ideas. This is where designers are inspired by different elements ranging from travel and art to culture, literature, an era and even space. It is also at this stage that the services of trend-watchers, researchers and venture teams who track consumer behaviour are required. For example, for the autumn/winter 2005 collection of Burberry Prorsum, the brand's Creative Director Christopher Bailey took inspiration from the strength of character and cultural revolution of the 1960s, triggered by Twiggy.

2 Screening of ideas involving a study of what is acceptable in the marketplace. This is an important aspect of product development and could lead to a negative impact if overlooked. For example, Chanel made a *faux pas* during its fashion show for the summer of 1985 where models showed dresses with design imprints of verses from the Muslim Koran. This prompted protests from the Muslim world and an apology and discontinuation of the design by Chanel.

3 Testing concepts and their feasibility. For example, the use of specific materials that are both appealing and acceptable, for products manufacture. This is a key aspect of product development as the wrong choices could lead to a negative impact. An example is the use of animal fur which sometimes provokes protests from consumers.

4 Business analysis to ensure that the product has the potential for generating profits. For example, the Louis Vuitton Murakami leather goods line was a huge success when it was launched in 2002/2003 because the brand had evaluated its success potential.

5 Development of the product through design prototypes. This provides a first-hand look of the final product and an opportunity for modifications.

6 Test-marketing involving the complete or partial launch of products in a specific market. This is practised by luxury brands that avoid launching certain products uniformly in all the markets where they operate.
7 Launching and retailing of the product.

Product management

Creating new products is only the beginning of the Product Manager's job. Products need to be managed so that they can remain relevant and appealing. The product management system that a brand adopts depends on the range of the product portfolio. For example, brands with a **mono-product** range such as Manolo Blahnik who designs and manufactures purely footwear could handle product management through a single product-planning division. Other brands with a **multi-product** range such as Celine, which has bags, shoes and apparel in its product range, would have a broader product management system. Yet other brands that have diversified their range to include products and services with sub-brands such as Armani, which has a **multi-brand** portfolio ranging from Emporio Armani to Armani Exchange and Armani Casa, among others, would have a more extensive product management system. Another category comprises of a brand like Louis Vuitton, which has maintained a **single-brand** approach while extending its product range and introducing services such as an art exhibition centre.

In order to clearly craft an effective product management strategy, it is important to first understand the structure of the products in a brand's range. The product structure comprises of the **length** of the product, which indicates how many types of major product groups are in the brand's complete range. The second component is the **breadth** of the product, which indicates how many different sub-products are within each major product group. The third is the **depth** of the product, which shows yet how many types of products are within these sub-product groups.

To clarify this structure, let's take a look at the product range of a typical luxury brand. The examples of products shown are divided into broad product and sub-product categories, to act as a basis for a general overview of luxury products and are not definite in nature. The information in Figure 5.6

Figure 5.6   *The luxury fashion product classification*

uses the product portfolio of Jimmy Choo, which is a mono-product (leather-goods) brand to illustrate the relationship between the product length, product breadth and product depth.

An additional approach to the assessment of luxury products according to their categories and functions is through dividing them into groups and sub-groups, as shown in the following section.

Major product groups

The following are examples of goods that can be found in the major product groups:

1 **Leather goods**: bags, shoes, belts, small leather-goods, luggage and accessories.
2 **Apparel**: *haute couture*, *prêt-à-porter*, sportswear.
3 **Eyewear**: sunglasses and prescription glasses.
4 **Timepieces**.
5 **Jewellery**.
6 **Children's clothing and accessories**.
7 **Animal accessories**.
8 **Furniture & home decoration**.
9 **Services**: hotels, cafes, clubs.

Sub-product groups

The products below are examples of goods that can be found in the sub-product categories among the major product groups:

1 **Bags**: day bags, shoulder bags, clutches, evening bags, bridal bags, sports bags, briefcases, and so on.
2 **Shoes**: evening shoes, day shoes, sandals, and so on.
3 **Accessories**: hairpieces, key rings, mobile phone straps, iPod cases, animal accessories, and so on.

In order to effectively manage luxury products, it is also important to categorize them according to the commercial role they play for the companies that own the brands. This can be done using the well-known product management model developed by the Boston Consulting Group, known popularly as the BCG Matrix. This model aids in product portfolio planning and management. The BCG Matrix features a cube that comprises a four-boxed dimension of products that are labelled: Dogs, Cash Cows, Stars and Problem Child. These are further measured against two major market elements: Relative Market Share and Market Growth Potential.

Dogs are products with a small share of a slow-growth market. Products in this group do not generate cash for the company but tend to absorb it and therefore might need to be removed from the product portfolio. In the luxury goods sector, these would include haute couture, which several brands have gradually removed from their portfolio.

Cash cows are products with a high share of a slow-growth market. The products in this group generate high sales and profitability for their owners; more than the investment made in them. It is therefore important to keep them in the product portfolio. An example is jewellery.

Stars are the products that have a high share in high-growth markets. They also generate huge income and contribute substantially to the profitability of the brands. The stars are the key products of brands and should be kept and rejuvenated at all costs.

Problem child products are those with a low share of a high-growth market. They consume high capital resources and generate few sales and profits in return. They also need huge investments of time, money and effort in order to increase their market share. These include products like timepieces.

In balancing the role of products within the portfolio, there should be equilibrium in investments and management time. This means the removal of the Dogs, the maintenance of Cash Cows, and the boosting of the Stars. Usually, the funds from Cash Cows are invested in Problem Child products to turn them into Cash Cows or Stars. If, however, the Problem Child product potentially becomes a Dog, then it ought to be removed from the product portfolio.

The BCG Matrix is also useful as a platform for performance measurement for luxury companies with multiple brands in their portfolio, as shown in Figure 5.7.

The next major task after defining and charting out the product range of a brand is to actually manage the products. The decisions that are made regarding product management consist of product naming, product classification, product extension, product alignment to the brand image, marketing research, trend tracking and analysis of the consumer response to the product offerings

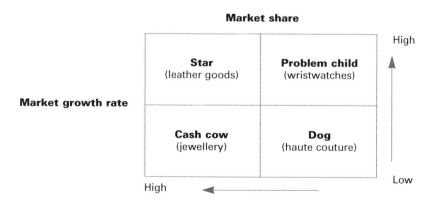

Figure 5.7   *The Luxury Fashion Product Classification using the BCG Matrix*

of the brand. Other decisions are related to customer relationship management and sales response.

In several luxury companies with a wide product portfolio, the function of product management is often divided according to the particular product group or sub-brand group. This is where product category managers have the role of coordinating the mix of diverse product ranges and lines within the general product portfolio and also evaluating new product additions. In this setting, there are also brand managers who manage the different brands within a single or multi-product category. Their responsibility also includes coordinating the extensive marketing mix and aligning them to the overall brand strategy.

There are two significant decisions that are made in product management of luxury goods. They are luxury product naming and luxury product and brand extension.

Luxury product naming

Every fashion season, consumers are introduced to new products from luxury brands. These products include apparel and accessories like bags, shoes, eyewear and timepieces. Others are fragrances, make-up and cosmetics. A number of these products, notably the leather goods, usually come with product names. Some of the names are remarkable because they have a 'background story' while others are forgotten by the next season when new products are launched with yet more names. Examples of luxury product names include Alexander McQueen's debut Novak bag; Ralph Lauren's Ricky bag launched in the 2006 spring/summer collection; Jimmy Choo's Tulita and Theola bags and Louis Vuitton's Speedy and Musette bags that are often re-launched with different materials. Other brands with product names include Furla, which has names for almost all the leather goods in its collection. Among them are the Patricia, Susy, Greta, Phoenix, Lutetia, Hope, Penelope, Norma, Nicole, New Divide and a host of others. In addition, Tom Ford's recently launched eyewear range have products named after film and fashion icons such as Farrah Fawcett and Ryan O'Neil and also after people personally close to him such as the De Sole, the Buckley and the Whitney glasses.

Product naming is an aspect of product management that should be approached from a strategic perspective. Although this practice is not new in the luxury goods sector, its current rampant application raises several questions. These questions are related to the motive behind naming the products and the objective these might serve for the brands and consumers. On the surface level, products could be used by brands to tell 'a story' and give some meaning to consumers regarding the particular product. However in most cases, this objective of product naming is unmet due to poor execution. In other instances, the aim of product naming is to replace product references. This strategy however doesn't provide an optimum positive impact as consumers are left confused and overwhelmed by the numerous product names.

Product naming of luxury goods needs to be credible to consumers. This means that there should be a reason behind the product name, which should be communicated to and understood by consumers. Several luxury brands seem to have caught the 'product-naming bug' and are rampantly naming products in order not to be left behind by the competition. Some of these product names also seem to have no tactical purpose and therefore are meaningless to consumers. Product naming should be approached tactically, whether the names are for fragrances, which require naming for their existence, or leather-goods, wristwatches, and sunglasses, which can exist without names.

While product naming is an excellent strategy for selling luxury, the product itself should be distinctive, innovative and highly appealing. When a catchy and meaningful name is added to an appealing product, it acts like a complement and contributes to the staying power of the product in the market. For example, the Hermès Birkin bag is named after famed actress Jane Birkin while the brand's Kelly bag is named after Grace Kelly. These bags that were created several decades ago have remained sustainable and continuously generate long purchase waiting lists due to their appealing and classic nature. Also, Mulberry's Roxanne bag, which contributed significantly to the brand's return to the luxury arena, has been highly successful as a result of its innovative and enchanting design and name. Yet other products with potential lasting power include the Chloé Paddington bag, named after London's Paddington district, the André Ross Champs Elysées bag, named after Paris' Avenue des Champs Elysées and the Gucci Jackie bag, named after US former first lady Jackie Kennedy.

Figures 5.8–5.13 show some of the signature bags of luxury brands that have been strategically named or connected with specific associations, which have turned them into iconic items.

Figure 5.8   *The Chloe Paddington bag named after the Paddington area of London*

Figure 5.9   *The André Ross signature Champs Elysees bag, named after Paris' Avenue des Champs Elysées*

Figure 5.10 *The Louis Vuitton classic Speedy bag in the brand's signature monogram*

Figure 5.11 *The Mulberry signature Roxanne bag*

Figure 5.12 *The Hermès classic Birkin bag named after actress Jane Birkin*

Figure 5.13 *The Gucci Jackie bag, the original version of which was named after US former first lady Jackie Kennedy*

Although product naming is important albeit not imperative in the luxury marketing and branding strategy development, when adopted, it should be approached with tactical objectives and implemented with caution. Above all, the consumer audience should understand what the name stands for and associate the product with its name.

Product and brand extension

The news of luxury product and brand extension is everywhere in the fashion press with numerous examples. Roberto Cavalli is now into hotels and cafés and has also launched branded Vodka. Giorgio Armani has added the ownership of several restaurants, cafés and a nightclub to his fashion empire. This also includes a recent venture with EMAAR Hotels & Resorts to build seven hotels and resorts within the next decade. Missoni also plans to build a hotel chain across the world. Salvatore Ferragamo owns luxury Hotel Lungarno in Florence and Bvlgari has hotels in Milan and Capri. Versace has also added hotel services to its range with the Palazzo Versace in Australia and a second hotel slated to open in Dubai in 2008 with six more hotels planned in Asia, North America and Europe. Nicole Farhi's offerings also range from fashion goods to restaurants, furnishings and home accessories. Pierre Cardin owns the highly successful Maxims hotel, restaurant, bar and club in Paris, Monte Carlo, New York, Mexico, Shanghai and Peking. The list of examples could go on for several pages.

Other luxury brands, from Gucci to Bottega Veneta, Ralph Lauren, Nino Cerruti and Paul Smith have all extended their product ranges to include home decoration, furnishings and more. Yet other product extensions include Prada and Nicole Farhi's debut fragrance launch in 2005 and Missoni's 2006 fragrance range launch. Gucci and Louis Vuitton have also included writing materials in their offerings and Tod's plans to launch its first ready-to-wear range in 2006. Also crystal brand Swarovski and jewellery brand Cartier have added leather goods such as handbags to their product portfolios. In addition, several luxury brands have included iPod covers in their product ranges as a response to the new MP3 player market.

Product and brand extension has brought a new dimension to luxury branding. New product and service categories that include a total lifestyle concept make up the new business arena that luxury fashion is being stretched into. Consumers now have the possibility to dress their homes with luxury products from brands like Versace and Armani; to grab a drink at Just Cavalli café in Milan; to have lunch or dinner at Nicole Farhi's restaurant in London or New York while shopping in the unique concept store; not to forget getting down to some dancing at Armani's nightclub in Milan. Product and brand extension has provided an avenue for luxury brands to offer a complete 360° lifestyle provision for consumers.

This diversification strategy of product and brand extension is an important means to extend the luxury brand from 'fashion' to 'lifestyle' through offering home furnishing and hospitality services to complement fashion and accessories. While diversification breeds growth, it is imperative to infuse a strategic approach in the diversification process of luxury goods. This means that for product extension to be successful, there should be an equal blending of solid managerial ability with artistic skill and an understanding of customer needs. Although several luxury brands have achieved success through this approach, the sector still lacks adequate streamlining and clear positioning of the diverse products and services offerings.

The creative talents of the designers at luxury brands are a part of the core make-up of the brands but must be complemented with business proficiency especially in the management of product extensions such as hotels and restaurants, which require a completely different set of skills. For example, the atmosphere and service level at Pierre Cardin's restaurant in Paris, Maxims, is the epitome of opulence, distinction and exceptionally high standards. This description doesn't exactly fit the brand's products like the licensed perfumes sold at several Parisian supermarkets.

Every luxury brand has the creative capability to turn out desirable extended products and services but not every brand has the capacity to effectively extend its product range. Before product extension can be successful for a luxury brand, the brand should have achieved a clear and concrete positioning in the market and most importantly in the consumer's mind. There should also be an apparent consumer following through a loyal consumer base. For example, consumers that are most likely to stay at the Palazzo Versace hotel are those that have an affinity with the Versace brand and are attracted to what the brand represents. In the same way, home furnishings designed by Missoni are likely to be purchased by consumers that also buy Missoni fashion or are attracted to the brand.

The implication of product and brand extension for luxury brands is that this strategy creates opportunities for growth and also for a broader level of brand experience and a deeper level of brand affiliation. The risk factor of brand extension is also high and rests with the company's capabilities and resources. Product and brand extension provides a channel for growth but should only be adopted if a possibility of competitive advantage is envisaged.

Pricing

Pricing is an important aspect of the marketing and branding strategy as it is one of the first indicators of a brand's positioning to consumers. It is also the most flexible of the Six Ps as it can be easily modified.

Luxury and prestige brands have traditionally adopted the premium pricing strategy to emphasize the brand strength, high quality and exclusivity associated with luxury goods, and also to differentiate them from the mass-market fashion brands. The luxury target audience is less price-sensitive and actually expects luxury goods to be premium-priced rather than economically priced. Pricing forms a part of the branding process as consumers often judge the position of a brand and the value of a product in terms of price.

To explain further, luxury brands are those brands whose ratio of functionality to price is low while their ratio of intangible and situational utility to price is high. This means that the price of luxury products is significantly higher than the price of products with similar tangible features but the high intangible characteristics and benefits of luxury goods justify the high price.

Pricing is the most elastic element of the marketing and branding mix as it can be changed at will. However, the strategy behind pricing decisions for luxury products requires meticulous evaluation and control. Pricing is also the only direct revenue generator among the Six Ps. This gives it a delicate position

Product quality

	Low	Medium	High	
Low	Economy Pricing	Value Position	Penetration Pricing	
Medium	Poor value Position Pricing	Medium Value Position	High value Position Pricing	**Price**
High	Price Skimming	Poor value Position Pricing	Premium Pricing	

Key: ■ Traditional luxury goods pricing strategy
▓ Extended luxury goods pricing strategy

Figure 5.14   *The extended strategic pricing model*
Source: Adapted from *Principles of Marketing* by Brassington and Pettitt (2003).

and calls for a clear set of objectives behind its strategy. Overall, companies set prices to maximize profitability, return on investment, increase cash flows and market share as well as optimize the production capability. Since luxury brands are premium priced, the pricing objective and emphasis is on profitability and return on investments. This is because prices between premium and economy differ by at least a factor of ten and the profit margins are even higher.

The process of calculating and equating costs to pricing is not very simple. This process is often done using the 'Extended Strategic Pricing' model, which is presented in Figure 5.14. It indicates a high, medium and low level of measurement in pricing versus product quality. This model is appropriate for luxury brands especially in the current luxury market context where offerings from several brands currently feature a gradual gravitation from premium-pricing towards the medium-pricing range for certain products.

The pricing strategy also includes an evaluation of the key objectives behind the chosen strategy to determine its success potential. The elements of this analysis consist of the pricing for the brand's products, the features of its customers, and the stance of its competitors. The customer aspect involves ensuring that there is a ready consumer market willing to pay the set price for the products and services offered. Price and cost are relatively different. The total cost of purchasing a product for a consumer incorporates the price-tag on the product as well as several other 'costs' such as time, energy, transport, mental effort and psychological costs. These factors are important in evaluating consumer responses to pricing. In the case of luxury brands, customers generally accept the premium pricing strategy.

Secondly, pricing has to be checked against those of competitors. For example, the classic Hermès Birkin bag retails for approximately €4,000 while its considered equivalent at Chanel costs about €2,500. For some customers, this could mean that the Hermès bag has more value than the Chanel bag while others might perceive the Hermès bag as overpriced. Thirdly, the overall costs of obtaining the product must be evaluated. In addition, the pricing strategy could be utilized as a publicity generation tool. An example is the one-off Eunis bag produced by André Ross, which was sold for US$88,888

Another important factor in pricing decisions is analysing the external market demand factor. This involves the responsiveness of the level of demand to changing or increasing prices. In technical terms, it is done through checking the price elasticity of demand. This is a measure of the degree of change in demand for a product when the price changes. If the change in demand is high in proportion to the change in price, demand is said to be elastic. If the change in demand is low in proportion to the change in price, demand is said to be inelastic. In order to implement an effective pricing strategy, these essential factors including costs, customers, competitors and demand ought to be thoroughly evaluated.

The place of distribution

The place of distribution refers to the channels that are used to make products and services available to customers. Retail channels are most effective when they meet the consumer's expectations in terms of location, convenience and product assortment. For luxury brands, there's the additional task of brand protection in the distribution channel choice. This is because one of the important features of luxury brands and any brand that desires to maintain an exclusive brand aura is a tightly controlled distribution channel. This means avoiding or minimizing the use of middlemen and licences or franchises in order to retain control of where the products are sold. For example when Gucci and Burberry licensed their brands to multiple manufacturers and distributors, their brand values plummeted downwards. However, the buying back of the licences led to the increase of the brands' strengths and appropriate brand positioning.

Tightly controlled distribution is nonetheless not a magic formula for the success of luxury goods distribution. There are other relevant calculated factors that have to be considered in the design and implementation of distribution strategies. Luxury brands currently utilize four broad strategies in products and services distribution:

1 Directly Owned Stores (DOS), which could be in the form of stand-alone stores or retail spaces within high-end departmental stores.

2 Licence operations through third parties, which is challenging to control and often leads to a diminished luxury status.
3 The Internet, which is a new channel and one of the strategic challenges luxury brands currently face.
4 Catalogue mail-order, which is a strategy used before the introduction of modern distribution channels.

The most appropriate medium of the distribution of luxury goods is the DOS both offline and online. This channel best preserves the brand qualities of exclusivity through controlled distribution, and prestige through brand image projection. Licensing is generally bad news for luxury brands in terms of quality and distribution control. This is the reason that several luxury brands such as Chloé and Gucci have either completed or are in the process of buying back their licenses from third party companies.

The distribution strategy of luxury brands also comprises of the tactics for the services distribution. These services include customer services and after-sales services. The services aspect of the distribution of luxury goods is often neglected and wrongly considered as an offshoot of the product. Luxury brands currently utilize three broad service distribution strategies, which are the following:

1 Customer service within the brand's store, wherever the store is located.
2 Customer call centres, which a number of luxury brands have outsourced to other companies.
3 Online customer services, which remains poorly handled by the majority of luxury brands.

As previously indicated, luxury brands have an exclusive distribution strategy. This is also technically known as the **vertical value chain system** and is represented in Figure 5.15. The vertical value chain system indicates that luxury brands manufacture, wholesale (where this applies) and retail their products and services with the minimal use of secondary distributors. This strategy involves both exclusive (single channel) and selective (approved and tightly controlled dealers only) channels.

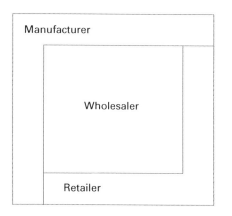

Figure 5.15 *The vertical chain distribution system adopted by luxury brands*

Unlike consumer goods, the distribution of luxury goods and services comprises of a one-track direction, making it easily manageable. In addition, several new distribution opportunities like the Internet provides optimal tools for enhanced services, long-term customer relationships and improved direct marketing methods. As noted in earlier chapters, luxury consumers desire personal attention and customized services and this can be achieved through online customer services powered by the Internet.

The choice of the appropriate distribution strategy results in increased sales and profitability, competitive leverage, customer satisfaction and brand loyalty. Most importantly, it portrays the language of the brand.

Promotion

Promotion involves communicating the message of a brand to consumers through various means. The means of communication include advertising, personal selling, sales promotion, public relations, sponsorships, cold-calling and several others. Additional 'new' promotional methods are online banner advertising and pop-ups; e-mail alerts and mobile phone alerts; movies, music and books; celebrity collaborations; and the recent iPod-casting.

Traditional brand promotion is a one-way process while communications is a two-way process that emphasizes exchanges with consumers. Communication with consumers features receiving feedback when brand messages have been effectively delivered. This is what yields the most benefits for brands. The communications strategy is an offshoot of the branding strategy.

The communication strategy has the following features:

1 The Push Trade promotion, where the brand is promoted to the market. An example of this is the traditional print advertising.
2 The Pull Customer promotion, where the market is pulled to the brand. An example is the various Internet promotional methods.
3 The Profile Stakeholder promotion, where the wider market environment is targeted for the promotion.

Luxury brand promotions follow the conventional promotion pathway where a brand sends a message to the consumer who receives and interprets the message. The complete process involves the sender (the brand) encoding the message through a package of images, colours, moods, feelings, sound and other elements that reflect the underlying message before sending it out. The receiver (the customer) then processes and decodes the message received from the brand. This process sounds simple but is oftentimes ineffectively implemented by several brands. Some of the hitches of effective brand communications can be found in four broad cases:

1 When the wrong message has been designed for the target audience.
2 When the right message has been designed and sent to the wrong audience.
3 When the target audience misinterprets the message as a result of failed sender encoding.
4 When the wrong medium has been used to send the message.

In designing promotional messages, it is imperative in all cases to define and target the right audience. Luxury brands have the additional task of conveying the brand's essence and all its elements in each communication. This means that the appropriate message, channel and execution style should be utilized in addition to the communications design itself. The identified effective promotional mediums suitable for luxury brands are:

1 Advertising
2 Direct marketing
3 Personal selling
4 Public relations
5 Sponsorships

Advertising is often defined to be a way of reaching a mass market because it utilizes the mass media. It is also often wrongly implied that advertising is non-personal and non-targeted. The reality is that although advertising luxury products through the mass media such as magazines and television is viewed by a mass market, the message within the advertisements are often targeted to a narrow group, that is the luxury consumer market.

Luxury brands are niche brands and their advertisements are tailored towards a specific consumer market. In addition, the advertisements of luxury brands are a means of communicating the brands' story, starting from their history and development to their personality and image, products and services.

Advertisements are highly important in the luxury goods sector, as they enhance the visibility of luxury brands. As a result, luxury brands allocate a large percentage of their earnings to advertising. The annual advertising budget of the average luxury brand is between US$14 million and US$50 million, representing between 5–15 per cent of revenue in most cases. This budget increases to approximately 25 per cent of the sales revenue with the inclusion of other aspects of communications such as public relations, events and sponsorships.

Traditionally, advertisements of luxury brands are mostly featured in fashion magazines, business publications, airline in-flight magazines and other high-end publications. This is because these publications are the most widely read by the target audience. Current statistics from *Luxury Briefing* indicate that *Vogue*, which is the foremost women's fashion magazine, circulated more than 2.1 million copies of its UK edition between January and June 2005.

Also more than 9 million people read its US edition in the first quarter of 2005. Furthermore more than 5 million people read men's fashion and lifestyle magazine, GQ, in the first quarter of 2005 in the USA alone. These examples represent a small fraction of the numerous fashion and lifestyle magazines that exist in different parts of the world. The indicators point towards the importance of the print media in advertisement and its influence on the luxury fashion consumer market.

Also, the glamorous nature and credibility of fashion magazines complements the characteristics of luxury brands. Fashion magazines also reinforce creativity through their high visual quality and long-lasting nature. The same can be said of television advertising. Although television advertising is used minimally by luxury brands, its prestigious nature complements luxury brands. It can also provide both entertainment and excitement through high-impact messages that utilize visuals, movement and sound.

Luxury brand advertising is significantly different from consumer goods advertising because they address different audiences. Sometimes however, several luxury brands wrongly adopt the same advertising channels as consumer goods. Other brands copy their competitors' media and style without understanding the strategic reasoning behind the choices. For example, it is common to find the advertisements of luxury products on street billboards and bus-stands in France, although these media are considered to be advertising domains of Fast Moving Consumer Goods (FMCGs). However, it can be argued that these media do not diminish the brand image of luxury brands in France because luxury fashion is an embedded aspect of French lifestyle and culture. However, if this strategy were transferred to the United Kingdom, where the majority of luxury consumers do not commute by bus, then the adverts would be addressing the wrong audience and its objective would be misplaced. On the other hand, in a city such as London where the majority of luxury consumers in full-time employment use the public underground train system in and out of central London on a daily basis, luxury brands might achieve a strategic objective by advertising at the train stations where their target consumers commute. Other advertising media that several luxury brands utilize, which require assessment and revision, are the bodies of taxis and buses (Figure 5.16).

The second issue to be determined after choosing the medium of advertising is selection of the products to advertise through each specific medium. In order to do this, it is important to ascertain whether the advertisement is product-specific or brand-specific. This factor indicates whether the advertisement aims to emphasize and reinforce the brand or if it seeks to promote a particular product in the market or both. For example, an advertisement of a fragrance might be placed at a bus-stand as a means of targeting the consumer group who commute by bus. In this case, the product (fragrance) is used as a tool to attract and invite new or old consumers to interact with the brand. This means that the advertisement is product-specific. On the other hand,

Figure 5.16 *Who do luxury brands target when they choose bus-stands, train stations and street billboards as advertising media, such as these found in different French and United Kingdom cities?*

placing the advertisement of a product such as expensive jewellery or leather handbag on a billboard in a highly tourist district of Paris could be a tool to invite wealthy tourists to purchase the particular product or to visit the brand's store while in Paris. In this case, the advertisement is brand-specific. Advertisements could also have a hybrid objective between brand and product specificity but if the objective is not set prior to deciding the medium, then the result could be counter-productive.

Luxury brands often feature products, models, celebrities and society personalities in advertising to reflect the brand essence and message. In addition to these, other tactics that generate rapid and instant publicity or rejuvenate the brand have been adopted. For example, Tom Ford has been known to use the 'Sex' concept to sell luxury. As the Artistic Director of Gucci, he oversaw the use of a controversial print advertisement in February 2003 featuring a female model displaying her pubic hair shaved into the Gucci logo. The picture shows the model pulling down her underwear to reveal Gucci's G logo, with a male model crouching between her legs. Needless to say, this advert generated great public coverage. Tom Ford again applied the 'Sex' advertising concept by featuring pornography stars as models in the 2006 print advertisement for his own branded sunglasses. Reports indicate that the models were also paid to have private sex on the set of the photo shoot in order to effectively transfer the 'feel' of sex onto the print adverts.

Additional advertising tactics include the use of a brand's origin, location, history and heritage as a source of its credibility and communications. This could be done through pictures, words and products. For example, Bally includes the tagline '*Since 1851*' in its print adverts to reinforce its history; Lacoste's print advert has featured a 1921 picture of company founder Renee Lacoste playing tennis, to underline the brand's long history and sports association. Also Burberry used images of London, the English lifestyle and a British celebrity, Rachel Weisz, to advertise its 2006 fragrance Burberry London (Figure 5.17); and Jean-Paul Gaultier uses a similar tactic of selling 'Frenchness' in its Spring/Summer 2006 advertising campaign.

The effectiveness of advertising can be measured in different ways. The factors that are considered in this exercise are the following:

- The persuasion level of the advertisement in terms of creating a favourable consumer predisposition towards the brand and its offerings.
- The accomplishment of the message delivered in terms of understanding and conveying the brand essence.
- The level of delight and enjoyment of the advertisement to consumers.
- The result from tracking the pre- and post-awareness level of the brand and products.
- The result from a panel research regarding the long-term advertising effectiveness.
- The impact of the advertisement compared with those of competitors.

Figure 5.17
Burberry emphasizing its English heritage through using a British actress to depict the quintessential English lifestyle. (2006)

In order to achieve a high level of effectiveness in luxury advertising, it is important to differentiate the general style, message and execution of the advertisement. The luxury goods sector is highly competitive and as brands strive to get noticed, they end up falling into the trap of sameness. It is not uncommon to look through the pages of a fashion magazine and find advertisements of several brands that are so similar that if the brand names were concealed, they could pass for the same brand. Consumers long to see fresh and distinctive advertising that has high and lasting appeal and this is only achieved through differentiation. The message of the advertisements also ought to be deeper than the surface beauty of a pretty model flaunting a desirable product. Luxury brands have differing underlying personalities but their advertising messages sometimes reflect the same brand image and personality which is wrong. The distinct brand images could be effectively portrayed with a more focused attention on insight, innovation and imagination.

Also, the concept and style of the advertisement of the sunglasses product of Armani, shown in Figure 5.19, has been adopted by several luxury brands.

Figure 5.18 *The Dior Crystal Watch advertisement (2005/2006), which focuses on the product features and design to accentuate its luxury status. The advertisements of other luxury products like the Chanel Camelia watch advert (2005) and the Hermès Cap Cod watch advert (2006), have also applied the same advert design and strategy concept. This depicts sameness, which is contrary to the quality of substance that consumers seek. Luxury brands have distinct identities, personalities and images and these are required to be reflected in all aspects of marketing communications, including print advertising*

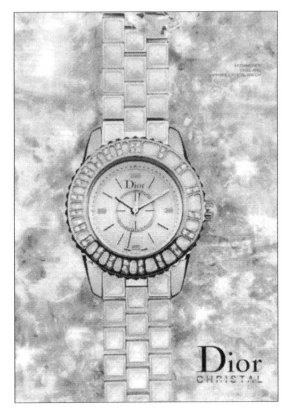

Figure 5.19 *The Emporio Armani eyewear advertisement, 2006. Several luxury brands have applied the same concept and style in their eyewear advertisements, depicting 'sameness'*

This depicts similarity in terms of products and brand personality portrayal. Consumers are bored with this level of sameness and monotony and now have higher expectations from luxury brands.

In response to the monotonous images and messages often found in luxury goods advertisements, several luxury and mass fashion brands constantly devise innovative advertising means and messages that act as 'firsts' in their categories. A notable example is the spring–summer 2006 advertising campaign of premium leather-goods brand Furla, which features its own employees as models (Figure 5.20). The strategic aim of this advertisement for the brand was to 'express the spirit of the brand' and to show that the brand understands its consumers' real needs. This tactic represents a new approach to fashion advertising. It portrays the employees of Furla as 'brand stewards' and 'brand ambassadors', who are attuned to serving their customers and fulfilling their expectations. This is an effective representation of perceived product efficiency and customer services. Another advantage of this advertising tactic is that it gives the brand a 'face' through revealing the dynamic and creative team behind the products and their complement to the brand's personality. This advertising method could however raise other questions related to the 'fantasy' aspect of a luxury brand's image projection to the public.

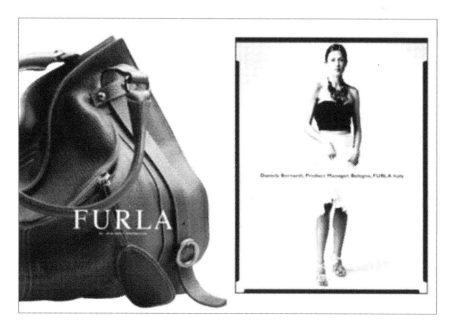

Figure 5.20 *Furla's advertisement featuring employee Daniela Bernardi (2006). This is an innovative advertising technique that shows the brand's employees as its ambassadors. However, it raises the question of whether luxury consumers relate more to the people who represent the brand or to the 'fantasy' and 'desire' aspects of luxury goods*

Figure 5.21
Oscar de La Renta (Spring 2006) advert, featuring Liya Kebede, effectively captures the brand's essence of stylish and modern chic, (2006).

Photographed by Craig McDean

While striving for differentiation in the luxury market, it is also important to critically evaluate the impact of an advertising campaign on a brand's positioning and image. This evaluation should also feature customer expectations and the effect of the advertisement on their perception of the brand.

Luxury and high-end fashion consumers constantly seek to be enticed and excited through desirable goods and dazzling models or celebrities in advertisements. While consumer goods like detergent and toilet paper project a sense of reality to their consumers, luxury brands project a sense of fantasy. These contribute to creating the 'desire' and 'lust' that propel consumers to seek luxury goods. However, when consumers are exposed to a different form of advertising, it is essential to ensure that they understand the underlying message.

Figure 5.21 shows a luxury brand advertisement that has effectively applied advertising communications to recapture the major qualities of the brand.

Direct marketing is defined as direct communication between a brand and a consumer designed to generate a purchase behavioural response. The response could be in the form of information request, a visit to the brand's store or website or actual product purchase. The goal of direct marketing is to lead consumers to interact with the brand. Its methods include the age-old mail-order selling technique through catalogues and direct mail. Others are telemarketing and home shopping, although these are rarely used in the luxury sector.

Direct marketing is one of the fastest growing media of communication among fast moving consumer goods, but their application in luxury goods promotions is minimal. This minimal use arises from several discrepancies in its utilization. For example, several luxury brands produce product catalogues designed for consumers but there is a continuous inconsistency over how, when and to whom these should be distributed. Several brands such as Roberto Cavalli and Gucci offer their catalogues to consumers on request and at no cost. Other brands such as Louis Vuitton sell their catalogue to consumers for a small fee. Yet others like Coach provide the possibility to order a free print catalogue from their website, in addition to the online version. Also, Jimmy Choo provides an online downloadable catalogue in PDF version that consumers can print. Most of these online and offline catalogues often do not make provision for product purchase although they provide product information.

One of the challenges that luxury brands face in using the direct marketing strategy is the retention of the 'exclusivity' and 'prestige' qualities while pushing products commercial-wise. This challenge raises the question of the range of products to present through direct marketing.

Direct mail has several disadvantages in addition to its numerous gains. The first disadvantage is the risk of overwhelming consumers with information which they might not be interested in; the second is related to ethical marketing concerns like seeking consumer permission prior to utilizing personal details for direct marketing purposes of the brand and its partners.

Personal selling is the most direct and longest established means of promotion in the promotional mix. It is the presentation of products and associated persuasive communication to potential clients. Personal selling is widely used in business-to-business exchanges where products or services demonstrations are required. However, it can also be an effective promotional tool for luxury brands.

Personal selling is manifested in several ways in the luxury goods sector. These include private shopping programmes, special customer events, private product previews, online privileged information access, fashion show sales and so on.

Personal selling in the luxury sector usually requires the presence of the product creator or other specialists that understand the product components, history, use and care. Specialized information and one-to-one interaction is the core of the personal selling strategy. It is also one of the avenues of providing personalized and customized customer relations services. This strategy is also effective for collecting customer data that could be utilized for data mining and re-designing products and services according to customer needs and expectations.

Public relations involve the planned and sustained effort to establish and maintain goodwill and mutual understanding between a company and its target audience. The aim of public relations is to influence and in some cases, change people's knowledge and feelings regarding a company and its offerings, including its identity and image.

In the luxury goods sector, public relations is a promotional tool used to persuade consumers and the public of the authenticity of the brand, while also facilitating understanding between the brand and the public. It is a means of building good relationships with not only consumers but also all the stakeholders of the company. The stakeholders include shareholders, associations, partners, collaborators, suppliers, distributors and competitors. For example, representatives of several luxury brands are often invited to their competitors' events and fashion shows and they are expected to share the goodwill of their brands during these events. This is because consumers and other stakeholders are influenced by the information they receive about a brand from different sources; therefore the brand must maintain positive associations at all times.

Public relations messages are often more credible than paid advertising because they involve a story that frequently leaves a lasting impression with the public. They also create a continuous buzz around a brand or a product. This contributes to a positive image for the brand and fuels word-of-mouth publicity. It also helps luxury brands to stay in the limelight through exposing their good deeds. The deeds can range from humanitarian acts to those concerning environmental protection. For example, in 2004, Jimmy Choo launched the coffee table book, *Four Inches*, featuring photographs of celebrities and models wearing nothing except Jimmy Choo shoes. The photographs were sold by auction in London, Los Angeles and New York and raised more than £1.6 billion. The proceeds went to the Elton John AIDS Foundation, which particularly benefits women and children with AIDS in Africa. Also in 2005, Salvatore Ferragamo celebrated the tenth anniversary of its Beijing store with a fashion show and gala night. The proceeds from the events were donated to the China Welfare Fund for the Handicapped. These are effective public relations tactics.

The Internet provides an additional effective medium to advertise and inform the public of public relations deeds. For example the corporate section of websites is an avenue to feature public relations deeds particularly on the 'News and Highlights' pages.

Among the main objectives of public relations in the luxury fashion sector, the following are the most prominent:

- Bringing attention to a brand's good deeds. For example, Stella McCartney supports the anti-fur movement and this is known as a part of her brand legacy. Burberry also supports the Breast Cancer Awareness project through donating a percentage of specific product earnings to the cause.

- Enhancing the image of a city, region or country. Several Italian and French luxury brands are involved in initiatives that promote their countries as fashion and art centres.
- Introducing new products or sub-brands to the public such as the 2005 co-branding collaboration between Zac Posen and Jaguar for the design of a limited edition driving gloves collection for the launch of the Jaguar XK Sports Coupé. A percentage of the sales turnover was donated to the Teachers Count charity.
- Influencing government authorities and legislation. Louis Vuitton is one of the luxury brands actively involved in initiatives such as lobbying to aid governments in fighting counterfeit luxury goods.

In order to execute an effective public relations strategy, it is imperative for a luxury brand to have a clear set of objectives and a specific target audience. An analysis of the brand's current position in public relations, the competitors' activities and the public's expectations is also important.

Public relations effectiveness can be measured in several ways. These include internal assessments, brand preference research and media coverage generated by public relations activities.

Public relations deeds are increasingly important especially among the current consumer base who are more ethically and environmentally aware and therefore seek substance and depth from luxury brands.

Sponsorships can be considered as an extension of public relations because they both aim to achieve similar objectives such as providing a good image and reinforcing a brand's credibility. Unlike public relations, sponsorship initiatives involve the provision of financial support channelled towards funding an event often relating to art initiatives, sports and goodwill. These actions generate a lasting positive impact among consumers and the public towards the brand. It is also a great source of brand loyalty especially among the consumers that have enjoyed the event or have an affinity with the specific activity that has been sponsored. For example, Louis Vuitton has been known to sponsor several young artists, painters and photographers. The brand also has an exhibition centre at its flagship store in Paris, dedicated to exhibitions by various artists. Other brands such as Pierre Cardin provide art and history exhibitions through the brand's private museum. Yet other non-fashion brands are implementing sponsorships through fusing fashion and gastronomy. An example is the champagne brand Moët & Chandon, which often sponsors and promotes fashion-related deeds. Every season, the brand commissions a designer to create a dress that would reflect the qualities of the Moët & Chandon brand. Past designers include Roberto Cavalli and John Rocha. The brand also sponsors the Fashion Tribute Award.

Sponsorships are also a way to target specific market segments. For example, Louis Vuitton sponsors the annual American Yacht Regatta competition, and in exchange the trophy has been named the Louis Vuitton Cup. The company also receives immense positive publicity and access to some of the world's wealthiest individuals through this sponsorship venture.

One of the major benefits of sponsorship is that it is a precise way of marketing because it provides a brand with its own specific territory. This makes both the brand and its message stand out. It is also a great way to attain competitive advantage. Like public relations, the sponsorship programme should involve an analysis of the current company situation, a definition of a clear set of objectives and the identification of the target audience. This will provide a guideline for mapping out and clarifying the strategy and its resources and performance measurement.

Some important points to remember in the development of sponsorships and other promotional tactics are the following:

1 Be distinctive and innovative.
2 Be consistent in portraying the brand personality and image.
3 Understand who the target is and satisfy them.
4 Analyse competitors' strategies and differentiate from these and avoid sameness.
5 Understand that each brand is unique and different and therefore promotional messages should correspond to the unique nature of a brand.

The celebrity connection

Celebrity endorsement of luxury fashion is hardly a new phenomenon but has been in practice for several centuries. Charles Worth, the man who invented haute couture in Paris in the nineteenth century understood the importance of linking celebrities to brands, even before this was recognized as an important marketing communications tool. To promote his fashion house, La Maison Worth, he sought a high society lady and influencer of court fashions Princess Von Metternich, wife of the then Austrian ambassador to France and close friend of Napoleon's wife Empress Eugenie. This celebrity's patronage and connection with La Maison Worth contributed immensely to the success and status of Charles Worth's couture house as the most influential in the world at this time.

Celebrities are highly important and valuable to brands especially in the luxury fashion sector. There is no argument about this. They wield enormous power in fashion circles and can contribute to making and breaking brands. Fashion designers pamper them and brand managers recognize their potential to brands and utilize this effectively. For example, Marilyn Monroe's declaration that she wears only Chanel No. 5 to sleep, contributed to making the fragrance an unequalled icon. Celebrity endorsement does not however begin and end with shooting and printing the photo of a beautiful star with a luxury product, in a fashion magazine. There are several factors and dimensions involved in choosing a celebrity to endorse a brand. It is however worthwhile to establish the scope and true value of celebrity endorsement.

First of all, who are celebrities? Celebrities are people that exert significant influence in several facets of the society ranging from arts, music, movies and television, sports, culture, education, politics, government and also religion. They range from film and television stars to musicians, sports personalities, scientists, engineers, royals, politicians and also socialites who have no defined careers apart from looking beautiful and attending the right events. In the fashion world, this list of celebrities would include designers, their muses, models, photographers, image consultants, style advisers and any famous person involved in the artistic aspects of fashion such as make-up artists, fashion consultants and also fashion experts like Mark Tungate whose book *Fashion Brands: Branding Style from Armani to Zara*, was published in 2005. The celebrities most utilized in the promotion of luxury fashion brands, however, are those in the film and music industry as a result of their high visibility and the prominent role that fashion plays in the entertainment sectors.

According to recent research statistics from advertising and marketing services company WPP, the number of celebrity advertisements has doubled in the past ten years. *The Guardian* also reports that one in four adverts currently features celebrities compared with one in eight in 1995. Although this statistic is related to a broad range of goods and services, there has also been an increase in the use of celebrities in the brand message communications of luxury brands. Several recent examples show evidence of this practice. Italian luxury brand Versace featured music icon Madonna and Hollywood stars Demi Moore and Halle Berry in its print adverts between 2005 and 2006. Likewise Julia Roberts appeared in the 2006/2007 print advertisements of Gianfranco Ferre; Sharon Stone and Monica Bellucci in Dior's and Jennifer Lopez, Scarlet Johansson and Uma Thurman (Figure 5.22) have all been the faces of Vuitton at different times. Also luxury watch brand Baume & Mercier adopted celebrity endorsement in 2005 in its advertising campaign featuring actors Meg Ryan and Keifer Sutherland. Non-luxury brands such as Gap and H&M are also catching on. Gap featured television and movie star Sarah Jessica Parker in their 2005 advertisement and H&M featured Madonna and her crew in their 2006 print advertisement. The use of celebrities from an earlier period is also not left out in luxury brands endorsements. For example, to celebrate the 100th anniversary of the birth of silver-screen actress Greta Garbo, Mont Blanc designed a special edition pen named after the deceased actress.

The reasons that these personalities are used in brand communications are: to make the brand's message stand out among the clutter of advertising and

Figure 5.22   *Uma Thurman for Louis Vuitton (2005)*

offerings from competitors; and to convince customers of the credibility of the brand's offerings. In addition to these, celebrity endorsement is important to luxury brands for the following reasons:

- Celebrity endorsement is a great brand awareness creation tool for new brands.
- Endorsement by celebrities helps to position and re-position existing brands.
- Celebrities contribute to sustaining a brand's aura.
- Celebrities are used to revive and revitalize staid brands.
- Celebrities generate extensive PR leverage and opportunities for brands.
- Celebrities are used to reach a global market.
- Celebrities promote a brand's products and appeal.

There are several ways that celebrities can be utilized to either endorse a luxury fashion brand or show some connection to the brand. The classic and most widely used method is the paid-for media advertisement mostly found in fashion magazines and on television. This is when a celebrity is photographed or filmed with an often-appealing product of the brand in question. The themes of these advertisements vary but the underlying message is uniform and gives an indication of a direct connection between the brand, its products and the celebrity. The ways that celebrities are used to endorse brands include the following:

- Print media advertising found in various magazines such as the 2005 spring/summer and autumn/winter adverts of Versace that featured Hollywood stars Madonna and Demi Moore respectively.
- Television advertising such as the video clip advert of the Chanel No. 5 perfume featuring Nicole Kidman, which ran from 2004 to 2005.
- Product use in movies and television programs, sitcoms and soap operas such as the 1984 film American Gigolo, which was a showcase of Armani designs and contributed to the global appeal of the brand. Other movie brand promotion includes Legally Blond II for Jimmy Choo, Le Divorce for Hermès, Miss Congeniality for Fendi and Dolce & Gabbana and the sitcom Sex & The City, which patently promoted both Jimmy Choo and Manolo Blahnik, among others.
- Fashion spreads showing celebrities in the apparel and accessories of luxury brands at different events and locations.
- Photographs of paid celebrities casually using the products of a brand. This tactic involves brands paying a highly photographed celebrity to appear with their products in an indifferent manner indicating that the product and brand is a part of their daily lives. Although this practice might be thought uncommon in the luxury goods category, as luxury products are highly desirable even to celebrities, it is frequently utilized. It is also highly effective as it portrays a true lifestyle which the public can relate to better than a glossy advert.
- Photographs of unpaid celebrities using the products of a brand. This is called 'gratis' product placement. It occurs when a celebrity embraces a product or a brand they truly like and visibly uses these products in public. Since these celebrities are often photographed, they become promotional tools and grant the brands exposure that yields both short-term benefits and long-term rewards. This aspect of celebrity endorsement is however becoming rare, as celebrities have got wise to their powerful influence over consumers and increasingly use this influence to their own advantage.
- The mention of luxury brands in music lyrics such as the inclusion of Jimmy Choo in the lyrics of Beyoncé. Another example is that of Maria Carey, who sang extensively of Louis Vuitton in her last album. In some cases, luxury brands pay the musicians to mention them in songs while in other rare cases the musicians voluntarily adopt the brands. Music celebrity endorsement of brands is increasingly used by both luxury and non-luxury brands. The concept has become so commonplace that a chart called *The American Brandstand Chart*, has been created by a company that tracks the mentions of brands in music lyrics. The chart indicates the hierarchy and level of influence of the brands that have been mentioned in song lyrics.
- Inviting celebrities to be co-creators and partners in designing specific products. Japanese designer Samantha Thavasa adopted this strategy through her collaborative bag designs with Beyoncé, Penelope Cruz, Victoria Beckham, Maria Sharapova and Paris and Nicky Hilton. Louis

Vuitton also teamed up with American rapper and music producer Pharrel Williams to create a limited edition sunglasses line in 2005. Also non-luxury fashion brands like Dorothy Perkins have collaborated with stars Sienna Miller, Nicole Kidman, Sharon Osbourne and Charlotte Church to create a T-shirt collection in aid of breast cancer research.

- Naming products after celebrities, (with their approval of course). Gucci has the Jackie bag, named after Jackie Kennedy and Hermès has both the Kelly and Birkin bags named after actresses Grace Kelly and Jane Birkin. Tom Ford also named one of his newly launched eyewear after celebrated actress, Farrah Fawcett.
- Other creative cross-marketing methods such as Jimmy Choo's book *Four Inches*, which featured photos of several celebrities including Paris Hilton, wearing nothing but Jimmy Choo shoes. Also, Pamela Anderson posed as a nude mannequin at the window of Stella McCartney's London store. The two endorsements were aimed at promoting several social courses but also generated immense publicity for the brands in the process.

Celebrity endorsement entails that the personality and status of the celebrity as successful, wealthy, influential and distinctive are directly linked with the brand. Other personality attributes that the celebrity may have such as glamour, beauty, talent and style will also be ultimately linked with the brand. This factor however appears to be required less among luxury brands than consumer brands because luxury brands already have well-defined and strong brand personalities. The reality is that luxury brands need to define the connection between their brands and celebrities. This fact raises the question of the choice criteria of a celebrity for a luxury brand. How can the right celebrity be matched with the right brand in order to achieve the desired maximum impact and results? The following five rules of celebrity endorsement for luxury brands provide an indication of this.

Rule 1: Credibility   The celebrity must be credible. This means that he/she must have a high level of expertise and talent in their field. These merits bring value to the brand and indicate the intent of the brand to be associated with the very best. Actors Tom Cruise, George Clooney, Nicole Kidman and Hilary Swank have star power because of their talent.

Rule 2: Global Appeal   The celebrity must have global appeal. This means that the celebrity must not only be known worldwide but must also be appreciated and liked by the majority of the people in the consumer and fashion societies. Charlize Theron and Halle Berry are two actresses that satisfy this criterion effortlessly.

Rule 3: Personality   The celebrity's personality must match the brand's personality. Several brands often wrongly choose a celebrity to endorse their brands based on their popularity and appeal. Although these attributes are important, it is essential to understand the significant role that a celebrity's personality brings to the brand. For example, a classic brand such as Hermès is most likely to give a clear brand message by using a celebrity who portrays the quality of 'classic chic' rather than one who exhibits non-conformism. In the case where luxury brands use a celebrity that portrays a different brand personality, it should be for a strategic purpose such as brand re-positioning, new product launch or brand extension. When the celebrity's personality matches that of the brand, the result is often an enhancement of the brand's image. For example, there is a definite match between Nicole Kidman and Chanel; and between Uma Thurman and Louis Vuitton and these celebrities brought a positive brand enhancement at the time of their endorsements of the luxury brands.

Rule 4: Uniform Power   The celebrity must not overshadow the brand. This is particularly important for new and up and coming luxury brands. Several established luxury brands already have powerful brand personalities, making it a challenge for celebrities to outshine the brand. However other brands that are yet to ascertain a high level of brand strength have to be careful in choosing a celebrity whose strength doesn't surpass that of the brand.

Rule 5: Constancy   The celebrity must have constancy and lasting appeal. This means that the celebrity should have sustainability and the knack to maintain their image and career accordingly. It is often based on how predictably successful a celebrity's career and role as a star is projected to be. This is quite similar to the sales forecast projections that companies make using previous and current cash-flows. Several stars that have been successful in their careers for decades might at the same time lack constancy and appeal, which cannot be ignored if they are to endorse a luxury brand.

Luxury brands that utilize celebrity support must also maintain high appeal through their product and service offerings even after the celebrity campaign is over. Celebrity endorsement facilitates an increased customer expectation level and this expectation must be constantly met and exceeded. Also, the use of celebrities to promote a brand shouldn't be a one-off strategy but should be revisited periodically.

Luxury brand managers constantly evaluate celebrities through unclear criteria. This is largely because this strategy has been viewed for a long time as one that doesn't require complex business decision grids. The increasingly sophisticated global business scene especially in the luxury fashion sector, however, calls for clear and structured decision criteria in managing the celebrity endorsement strategy. The closest evaluation measurement that exists today is *The Davie-Brown Celebrity Index* developed by Davie-Brown Entertainment and i-think Inc. This index evaluates the worth of celebrities through a systematic and controlled method that resembles financial brand valuation and forecasting. It aims to remove the ambiguity that surrounds celebrity appeal and acts as a guideline for celebrity choice in advertising.

Celebrity endorsement is not rosy at all times. Several risks are associated with this brand communications strategy; therefore luxury brands should meticulously evaluate all the inter-connecting elements related to this strategy. The following list covers some of the potential hazards involved in celebrity endorsement:

1 Celebrities can get into public controversies that might harm the brands they endorse.
2 The image of celebrities can be damaged as a result of professional or personal circumstances. This is automatically transferred to the brands they represent.
3 Celebrities can disappear from the spotlight of their careers even before the advertising campaign is over.
4 Celebrities can become over-exposed and lose their star appeal as a result of endorsing multiple brands in different categories. For example, Kate Moss has represented luxury brands Louis Vuitton, Burberry, Dior, Yves Saint Laurent and Chanel but also mass cosmetics brand Rimmel, which is sold in supermarkets.

   As a model, Kate Moss is performing her professional duties by endorsing various brands but when her status transcends to that of a celebrity, then the luxury brands' image balance with her celebrity status should be checked.
5 Celebrities can also decide to change their image, which might sometimes be a contradicting image to the brands they currently endorse.
6 Celebrities can decide to intentionally damage a brand if they feel that the brand did not meet their (sometimes extraneous) demands or did not give them the star treatment they desired.

As earlier identified, a key aspect of celebrity endorsement is related to the issue of the over-exposure of celebrities who endorse multiple brands within a short time period. This is often found among celebrities that are in 'popular demand' at a particular time. The multiple brand endorsements could lead to an over-exposure of the luxury brand or an undermining of its brand perception. This is because consumers could associate the luxury brand with the overall package that the celebrity and the multiple endorsements represent. If the multiple brands that the celebrity represents constitutes of mass-market brands or 'low-value' brands in other product categories, the damage on the luxury brand's equity could be worse. For example, the talented musician Madonna has represented luxury brand Versace as well as mass-premium brand H&M. Do her multiple endorsements affect the brand equity of the luxury brands she represents? In the evaluation of these endorsements, it is important to understand whether the two brands and adverts address the same group of consumers. It is also essential to ascertain what impact Madonna's brand endorsements could have on the brand equity of the two brands and on Madonna's own personal brand as a celebrity.

Celebrities are getting wise to the branding leverage their star strengths and powerful appeal provide them and are also more inclined to use this in branching out in their careers. They now understand the importance and influence of personal branding and are exploiting and extending it to commercial branding. As a result, several celebrities have ventured into the fashion and accessories businesses and more are on the way. Examples include Jennifer Lopez, Sean Combs, 50 Cents, Eminem, Sadie Frost, Gwen Stefani, Pamela Anderson and Jessica Simpson who all have clothing or accessories brands. Others are Kylie Minogue who owns a lingerie brand, Victoria Beckham who recently began designing jeans and Elizabeth Hurley, who launched a swimwear brand in 2005. In addition, the list of celebrities that have launched perfumes named after them is steadily increasing including Jennifer Lopez, Britney Spears, Paris Hilton, Celine Dion, Elizabeth Taylor, Michael Jordan, Naomi Campbell, Jessica Simpson, David and Victoria Beckham, Antonio Banderas, Donald Trump and Cindy Crawford, among many others.

The fashion business ventures of celebrities could also affect the brands they endorse in terms of image and competition. For example Sara Jessica Parker, who featured in the extensive global advertisements of Gap in 2005 was also the model in the advertisement for her own fragrance shortly afterwards. Also, Jennifer Lopez who appeared in Louis Vuitton advertisements in

2003/2004 (Figure 5.23) has also featured in the advertisement of her own branded fragrances before, during and after this period.

These product and brand launches result in an increased and steady source of revenue income for the celebrities and is also a way of increasing their visibility in the already cluttered celebrity market. However,

Figure 5.23   *Jennifer Lopez for Louis Vuitton (2004). The celebrity has also appeared in several advertisements for her own branded fragrances before, during and after this advertisement*

being a celebrity doesn't mean an automatic success potential in fashion branding. The real issue is to apply effective business strategies required in the development, management and sustenance of a brand because relying on a celebrity name alone to uphold a business venture is the fast lane to business failure.

Endorsement of luxury fashion brands by celebrities is a strategy that undoubtedly has great importance in the luxury goods sector. Although the short-term results are difficult to accurately measure, if managed effectively, this strategy often yields long-term benefits such as increased brand loyalty and brand equity, which ultimately translate to higher sales turnover and brand value.

People

People in the luxury branding mix refers to everyone that is affected by the brand and everyone that affects the brand. These include those involved in the development of products and services, brand management and the employee-wide staff involved in the daily business processes. People also constitutes customers and the general public whose attitudes and predisposition towards a company and a brand affects its performance. People are the most important element of any service because the experience they have with a brand influences their relationship with that brand and is transmitted to the customers.

People in the luxury sector can be categorized into three broad groups.

1 Customers, who have been extensively discussed in Chapter 3
2 Employees
3 Brand ambassadors

Employees such as retail store sales representatives and customer services staff are usually the first direct interface between consumers and the brand they represent. They are the representatives of the brand and reflect the spirit of the brand wherever they are located and under every circumstance. The luxury sector retails high-involvement goods and therefore the service expectation is high. The people who sell luxury products to consumers in the stores are consequently required to be professional, exhibit expert knowledge, be sufficiently stylish and emanate the brand's aura. This places a high level of responsibility on the employees of luxury brands.

There is a general consensus among a large percentage of luxury consumers of the negligible and sometimes poor level of customer services provided by the staff of luxury brands within the stores or after-sales. Consumers often complain that several representatives of luxury brands provide a 'cold' and 'aloof' service in their bid to maintain the 'prestige status' of the brand and a cool distance from consumers. This attitude spells unprofessionalism and neither inspires nor endears the customer to the brand. The customer interface and after-sales staff are important in luxury retailing and brands ought to invest heavily in them through expert training in sales, personal selling, customer service and brand stewardship.

Ambassadors of a luxury brand are the people that provide the brand with life. They are used by luxury brands in a peculiar way to promote the brand through 'giving it a face'. This involves using strong personalities that are connected with the brand to act as either the brand ambassadors or a symbolic figure linked with the brand. These personalities range from the designers and creative directors of luxury brands, to chief executives or prominent figures in the brand's management team. They could also include external public figures that are not involved in the brand's product design or management but have been adopted by the brand to become a part of its 'face'.

There is a difference between 'People' in the luxury branding mix, such as ambassadors and the 'People' that feature in the advertisements and other promotional activities of luxury brands. The people we are talking about here have a consistent and long-term relationship with the brand. As ambassadors of brands, they are a permanent part of the brand unlike the people used in advertisements who could be changed seasonally.

The people who act as brand ambassadors include creative directors such as John Galliano of Dior, Marc Jacobs of Vuitton, Jean-Paul Gaultier of Hermès and Karl Lagerfeld of Chanel and Fendi. Others are chief executives and senior managers such as Sidney Toledano of Dior; Bernard Arnault of LVMH and Frédéric de Narp of Cartier. Yet there are those that are both presidents or senior executives of luxury brands and at the same time the creative directors. This group includes Giorgio Armani, Muiccia Prada, Donatella Versace and Tamara Mellon of Jimmy Choo, among many others.

Brand ambassadors often become household public names and sometimes celebrities in their own right with a personal brand value. They represent the brands both in their personal and public lives and are the expected faces at all public events involving the brand or the wider fashion industry. For example Donatella Versace acceded in an interview that it is impossible for the Versace brand to function without her because there is nobody that can represent the brand the way she does. She is also widely believed to be a fashion diva, which is an indirect definition of a celebrity. On the personal level, her home in Italy is an extension of the Versace brand. Donatella represents Versace just as Tom Ford represented Gucci and Karl Lagerfeld currently represents Chanel and Fendi.

There is yet another small group of ambassadors who are not directly linked with the creative or business aspects of luxury brands but have become 'muses' or 'eyes' or 'noses' for the brands. Their principal role is to bring inspiration and fresh ideas to luxury brands through their fashion vision, wealth of knowledge, worldliness and high aesthetic sensitivity. This group includes the likes of Sofia Coppola who acts as Marc Jacob's muse and Dita Von Tesse who is connected with Louis Vuitton.

The final group of the faces that act as ambassadors are the models through whom a brand's products are displayed both on the runways and in advertisements. The concept of fashion models was introduced in the nineteenth century by La Maison Worth and since then the popularity of models has grown. However, for a long time, models were not celebrated in the fashion sector until the era of the Supermodels of the 1980s, mainly promoted by the late Gianni Versace. Since then, luxury brands have promoted and even celebrated models such as Eva Herzigova, Cindy Crawford, Heidi Klum, Kate Moss and more recently Gisele Bundchen and Daria Werbrow.

The challenge faced by luxury brands in managing ambassadors is to know when the brand's ambassador should be promoted as a personal brand and if this is a positive factor for the luxury brand or not. For example, during Tom Ford's tenure as the Creative Director of Gucci, his celebrity status and personal brand power seemed so strong and influential that the thought of Gucci without Tom Ford and vice versa was unimaginable. On the other hand, both Stella McCartney and Phoebe Philo were highly successful as the Creative Directors of Chloé but never quite overshadowed the brand.

It has often been argued that luxury brands should avoid celebrity or star designers in order to contain the risk of the designer overshadowing the brand. The proponents of this opinion believe that instead of promoting the designers, luxury brands should channel their resources into sustaining their brand equity. This debate could be approached from two viewpoints. The first point of view is the definition of the strategic role of the designer. The designer's role for a luxury brand depends on the position of the brand when the designer joined the company. Using Gucci as an illustration, Tom Ford as a star designer played a key strategic role in resuscitating the prestige brand aura of Gucci and elevating it once more to the luxury fashion brand status after the brand depreciated for several years. In this case, the star designer is imperative. On the other hand, Karl Lagerfeld's role at Chanel and Marc Jacobs' at Louis Vuitton are more aligned towards promoting the identities and 'spirits' of the brands and enhancing their value and less about defining the brand character and strategic direction as Tom Ford did for Gucci. Other rising designers such as Tomas Maier of Bottega Veneta who currently plays a purely creative role might be elevated to star or celebrity status according to the needs of the brand and the requirements of the market environment.

To say that a brand doesn't need a designer with celebrity status would be wrong but the presence of a star designer should be to play a key strategic role at the required time for the brand. This is one of the reasons for the importance of brand ambassadors.

Positioning

Positioning is the strategic placement of a company or brand in a clearly desired position measured against that of the brand's competitors. Positioning as part of the luxury branding mix is different from brand positioning already discussed in this chapter, which is a source of brand equity and brand value. In this context, Positioning refers to the choices that a brand makes, which determines where and how it competes in its market. In the consumer goods category, this would mean defining and targeting a specific or several market segments, which would act as a guide in designing other elements such as pricing and product features.

Positioning on this level deals mostly with products, services and pricing. Since luxury brands have a clearly defined and highly specific market, the positioning strategy serves mostly as a strategic tool for external competitor intelligence and sector benchmarking. It is also a guide for evaluating internal product decisions such as product extensions and diversification.

Positioning is applied through positioning maps. This could be done internally through mapping products and services together on a positioning map. It allows the products to be compared and contrasted in relation to one other and those of competitors. On the external level, positioning could be done through using market indicator factors such as appeal and pricing as labels for the positioning map. The most feasible competitive position, which enables a brand to distinguish their own products from the offerings of their competition is then selected and executed.

In the development of positioning maps, two or multiple axes are used depending on the length and breadth of the brand's portfolio. After determining the number of axes, they are labelled with relevant factor indicators. These factors could be represented through 'pricing' as one variable and 'quality' as another variable. Other possible labels include 'design' as one variable and 'image' as another. The individual products are then mapped out next to each other and gaps are usually identified at this stage. These gaps could be regarded as possible areas for new products or product re-launches. An example of a positioning map is shown in Figure 5.24.

It is highly essential for luxury brands with low market awareness to have a well-crafted positioning in terms of product, services and branding. This is one of the fastest routes of appropriate placement in the market. The Tom Ford brand can be used to illustrate the dimensions of positioning. Tom Ford, the former Creative Director of Gucci has recently launched two products. The first is an eyewear range branded *Tom Ford Eyewear* and the second is a fragrance and cosmetics co-branding venture with Estee Lauder branded the *Tom Ford Estée Lauder Collection*. Since Tom Ford is a household personality in the luxury fashion arena with a clear image that needs no introduction, the recognition level of products associated with his name is likely to be high. However, on the branding sphere, there is some message disparity regarding

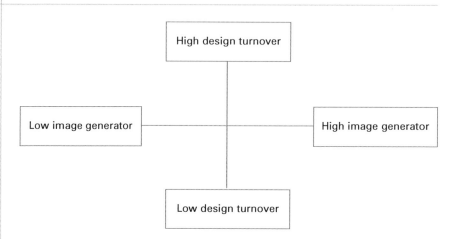

Figure 5.24 *The positioning map*

the simultaneous brand launch of the Tom Ford brand and its co-branding venture with Estée Lauder. It is important for consumers to understand from the onset whether Tom Ford is a new luxury brand or a co-brand of Estée Lauder. If it is a new luxury brand, what is its product range? Where is its market and which consumers does the brand target? What is its identity and positioning? These questions need to be clarified for consumers as co-branding is a strategic move that requires clarity with consumers. However, the strategy that Tom Ford adopts ought to be clear and understandable to consumers from the moment the brand is introduced in the market.

The Positioning of luxury brands is important for competitive leverage. It should also incorporate research and benchmarking, with the objective of creating value for consumers.

The confusion and clarification of fashion co-branding

Co-branding occurs when two different companies pair their brand names in a marketing context. This could include new or revived products, services or ventures as well as advertising or distribution outlets. The tactic of co-branding has been rare in the luxury goods sector mainly due to the high level of competition and brand protection among luxury brands. It is however currently gaining acceptance and popularity.

The attempt at co-branding is believed to have been started by *haute couture* designer Pierre Cardin in 1959, through his attempt to fuse luxury fashion and mass fashion. He fused his then highly luxurious brand name with then supermarket Printemps, where he presented his first *prêt-à-porter* collection to the shock of the world of high fashion. As a result, he was expelled from the French fashion governing body La Chambre Syndicale and was regarded as a sell-out.

Fast-forward to 1987 and venerable Japanese luxury fashion designer Yoji Yamamoto designed his first sportswear collection for Adidas under the brand name Y-3. This generated a buzz in the fashion press and several 'analysts' tried to understand the motive behind the collaboration apart from the commercial gains. This action was promptly termed the *'commercialization of exclusive fashion'*. The partnership remains in existence and has broadened to a product range including apparel, footwear and accessories. Adidas is also collaborating with Stella McCartney in designing stylish but functional sportswear.

In the autumn of 2004, however, something groundbreaking happened in the fashion-branding arena. Respected and often revered king of the catwalk and creative director of Chanel and Fendi, Karl Lagerfeld designed a limited edition collection for Swedish mass-fashion brand H&M. Lagerfeld's reason for accepting this one-off collaboration with H&M was his desire to bring high fashion to normal people. His designs turned out to be a hit among consumers worldwide and a retail innovation for H&M. Several items in the collection were sold out within hours of their launch. H&M also experienced same-store sales increase of 12 per cent in the first month following the launch, and also higher profits.

A repeat episode occurred in the autumn of 2005 through another one-off design collection for H&M by Stella McCartney. This time, there were reported queues in front of several H&M stores all over the world, the night before the collection's launch. Some consumers were even injured in the frenzy and near-fights that ensued in the stores. Needless to say, this collaboration was a huge success not only for H&M but also for Stella McCartney who launched her high-end brand just five years ago. The third collaboration is with Viktor & Rolf in autumn 2006. H&M has also indicated its interest in working with other luxury designers.

Other examples of co-branding abound between luxury brands and other brands. Puma, another sporting goods brand, has collaborated with Japanese designer Mihara Yasuhiro in shoe designs; supermodel Christy Turlington in yoga wear through the Nuala sub-brand name; Richemont-owned Shanghai Tang in footwear through another sub-brand called Shanghai Tang Peony, and more recently in spring 2006, Alexander McQueen to create men and women's sports footwear. In addition, American music star Sean Combs signed a deal in 2004, to collaborate with Estée Lauder in the production of a fragrance line. Prada has also co-designed jewellery with Fred Leighton, the first between a jewellery company and a fashion brand. Jewellery brand Tiffany also hosted a first-ever fashion show in New York in September 2004 showing the designs of clothes designer Behnaz Sarafpour. In 2005, hosiery company, Wolford collaborated with luxury designers Zac Posen and Missoni to design a limited edition range of tights collection. Also in February 2006, American supermarket Target launched an accessories collection by British high fashion designer Luella Bartley.

There have also been co-branding activities between luxury brands and companies in the non-luxury sector. For example, British designer Ozwald Boateng redesigned the charge card of Coutts bank, United Kingdom as part of its re-imaging project in 2004. Alexander McQueen also created a new version of the American Express Centurion exclusive credit card as part of its fifth anniversary in 2004. Remarkably, Giorgio Armani designed a limited edition CLK for Mercedes-Benz in 2003 and Emilio Pucci linked up with Champagne and fine wines brand Veuve Cliquot in summer 2004 to create a limited edition packaging design for Cliquot's La Grande Dame 1996 vintage wine. Also in 2004, LVMH owned Moet & Chandon teamed up with Swarovski to design an edition of the champagne bottle decorated with Swarovski crystals. Versace also recently collaborated with private charter airline TAG Aviation to redesign the interiors of its airplanes.

In addition, Coca Cola and luxury cosmetics brand Shisheido have signed a deal to create a health drink and a new cosmetics and drinks brand. Kate Spade also took the co-branding exercise beyond the fashion arena by collaborating with stationary company Crane & Co. to create personalized stationery and wedding invitations, which were launched in January 2006. Also designers Versace redesigned the limited edition version of the Nokia 7270 mobile phone in 2005, while Dolce & Gabbana designed a limited edition version of the Motorola V3i Gold in 2006. In addition, designers Christian Lacroix, Philippe Starck and Nicole Farhi collaborated with Danish pedal bin company Vipp between 2005 and 2006 to design a special collection of bins, which were auctioned for charity. The list goes on . . .

The important strategic questions related to co-branding are the following:

What is the tactical objective behind these collaborations and what implication do they have for individual luxury brands and the luxury goods sector as a whole?

Co-branding is a new phenomenon that indicates the departure of luxury brands from the core single-brand strategy. This co-branding strategy was previously termed 'controversial and risky' and was generally unacceptable until this decade. It was viewed as having a potentially negative impact on the 'luxury' and 'exclusive' image attributes of luxury brands. However, the changing luxury market environment and democratization of luxury are factors that co-branding addresses in addition to providing competitive leverage for the brands.

There are four major methods of co-branding for luxury fashion brands:

1 Co-branding among luxury brands such as between Swarovski and Moët & Chandon.
2 Co-branding between luxury brands and mass fashion brands like Karl Lagerfeld and H&M, which has generated much discussion and analysis.

3 Co-branding between luxury brands and celebrities such as the collaboration of Sean Combs and Estée Lauder; and Samantha Thavasa and Penelope Cruz.
4 Co-branding between luxury brands and companies in other categories of goods such as Alexander McQueen and American Express.

These types of co-branding are increasingly gaining acceptance among luxury brands. However, co-branding should be approached cautiously as it could have adverse affects on the brand image and brand loyalty. The effect of co-branding on the consumer ought to be paramount in decisions concerning this strategy. The following tactical guidelines are essential in developing co-branding strategy in the luxury sector:

• There must be a strategic purpose behind the co-branding activity. In other words, brands shouldn't team up without a concrete and significant reason. When H&M collaborated with Karl Lagerfeld and Stella McCartney, it was to address the consumers' changing needs and expose them to luxury fashion in anticipation of 'trading up'.
• The co-branding should be a win–win situation for the brands involved. Again, the H&M venture had the advantages of endearing mass fashion consumers to luxury designs and embracing mass fashion brands as complementary brands of luxury brands rather than being viewed as competitors.
• The collaboration should be controlled through a limited edition or a one-off collection. Karl Lagerfeld's design for H&M was a thirty-piece one-off collection. This retains the luxury aura of Lagerfeld, which extends to his own brand and the luxury brands he designs for. It also ensures that H&M is not misinterpreted by the consumer as a luxury brand, which is not the company's objective.
• There must be a clear synchronism between the brands in the co-branding process. Co-branding sometimes involves two brands with different brand associations. However, the target audience must understand these two brand messages and be able to see their joint benefit. This benefit must be favourable otherwise the exercise is pointless.
• The co-branding activity must increase the brand equity of the brands involved. Brand equity is the effect of brand knowledge on consumer response to the brand. One of its sources is brand loyalty, which is a result of a psychological process of affiliation and attachment with a brand. Co-branding should be designed to increase this element in consumers.

Finally, to ensure the success of co-branding, the brands involved in the venture must communicate the co-brand promise and its differentiated features in a clear and consistent manner. The brands ought to also enhance the esteem and loyalty of the customer groups.

The menace of fake luxury goods

To commence the discussion of this highly important topic, it is imperative to set the record straight by defining counterfeiting and its boundaries. There are four levels of the luxury faking business:

1 A **counterfeit product** refers to a 100 per cent copy of the original product made to deceive consumers into believing that it is the genuine product.
2 A **pirated product** is a copy of a genuine item but produced with the knowledge that the consumer will be aware that the item is fake.
3 An **imitation product** is not 100 per cent identical to the original product but is similar in substance, name, design, form, meaning or intent and consumers are often aware that it is not the original product.
4 A **custom-made product** is a replica of a trademark design of branded products made by legitimate craftsmen who may have some connection with the brand.

Having clarified these definitions, it is obvious that the luxury goods sector battles all four groups of fake products, albeit in differing degrees. On the first level, counterfeit goods are sold in some markets by people who claim to be authorized agents of luxury brands. These goods are traded every-where, from the kitchens of housewives in San Francisco to side-street stalls off Oxford street in London; Canal street in Manhattan and various market 'hot-spots' in Hong Kong like the Temple street market; and also in China and Taiwan. Imitation and custom-made fakes hold a minor proportion of the trade in fake luxury goods. For example, the Hermès Birkin and the Vuitton Speedy bags have been greatly copied by other non-luxury designers who have quoted the brands as their sources of inspiration. Do these products represent fakes?

Fake products, whether counterfeits, imitations, pirated or fake custom-made pose an ongoing problem for luxury brands. Apart from the legal impli-cations, which are important, fake goods cause enormous harm to brands, consumers and also their vendors and manufacturers. It damages a brand's image, over-exposes high-end brands, reduces a brand's equity and costs companies a lot to curtail. Fake goods also lower the self-image of counter-feit product consumers and add to their mental stress by creating an increased desire for products that they might not be able to afford. For the vendors and manufacturers, there is the continuous fear of being caught by increasingly vigilant authorities.

These adverse effects not only exist within the luxury sector, they also affect governments and economies. In 2003, the counterfeit goods market cost New York City more than $1 billion in taxes, an immense weight on the state's economy. This led to increased vigilance and seizures of counterfeit goods across the USA. Counterfeiting of fashion goods is a menace and has no justification. It is similar to pirating CDs, DVDs and Video Games and also stealing intellectual property like Copyrighted materials.

Counterfeits have been a problem for the luxury and prestige industry for centuries. In 2005, the international trade of counterfeit goods was estimated to be worth €500 billion, which is a significant jump from its 1997 worth of $90 billion. New York City alone accounted for $23 billion in sales of counterfeit luxury goods in 2004, while Italy has an annual counterfeit goods trade of approximately €3.1 billion. This rapid growth rate is also evident in several Asian markets and shows no signs of abating. In Hong Kong, there is a high demand for counterfeit luxury goods mainly from white-collar workers between the ages of 25 and 34 and other age groups. In China, the case is more serious and although statistical evidence remains inaccurate, it is considered a major world centre for counterfeiting and the worst violator of intellectual property rights. However, the Chinese government has recently taken measures to contain the trade through introducing new laws and launching visible raids on factories. Other major producers of counterfeit luxury goods are found in Turkey, Thailand, Morocco and South Korea.

The ongoing question of how to curtail counterfeiting in luxury fashion seems to have received no clear answer. Several luxury brands believe that this is a losing battle so instead of trying to win against the violators, they have initiated different means of making the trade more expensive to operate. Luxury brands such as Louis Vuitton and Burberry have proactively channelled substantial resources towards dealing with the supply aspect of fake luxury products but have almost ignored the growing demand facet. These brands work in collaboration with law enforcers such as the New York Police Department's Trademark Infringement Unit and the Chinese government authorities. They often raid stores and factories; and arrest counterfeit goods suppliers and distributors. An example is the recent closure of the Shanghai Xiangyang Road Market, which is considered an abode for replicas of luxury brands, by government authorities. Other brands such as Hèrmes have warning messages on their website informing consumers that products are sold exclusively in Hèrmes Boutiques, approved retailers and on the official Hèrmes website and therefore purchase of Hermès goods outside these three channels would not guarantee that the products are genuine. The result of these efforts is that the counterfeiting trade is now more expensive for the suppliers but despite this, the demand continues to grow.

So how can the demand aspect be curtailed in addition to the supply of fake luxury goods? An example of how this may possibly be done can be taken from the French government, which is a notable pioneer of curbing the demand for fake luxury goods. While several government authorities have made the manufacture and sale of fake luxury goods illegal, the French government has gone a step further. It has introduced legislation covered under criminal and customs law which makes not only the manufacture and distribution of fake luxury products a crime, but also their ownership and possession. Therefore a consumer possessing a fake Louis Vuitton bag can be arrested on the streets of France and stands the risk of spending a minimum of two years in jail. Although this measure may be perceived as drastic by some authorities, it has guaranteed an almost 100 per cent absence of fake luxury goods in France. Italy is also another country that has shown seriousness in fighting counterfeiting although the country is also a manufacturing centre of fake luxury goods. Representatives of several Italian luxury brands are often found at major Italian airports informing travellers of their risk of being fined for purchasing fake luxury goods whether at home or abroad.

Luxury brands however need to move beyond focusing on winning the battle against the suppliers of fake luxury goods. Making the ownership of fake luxury goods illegal just as pirated CDs and DVDs is a step towards this. In addition, an understanding of the demographic and behavioural profiles of the counterfeit luxury consumers will provide a platform for creating better counter-strategies to eradicate the demand for the goods.

Interestingly, a large proportion of luxury consumers in different markets are opposed to the sale of fake luxury goods and several consumers are even willing to join in the battle against this practice. Yet numerous other consumers would consider purchasing fake luxury goods if presented with an opportunity to do so while on holiday. In Hong Kong for example, one of the popular tourist activities is a visit to the fake luxury goods markets. This is perilous for the luxury industry and shows that even core luxury consumers could contribute to the demand for counterfeits. However, if the ownership of fake luxury goods becomes illegal, consumers will be wary of being found with counterfeit luxury goods. Luxury companies therefore must collaborate with various governments in order to make the ownership of counterfeit luxury goods illegal.

One of the biggest problems of counterfeiting is that consumers do not view the trade as a crime similar to selling fake drugs because they believe that there are no serious victims. The only casualties they see are the brands but these brands are perceived as highly profitable companies therefore consumers assume that the problem of counterfeit trade has no drastic consequences. The reality is that the problem of fake luxury goods is grave both for consumers and for brands.

Several consumers and brand analysts have argued that counterfeiting has numerous advantages. Prominent of these is the theory that if a brand is copied, it means that the brand has a strong reputation. Others have said that fake and counterfeit products are an extension of the advertisement of the true brand. Yet others have indicated that counterfeit trade provides employment opportunities for poor people in the countries where they're manufactured. These justifications have no concrete basis just as defending an apparent crime in front of a jury stands no chance.

Counterfeiting is theft irrespective of the way it is evaluated. It is similar to purchasing a fake ticket or a fake property. The buyer supports crime, steals money from the brand and governments and lies to other people and some-times even to themselves. Contrary to popular belief, when consumers buy counterfeit goods, they are indirectly funding crime as most counterfeiters belong to organized criminal groups that are also involved in other perceived 'more serious' crimes such as drug trafficking and prostitution. Also buying fake luxury goods does not increase employment opportunities in poor countries. On the contrary, it creates misery and hardship for the people forced to take part in these criminal activities and exposes them to the risk of being caught and penalized. Luxury goods counterfeiting is theft of intellectual property and the creativity of others. To illustrate this point, let's use a piece of literary work produced by a writer after months of tenacious writing and editing that results in the creation of a masterpiece. After finally getting it published criminals steal the script and begin to illegally reprint it to sell for $1. If you think this is unacceptable, then luxury goods counterfeiting is ten times more unacceptable. Another way to look at the theft of creativity and intellectual property (to which luxury goods belong) is through the work that went into this book, which you have in your hands which included years of extensive research, writing, editing and finally publication. It involved count-less hours behind the computer screen, endless days spent at libraries in different cities, constant travel, interviews, exchanges and continuous full-time work in the luxury goods sector. Some nights I had to forgo sleeping in order to meet deadlines. Now, after going through all these relentless efforts to get the book published and available in the market, would it be a source of pleasure to discover that a vendor somewhere has reproduced it and is selling it at a fraction of its price to enrich himself? This case is similar to the sale of fake luxury goods.

> *Think-point for consumers*: If you condemn drug trafficking, prostitution or the sale of fake prescription drugs but you turn around and purchase fake luxury goods, you are no better than the people who engage in the activities you condemn.

Several luxury brands such as Louis Vuitton are visibly working hard to contain counterfeiting. As one of the most copied luxury brands in the world and a favourite for consumers of fake luxury goods, the company has shown a firm commitment to the battle against counterfeiting. Louis Vuitton spends approximately €10–15 million a year on the battle against fake products. A part of this budget is channelled towards lobbyists, who try to persuade differ-ent governments to protect brand rights. A team of counterfeiting and intel-lectual property specialists has also been established at the Louis Vuitton offices in Paris and abroad, to counter this menace. The company also employs agents who scour the world in search of counterfeiters' factories and export operations, which are then reported to local authorities. Louis Vuitton has also joined forces with various French and international professional associations to educate consumers and raise awareness of the risks inherent in purchasing counterfeit goods. In addition, the company was one of the key players in the formulation of the legislation that makes the ownership of luxury goods illegal in France.

Louis Vuitton assists in seizing and destroying counterfeit materials and finished products. In 2003, the company conducted a total of 4,200 raids, leading to the arrest of nearly 1,000 counterfeiters. Louis Vuitton also helped the US Customs Service seize 100,000 fake Louis Vuitton products that were being imported from South Korea. In 2004, more than 6,000 additional raids were conducted worldwide and over 8,200 anti-counterfeiting complaints were filed by the company. One of the numerous counterfeiting victories won by Louis Vuitton is the April 2006 court ruling against French (incidentally!) supermarket group Carrefour, which was ordered to pay Louis Vuitton more than US$37,000 in damages for selling fake Louis Vuitton bags in one of its Shanghai stores.

In addition to these, Louis Vuitton continues to devise new strategies for fighting counterfeits. The company now targets landlords who rent their premises to vendors of fake Vuitton products, through filing complaints against them for turning a blind eye to criminal activities on their property. In April 2005, Louis Vuitton won a major victory against a New York landlord who owned seven stores in the counterfeit hot zone, Canal Street. This led to the eviction of the tenants and the prohibition of further fake goods retail, among other actions. The objective of this strategy is to discourage proprietors from leasing their property to fake luxury goods vendors, thereby making the business either impossible or more expensive to operate. These examples ought to be emulated by other luxury brands.

The luxury branding death-wish list

Managing luxury brands is a fascinating business. However, the development and implementation of effective strategies is a challenge that needs constant revision and high adaptability. Luxury brands must remain innovative and creative in their branding, marketing and retailing design. More importantly, there should be clarity and consistency in delivering a luxury brand's message to its audience.

Every luxury brand worth their place in the market ought to ingrain brand knowledge and management methods in their company's DNA. As the most powerful and single most important asset of a company, the brand should be the blueprint, organizing principle and the basis for every decision made within the company.

In conclusion of this interesting chapter, which has provided the tools and techniques for effectively managing a luxury brand, let's take a quick look at the luxury branding death-wish list. The death-wish list consists of factors that often lead to a brand's death, therefore when a luxury brand decides to commit suicide, it should adopt these strategies. If, however, the brand desires to have a long and profitable existence, it ought to apply the opposite of these suggestions. The death-wish list of luxury fashion branding is the following:

1 Do not have a clear brand identity and image.
2 Do not fight counterfeiters.
3 Believe that you don't need to reinforce your brand aura.
4 Do not have a strong web presence.
5 Do not have an e-boutique.
6 Retail your goods through low-end retail locations.
7 Do not track market trends and consumer behaviour.
8 Overlook your competitors' branding strategies.
9 Believe that branding is the same as marketing.
10 Believe that marketing is the same as advertising and promotions.

Chapter 6
Digital luxury

'Luxury brands have been slower than most to unlock the potential of
e-retail. They have struggled to overcome the challenge of making
their digital environments as alluring as their stores.'

Mark Tungate, writer and branding specialist and author of
Fashion Brands: Branding Style from Armani to Zara

The case for e-retail

Technology has definitely changed the landscape of consumer behaviour and
the way business is conducted, including luxury fashion management. The
impact of the digital revolution on consumers in the last ten years is overwhelming. The Internet has empowered consumers more than ever before and
has elevated their product and brand expectations. The Internet also provides
online consumers with instant information, and lower switching costs in
terms of time, information, product comparison and purchase. As a result, the
task of retaining the attention and loyalty of consumers has also become more
challenging.

The Internet as a means of information and retail distribution has established e-retail as a core aspect of global business. E-retail is now an indispensable complementary sales channel for offline retail activities in several
categories of goods, including luxury fashion. It is also an effective avenue of
enhancing brand awareness, reaching new markets and creating competitive
leverage and differentiation for luxury brands. The internet provides a unique
opportunity to access the huge market constituting of millions of people that
make up the online consumer population.

The Internet plays a significant role in fuelling the universal appeal of
luxury brands to a global consumer group. Just as the language of fashion
branding is universal, the e-retail community is also worldwide. Since luxury
fashion goods don't need introduction or clarification in the global marketplace, the allure of their highly creative products on consumers is identical,
wherever the consumers may be located. They are uniformly appealing to an
international consumer base that stretches from San Francisco and New York,
to Paris and Moscow, Hong Kong, Sydney and beyond. In the same way, the
drawing power of the brand aura is consistent among a worldwide consumer
group. Several brands like Christian Dior, Gucci and Burberry have a high

awareness level in the global fashion society and beyond and this global presence is reinforced on the internet. The internet also contributes to attaining a higher level of brand equity and creates multiple opportunities for developing deeper relationships with consumers.

However, the Internet has evolved from a medium for enhancing brand awareness and disseminating information to an essential channel of retailing. Although the online sale of general consumer goods such as books and CDs have been highly successful, the sale of luxury goods online has been the subject of constant debate. Since e-retailing of other goods became prominent, there has been a wide credence of the near impossibility of successfully retailing luxury fashion goods on the Internet. This is as a result of the perception that e-retail has a strong negative impact on the innate attributes of luxury brands such as 'prestige' and 'exclusivity'. Also the sale of luxury goods relies heavily on aesthetic and sensory appreciation and this factor has raised questions regarding the reproduction of a prestigious atmosphere and the sensory attributes of luxury products online. These issues are yet to be fully addressed. However, several advancements in e-business strategies have made the e-retail of luxury goods currently feasible. The tools and techniques that enable this are extensively analysed in the following sections of this chapter.

As earlier indicated, the adoption of the internet as a sales channel is now essential for luxury brands that aim to maintain a competitive edge. The important nature of the internet is being propelled by several factors, such as the increasingly complex and accelerated nature of global retailing and the rapid dissemination of information. The internet has also closed the information gap and consumers worldwide now have uniform awareness of products and services in real-time. This means that if Givenchy launches a new product in Paris today, consumers in Dubai, Tokyo, Mumbai or Johannesburg are aware of the new product uniformly, mainly through the internet. The direct consequence of this is that the consumer desire for additional information and purchase possibilities of the product and instant gratification is heightened. Since the product information is uniform and accessible globally, the expectation of product availability is also uniform, irrespective of the geographical location of the consumer. One of the most effective means to providing global consumers with products and instant customer satisfaction is through e-retail.

The fast flow of instantaneous information across the globe has also provided the luxury consumer with a wide variety of choices in product offering and more access to viewing and purchasing them through the internet. To illustrate this point, a standard scenario involving a luxury consumer who lives in Mumbai, India is reproduced below:

A wealthy consumer buys a fashion magazine where she sees the advertisement of a new product of Christian Dior. She immediately visits the Dior website and to her delight finds the product and its exact specifications. As a devotee of Dior she's often willing to spend thousands of dollars on Dior products and would like to make an immediate purchase of this new product. However, she lives in Mumbai, India, where there is no Dior store. In order to purchase the product, she would need to travel to New Delhi, where the only Dior store in India is located and hope that she would find the product in the often limited stock. The possibility of travelling to New Delhi was however remote since she had a busy work schedule and would hardly have adequate spare time for the trip. A second alternative would be to purchase the product during her summer shopping vacation trip to Europe in several months' time but she didn't want to wait. Another option was to ask a friend who lives in London to purchase the product and ship it to her. This would however entail finding the fastest means to send money to her friend and also dealing with shipping requirements. She was already becoming irritated by the envisaged inconveniences but however decides to give her friend in London a call. If the process became too complicated, she might start thinking of alternative brands with more accessible means of purchase.

This scenario provides a backdrop to the changing attitudes of the current luxury consumers towards the accessibility of luxury goods. A large proportion of luxury consumers currently seek alternative luxury brands rather than alternative means of purchasing products from a single brand. The likely conclusion of the recounted scenario would be that the consumer would visit the website of a luxury fashion e-retailer like yoox.com, choose an alternative luxury brand, make the purchase online and receive the product at his or her doorstep. The result would be satisfaction on the part of the customer; enhancement of the relationship with the brand selected online and the possibility of the dissipation of the brand attachment to Dior.

This illustration indicates that luxury consumers are losing patience with brands that are distant. Consumers now have access to multiple brands and products through one click of the mouse and this has made product accessibility one of the key decision factors in the purchase of luxury fashion goods. This factor gives old luxury brands the necessity to adopt e-retail and new brands the potential of becoming global brands within a short time period.

E-retail indicators

Internet penetration in several countries is growing at a fast rate. In most developed economies, the percentage of the population with internet access is as high as 95 per cent. In the United Kingdom, more than 11 million people consider themselves as 'heavy' web users and this trend is similar in other countries. Other indicators show that by the end of 2006, more than half of the entire UK, German, French and Italian populations will be online, almost a 100 per cent increase from 2000. The number of broadband connection in Europe also increased by 136 per cent between 2004 and the first quarter of 2005. This is excluding the increase in the number of consumers connected on high-speed Wi Fi systems and those still using the dial-up internet access. In France the adoption of the Wi-Fi system has become almost a national obsession. The governing authorities of Paris strive to make the city the Wi-Fi capital of the world with 3,000 'hotspots' implemented by the end of 2005, including bus routes and underground train stations. These are in addition to the wireless spaces provided by telecommunications companies such as Orange. The increasing availability of internet connection directly impacts the retail of goods online. It is also fuelling the rapid increase of the e-retail economy, which is currently growing at a rate of 45 per cent year-on-year, according to IMRG.

The adoption of the internet is spreading among different age segments of the consumer society that has extended beyond young consumers. For example, the number of European seniors with Internet access was 15 million in 2005 and this figure is on a steady rise. This consumer group also has the highest disposable income in Europe and more shopping and leisure time; therefore they constitute an important online luxury consumer segment.

The United States, which is the largest global retail market, also has the highest growth rate of both internet penetration and e-commerce. In 2000, more than 40 million US households had online access. In 2006, more than one-third of all households in the entire US population make at least one online purchase each year and this figure is expected to increase steadily. Internet retailing is also the US retailing industry's fastest-growing distribution channel. Retail sales on the internet totalled $87.5 billion in 2004, an increase of 25 per cent from the $70 billion figure in 2003 and an increase of 62 per cent from the $54 billion in 2002. Also, the Internet is now the primary communication medium for US teenagers who constitute an important future market for luxury brands. In a recent poll by AOL, 46 per cent of 12–34-year-olds voted the internet as the most essential communication medium to their lives. Wireless network is also gaining popularity in several US cities and major software and telecommunications companies are installing 'hot-spots' in thousands of locations enabling the access and convenience of online shopping.

Current indicators also show the online consumer population is growing steadily and rapidly. A large proportion of these online consumers are wealthy and they make frequent purchases online. For example, approximately one-quarter of the US online population in 2000 had annual incomes of over US$75,000. This figure has doubled in the last five years, indicating an increasing online luxury consumer market. Also the US had a forecast online retail sale projection of $316 billion in 2005, an increase of more than 100 per cent from 2004, indicating a substantial growth rate, fuelled by online consumers. Also, the e-retailing sectors in the UK, France, Germany, Spain and Italy are increasing rapidly.

E-retail is also currently a part of the daily activities in several Asian countries. For example in South Korea, which has one of the highest Internet penetrations in the world, 23 million out of 30 million cell phones were internet enabled by the end of 2005. This factor fuels product accessibility, e-shopping and instant information dissemination. The Internet has also over-taken television as the most heavily used communications medium among young consumers and teenagers in Hong Kong. In Shanghai, there are several WiFi 'hot-spots' around the city including several retail outlets and eateries like Starbucks cafés.

These indicators show that a growing number of consumers currently have internet access at their fingertips and therefore the possibility to shop at will.

In addition to online penetration and e-shopping of general consumer goods, the demand for the e-retail of luxury fashion goods is on the increase. As earlier indicated, a large segment of the world's wealthy consumers has constant internet access and are increasingly making online purchases. In several countries, the ratio of wealthy people who have bought products worth above US$250 online versus the rest of the population is 3:1. This provides evidence of the viability of the e-retail of luxury goods. It also raises the following question:

> Why are the majority of luxury brands reluctant to satisfy the consumer demand for the e-retail of luxury fashion goods?

The answer is mainly that luxury brands have a major concern related to the possible loss of the brand aura on the Internet. Other reasons include the lack of e-business planning and implementation know-how of online luxury. The subsequent sections of this chapter aim to clarify the major strategic issues related to the e-retail of luxury goods.

E-retail attributes

The internet as a retail platform is uniquely different from conventional bricks and mortar retailing. The key attributes of e-retail are shown in Figure 6.1.

The internet as a retail location

The internet is the most accessible platform for retailing the products of global brands as well as enhancing brand equity and customer relationships. This includes luxury fashion brands, which thrive on global awareness and operations.

The famous retailing adage, which states that '*the three most important things in retail are location location location*', recognizes location as the central aspect of retail, and this reasoning can also be applied to the internet,

> **E-retail characteristics**
> - Fast and convenient shopping
> - More product variety and access
> - Global availability
> - Mass online class
> - Lack of human contact
> - Low switching cost (1-click)

Advantages of e-retail

For the e-retailer

- Convenient location
- Cost-effective
- Global audience
- Round the clock service
- Opportunity for data mining and relationship marketing
- Small to large scale operations
- Competitive advantage services

For the consumer

- Saves time
- Extensive product variety
- Convenient
- Easy to use
- Up-to-date information
- Round the clock availability
- Product personalization
- Favourable prices
- Instant gratification

Disadvantages of e-retail

For the e-retailer

- High capital investment and ongoing costs
- Complex logistics (related to global deliveries, returns, exchanges and refunds)
- Low impact sales
- Less impulse purchase
- Legal complications
- Challenging post-sales

For the consumer

- Security worries
- Delivery timing
- Delivery costs
- Lack of human contact
- Non-physical goods
- After-sales services difficulties
- E-CRM inaccessibility

Figure 6.1   *E-retail attributes*
Source: Adapted from Dennis, Fenech and Merryllis (2004) *E-Retailing*, Routledge, London.

as a retail location. Although the internet is an important retail location, a large number of luxury fashion brands do not recognize it as such. The few brands that acknowledge and utilize the Internet as a sales channel mostly provide a sparse product range and limited delivery to a few destinations. Also there are some luxury brands that have shown such a low commitment to e-retail that they have implemented a website constituting of one page, with neither information nor e-retail. The brands that have adopted this stance also do not recognize their website as a retail location in their print media advertisements.

The offline store

Figure 6.2 *Louis Vuitton Stores are found in exclusive luxury locations like the Sandton City Shopping Centre in South Africa (2004)*

The online store

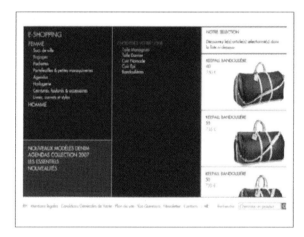

Figure 6.3 *Louis Vuitton's 'exclusive' online store for the European market. The exclusive retail strategy is yet to be implemented in the US market (2006)*

The e-retail of luxury fashion goods is still in its early introductory phase. The current situation indicates that the majority of luxury brands are yet to realize and tap the enormous market potential that exists in the e-retail economy. As a sales platform, the internet is almost unexploited by luxury fashion brands and the few who have done so, approach it with apprehension. The reluctance of luxury brands to adopt e-retail is mainly from a fear of diluting the brand image through more product accessibility, and negatively affecting the offline sales channels. Several luxury brands are also concerned that the luxury retail atmosphere and overall high-impact experience cannot be reproduced online. Another point of view is that since luxury goods are sensory in nature and involve an innate emotional response, they cannot be sold online because of the difficulty of reproducing the sensory attributes required in their appreciation. As a result, several luxury brands including Chanel, Versace and Valentino are yet to adopt e-retail through their own websites. Other brands like Hermès and Armani have launched limited e-retail websites with a narrow product range distributed in a small number of markets. Yet the products of other brands like Chloé and Roberto Cavalli are retailed through separate e-commerce websites and e-malls. However, the majority of the global luxury fashion brands have not currently implemented e-retail activities.

The *sensory* nature of luxury goods has been particularly cited as one of the major reasons for the slow adoption of e-retail by luxury brands. This is because luxury consumers are known to appreciate the high aesthetics of luxury products when viewed physically, through the utilization of the human senses of sight, touch and feel. These senses also draw out the emotional and psychological brand responses from consumers. As a result, luxury products such as apparel, leather goods, jewellery, wristwatches, fragrances, cosmetics and other accessories are classified as sensory goods. The online reproduction of the sensory elements required for luxury goods retailing has been a major source of concern for luxury brands. Also, the conventional luxury shopping experience, which is summed up in the store visit, the immersion within the highly creative and prestigious retail atmosphere and the interaction with the products is sensed to be lacking online. The majority of luxury brands are of the opinion that the e-retail shopping experience lacks these prominent features and that a computer screen cannot reproduce the level of interaction required for luxury goods retailing. The reality, however, is that the value of luxury goods to consumers does not decrease as a result of the lack of some of the sensory elements online. Also, there are current e-retail strategies that can be used to replicate the sensory elements online, compensate for the lack of human presence and enhance the shopping experience.

The current global retail environment requires e-retail as an indispensable aspect of retailing and a means of reaching and satisfying luxury consumers. The issues related to physically viewing and interacting with products before purchase is becoming less important for consumers especially those with prior experience with the brand. In addition, consumers increasingly utilize both the offline and online channels in a single purchase, making e-retail a complement of the overall shopping experience.

The major factor that has currently made the e-retail of luxury goods mandatory is the luxury consumer psychology which has changed. Convenience and accessibility which are both prominent benefits of e-retail now rank high among their expectations. A wealthy luxury consumer living in a Scottish village castle no longer wants to be obliged to travel to Edinburgh or London to purchase luxury goods. Consumers desire to have the luxury retail experience online and in the comfort of their homes or offices. Since they now frequently interact with the internet, their level of expectation of convenience from luxury brands has increased. The luxury consumer group has comfortably adapted to technology and is currently evolving to adapting technology to their needs and their lifestyles.

The time has come for luxury brands to change their stance regarding e-retail. There is a current need for luxury brands to design merchandizing, retailing, marketing and logistics strategies to incorporate the internet. This will form an effective tool for integrating the online and offline retailing activities. The prevailing issue is whether it is realistic to imagine that the physical luxury retail store environment can be replicated on the internet. Or that luxury goods can be successfully sold online without diluting their brand aura and brand equity.

The challenge of selling luxury goods online is evidently enormous as the online luxury shopping experience is considerably different from the conventional physical shopping experience. Also the sensory nature of luxury goods requires a face-to-face contact rather than the face-to-screen contact provided by the internet. The internet also seemingly lacks the exclusivity and prestige qualities of the offline locations of luxury fashion stores. In addition, the online luxury consumer has a different set of needs from the offline luxury consumer although some of the offline consumers also shop online and vice versa. These needs have to be understood and satisfied by luxury brands.

Therefore the questions relating to creating a high-status website atmosphere, replacing the human senses in the virtual environment, satisfying the high demands of online consumers and matching 'high class' with the 'mass class' of the internet world are justified. However, the application of feasible e-retail strategies makes the successful e-retail of luxury goods possible. Prior to investigating these strategies, let's take a look at the online consumer and understand how their evolution has affected e-retail.

Online luxury fashion consumer behaviour

The existence of an online luxury consumer population is no longer in question and this consumer segment is also growing rapidly and steadily. Luxury fashion consumers frequently make online purchases through the limited available luxury e-retail websites. They are also more willing to make continuous online luxury purchases than offline. For example, apparel is one of the fastest growing e-retail product categories globally. An indication is that in the USA, online sales of apparel were forecast to generate revenues of $12.5 billion by the end of 2005, an increase of 23 per cent from 2004.

Consumers of luxury goods are among the global consumer population that crave continuous internet access. They represent a substantial proportion of the 600 million + consumers worldwide who currently see online access as an absolute necessity, in the same manner they view eating and sleeping. This is excluding the estimated near 1 billion online users exposed to e-retail. A large portion of this online population represents high net-worth individuals who have the resources and willingness to purchase luxury fashion goods on the Internet.

The evolution of e-retail since the DotCom crash of the late 1990s and early 2000s has enabled a prolific environment for e-retail. The widespread adoption of high-speed internet connections has changed the perception of consumers to online shopping. Also, the introduction of secure payment systems and development of e-CRM methods have dispelled consumer fears related to payments, refunds and after-sales services. As a result, consumers currently exhibit a high level of confidence in online shopping and in spending vast sums on the internet.

However, consumers that are likely to purchase luxury goods online are those with a prior offline relationship or exposure to the brands. This is because consumers are influenced by their previous shopping experiences and brand relationships both online and offline. This experience affects their assessment of the current online purchasing process. If the consumers already have a positive brand experience, it enhances their evaluative process and the decision to buy the products of the brand online. At the same time, the website must satisfy consumer needs and exceed their expectations.

The website of a luxury brand is expected to meet more than the minimal requirements of e-shopping, like ease of navigation and appealing design. This is because the luxury-purchase decision process utilizes a high dose of emotions and irrationality which are boosted by high-impact experiences. The emotional responses of online consumers must be enhanced through capturing the right moods and feelings on the website. This is key to ensuring the ultimate goals of increasing online shopping traffic, high sales turnover and profitability!

The online buyer behaviour is comparatively different from the offline behaviour in several aspects. The conventional offline consumer buying decision-making process starts from recognizing the need for the product to the product information search, purchase, utilization and after-use evaluation. Shopping for luxury goods both online and offline however does not follow this path as a result of the significant role that sentiments and psychology play in luxury goods purchasing decisions. In addition, the online consumer attitude is shaped by an auxiliary series of emotions and feelings, indicating a distinct process, especially in relation to luxury goods. These feelings include the total web experience and prior relationship with the brand, among others. Luxury fashion consumers have an emotional affair rather than a cognitive bond with luxury brands. This factor is also reflected in the online product evaluation and consumer behaviour.

The online luxury buying decision-making process has been excellently captured in the 'Experience Hierarchy' model of R. Mohammed *et al.* (2002), in their book, *Internet Marketing*. This model follows a four-stage process and is based on the principle that the sum of the consumer experience while shopping online determines their evaluation of the website, which subsequently

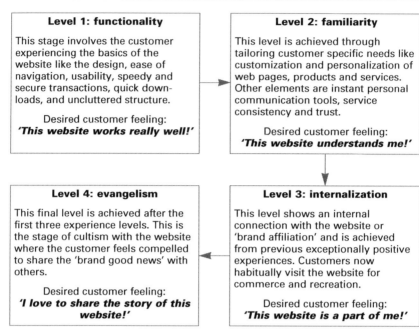

Level 1: functionality

This stage involves the customer experiencing the basics of the website like the design, ease of navigation, usability, speedy and secure transactions, quick down-loads, and uncluttered structure.

Desired customer feeling:
'This website works really well!'

Level 2: familiarity

This level is achieved through tailoring customer specific needs like customization and personalization of web pages, products and services. Other elements are instant personal communication tools, service consistency and trust.

Desired customer feeling:
'This website understands me!'

Level 4: evangelism

This final level is achieved after the first three experience levels. This is the stage of cultism with the website where the customer feels compelled to share the 'brand good news' with others.

Desired customer feeling:
'I love to share the story of this website!'

Level 3: internalization

This level shows an internal connection with the website or 'brand affiliation' and is achieved from previous exceptionally positive experiences. Customers now habitually visit the website for commerce and recreation.

Desired customer feeling:
'This website is a part of me!'

Figure 6.4   *The four-phase online customer* Experience Hierarchy
Source: Adapted from Mohammed *et al.* (2002) *Internet Marketing*.

affects future visits. The online experience also affects the consumer's over-all perception of the brand, which will determine the direction of future inter-action with the brand.

The stages of the Experience Hierarchy model begin from the moment a potential online shopper clicks on the homepage, to his post-purchase evalu-ation process. The model is presented in the Figure 6.4.

This customer experience assessment highlights the need for luxury fash-ion brands to create a compelling, memorable, enjoyable and positive total customer experience for online shoppers. The website should also be consis-tent with the overall brand strategy in order to maintain a parallel customer perception of the brand associations. Fortunately, the high brand awareness of several luxury fashion brands provides a fast route for online luxury consumers to attain the level of 'Brand Evangelists'.

The key to attaining enhanced customer experience is to develop a website that places an emphasis on accentuating the brand characteristics and also has an unwavering focus on creating a superior customer experience for every online shopper. Luxury brands generally have desirable products but the brands that will succeed with acquiring and retaining loyal customers through e-retail are those that apply the right mix of branding, marketing, customer relationship management and transactional strategies to enhance customer experience. This is a challenge that can be overcome through the implementation of feasible e-retail strategies discussed further in this chapter.

In order to execute effective e-retail strategies, it is important to understand the characteristics of online luxury consumers. Online consumers are intelligent and should never be underestimated. They are also empowered with a low switching cost because they can move from one e-boutique to the other with a click of the mouse. This means that they are equipped to view and compare product variety, to shop conveniently and to receive delivery of goods without the extra time cost of travelling to the store. Online luxury consumers also have high expectations. This includes their opinion that although the luxury e-boutique is available to the masses, it should be designed to feel appropriate to only a niche segment, to which they belong.

Several attempts have been made by different researchers to segment the online consumer population according to their key purchasing influences. Other efforts have been in differentiating the offline and online consumer behaviours. Although a standard online consumer behaviour model is yet to be developed, a suitable model of offline consumer segmentation, which can be applied to online consumers, is that of J. Nielsen produced in his book, *Designing Web Usability*, where six groups of consumers were identified:

1 **Social shopper:** those who associate shopping with pleasure and social meetings. They are the least likely group to shop online.
2 **Habit shopper:** those that only visit the same stores and shop through the same medium. This group will stick to offline stores for a long time.
3 **Ethical shopper:** those more concerned with ethical associations of shopping like material sources and employee working conditions, than with shopping medium. They have medium online shopping potential and require websites to meet their ethical expectations.
4 **Value shopper:** those who seek value from an overall combination of product and service quality and cost. They are likely to scout for these features online.
5 **Experimental shopper:** those who are not afraid to try new stores and shopping media. This group has a high potential for shopping online.
6 **Convenience shopper:** those who appreciate shopping without time delays. This is the best target group for online shopping.

A large proportion of the current online luxury fashion consumer group fall within the 'Convenience' and 'Experimental' shopper segments. Their characteristics include high literacy and mobility and inter-cultural awareness as well as being high net-worth individuals. Their expectations from e-retail range from security and convenience to personal and instant satisfaction. Their chances of switching between brands are also high. This is as a result of their experimental nature and the ease of viewing numerous brand alternatives and product offerings online. Other characteristics of the current online luxury consumers comprise the following:

- Restless
- Empowered
- Fashion-savvy
- Highly demanding
- Disposable nature
- Convenience-driven
- Cash-rich and time-poor
- Media and brand saturated
- Individualistic and independent
- Informed, knowledgeable and educated
- Financially, socially and environmentally aware
- Less attuned to brand loyalty and more attuned to brand-hopping
- Busy Busy Busy Busy Busy Busy Busy Busy Busy Busy Busy Busy Busy

Although online consumers are attuned to switching between brands, they are also likely to be repeat visitors and repeat buyers if they find a website visit enjoyable. At the same time, they are less likely to return to a website which they found unsatisfying than they are to return to a physical store. This is because the physical store could be located in the same vicinity as other retailers the customer visits or other activities the customer partakes in. This factor is however inapplicable online.

Online consumers are unique because they are easy recruits as 'brand evangelists'. Current pointers show that the chance of 'word-of-mouth' promotion of effective websites versus effective offline distribution channels is more than 50 per cent. Also, viral marketing or 'word-of-mouse', which involves forwarding web pages to others, is most effective with satisfied online consumers.

The acquisition and retention of the sophisticated and savvy online consumer set might seem impossible through the internet, which lacks the human charm and interface. However this objective could be approached through the four-step process of marketing communications, as follows:

Attention >>Interest >> Desire >> Action

This framework may sound simplistic or indicate a transactional outlook but it is an important tool in the process of online customer persuasion.

Attention is the first step to online purchase probability. How does a website grasp a consumer's attention? This can be attained through a captivating homepage design, ease of navigation, excellent functionality, interactivity and clear and concise text and contents. These features lead to the 'stickiness' of consumers to the website.

Table 6.1   The effect of Internet features on consumers

Web element	Effect on consumers
Interactivity	Compensates for the lack of human presence
Fast service	Saves time
Convenience	Provides goods and services anytime and anyplace
Personalization	Empowers consumers to be co-creators
Customization	Gives a sense of individual recognition
Privacy	Associates the brand with ethics
Real-time communication	Shows excellent customer relationship management
Security	Breeds brand trust and loyalty
Instant product availability	Provides instant gratification
Low transaction costs	Saves mental energy and time
Additional features	Creates an enhanced experience, personal enhancement, education and social benefits

Source: Adapted from Mohammed *et al.* (2002) *Internet Marketing*.

Interest in a website is achieved when a consumer senses that a website has the potential of fulfilling their needs. Creativity in visual and interactive elements is a fundamental requirement to achieve this.

Desire for the product and service offerings of a website are as a result of creative product and service designs and also ingenuity in their presentation, merchandizing and transactional process. The products must emanate desire and reflect the brand's persona.

Action is when the actual purchase is made, as a result of a positive customer experience. This leads to repeat-action during subsequent visits.

In addition to the online customer persuasion tactics, the design of an effective e-retail strategy involves an understanding of what luxury fashion consumers look for in a website. This is summarized in Table 6.1.

Luxury fashion e-retail strategy

In order to implement a successful e-retail strategy, it is important to have a clear plan, which is in line with the organizational long-term branding and marketing goals. Global luxury fashion brands often have excellent offline brand positioning strategies but repeatedly ignore or underplay the effect and importance of strategic online branding. Several strategies have been identified for the successful e-retail of luxury fashion goods. They are discussed further in this chapter. The appropriate application of these tactics will contribute to e-retail success through generating online traffic, high turnover, profitability and brand asset value.

   An effective e-retail strategy plan should incorporate aspects of marketing and branding in addition to the e-retailing tactics. The chart of Figure 6.5

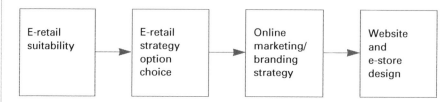

Figure 6.5   *The process of e-retail strategy development*

illustrates the process of e-retail strategy development. As indicated in the chart, the first step in the formulation of a feasible e-retail strategy is to determine the suitability of luxury goods to be retailed online. This leads to the question in the following title.

Are luxury fashion products suitable for e-retailing?

The early part of this chapter identified the major reasons for the late adoption of e-retail by luxury fashion brands, ranging from concern over diluting the brand aura to the popular consensus of the incompatibility of sensory goods and the web. Although these arguments have some logical business credibility, the reality is that it is possible to sell luxury goods online profitably. As proof to this, luxury brands like Louis Vuitton, Christian Dior and Gucci are pioneering e-retail in the industry and currently reaping substantial online sales turnover in the process.

An effective method of gauging the suitability of goods for online sales is through the 'Electronic Shopping Test' or ES test framework, devised by M. de Kare Silver in his book, *E-Shock: The New Rules*. The ES test quantifies the likely e-retail potential of certain products and estimates the proportion of the target customers that are likely to buy the goods online. This strategic tool, when frequently utilized, acts as an aid in the development and revision of e-retail strategies. It utilizes a three-factor test criterion based on (a) product characteristics; (b) familiarity and confidence; and (c) consumer attributes.

Product characteristics

The product characteristics are classified in terms of their physical and virtual attributes. The products, which appeal to one or more of the human senses of sight, sound, taste, touch and smell are grouped as physical goods. Those that require a minimal use of the human senses and a high level of 'intellect sense' are classified as virtual products. Luxury fashion goods naturally fall within the physical goods group while services such as travel and banking fall within the virtual products classification.

The test measures product characteristics through scoring them between 0 points (lowest) to 10 points (highest). The more virtual a product is, the higher its e-retail appeal and therefore the higher the score. In the same manner, the more physical a product is, the lower the e-retail appeal and therefore the lower the score. This evaluation is based on the principle that virtual products are more suitable for e-retail than physical products. For example, products such as clothing and shoes that could require the utilization of the senses of sight and touch have a lower score than products that are more virtual such as insurance and banking.

In the framework of this test, however, we can say that luxury goods can be classified as 'virtual' because consumers evaluate them mainly through the abstract qualities of brand perception and brand relationship. Also, the utilization of atmospheric elements in the e-store design influences the 'virtual' nature of assessing luxury goods online.

Familiarity and confidence

This criterion is measured by considering the consumer's feelings of familiarity and confidence in products and services based on previous use, satisfaction and brand reputation. A consumer who is confident about the products of a brand is likely to purchase them online without feeling a strong need to physically handle the goods pre-purchase. This relates to the fact that luxury consumers that are most likely to purchase goods online are those that already have an existing relationship with a brand.

The scoring in this category ranges from 0 points (lowest) to 10 points (highest). Sensory goods are scored high as there is often an advanced level of familiarity and confidence towards them. For example, consumers are more likely to buy sensory goods like fragrance, cosmetics or leather goods from brands that they are already familiar with.

Consumer attributes

Consumer attributes identify the characteristics that shape online consumer behaviour. This factor is weighted higher (0–30 points) because consumers' attitudes have greater influence on purchase decisions. It measures the percentage of the target consumers' responsiveness to e-retail. It is scored from 0 (non e-responsive) to 30 (90 per cent e-responsive).

A sample ES test is provided in Table 6.2. It highlights the e-retail potential of sensory goods. A total score of 30 and above indicates likely e-retail success.

The sample ES test indicates that several goods in the portfolio of luxury brands are suitable for e-retail. This shows the viability of the e-retail of luxury fashion goods.

Table 6.2   The ES (electronic shopping) test

Product	Product characteristics (0–10)	Familiarity (0–10)	Consumer attributes (0–30)	Total
Women's wear	7	7	21	35
Men's wear	5	6	19	30
Handbags	8	8	25	41
Luggage	8	7	22	37
Shoes	5	5	20	30
Timepieces	5	5	10	28
Eyewear	5	7	17	21
Jewellery	3	5	10	18
Fragrance	2	9	19	30
Home items	5	6	14	25
Cosmetics	6	9	22	37

Key:
Black: Low ES potential
Red: Medium ES potential
Blue: High ES potential

Source: Adapted from Harris and Dennis (2002), *Marketing the e-business*.

E-retail strategy options

The next step after determining the suitability of the e-retail of luxury fashion goods is the selection of the appropriate e-retail strategy option. The core of the e-retail strategy is the choice of the approach to adopt towards e-retail. Several luxury brands often fall into the unfounded conclusion that internet presence and a strong brand identity equals guaranteed online sales. This is one of the biggest misconceptions of luxury e-retail. Success on the web is unachievable without a defined e-retail strategy that fits with the overall branding and marketing strategies. This factor cannot be overemphasized. If a brand doesn't have a clear e-retail strategy that is aligned to its offline strategies, it runs the risk of losing consumer loyalty in the long run. Also in addition to website design and execution, e-retail has implications for other channels of distribution in respect of supply chain, logistics, product orders and delivery, taxes, payments and security, returns, refunds and exchanges. These important factors ought to be considered in the choice of an e-retail strategy.

The classified strategic e-retail options are shown in Figure 6.6 followed by an explanation of the implications of each strategic choice.

Strategic option one: e-retail only

The main activity of the luxury fashion retailers that have adopted this strategic option is that of exclusive e-retailing of luxury fashion goods. As a result,

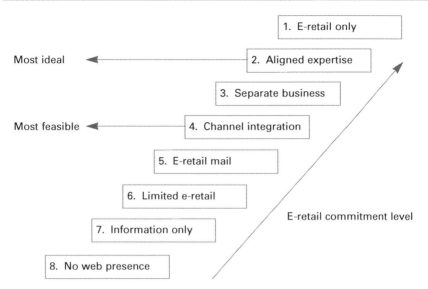

Figure 6.6   *The e-retail strategic options*
Source: Adapted from Harris and Dennis (2002) *Marketing the e-business.*

all of the company's strategies are developed and attuned to online customer requirements and the e-market environment. This indicates a high commitment level to e-retail.

As of the time of writing, no luxury brand has adopted this strategy. However, several independent web-based retailers of fashion goods have emerged in different markets. A notable example is Italy-based Yoox.com, which has a global e-commmerce platform and distribution. Yoox.com is also the exclusive authorized e-commerce partner of some of the most prestigious luxury fashion brands like Roberto Cavalli (Figure 6.7), Armani and Dolce & Gabbana. The e-retailer also has the differentiating factor of a product range that includes exclusive ranges, limited editions by young designers and precious vintage items. The e-retailer also has an online design studio with a selection of books and a fully localized website in seven languages. Another luxury goods e-retailer with global distribution is U.K.-based Net-A-Porter.com, which hosts the online boutiques of Chloe and Jimmy Choo in addition to retailing products of other brands.

Others independent e-retailers are bluefly.com, glam.com and forzieri.com. Some of these e-retailers sell products exclusively from luxury brands while others have a mix of luxury, premium and mass fashion brands in their portfolios. Also some of the independent e-retailers like Net-A-Porter.com sell the goods that feature in the current season's collection of luxury brands while other e-retailers sell the products from the previous season's collections at discounted prices. Some of the products that can be

luxury fashion branding

Figure 6.7   *Roberto Cavalli at Yoox.com (May 2006). Yoox.com is also the official e-retailer of goods from Armani, Dolce & Gabbana, Versace and numerous other luxury brands*

found on several e-retail-only websites include those of brands like Giorgio Armani, Prada, Fendi, Burberry, Versace, Valentino, Diesel, Anne Klein, Chanel, Gucci and Chloé, among several others.

The sale of luxury goods through secondary e-retail-only websites is a source of high sales revenue and industry partnerships. It is also an avenue for the enhancement of the luxury brand aura through highly functional and interactive online experiences. However, this strategy ought to be managed by luxury brands with tact in order to avoid long-term negative results. This is because e-retailers who sell a mix of luxury and mass fashion brands could expose the luxury brands to brand dilution in the long-term. Also independent e-retailers that sell luxury products at discounted prices could foster a possible loss of pricing control for luxury brands. This means that in some cases, luxury brands that implement a 'no-discount' policy might not be able to control independent e-retailers who practise price discounts. Therefore there should be synergy between the strategies of the luxury brands and those of the e-retailers. For example, in May 2006, notable e-retailer designersimports.com featured the Fendi Zucchino Hobo bag with a price tag of US$269, marked down from its original US$795 retail price. Another noteworthy e-retailer bluefly.com has also featured several Gucci products sold at discounted rates of up to 40 per cent. If Fendi and Gucci both implement strict pricing strategies that do not include discounting, this could have a negative impact on the brand equity. However, the discounting strategy is often an agreement between the luxury brands and the independent retailers. From the strategic viewpoint nonetheless, a consistent branding message ought to be provided to the brands' customers irrespective of the retailer or retailing channel.

In addition, there are several websites that retail counterfeit luxury goods, with a claim of authenticity. Consumers may confuse the authorized e-retailers with the counterfeiters, if the luxury brands don't take measures to control the online distribution of their goods and educate consumers on where to purchase the authentic goods. Brands and e-retailers must therefore have an agreement in e-retail practices and above all, the message to consumers should be clear.

The 'e-retail only' strategy is still in its introductory phase in the luxury fashion sector, therefore its long-term effect on the luxury brand equity is yet to fully materialize.

Option two: aligned expertise

The aligned expertise strategy identifies e-retailing as a major source of the core competence of luxury brands. This strategy indicates a high commitment to the development of e-retail. It combines expertise in offline and online retail strategies to produce a continuous outstanding experience for consumers. It recognizes the internet as a key sales channel and gives it a prominent position alongside offline retailing in the company's overall strategy. This e-retail option is capital-intensive and brands that adopt it must invest in technological expertise for integrated retailing and customer service management. The overall goal of this strategy is to provide a uniform high level of satisfaction through integrated advanced technology, whether the consumer is shopping online or offline. This is the most ideal e-retail option for luxury brands but unfortunately, at the moment, no known luxury brand has adopted this option.

Option three: separate business

The brands that apply this strategic option recognize the importance of e-retail but approach the channel with caution. The e-retail activities are therefore developed through a separate and independently managed company. An example is eluxury.com owned by Louis Vuitton Moet Hennessey (LVMH), the parent company of Louis Vuitton. LVMH uses eluxury.com as a platform of e-retail in the US market for the products of several brands in its portfolio such as Louis Vuitton, Christian Dior, DKNY and Marc Jacobs, among others. This strategy differs from the e-retail strategy LVMH executes for some of its brands like Louis Vuitton in the European market. Although this strategic option provides a risk-free entry into e-retail, it also poses a risk of compromising the unique individual brand identity through the mixed message communications of the separate e-retail company and the luxury brand. This strategy is most effective when both the online and offline retail activities are aligned with similar marketing and branding strategies.

Option four: channel integration

Channel integration involves the effective streamlining of both the online and offline retail channels. Brands that adopt this option recognize the presence of an online consumer group and provide a trading platform to satisfy them without compromising the strong emphasis placed on offline retail activities. This e-retail option is the most feasible for luxury fashion brands at the moment as it effectively aligns the online and offline retailing activities and utilizes internal resource fits in its management. This option also recognizes that real space (offline) and cyberspace (online) are not mutually exclusive because frequently, consumers use both spaces during their purchase evaluation process. For example, a customer may obtain pricing information online and visit the store for the 'purchase experience' while others may visit the store to 'feel and look' at the products and then purchase online at their convenience. An additional indicator is that e-retail continuously influences offline store visits both for shopping and through return and exchanges of purchased goods. Consumers are also likely to make a purchase in the store while returning or exchanging a product they bought online. Although several luxury brands are yet to adopt complete channel integration, the brands that have shown the most inclination to this strategy are Dior and André Ross (Figures 6.8 and 6.9). At the time of writing, Dior had implemented a multi-country e-retail strategy

Figure 6.8 *The Dior online boutique (October 2006)*

Figure 6.9 *The André Ross online boutique (August 2006)*

These brands are closest to adopting the Channel Integration strategy. They also indicate the highest commitment to e-retail in the luxury goods sector so far

covering the USA, the UK and France with other planned markets like Germany; while André Ross had adopted product delivery to the global market.

Option five: the e-retail mall

The e-retail mall is a website that sells the products of multiple luxury brands with a single check-out point. This strategy has been adopted mostly by offline luxury departmental stores such as Macy's and Neiman Marcus; and by pure-play e-retailers like net-a-porter.com, yoox.com and eluxury.com. Another notable company that has implemented the 'e-retail mall' strategy in an elevated manner is glam.com. The website innovatively and creatively combines the different aspects of fashion retail that online consumers seek. These include fashion and trends information, style news and celebrity features. They are provided in a unique space that also includes links to the websites where the featured items are retailed.

The e-retail mall streamlines the shopping experience for the consumer by grouping different brands together in one website. It could however lead to the opposite effect if mismanaged. This could happen when elements that enhance the online customer experience have not been effectively implemented.

High-impact web experiences are more challenging to produce in an e-retail mall than in a single brand e-boutique. This is because e-malls focus more on functionality and managing multiple brands than on creating a pres-tigious website. Also, a customer who intends to purchase the product of a particular luxury brand might not appreciate clicking through a website with multiple brands and products such as an e-retail mall. At the same time, some online consumers appreciate the variety of product offerings that e-retail malls offer. This poses a paradox that requires an appropriate strategic balance.

Online luxury consumers lack both physical contact with the products retailed online and human contact with the sales personnel; therefore their interaction with the brand is summed up in the visit to the e-store. This means that online customers would have a higher expectation for an enhanced brand experience with the brands they encounter online. The elevated brand experi-ence is more difficult to attain in a website that features numerous brands but innovative companies like glam.com (Figure 6.10) have implemented tactics to overcome this through providing e-shoppers with links to luxury brands' websites.

A major challenge of the e-retail mall strategy option is that the aura of a luxury brand could be downgraded if the e-mall retails a mix of products from high-value and low-value brands. For example, the products of Louis Vuitton, which is considered the most valuable luxury brand in the world, are retailed on eluxury.com where products from little-known mass fashion brands with lower brand value are also found. This factor could affect the luxury brand equity in the long term.

Figure 6.10   *Glam.com provides a combination of fashion, celebrity, trends and style news with direct links to e-retail the websites (May 2006)*

The offline retail location choice of luxury brands is often in the most exclusive and prestigious districts of the world's fashion capitals, and the same principle of exclusive retail location ought to be applied online through exclusive websites. Streamlining offline and online retail strategies is crucial to generating online traffic and retaining brand loyalty.

Option six: limited e-retail

This e-retail strategy option recognizes the value of e-retail in specific markets while overlooking other markets. Luxury brands that adopt this option implement e-retail in a single or few markets and often leave an unfilled market gap in other regions with a ready online consumer population. Limited e-retail also provides a narrow range of products online, rather than the complete product range. This strategy is currently the most widely adopted by the few luxury fashion brands that have implemented e-retail. For example, luxury brands like Louis Vuitton, Gucci and Dior (Figure 6.11) have e-retail activities for a few markets while other brands like Giorgio Armani (Figure 6.12) and Hermès provide a limited range of products for their online boutiques although the brands have plans to extend their e-retail offers. However, the limited e-retail approach is akin to telling consumers that 'we know it is possible to make life easier for you but we won't'. This strategic option indicates a rather low level of commitment to e-retail.

Figure 6.11 *Dior online store is available in France, UK and German markets and in the USA through eluxury.com (Spring 2006)*

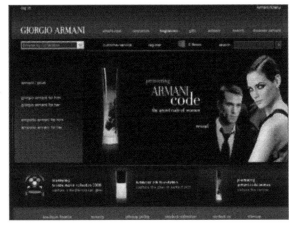

Figure 6.12 *Armani's US-only online store retails fragrance, cosmetics and timepieces; however, Armani products are sold on several other independent websites (Spring 2006)*

However, since the e-retail of luxury goods is still in its introductory phase, rapid expansion of e-retail by luxury brands is envisioned. Several luxury brands are currently evaluating the possibility of extensive e-retail operations.

Option seven: information only

This e-retail option provides solely product and corporate information for customers and the public through the website. The majority of the global luxury fashion brands such as Chanel and Versace fall within the group of luxury brands that have this approach to the internet. This option shows a low commitment to e-retail and doesn't address the online consumer and their needs. While this approach may be intended to protect the brand integrity of exclusivity, it is no longer applicable in the current global luxury fashion marketplace.

Option eight: no web presence

The 'no web presence' e-retail strategy indicates an aversion to the use of the internet for e-retail and also for information provision. Some luxury brands that currently adopt this approach are Prada, which has a single-page website with no information, although it occasionally features pop-up messages of news and events related to the brand. Other luxury brands like shoe designers Christain Louboutin and Manolo Blahnik don't have independent websites although their products are retailed from the websites of e-retailers like neimanmarcus.com. There are often several reasons for the non-adoption of the internet medium as an information or retailing channel, which might vary among brands. The fact remains however that the internet is the biggest potential of global commerce and any luxury brand that intentionally ignores this medium has literally signed a long-term death wish.

Case Analysis
Louis Vuitton and Eluxury.com

Louis Vuitton is the most valuable luxury fashion brand in the world. Its brand value asset has been placed at above US$ 17 billion and its consumer following is likened to a cult. The brand characteristics include innovation, creativity and exclusivity. Louis Vuitton also implements stringent brand developmental strategies such as a 'no price discount' principle, rigorous product tests and the destruction of unsold goods. The brand's stores are located in the most exclusive areas of the world's major cities and its clientele range from the rich and famous to the new luxury mass consumers. Louis Vuitton stores are also neither located in the same vicinity as mass fashion brands nor in shopping centres. However on the internet, the goods of Louis Vuitton are retailed on eluxury.com, which is a pioneer fashion retail mall that also retails the products of more than fifty brands ranging from luxury to premium and mass fashion. Some of the brands retailed on eluxury.com have low brand awareness. This strategy raises several questions.

Does this e-retail strategy represent the 'exclusivity' and 'high status' brand attributes of Louis Vuitton? Does it enhance the equity of the brand?

Luxury fashion e-marketing and e-branding strategy

Consumers decide to visit websites according to the information and products they seek but they re-visit websites according to the experiences of their previous visits. These experiences are shaped by effective e-marketing and e-branding strategies. The internet is a pull marketing medium, which contrasts with the push medium used in offline marketing. This is because internet activities function on the premise of drawing or 'pulling' consumers to visit websites while traditional marketing platforms 'push' consumers to make purchases. The marketing strategy used for the internet should therefore focus on the acquisition and retention of website visitors.

E-marketing strategy

Marketing is often wrongly summed up as marketing communications, in other words advertising and public relations. From a tactical viewpoint, marketing strategy comprises of a holistic approach that incorporates the development of products, pricing, distribution and promotional techniques. There are also important additional elements of the marketing strategy like the assessment of the competitive and consumer market environments and factors that contribute to competitive leverage.

The online marketing strategy borrows some of the major elements of the offline marketing strategy and adapts them to the internet environment. However, rather than focusing on the product and services aspects of a brand's offerings, the elements are re-aligned with a strong concentration on the customer experience. This is because the internet is a virtual medium that lacks human interface and this factor ought to be overcome. The shortcoming is compensated through the application of strategies that provide an overall high satisfaction for the online customer. The online marketing strategy therefore captures the internet marketing strategy as a customer-oriented technique rather than a product-oriented method.

The major element of the luxury fashion e-marketing strategy is known as the e-marketing mix. It is a model that has been adapted from the e-marketing-mix concept found in the works of Lauterborn (1990); Harris and Dennis (2002); and Mohammed *et al.* (2002). The e-marketing mix features a set of factors that offer the optimal value to the online customer, when effectively implemented. The elements of the e-marketing mix are also known as the 10 Cs of Luxury Fashion E-Marketing and are presented in the following section.

The 10 Cs of luxury fashion e-marketing

The 10 Cs that comprise the luxury fashion e-marketing mix are the following:

1 Customer value
2 Convenience
3 Cost
4 Communication
5 Computing
6 Customer franchise
7 Customer care
8 Community
9 Content
10 Customization

Customer value

Consumers seek satisfaction from a brand's products or services through obtaining solutions to their needs and wants. In the case of luxury consumers, these might include emotional and psychological needs. When a luxury fashion consumer purchases a new timepiece from Rolex, the overall pleasure he obtains from the product not only originates from the physical attributes of the wrist watch itself, but also emanates from a package of contentment gained through the total brand experience which the product is a part of. This is what the customer interprets as benefits and value, and the satisfaction obtained is called 'customer value'. In the offline marketing mix, its equivalent is the 'product' element. However, rather than focus solely on the product features as a source of customer satisfaction, 'customer value' emphasizes the creation of a powerful brand experience in addition to the satisfaction gained from the brand's products and services.

The creation of customer value for the online consumer can be achieved through providing the required product range and adequate tools to viewing them and also enhancing the web atmosphere. Several luxury brands wrongly offer a narrow product range in the e-store. Others provide end-of-season products or goods that no one would buy in the physical stores. For example, Hermès is best known for its highly coveted leather goods, but the brand's website neither provides a means to purchase this product range online nor information regarding its offline sales. Ideally, luxury brands ought to offer a complete product range online with a few exceptions such as limited edition products or other specially-made goods that retain the brand's aura.

Convenience

Convenience is one of the most important advantages of e-retail. The internet provides online consumers the comfort to buy what they want, when they want it through an e-store that is open round the clock. Online consumers also have the benefit of combining online shopping with other activities. The internet also offers a retail location without associated problems like accessibility and transport. Convenience replaces 'Place' or 'Distribution' in the offline marketing mix.

In order to make the 'convenience' experience complete for the consumer, luxury fashion brands are required to integrate the offline retail offers with the e-retail strategy. As indicated earlier, real space and cyberspace are not mutually exclusive but are inter-related and this factor should be reflected in providing convenience to consumers. This is because several luxury consumers are multi-channel shoppers who may visit both the website and the offline store before making a purchase from either or both of the retail channels. The convenience element should also include effective website usability and streamlining the after-sales service to include returns, refunds and exchange of goods in physical stores, despite online purchase.

Cost

The cost of purchasing a product is not the same as the product's price-tag. The real cost that consumers bear includes the price of the product and additional costs like transport cost and travel time to and from the store, time lost in parking, time spent in the store, time spent at checkout points, the mental cost of shopping and in some cases the monetary cost of parking. E-retail saves the online consumer these costs and hassles.

An additional 'cost' factor in the online sale of luxury goods is the issue of price discounting. Consumers generally perceive the internet as a price discount destination due to a wide range of goods that are often on 'sale' on the internet. As a result, they transfer the expectation of online price discounting to luxury goods. In response, several luxury brands have adopted the strategy of online product discounting or end of season sales promotions. This strategy neither enhances brand integrity nor sustains brand equity for luxury brands. Ideally luxury brands ought to maintain a strict and consistent pricing policy both online and offline. This means that if a luxury brand does not discount the price of its products offline, the same policy should be applied online.

Communication

Communication is a two-way cooperative process between a company and its consumers. It provides access to feedback and more importantly to insight into consumer needs and expectations. Marketing communication adopts several methods in the exchange of information such as through customer services. The internet enhances customer services through instant information exchange with online consumers using emails and live chats. Communication is the equivalent of 'Promotion' in offline marketing. However, unlike promotion, which focuses on convincing consumers to make purchases, communication concentrates on exchanges, which eventually leads to conviction.

Luxury fashion brands can exploit internet tools like exclusive online clubs, permission marketing (opt-in and opt-out), viral marketing, email news and other customer data collection techniques to enhance communications with the online consumers.

Computing

Computer and logistics systems are fundamental in the effective functioning of the e-retail elements. Computing is required for effective control of the product range, orders and dispatch. In order to manage logistics like timely deliveries of goods in the right quantity and size and to the right location, effective computing and category management systems must be put in place. Other related issues such as electronic billing, taxation calculation and secure payments can only be achieved through competent computing coordination. Creating computer networks between suppliers, manufacturers and retailers is one way of accomplishing effective computing management.

Effective computing is essential in e-retail particularly with the rapid change of the online product variety. This is because luxury brands currently have an increasing variety in product offering and a decreasing product life-cycle. The implication of this is an enlarged assortment of goods that require effective management online. In addition to product management, luxury brands can also extend computing systems to empower customers through providing tools for online order tracking and mapping for store directions.

Customer franchise

Customer franchise is the sum of the associations of trust, confidence, image and overall feelings that a consumer has developed in relation to a brand, as a result of their experiences with the brand online. Customer franchise can be directly linked with brand positioning and brand equity, which have been extensively discussed in Chapter 5 of this book. The branding element is of paramount importance to luxury fashion brands because the brand strength sustains the online experience with the customer. In order to build trust with the online consumer, a high customer franchise is essential.

Customer care

Customer care and customer services are among the current buzzwords in the business vocabulary. Excellent customer service does not begin and end with placing pleasant looking employees behind polished desks to respond to queries. Effective customer care is extended to every aspect of a customer's contact with a brand. The current reality is that the majority of luxury brands have a poor rating among consumers with regard to the provision of customer services both online and offline. This is because, for a long time, the luxury sector focused on product sales rather than customer experience enhancement as a source of advantage. The internet has however made the challenge of achieving consistent and efficient customer services easy.

Online consumers lack the human interaction of offline retailing and this factor must be compensated to enhance the web experience. Some ways of achieving this and enhancing customer services online are the following:

- Fast and reliable delivery of goods.
- Quick returns, refunds and exchanges of goods.
- After-sales services both online and offline.

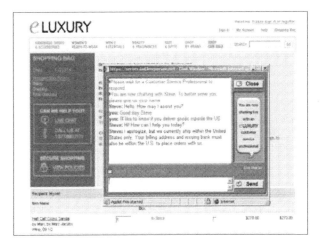

Figure 6.13
Eluxury.com's live chat facility provides instant shopping assistance in an efficient manner (June 2006)

- Live online chat with a customer services representative.
- Direct telephone link facilities from the website.
- E-notes facilities for message posting.
- Online bulletin boards.
- Online personal shopper.
- E-news subscription.
- Instant online fashion coordination.
- Extensive product view and description.
- Exclusive subscription offers to fashion shows and product previews.
- High security transactions.
- Viral marketing tools.
- Permission marketing tools.

Online customer services programmes also provide an excellent medium of developing a customer database and gathering feedback from consumers. The majority of the existing luxury brands are far from implementing effective e-CRM strategies. A few exceptions are Gucci.com and Eluxury.com (Figure 6.13) which have implemented efficient means of interaction between their online customers and an available customer services staff.

Community

The online consumer society consists of several communities of consumers with shared interests. The internet has equipped consumers with the tool to develop platforms where they can share stories of positive and negative experiences with different brands. These are called user-to-user communities. These communities have sprung up in the luxury fashion arena, although they have been prevalent in other sectors such as the airline industry. A notable example is the Louis Vuitton fan website at 'www.lying-awake.net/vuitton'. Consumer fans of Louis Vuitton use this website as a platform for sharing experiences and discussing issues connected with the brand. The website had 1,322 official members as of May 2006. This platform for sharing brand experiences is an effective tool that luxury brands can adopt to build stronger relationships with consumers.

In order to optimize the opportunity created by online communities, luxury brands can proactively incorporate internally managed user communities to their websites. Although luxury brands have yet to initiate this level of customer relationship, casual fashion brand Lands End has pioneered a simultaneous shopping possibility called '*Shop with a Friend*', where two shoppers can browse the website, share notes and purchase goods at the same time. Other examples outside the luxury fashion sector that enable user communities include Orange.com and Microsoft.com. An effective brand community helps to build a closer relationship between consumers and brands.

Content

The contents of a luxury brand's website are significant in sustaining the brand's image. The corporate, product and services information provided on the website should be up-to-date and highly interesting. The presentation style using text, images, video, sound and colour scheme are also expected to be well coordinated. In addition, other pleasantly surprising features that contribute to an enhanced customer experience should be incorporated in the website. This could be in the form of a brand's product manufacturing process or an audio/video greeting from the brand's ambassador. These tools are called 'social benefits' and their role is to boost the functional benefits provided by a website. The social benefits that some luxury brands have provided on their website at different times include product manufacturing video clips at Vuitton.com and an animated picture story of the Gucci's La Pele Guccissima in production at Gucci.com.

Customization

The demand for customization of products, services and web experiences is an aspect of the increasing expectations of online consumers. In the present luxury market, consumers desire to be recognized and provided with personal attention. In line with this, they expect the websites of luxury brands to provide tools to customize and personalize their experiences with the brands. One method of achieving this is through implementing techniques that aid in manipulating features of web pages such as background colour, wallpaper and text size. These could leave powerful lasting impressions on consumers. Another technique is the provision of multiple background music choices. Other methods of customization and personalization could be derived from the

digital luxury

Figure 6.14
Anya Hindmarch's website provides tools for product customization, which boosts the overall web experience and enhances customer value (Summer 2006)

shopping habits and product preferences of a brand's consumers. A notable example of a luxury brand that uses customization as a means of providing a superior web experience is Roberto Cavalli. The website attains this through providing customizable wallpaper and multiple background music options.

In addition, the internet could be used as a means of making products and services customization available to a broad consumer group. This strategy is, however, lacking in the luxury sector as the majority of the existing luxury brands provide product customization only to a select clientele. There are a few exceptions, though, including British luxury brand Anya Hindmarch which pioneered the provision of product customization through its website as a means of enhanced customer value (Figure 6.14).

E-branding strategy

Branding and marketing on the web have often been misinterpreted as one and the same thing. While the branding and marketing concepts complement one another, their application is hardly identical. As has been repeatedly emphasized throughout this book, a brand is the sum of all the feelings, perceptions and experiences a person has as a result of contact with a company and its products and services. This means that branding strategy constitutes of factors that can be linked to consumers' minds, where the branding associations reside.

Several luxury brands have defined both their online and offline marketing strategies but are often found wanting in the aspect of online branding. This is mainly because attaining the desired brand perception and brand position-ing on the web is a challenge that requires clear-cut strategies. However, a

Case Analysis
Coach.com and the 10 Cs

Customer value   It is not clear if the full product range of Coach is available online; what is clear is that the online shopper has a wide selection (including limited editions!) and ease of navigation to view them. Products are categorized for easy retrieval through uncluttered pages. There is also a search facility for a quick tour. There are multiple tools for product views such as zoom, image enlargement, colour selection, complementary product selection, avatar product view and an online flip over catalogue!

Cost   Coach maintains a consistent online and offline pricing strategy. Nowhere on the website are products marked with 'Sales' or 'Discount' signs.

Convenience   The Coach e-store as a retail destination offers several features that enhance and stimulate an enjoyable shopping experience, except sound. The website can also be found easily on search engines.

Communication   Coach.com provides visible ways of communicating with the online customer. The Customer Services telephone number appears on the homepage and on all subsequent pages. Links to customer services, email sign-up and store locations are also visible on multiple pages including those in the online catalogue.

Computing   Coach has made excellent use of computing technology to design an effective website. Orders are shipped within two to three working days of purchase and the customer can track the status of their purchased merchandise online. There is also a facility for express shipping.

Customer franchise   Coach.com communicates a consistent brand image through its website. The overall experience of the customer after each visit is expected to be positive. The service is quick, well-organized and provides value and a high satisfaction level.

Customer care   The online customer care of Coach.com is one of the most efficient in the luxury fashion industry. Online customers are offered the possibility to return or exchange new and unused merchandise either at a Coach store or through shipping. Merchandise can also be exchanged for store credit. Provisions are also made for telephone contact, email contact, free catalogue order, viral marketing and product registration. Consumers also have the possibility to purchase and check the balance of gift cards online.

Community   At the time of writing, neither Coach nor its consumer group had developed a visible user community platform.

Content   Coach.com features relevant corporate and product and services information, presented in a highly functional and uncluttered layout. However the website is deficient in social benefits.

Customization   The website of Coach lacks customization features for products, services and web contents.

well-defined offline brand strategy can be streamlined into the online branding strategy. This boosts the response of consumers because when the brand perception and equity are positive, the consumer response to new channels of sales is likely to be high. Online branding can prove to be an indispensable brand power booster, when expertly managed.

In the development of online branding strategy, the online consumer forms the central point from which the strategy is built. The aim is to enhance the brand's perception in the consumer's mind. Consumers have exceptionally high expectations from luxury brands on the internet. In order to meet their needs, luxury brands need to apply effective strategies to differentiate the luxury brand's website from the clutter of millions of existing websites.

The following questions are particularly important in the development of an online luxury branding strategy:

- Does the website capture the interest of the consumer through its design, layout and structure?
- Will each visitor to the website experience a high impact through the key brand associations?
- Does the website epitomize the key characteristics that make up the brand identity, personality and image?
- Does the website evoke the desired luxurious atmosphere?
- Will the website have a positive impact on the brand equity and increase the brand value?

Dior.com can be used to illustrate the points raised above. The website successfully captures the brand essence of Christian Dior. The cool and

trendy yet luxurious elements of the brand are apparent on the homepage and on all the subsequent pages. The website's atmosphere exudes every emotion experienced in a Dior store, which gives it authenticity. This effect has been achieved through the use of online branding elements such as atmospheric features like visuals, flash animations, videos, sound, pictures, navigation, layout and customer care (Figure 6.15).

Figure 6.15   *The Dior website captures the brand essence through its design and functionality features (May 2006)*

Website and e-store design

A crucial aspect of the online branding strategy development of luxury goods is website and e-store design. Luxury fashion website and e-store design ought to aim to achieve more than basic, functional requirements, through a focus on an enhanced web experience for every visitor to the website. This is because e-retail involves a constant flow of innovative concepts of differentiation to meet the high expectations of the online consumer.

One of the most powerful pioneering tools of designing high-impact websites and e-stores is called 'web-atmospherics' or 'webmospherics'. It is the creation of a luxurious atmosphere on a brand's website to emit the prestigious atmosphere found in the physical stores of luxury brands. Webmospherics is achieved through the utilization of specific elements to reproduce the intricate 'look and feel' associated with luxury brands. The concept of webmospherics was made prominent by Knowles and Chicksand at the 2002 IBM E-business Conference in Birmingham; and Harris and Dennis in their 2002 book, *Marketing the E-Business*.

The elements of webmospherics are adaptations to the five human senses which, when applied, contribute to a more sensory online consumer experience. They are the following:

1 Visuals such as text, graphics, pictures, design, colours, videos, 3-D view and zoom.
2 Sound such as music, clicks and other effects.
3 Smell such as fragrance and perfume samples.
4 Usability such as interactive tools, navigation ease, 3-clicks purchase, video and sound control buttons, quick downloads, avatars, instant messaging, chat groups, message boards, online shopping assistance, complimentary products, collaborative filtering and virtual changing rooms.
5 Personalization and customization of web pages, products and services.

The objective of webmospherics is to create a high-impact web experience, increase purchase probability, aid in subsequent brand and website memory recall and retain customer loyalty in the long-term. In order to achieve the optimal effect, the features of webmospherics must be aligned and applied with exactitude according to a brand's specific attributes.

Visuals

Sight is the most powerful medium of attracting and retaining the interest of online customers. Visuals involve the use of tools and aids that luxury brands can manipulate to create a memorable web experience. These tools include the colour scheme, pictures, video clips, slide shows, three-dimensional product views, zoom facilities of whole and parts of products, text font, style and size, interactive flash media, full screen mode and graphics.

The **homepage** of a luxury brand's website is the first point of contact between the brand and the online luxury shopper. The homepage introduction must be powerful in order to create a high impact and reinforce the prestige attributes of the brand. Several luxury brands such as Roberto Cavalli, John Galliano, André Ross and Valentino have implemented highly graphical and attention-grasping homepages, while the majority of luxury brands have homepages that are far from powerful. It is also important for a luxury brand's homepage to reinforce the brand's attributes such as the brand's personality and heritage. Chanel captures this feature effectively on its website's home-page, which opens with the Chanel double C logo in the brand's classic black and white colours. Also, the homepage should be constantly updated and must maintain consistent impressive features in the course of the updates. Louis Vuitton is one of the few luxury brands that has maintained a steady use of visually-arresting and regularly updated pictorial images on its homepage to create high impact (Figures 6.16–6.19).

Figure 6.16
Vuitton.com
(Spring 2004)

Figure 6.17
Vuitton.com
(Spring 2005)

Figure 6.18
Vuitton.com
(Spring 2006)

Figure 6.19
Vuitton.com
(Autumn 2006)

Another key factor in achieving a strong homepage introduction is the implementation of interactive rapid features such as flash animations to grasp the attention of the browser. It is also important to provide control tools for viewing and skipping introductory videos, animations and sound. Several brands ignore these important elements and website visitors are sometimes forced to wait for long homepage downloads or watch flash animations against their desire.

When improperly managed, the homepage has the potential of generating negative brand perceptions rather than brand and website enhancement. For example, some luxury brands shut down their websites during redesign and often replace the homepage with a message that reads along the lines of, 'Coming Soon' or 'Will be Back Soon'. This affects the online customer experience and dampens their high expectations. Versace.com, Fendi.com, Gucci.com and Elizabethhurley.com have fallen victim to this rather wrong strategy. The ideal situation is that a luxury brand's website should be kept in operation during its reconstruction, where possible. There is no strategic reason to remove access to a website while changes are being implemented.

The homepage establishes the online experience with the website visitor and its messages ought to aid brand enhancement and not the reverse.

In addition, the homepage message of luxury brands should also be aligned to the offline communications strategies. For example, in the spring of 2005, Versace.com was 'closed' and the homepage had a message indicating that the new site was 'in arrival'. During the same period, Versace launched a multi-million dollar global print advertising campaign featuring music icon Madonna. Several consumers that were exposed to the highly visible and appealing adverts would have likely visited the website either out of the desire to begin a relationship with the brand or reinforce the already existing brand relationship. The closure of the website and absence of an alternative shopping channel, could have led to stunting the consumer's perception and negatively affecting the brand's aura. Closing down a website can be likened to closing down a physical store without providing an alternative store.

The homepage of a website is often misunderstood as the brand's **welcome page**. The welcome page is different from the homepage in content, function and layout. Homepages house the major navigational toolbars for the website's functionality and interactive features to enhance the web atmosphere. Welcome pages on the other hand serve as the first page that welcomes the browser and ushers them into the website. Welcome pages are most useful for sectionalizing websites that have different localized contents in terms of language and region-specific information. While the homepage is indispensable for every website, the welcome page is optional and is implemented according to the requirements of the market and the expectations of the consumers. Luxury brands should ideally have welcome pages, especially the brands that feature multiple languages and regional market contents.

Another important visual element in webmospherics is the **video**. The use of short and relevant video clips adds colour and excitement to the online luxury atmosphere, and enhances the mood of both the e-boutique and the online shopper. Video clips also contribute to website stickiness. Website stickiness is the retention of the online consumer's attention to an extent that their time allocation to the website's visit is extended. Videos also contribute to memory recollection of the website and repeat visits. Most importantly, website video clips create a feeling of human presence and interaction and decreases the impact of the virtual interface in the web environment.

Several luxury brands such as Christian Dior (Figure 6.20) and Louis Vuitton have included video clips of their fashion shows on their websites. Other brands like Chanel and Dior have also implemented video clips of interviews with their creative directors Karl Lagerfeld and John Galliano at different times. Vuitton.com has also shown a video clip of the manufacturing process of its leather goods and Chanel.com has featured a video clip demonstration of its cosmetics use at different times.

In order to be relevant and appreciated by online consumers, video clips ought to be short, easy to understand and fast to download. They should also

Figure 6.20
*Dior.com 's
online video
clip of its
fashion show
(2006)*

have control tools and an option for skipping or enlargements. These provide
the website visitor with a sense of empowerment.

Interactive animation is yet another essential visual tool that contributes
to an enriched online retail atmosphere. There are several ways that animations can be used to feature products and services on a website. For example,
Jimmychoo.com and Coach.com have utilized the animation tool through
online flip-open catalogues, which provide a sense of human presence online.
Coach.com has also incorporated a feature for product-view on an avatar that
can be modified according to the height and weight dimensions of the shopper. This gives the online consumer a clear idea of the product size on the
human form. Coach's website also has tools that allow the shopper to view
handbags either on the shoulder or clutched in the hand. These elements
contribute to a high-impact online shopping experience.

Colour is also a highly important online visual element. This is because
the product attributes are most enhanced by their colour scheme, the quality
of the images and their placements. Luxury brands use colour heavily in the
product presentation, e-stores and online catalogue sections of their websites.
The appropriate colours should be applied on the homepage for a strong introduction and in the subsequent pages for a balanced result. In addition, some
background white space should be left on most or all the web pages to achieve
a harmonizing effect. The download time of colour pictures or online catalogues should also be kept short.

A factor that poses a challenge in efficient online colour management is the
representation of colour on computer monitors, which display colours in
varying tones. The colour display gradient and quality can be controlled with
colour management software like eColour, which has a cookie that reads a
monitor's output and advices on its settings adjustments.

Colour pictures are accompanied by product information and description through text. The **website text** should ideally be short and presented in an uncluttered format. At the same time, the product information should be in-depth and expert. The text font size, style, clarity of language and tone ought to be applied with consistency according to the tastes and expectations of luxury consumers. Ideally, website text should be restricted to a maximum of three sentences per paragraph. Small illegible text font sizes and uncoordinated language should be avoided at all costs. The language of the website should also be clear, concise and consistent in its tone through all the pages. Dark text colour should also be applied against a clear background and vice versa.

3-D and zoom product views are indispensable visual tools in the online sale of luxury goods as a result of the sensory nature of luxury products. Facilities for three-dimensional product views, zoom view and product-size enhancement provide a superior visualization of products and also empower shoppers to see products in their own individual mode. Also applying these features through slide shows contributes to a positive online web experience.

Sound

In offline retailing, sound is used to evoke and stimulate different feelings in the subconscious of the shopper. This is achieved through music type, volume, pitch, tempo and other sound manifestations. For example, in physical store retail, fast music is used to generate high shopping traffic inflow and spending; loud and funky music encourages impulse purchase; soft music such as jazz and classical music prolong the length of time that customers spend in a store; and slow tempo music reduces the pace of human traffic flow and increases sales volume. Also, familiar and nostalgic sounds such as waterfalls, chirping birds and Christmas carols stimulate emotions that lead to spending.

This retail strategy of influencing mood with sound effects can be transferred to the internet environment. Sound is also an important tool for entertainment while shopping online, and can be one of the strongest motivations for online luxury shopping. Sound is most effective when applied with a focus on the brand personality. Although all luxury brands are associated with prestige, each brand has its own distinct attributes. Therefore the choice of sound features such as music should be in line with the key associations of the brand and its consumer expectations. It is also vital to apply the sound element in moderation and appropriately through consistency in sound type. This is in order to avoid a negative effect that could lead to irritating online consumers with sound in all the website's pages. Sound effects should also have control tools to provide online consumers the empowerment to manage their sound choices.

Several luxury brands have currently incorporated sound within their

Figure 6.21 *The Furla homepage uses appropriate sound that is aligned to the brand's personality (August 2006)*

Figure 6.22 *Royal Elastics homepage creates a high impact introduction with music that accentuates its brand aura (August 2006)*

websites. Furla.com (Figure 6.21) has background music on its homepage while Chanel.com has featured background tempo instrumental music on its product presentation pages, which effectively creates a luxurious mood. Another website that has successfully implemented an effective online sound feature is sportswear brand Royal Elastics (Figure 6.22), which has music that complements its trendy brand personality.

Smell

Smell is a challenging human sense to transfer to the internet virtual environment because of the difficulty of reproducing aroma on the web. However, technological advancement aims to provide a means for online consumers to have a whiff of scent while shopping on the internet. One method is through a scent-smelling software called 'iSmell Personal Scent Synthesizer', still in development. This software is supposed to provide digital scent through a peripheral device plugged to a computer in the same manner as speakers. The device will receive and transmit smell from websites that have scent-emission tools. Luxury brands can use this mechanism to sell goods that rely heavily on the sense of smell such as fragrance and cosmetics.

The absence of the sensory element of smell online can also be overcome through offering samples of luxury products from the brand's website. Providing complete product or component samples from a website is a powerful way of guaranteeing future sales. This is because consumers who have tested or purchased scent-based products are usually likely to make regular future purchases as a result of an affiliation with the product's scent. In addition, scent can be easily recalled and attachment to particular scents is hardly outgrown. Therefore, there is a high probability of repeat online purchases of scent-based products. This is one of the reasons that perfumes and fragrances are among the most frequently purchased sensory goods online.

An additional strategy for the enhancement of the 'smell' element online is through providing a strong and comprehensive description of scent-based products. For example the following phrase might be used to describe the scent in a bottle of perfume:

> A soft and soothing scent that oozes energetic vanilla, with a hint of soothing lavender and powdery English rose that lasts all day.

Usability

Usability is the backbone of a website and crafts the online experience through navigation, functionality and interactivity. It is an essential element for a high-impact customer experience and can contribute substantially to a luxurious online atmosphere. The usability of a website is determined by its effective application of tools that enhance the ease of navigation, speed of operations and an overall pleasant web atmosphere.

Luxury consumers expect reliable and fast service online and at the same time, more value through a high level of website interactivity. The utilization of easy **navigational tools** makes the browsing experience effortless and will likely encourage the visitor to click through several pages on the website. Navigational tools include appropriate website design and layout and other elements such as full-screen mode and new window pop-up tools. Also important are multiple product download formats like PDF and Word versions of documents and catalogues. Another important navigational tool is the 'breadcrumb', which provides a sequential list of the pages that an online visitor has viewed. This aids the online consumer in tracking their movement on the website and retracing their steps where required. It is also imperative to provide the possibility to return to the homepage from all the pages of the website.

Simplicity in website layout and structure is an important factor in luxury fashion website design. Several luxury brands seem to underestimate this factor and end up developing websites cluttered with multiple pages and excessive information. The luxury fashion website ought to be easy to navigate in terms of product search and highly relevant in terms of information content.

Functionality involves elements that contribute to the flawless online shopping transaction process. These include the number of clicks from product view to the checkout point; product display and e-merchandizing techniques; the security of online transactions; payment method choices; currency conversion; and the overall shopping transaction speed.

The purchasing and transactional process should be quick without too many click-through pages. At the same time, customers should be given the possibility to store their product selection and return at will to order and pay. There should also be the possibility to check product stock and reserve goods to try on and purchase in the physical stores.

In addition, a website's functionality is enhanced through tools such as multiple language choices to satisfy the global base of luxury consumers. While it is impossible to provide alternative website text in all the languages understood by consumers, the ideal luxury brand's website should have an extensive language choice apart from the classic English, French, Italian and Japanese. The language options should also not be automatically restricted by the locations. This means that if a luxury brand has different web contents for different markets, the language choice given to the online consumer to view those contents should not be limited to the language spoken in that particular market. Thus the consumer could select their location and then select the language in which they would like to view the contents of the website in that location. For example, if a consumer is in France and would like to view the website in English or in Spanish, the website contents would display the information relevant to the French market in the language selected by the consumer. This is contrary to the assumption of several luxury brands that every consumer who lives in France automatically wants to view websites in the French language. Exceptions to this are Cartier.com and denim brand Levi.com.

Interactive features such as animations are also important usability tools which are highly valued by luxury consumers. It is imperative to retain a focus on the characteristics of online consumers and to design the website in accordance with their expectations. However, interactive features should be implemented in moderation and with a relentless focus on the brand's aura and long-term equity. Several brands are often carried away by incorporating high interactivity features on their websites without considering their brand personality and the requirements of their target audience which is quite wrong.

The usability and functionality choices made for the website should reflect the core strengths and purposes of the brand and add value to the online shopper's web experience. For instance, if customers expect reliable and fast service, it will be unwise to load up the website with interactive flash videos, and force the browser to wait for long downloads. This adds little value to the customer's experience and damages the brand image. On the other hand, if the website visitors expect a high-impact experience from a website, they will probably be more attuned to waiting for an interactive flash video to load. Website visitors should, however, not be forced to watch interactive animations against their desire. The choice of skipping the animation should be provided through control tools.

Other important tools that enhance usability are the following:

- Providing the current date and time on the web pages.
- The option of returning to the homepage from any of the successive pages.
- Placing arrows with links at strategic points on the website.
- Placing the navigational menu on the left side or the top of the web page. This enables clicking on page links in the same direction as reading.

There is, however, no standard criterion for the page placement of usability tools such as the navigation menu. Placing the navigational menu on the left hand side of the screen provides ease-of-use for the online consumer because the choice for clicking is in the natural direction of reading (from left to right). On the other hand, placing the menu on the right side of the screen is practical as most website visitors are right-handed. Also, with the menu on the right of the screen, the user will be forced to read the text and view the images on the page before clicking on the links, since their eyes move from left to right.

Consumers could also be given the ability to change the background colour of web pages and the font sizes of texts. These tools contribute to interactivity and are also beneficial to visually impaired consumers. In general, the application of the appropriate functionality tools aid in enhancing brand affiliation.

E-merchandizing

E-merchandizing involves product presentation and online selling techniques. These feature several methods that have been directly transferred from offline retailing and modified accordingly. They include the e-store layout and the product presentation style. Other tools of merchandizing like atmosphere enhancing features, ought to be implemented in the e-store to enhance the brand aura. For example Gucci.com, Vuitton.com and Dior.com utilize tools like zoom and alternate product view options to enhance the e-store, while Chanel.com uses these tools in product presentation although the brand has no e-retail activity. Other brands like Hermès and Ralph Lauren provide basic e-store layout and minimal e-merchandizing interactivity through their product presentation.

Interestingly, private luxury e-retailers such as Yoox.com and Net-A-Porter.com have implemented e-merchandizing techniques that are more feasible than those of the majority of luxury brands. Yoox.com enhances usability through an excellent product presentation featuring multiple view options of a single product mostly on a human mannequin. The website has other interactive tools like icons showcasing the previously viewed products, on the same page, a choice to view related items and save preferred products and viral marketing options. This gives a sense of shopping assistance and compensates for the lack of human presence online. There is also a viral marketing option tool that enables forwarding web pages to others. Yoox.com also shows customers the front and back view of products like apparel. This feature boosts the shopping experience through enhanced functionality and atmosphere.

Another fashion apparel e-retailer with impressive e-merchandizing and interactive tactics is US casual wear brand, Lands' End. Landsend.com enhances online customer interactivity through a virtual model called, '*My Virtual Model™*'. The model can be customized by online customers according to their height, weight and size dimensions and other features like facial characteristics, skin tone, hair style and hair colour. The customized Virtual Model wears and displays the outfits selected by the customer. The clothes can also be viewed on the model from a 360° angle point. The customized model can be stored for future visits and can also be forwarded through an e-mail form. This interactive feature significantly boosts the online customer experience and leads to memory recall, repeat visits and eventually customer loyalty.

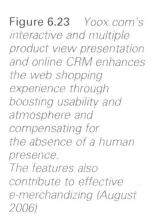

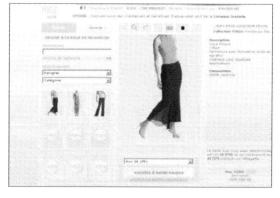

Figure 6.23 *Yoox.com's interactive and multiple product view presentation and online CRM enhances the web shopping experience through boosting usability and atmosphere and compensating for the absence of a human presence. The features also contribute to effective e-merchandizing (August 2006)*

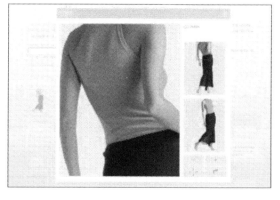

However, Landsend.com has a limited e-retail strategy of sales only in the US market.

The e-retail of luxury goods ought to be approached from a global distribution perspective rather than the widely practiced restricted sales to a few markets. This is because limiting e-retail by geography affects a luxury brand's perception as a global brand. For example, at the time of writing, the website of highly respected luxury brand Hermès had e-retail for only the US and French markets with a highly limited product range. The e-retail practice of a global luxury brand such as Hermès ought to be extended to other geographical markets.

Final notes

The major features of the website and e-store design are summarized in Table 6.3. These tips, while not conclusive, provide a guideline to developing a highly luxurious and functional luxury website and e-boutique.

Table 6.3   Dos and don'ts of website design

Dos	Don'ts
1. Have a great homepage	1. Avoid saving the best pages for last
2. Provide multiple language choices in addition to multiple location contents	2. Avoid multiple sequential click-through pages in the same section
3. Apply a clear colour management plan	3. Avoid cluttering pages with excessive information
4. Align website design to brand image	4. Avoid graphics that require long downloads
5. Apply 3-clicks to buy	
6. Provide the browser with 'breadcrumbs' as a tracking device	5. Do not for any reason close down a website during reconstruction or launch an unfinished or a 'coming soon' website
7. Use clear, concise and consistent language	
8. Provide expert and updated information	6. Maintain a consistent Marketing Mix strategy and brand exclusivity both online and offline
9. Provide short-cut navigation tools	
10. Provide homepage link on all pages	7. Do not retail luxury goods on non-luxury e-retail malls
11. Provide e-CRM link on all pages	
12. Enhance the web atmosphere through videos, sound and animations	8. Do not write long-winded text in tiny illegible font size
13. Apply quick downloads	9. Do not under-estimate or take the online consumer for granted
14. Provide control tools for videos, sound and animations	10. Dot Com companies failed for offering free and cheap products, managerial incompetence, mismanaged logistics, under-utilized customer database, and misunderstanding the e-retail market. Do not make the same mistakes!
15. Provide multiple product views	
16. Apply Viral Marketing, Permission Marketing and Collaborative Filtering tools	
17. Apply Micro Marketing tools like pop-up and banners moderately	
18. Leave some background 'white space'	

The luxury e-retail death wish list

If after reading this chapter you still subscribe to the primeval and unrealistic viewpoint that the internet and luxury goods are incompatible, then the e-retail death wish list below provides some guidelines for you. Good luck, you'll need it!

1 Do not have a website!
2 Have a website with only one page!
3 Have a website but do not sell your products online. Only provide your global consumers with product images and tell them to travel to your store in Paris to buy them!
4 Allow your products to be sold rampantly on the web at unauthorized websites.
5 Continue to maintain the viewpoint that luxury fashion and the internet are not compatible!

Chapter 7
Le new luxe

'The interpretation of luxury has become completely individual. No
one can define luxury for others any more.'

Aaron Simpson, CEO Quintessentially

A different fashion landscape

The definition of luxury has changed. Although the term 'luxury' is a paradox
in itself, the concept of fashion that is tagged 'luxury' is no longer the same
as it was as recently as twenty years ago. In the last several decades, the
luxury sector has undergone a significant evolution as a result of several
factors, which are carefully examined in this chapter. The analysis provides a
portrait of the current luxury environment and acts as a catalyst for strategy
development to manage the sector's present and future.

As indicated in the earlier chapters of this book, luxury fashion has always
been a fundamental part of history and society. From the beginning of the
nineteenth century when modern luxury fashion began, to the middle of the
twentieth century, the luxury fashion market was a small and specific niche
consumer sector made up of aristocrats, celebrities and the world's royals.
During this period, fashion sameness was the order of the day and luxury
fashion consumers were pleased to dress the same. In the present twenty-first
century environment, the story is totally different.

The transformation of the luxury scene has been due to several factors.
First, a mass group of wealthy consumers has emerged throughout the world.
In the last three decades, a vast amount of wealth has been amassed by individuals due to several economic, social, and technological breakthroughs.
This has created a multitude of wealthy people. For example, twenty years
ago China had no middle class but, presently, the growth rate of the country's
upper-middle class and young urban professionals is among the highest in the
world.

Secondly, the high entry barrier that the luxury sector guarded for
centuries has been lowered due to advancement in business and management
practices, driven by globalization and the internet. As a result of the lower
entry barrier, several luxury and aspirational brands have emerged in the last
few decades. In addition, 'mass' fashion brands have attuned their business
strategies to resemble those of luxury brands and now offer similar goods at

a lower price. These factors have also given luxury consumers more brand choices and variety than ever before, and have contributed to the changing consumer psychology.

Thirdly, the rapid growth of digital, information and communications technology has provided a completely different operational platform for both luxury brands and luxury consumers. The internet presents luxury brands the possibility to attain a global level of brand awareness within a short period of time. It also offers luxury consumers more empowerment to choose among a wide array of products, easier access to view their choices and lower switching costs. This influence has led consumers to be individualistic and experimental in their fashion choices. As a result, consumers have become self-stylists and bold enough to mix luxury and high-street fashion in one outfit; something that their mothers and grandmothers would have considered taboo in the past.

Fourthly, the luxury sector has been undergoing a deconstruction process since the 1990s as a result of changes in the investment and ownership structure of several luxury brands. As from this decade, financial institutions including investment firms, private equity holding companies and other non-luxury companies have realized the high intangible asset benefit of luxury brands. This has resulted in increased investments in the luxury sector through acquisitions, capital investments and brand portfolio development. These 'outside' companies include Italian equity funds company Charme, which owns Scottish cashmere brand Ballantyne; Equinox Holdings, which previously had a majority stake in Jimmy Choo; Starwood Capital, which owns Baccarat Crystal; Bridgepoint Capital, which recently sold Molton Brown to Kao of Japan; W Holdings, which owns Amanda Wakeley; and The Falic Group, among several others. These companies place an emphasis on return on investment and augmentation of shareholder value. As a result there has been increased pressure on luxury brands, for rapid sales and profitability. This has led to the introduction of several mass marketing strategies in the retail and brand management of luxury brands. These strategies have further led to the creation of an ambiguity in the definition of a true luxury brand. As a result, luxury brands have divided into groups of 'true luxury' and 'common luxury' or 'fashionable luxury'. Before this era, the branding and retail strategies of luxury brands were clearly different from mass fashion brands but currently, the line that differentiates strategies applied in the two sectors is a blur.

The effects of the changing environment

The results of the changing definition of luxury and other phenomenal transformations in the luxury sector are several. However, chief among these is clearly described by the frequently used phrase 'the democratization of luxury'. This expression means that luxury goods or goods that resemble luxury goods are now available to an increased number of consumers. This visible fact is also seen in the current consumer behaviour of 'trading down' in some categories of goods like basic consumer products in order to 'trade up' to acquire luxury goods. This behaviour is more evident among the new wealthy middle class with a higher disposable income than the middle class of the previous centuries. This group of consumers are also called the 'luxury mass class'.

Having seen the causes of the redefinition of luxury and how these are influencing the sector shifts, it is worthwhile to take a look at the effects they have on the market. This examination will act as an indicator of how the challenge of managing a modern luxury brand can be overcome.

Effect 1: the rise of the masses

The brands formerly known as mass fashion brands, like Zara, H&M and Top Shop, have gone through a dramatic change in the last few years. These changes have been rapid and innovative and the brands seem relentless in innovating new retail and branding techniques. For example, while the UK's Top Shop is busy taking fashion retail to the homes of fashionable Brits with its 'Top Shop To-Go' service, France's Naf Naf distributes free postcards to consumers and tourists, with images of gorgeous models in the latest Naf Naf creations; and Dorothy Perkins hosts special customer product discount events in its stores, along with free cocktails served by charismatic sales representatives. Also, low-priced UK fashion brand Primark, which for a long time was regarded as one of the lowest status fashion brands, is now a favourite for those attending the London Fashion Week. Top Shop also currently has catwalk shows at the London Fashion Week, alongside major luxury brands like Burberry.

In addition, Swedish fashion brand H&M showed retail innovation through its co-branding collaborations with luxury fashion designers, Karl Lagerfeld, Stella McCartney and Viktor & Rolf, as well as links with celebrities like Madonna. Also, Zara, which is considered the market leader among the mass fashion brands, is not left out in the fashion marketing innovation. Zara is reputed to have the fashion industry's most effective and responsive operations techniques, which enables the production of new designs approximately every three weeks. As a result, its stores have a high shopping traffic of style-conscious consumers. Although Zara is not a luxury fashion brand, it has achieved great success in several global markets, including France, where more than three quarters of the population are hard-to-please luxury fashion consumers.

On the American frontier, brands that formerly targeted the fashion mass market like Gap, Banana Republic, Wal-Mart and Target, are also elevating their offerings to include a 'premium' feel. Gap, for example, adopted a different communications strategy through celebrity endorsement advertising with actress Sara Jessica Parker in its 2005 advertising campaigns. This was aimed at revamping the brand's image to reflect a more 'luxe' appeal.

Brands in other categories like sports brands Adidas and Puma are also responding to the mass luxury fashion demand by upgrading their offerings. Others include traditional luggage company Samsonite, whose Creative Director, Quentin Mackay, formerly worked at Tanner Krolle and Loewe. Another example of mass fashion with luxury undertones is the collaboration between Yoji Yamamoto and sportswear brand Adidas, which resulted in the creation of the Y-3 sub-brand. The sub-brand is aimed at representing luxury style in the mass sportswear market and its collections are shown at the New York fashion week, alongside major luxury brands. The objective of these tactics is to infuse 'luxury' qualities into the brands.

The elevation of the status and offerings of mass fashion brands is one of the most visible changes in the luxury fashion arena. Mass fashion brands now have greater relevance because both luxury consumers and the luxury competitive environment have changed. For example, the changing interpretation of luxury fashion by consumers has led to the adoption of mass fashion by the same consumers which has unconsciously formed a pedestal for mass fashion brands to stand side by side with luxury brands. This factor has pushed the mass brands to devise strategies that have enabled them to successfully encroach on the luxury consumer arena. Their success has also changed the way they are defined and perceived. They are no longer considered as only 'mass fashion' brands but are now 'mass premium fashion' brands or 'high-end' brands in some cases. Although they remain focused on a mass market, it is no longer appropriate to consider these brands as low-end or middle-end mass brands.

As a result of the elevation of mass fashion brands from 'mass' to 'premium', these brands have become competitors of luxury brands, for the first time in the history of luxury fashion. Luxury brands, which offered products that were previously based on social status, have always had well-defined territories along which they operate. There had never been any question that they hold the strings in determining the consumers' behaviour until now. However, today, mass fashion brands offer consumers alternatives to their luxury products at better price-value. The mass brands have also found several effective and innovative means to make their offering attractive. Mass fashion brands are capitalizing on the changes in the luxury consumer psychology and their evolution beyond using luxury goods for ego needs satisfaction. For today's luxury consumer, the branded bag or watch is no longer required solely to enable the fulfilment of esteem needs. It is no longer a problem for a young wealthy consumer to combine a $50 pair of jeans from Zara with a $2,000 bag from Vuitton and a $3,000 watch from Chanel. Mass fashion brands are currently exploiting this development in the luxury consumer market.

The most noteworthy strategies that mass fashion brands have developed include the modification of retailing tactics to reflect a 'luxurious' appeal and the manipulation of similar branding and marketing mix strategies as luxury brands. The mass fashion brands have also developed advanced operations techniques to produce new designs within a short time period. The adopted strategies are presented below:

1 Fast design turnover, popularly known as 'Fast Fashion', which is a business model that encourages new designs in stores every few weeks instead of every fashion season. This ensures that consumers find something fresh every time they visit the store. Consumers are also encouraged to visit the stores frequently. Another benefit of fast design turnover for the brands is that fast fashion items are hardly placed on 'sales' or 'mark-downs', which means higher revenues for the brands. The fast fashion model is also beneficial to the wider economic environment through outsourcing of production. As a result of the need for frequent change of retail stock, several mass fashion companies presently outsource the production of goods to manufacturers and suppliers closer to their base in Europe instead of in Asia where the labour cost is lower. This creates more employment and gives a boost to the European textile industry. Although this model is prevalent in Europe, American brands have recognized its benefits and are adjusting their business strategies accordingly.

2 Limited-edition products, which is a spin-off of fast fashion. Rapid fashion design turnover means that the stores are not overstocked, which makes every product under the fast-fashion model a limited-edition product. Limited-edition products address the consumer need for individualism, customization and independence in style interpretation. Consumers no longer want to look the same but prefer to have a personal style. Limited-edition products ensure that each piece of clothing or accessory is viewed as individual.

3 Brand communications, luxe-style, which is exemplified by the high advertisement expenditure in fashion magazines like Vogue and Vanity Fair by both mass fashion and luxury fashion brands. This advertising medium was previously the sole domain of luxury brands but presently, the communications design, style and message of mass brands reflect a luxury feel. Examples can be seen from the concept, feel and style of the recent advertising campaigns of brands such as Mango and Marks & Spencer in the print media. Brand communications, luxe-style, is a contributing factor to the changing perceptions that consumers have of mass fashion brands and luxury brands. For example, when a consumer sees a similar looking Gap advertisement beside that of Hermès, it undoubtedly does something to their mind.

4 Celebrity product and brand endorsement. Several mass fashion brands are using the celebrity association, pioneered by luxury brands, to endorse

their products. Some of these celebrities also endorse luxury brands. For example, Mango has featured supermodel Claudia Schiffer in its print advertising while Sara Jessica Parker and Helena Christensen have both appeared in Gap advertisements. Musician and actress, Madonna has also appeared in H&M's advertisements. Also cosmetics brand L'Oréal features celebrities like Beyoncé, Aishwarya Rai and Eva Longoria, in its advertisements. These highly paid endorsers lend their images to several luxury brands, sometimes in the same periods that they do to mass fashion brands.

5 Prestige retail location through stand-alone stores and retail spaces in luxury departmental stores. It is now possible to find the stores of mass-premium brands in prestigious locations in the major fashion cities like Paris, New York, Milan, London, Tokyo, and Los Angeles, among others. They now utilize the same retail location strategies of luxury brands.

6 Co-branding with luxury fashion designers. Mass premium fashion brands presently collaborate with luxury fashion designers, to elevate their brand status. The most famous example of this co-branding tactic is H&M's collaboration with Karl Lagerfeld, Stella McCartney and Viktor & Rolf, in creating limited edition products. Other co-branding initiatives include American supermarket Target and British luxury fashion designer Luella Bartley; Adidas and Yoji Yamamoto; and Seven For All Mankind and Zac Posen. These collaborative efforts would have been unthinkable ten years ago but they have presently created a synergy between the two categories of fashion through acknowledging that they have consumers in the same sectors.

The results of these strategies include the rapid growth and expansion of mass-premium fashion brands spurred by high sales turnover and profitability; a shift in the global supply chain of fashion production from China to closer locations like East Europe for European brands and Mexico for North American Brands; and an ever-growing individual consumer style. Another result is the significant rise of the brand asset value of mass fashion brands. As an indicator, in 2005, Zara featured for the first time on the list of the Top 100 Global Brands Scoreboard by Interbrand/*Businessweek*. It was ranked no. 77, with a brand value higher than luxury brands Tiffany, Hermès, Cartier, Prada, Bvlgari and Armani. In 2006, its position rose to no. 73, with a brand value of $4.23 billion. The implication is that if these brands were placed on the stock market, the potential value of Zara would be higher than the luxury brands. On the other hand, it can also be argued that consumers have more interaction with Zara than the luxury brands because Zara is a mass brand; therefore the brand value is likely to be higher. However, what remains clear is that mass fashion brands are increasing their brand equity among consumers.

In an attempt to face up to the competition posed by mass-premium fashion brands, luxury brands have developed production and retailing models to increase the length and breadth of their seasonal products. This tactic guarantees frequent product change and shortens the shelf life of the luxury products in question. Some brands like Dolce & Gabbana, Chanel, Versace and Prada have adopted this strategy through introducing pre-collections, usually launched before the season's main collection. Pre-collections often yield better commercial gains and addresses the consumer need for 'early' and 'fast' products prior to the actual fashion season. As a result, luxury brands are placing less emphasis on runway shows and more attention on pre-collection shows. Other brands like Dior and Gucci have developed a 'capsule collection' and 'cruise collection', launched prior to the seasonal collections, to spur product rotation. This indicates that luxury brands are inclining towards the fast fashion model of mass fashion brands. However, the emphasis on creativity in product development should be the driving force of luxury goods creation, using the fast fashion model. This way, the creativity is ensured to meet consumer needs better.

Effect 2: from fast fashion to throwaway fashion

While fast fashion addresses the fashion consumer's demand for constant design change, a new spin-off trend called 'Throwaway Fashion' has also emerged. Throwaway fashion is directly linked with the disposable nature of the current consumer society towards products. This consumer attitude characterized by frequent disposing of goods has been transferred to luxury fashion from other product categories like basic consumer goods. Consumers presently have a throwaway attitude towards a wide array of goods due to the rapid rate of innovation in almost all categories of goods. This has made them view every purchased product as a temporarily owned item, to be discarded with the arrival of a new and better design. It has also contributed to increased expectations of consumers. As a result, fashion is now viewed as disposable. Fashion brands are also contributing to this attitude by constantly providing new designs. Since Zara, H&M and several mass premium fashion brands release new designs every few weeks, consumers have learnt to dispose of certain items in order to create room for the new ones. While most consumers can afford to adopt this attitude towards mass fashion products which have lower prices, the story is quite different when it comes to luxury brands.

Luxury goods are different because they are premium priced. Certain luxury products like bags and shoes, which fashion consumers purchase to complement their mass-premium fashion products like apparel, have an even higher price difference with mass fashion products. This means that consumers literally cannot afford to adopt the 'throwaway fashion' attitude towards luxury goods. Nonetheless, several solutions have been devised by innovative companies, to address the consumer need of 'throwaway fashion' in the luxury arena.

The most notable of these solutions is the provision of the temporary owner-ship of luxury goods to consumers. This service includes borrowing, exchang-ing or trading luxury goods between companies and consumers or among consumers, in order to allow the consumers to maintain fashion trends. Several independent companies in different parts of the world currently provide such services. They have applied the same concept that luxury brands have used for decades when 'lending' clothes and accessories to celebrities for special red carpet events like the American Oscar Awards. The difference is that in this case, consumers have to pay a fee to 'borrow' the goods. The companies that offer these services have created a platform for one-day borrowing of clothes and accessories to lending products that can be retained for weeks or months. The services also extend to style consultancy and advice. Foremost among the companies offering these services include Seattle-based Bag Borrow or Steal, which operates a designer bag-rental service for a monthly subscription fee, and Albright Inc. which specializes in weekly rentals of products from the top strata of luxury brands. Others are London-based One Night Stand which rents eveningwear, Paris' Quidam de Revel which operates an appointment-only luxury goods rental service, and Australia's Mila and Eddie (Figure 7.1), which operates a bag-loaning business based on private membership.

The second solution that luxury consumers have found to throwaway fash-ion is the purchase of second-hand and vintage luxury goods. Although this practice has been in existence for several decades, its commercial scope has expanded. Accordingly, speciality stores have sprung up all over the world to cater to customers that want authentic fairly-used luxury goods at low prices that are sometimes up to 80 per cent lower than the original prices. For exam-ple, several consignment stores on Rue Guisarde at the St Germain des Près district and others in the Ile Saint Louis district of Paris retail second-hand luxury products in excellent condition.

Also, websites that retail second-hand but authentic luxury goods have

Figure 7.1 *Mila and Eddie provides designer bag rental services. This addresses the 'throwaway fashion' attitude of consumers (August 2006)*

emerged, notably portero.com, which trades through the ebay portal. These websites have credibility because they operate on a company platform, rather than on an individual hawking position. The fairly-used luxury product trade is highly successful on the internet because it gives shoppers anonymity.

Effect 3: trend watching, trend tracking and luxury services

One of the main reasons that consumers have become marketing experts is their desire to be trendy at all times and in some cases, at all costs. The majority of luxury consumers now follow fashion trends religiously, which has led to their becoming self-fashion stylists. Their fashion knowledge has also led to an ability to interpret hidden branding and marketing messages that are targeted at their subconscious.

The need to be trendy is being fuelled by the mass media, notably fashion magazines and television shows, which hound consumers with fashion articles and features with non-stop lists and images of fashionable people. Also every season, multitudes of new fashion trends emerge, requiring different attitudes, moods and interpretations. Several brands have also developed pre-season collections, which sometimes conflict with the styles of the main collections. In addition, there is a continuous increase in the number of fashion brands around the world, with enticing product and services offerings. These factors have led to consumers being overloaded with fashion information and product choices. Consumers can hardly keep up with the frequent style changes in the fashion market. Consequently they seek a solution through tracking fashion and lifestyle trends. The information they obtain guides them in defining their own individual styles.

Trends information is increasingly found in the mass media and on the internet through fashion e-zines. Fashion magazines are often filled with product features of various luxury fashion brands and advice on how to wear them. Also, numerous websites and online fashion retailers offer free services on fashion styling and coordination. 'Style Advisers' and 'Style Consultants' have also become important roles in the fashion industry as a result of the growing consumer demand for trends services. Also the title of 'Style Icon', given to some celebrities has become as much a career as being an actor or musician. These avenues of trends information all provide consumers with the possibility of becoming stylish.

The need for fashion trends information has also extended from consumers to the luxury brands that provide the trends. This is because the luxury market has become highly competitive and brands are now required to be well-informed in order to stay ahead of the game. The trends information and analysis needs of luxury brands extends from consumer lifestyle trends to consumer attitudes towards fashion. These provide luxury brands with a framework to assess the consumers' potential interpretation and response to their products.

The demand for trend analysis by luxury brands has led to the emergence of a services sub-sector within the fashion industry, known as the 'Fashion Trend Service'. This service is provided by several companies like online-based Trendwatching.com, which supplies up-to-date information on consumer trends through individual trend scouts all over the world. Other companies like hintmag.com and jcreport.com offer fashion trends information through online magazines available by paid subscription. Yet other e-zines like Daily Candy provide fashion trends and news to the public for free. The fashion trend information service also extends to trend advice provided by the likes of Hong Kong-based Parisexchange.com. Another aspect of the trends service for consumers is Trend Analysis and Intelligence, being pioneered by London-based company, The Future Laboratory and Nice-based company, Style Vision. The utilization of fashion trends companies indicates that assessing consumer response is a key tool for the development of effective branding strategies.

Figure 7.2 *The luxury industry's leading information source,* Luxury Briefing Journal, *is available only by subscription through www.luxury-briefing.com. It addresses the luxury sector's need for relevant market information and analysis.*

Photography by Jonathan Glyn Smith

Figure 7.3
Quintessentially, the world's leading private members club and concierge service provides luxury consumers with up-to-date luxury fashion and lifestyle information through the Quintessentially magazine. This addresses the consumer need to be in the know about new trends.

In addition to trends tracking, several luxury services companies have emerged to provide services ranging from market information for both brands and consumers to concierge services for consumers. The information provided includes marketing intelligence, analysis and consumer lifestyle insights. Notable among these information sources are the pioneer luxury industry journal, *Luxury Briefing* (Figure 7.2), published by Atlantic Publishers, UK and available only by subscription; and High Net-Worth magazine, produced by London-based Ledbury Research.

Also, the world's leading private members' club and concierge service company, Quintessentially (Figure 7.3) provides a combination of private club and concierge services in addition to its magazine, *Quintessentially*, which is circulated among celebrities and the world's wealthy but is also available to the wider public by subscription.

Trend tracking is not a new concept in the fashion industry, as it has been practised as a part of marketing research for a long time. However, the current strong focus on trailing the rapid changes in the fashion sector by both consumers and brands has never been seen in the history of fashion. This is one of the effects of the new attitudes to luxury.

Effect 4: the new luxury brands

The entry barrier of the luxury fashion sector has been lowered, as pointed out earlier in this chapter. In the past, several decades were required for a new luxury brand to build its credibility and awareness among consumers. Today, however, the timeline has reduced substantially. The main factors that have contributed to this are the internet which provides rapid and uniform information to consumers worldwide making the creation of brand awareness easier; and the globalization of fashion tastes. Also, the increasing flexibility and experimental nature of luxury consumers increases the success potential of new luxury brands.

However, only a handful of the hundreds of brands launched annually are successful. The exceptional brands that have succeeded in establishing global awareness and credibility in the last two decades include British luxury leather-goods brand, Jimmy Choo; French luxury brand Paul & Joe; and British brand Ozwald Boateng. Also British brand Stella McCartney was launched in 2001, and in little over five years has achieved a global consumer following. Italian brand Piazza Sempione, launched in 1990, is also growing rapidly globally. Also highly successful Dolce & Gabbana is only 21 years old while Versace is a brand that is young at 28 years. These brands can be considered as being in their infancy when compared to brands like Hermès, which has a 168 years history, and Louis Vuitton which celebrated its 150 years in 2005. Despite the young age of the new brands, their level of success is immense, proving the point of the high success potential of new luxury brands.

Also in the current twenty-first century, two newly launched luxury brands currently apply strategies that make them brands-to-watch in the coming years. They are French leather-goods brand André Ross and the self-named brand of American fashion design icon Tom Ford. André Ross is based on the brand heritage of bespoke French craftsmanship, which is currently used to create products for a broader luxury consumer base. Tom Ford on the other hand has adopted a reverse positioning strategy of launching with lower-priced products like make-up, eyewear and fragrance rather than apparel and leather-goods collection.

Several other aspirational brands that have been launched in recent decades abound, all trying to create brand awareness and occupy a strong brand positioning in the market. Some of these brands will become successful while others will fail as a result of mistakes and unfeasible business strategies. However, the fact remains that adequate room has now been created for new brands to be launched in the current luxury fashion market without the back-up of a long history. Also new luxury brands currently have a high success potential with the application of appropriate strategies.

Effect 5: accessible luxury

Another important effect of the changing luxury scene is the increased accessibility of luxury fashion. Luxury fashion goods are now available to more consumers as a result of two major factors. First, the luxury consumer market has expanded and there are more people that can afford luxury goods, all over the world. Secondly, the product portfolio of luxury brands has undergone a modification as several products that previously had the 'exclusivity' attribute have been diffused to include lower-priced versions. Also, luxury brands have extended their product ranges to include lower-priced items like cosmetics, fragrance, eyewear and other accessories. These goods are designed to act as the brand's introductory points for new consumers and the retentive points for old consumers. Perfumes in particular play an important role in consumer relationship with the brand. It is considered the easiest point-of-entry product into the luxury market and has the fastest growth rate. It also generates high publicity, does not consume high capital, is a source of fast profits and has a long shelf-life and rapid stock turnover. Other aspects of the product extension include goods that reflect a 'lifestyle' such as furniture, interior decoration, restaurants and hotels. This product extension has broadened the scope of interaction between luxury brands and consumers. Consequently, there are now three distinct product groups in the luxury product portfolio:

(a) Lower-priced luxury products such as make-up, cosmetics, fragrance and writing materials.
(b) Medium-priced luxury products, such as restaurants, exclusive clubs, eyewear and in some cases wristwatches.
(c) Expensive luxury products such as leather-goods, apparel, jewellery, wristwatches, special edition products, hotels and spas.

Luxury brands usually launch their product range with expensive goods like leather products, which stamp their status of luxury. However, in order to access new consumers, both old and new brands now segment their offerings to include entry-level products like cosmetics, in addition to expensive products. An example of a brand that was launched with accessible luxury products such as eyewear is American brand, Tom Ford, which also has a co-branded cosmetics range with Estee Lauder. This product launch method is known as the reverse positioning strategy. Although it is an innovative way of launching a new brand and of entering new markets, it also raises the question of its suitability for the luxury goods sector.

Accessible luxury is also being spurred by specialist stores emerging all over the world, notably in New York, Paris and London. These stores would have been considered as junk stores twenty years ago but they are currently treasure islands for luxury consumers. They stock goods ranging from vintage apparel and accessories to designer home decoration pieces and other rare knick-knacks. Some of the stores have branded themselves as 'lifestyle concept' stores. An example is Collette located on Paris' Rue Saint Honoré, which stocks goods ranging from luxury branded clothes, accessories, make-up and cosmetics, books, CDs, DVDs and other funky lifestyle 'stuff'. The store has become both an institution and a tourist attraction. It also has an underground Water Bar that serves as a fashionable meeting point for savvy consumers. Stores like Collette provide an avenue for consumers to interact with luxury brands without the intimidation that is sometimes felt in the luxury brands' own stores.

Effect 6: intangible luxury

When the question, 'What is luxury?' was posed to several people, including professionals in the branding and luxury goods fields, their answers included intangible qualities such as time, family, health and well-being, rest, travel, peace, essence, desire and substance. Others say that luxury is a dream and this dream mainly comprises of intangible qualities that are lacking in consumers' lives. Yet others insist that luxury is now a question of personal perspective. These answers reflect two things. The first is that there is a change in the definition of what constitutes luxury for several consumers. The second is that the interpretation of luxury is now completely individual. The reasons for these changing definitions of luxury are fairly obvious.

The first reason is that consumers of the present generation have access to more wealth. They are much more likely to attain career success and wealth at early ages compared to their counterparts of previous generations. This is mainly as a result of the expansion of the corporate and business sectors due to global economic and technological advancement, which have created wealth acquisition avenues. The same group of consumers are also working more as a result of increased responsibilities. The implications include stress, chaos, lack of time, health problems and all the negative associations that come with being busy all the time. These effects are most evident among the group of consumers known as Young Urban Professionals (YUPs), High Net-Worth Individuals and Career Women with families. These groups of consumers desire an escape route from their chaotic lifestyles. As a result, they have come to perceive luxury as the intangible substances that they wish to have in their lives, such as simplicity, time, well-being, de-stressing services, freedom, space and peace of mind. Other notions of luxury by this group are elements that add true meaning, value and happiness to their lives, such as family, friends, community and charity work. These intangible qualities have become aspirations in the same manner that physical luxury goods remain aspirational goods for a large segment of the consumer population.

At the same time, luxury consumers desire innovative and inspiring luxury products to enable them to feel dynamic and alive. They view luxury as not necessarily the most expensive or the most lavish products, but the best that suits each individual and their outlook on life. Some wealthy luxury consumers also view luxury products like fine jewellery, well-crafted time-pieces and fast cars as conspicuous wastes. However, in general, the current luxury consumers use luxury products and services as sentimental and expressive tools. Consequently the luxury brand offering should offer an appropriate balance between the need levels of tangible and intangible benefits.

In addition to the intangible qualities that consumers currently relate to luxury, ethical and socially responsible practices are now linked with luxury brands. Current luxury fashion consumers have become morally conscious in addition to being intelligent and socially aware. These consumers are extending associated ethical practices to every aspect of their lifestyles, from the consumption of organic food, to the use of carbon-neutral products. They now read the labels on their clothes and are interested in the sources of the materials of luxury products and also the conditions under which they were manufactured. They expect the luxury brands that they endorse to show visible ethical practices and social responsibility. This factor has become an important strategic requirement for competitive advantage in the luxury market. For example, in 2005 the musician Bono, his wife Ali Hewson and New York designer Rogan Gregory, launched a socially conscious apparel brand called Edun. This fashion brand is based on the concept of fair trade and employment. The clothes are manufactured with only organic materials. Another fashion designer following this concept is Linda Loudermilk, who has an 'ecoluxury' apparel line made from organic and sustainable fabrics. The impressive consumer responses to these products and brands imply the high ethical value of luxury consumers.

One of the ways of effectively addressing the need of consumers for intangible qualities like purity and serenity is through extending a luxury brand's offering to include luxury services like hotels, restaurants and exclusive clubs. Luxury brands are reputed with appealing product attributes and these can be transferred to the service experience they offer consumers. For example, a consumer staying at the Palazzo Versace ought to experience an exceptional and rare service to fulfil their intangible needs.

In satisfying the intangible desires of consumers, it is important for luxury brands to emphasize their brand essence and integrity, irrespective of the product or service being offered. Also luxury brands need to readjust their practices to reflect the new luxury environment. This might include relinquishing certain old practices in favour of modern strategies that hold relevance for consumers. The new luxury requires creating the unexpected rather than the expected.

Effect 7: a borderline identity

As has been extensively discussed, the change in the luxury scene raises several questions about the real meaning of luxury. It also queries the criteria for defining the brands that can currently be tagged as authentic luxury brands and what they represent for luxury consumers.

In the previous luxury market scene, luxury brands were meant for a specific niche consumer group and there were only a handful of brands that could immediately be identified as luxury brands. This was the era when a three-tier pyramid could easily be drawn with luxury and prestige brands placed at the top-end, aspirational fashion brands placed at the middle level and mass market and supermarket brands placed at the lower level, as shown in Figure 7.4. Each of the levels addressed a specific social class in the consumer society. However, today the picture has changed.

In the current luxury environment, the market structure has been diluted so much that the pyramid is no longer relevant. For example, it would be difficult to place high-end brands with lower-priced diffusion lines or brands that collaborate with mass-market brands on the pyramid. Also, it would be inappropriate to categorize premium-mass fashion brands like Zara, Topshop and Gap as 'supermarket brands'. Also, sophisticated premium brands like Furla and Longchamp would be lost on the pyramid. Despite the current irrelevancy of the luxury pyramid structure, the following crucial questions remain unanswered:

1 Have luxury brands become mass brands as a result of increased availability and access to luxury goods?
2 Are fashion brands becoming luxury brands through elevating their branding and marketing strategies to reflect premium appeal?

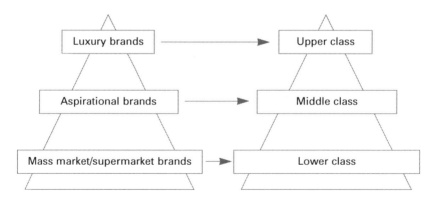

Figure 7.4 *The previous market hierarchy structure of the luxury goods sector in relation to customer strata in the society. This hierarchy has lost its relevance in the current market environment.*

3 Where can the lines between luxury, prestige, aspirational, premium and mass fashion brands be drawn?

There are no black and white answers to these questions. However, to lessen the confusion, some definitions will be given.

Luxury and prestige brands represent the highest form of craftsmanship and product quality and command a staunch consumer loyalty base that is not affected by trends. These brands create and set the seasonal fashion trends and have the ability to retail an item for €20,000 and another for €300 to different consumer groups. They are the epitome of prestige and are capable of pulling all of their consumers with them wherever they are located. Brands in this group include Bvlgari and Hermès, among others. True luxury and prestige brands do not utilize mass-market strategies in order to become mass-market brands. Rather, they have recognized the changes in the luxury marketplace and are attuning their strategies accordingly, without sacrificing their core heritage and brand essence.

Premium brands are those brands that aspire to become luxury and prestige brands but their marketing mix strategies are more attuned to a mass market, albeit a luxury mass market. The brands in this group are also sometimes referred to as **mass-premium** brands, **aspirational** brands, **mass-luxury** brands, **designer** brands or simply **high-end** brands. The group of premium brands has a broad scope, which makes narrowing them down challenging. Several of the brands in this group also have different levels of operations. Consequently they have been categorized as follows:

(a) High premium brands, such as Calvin Klein, Tommy Hilfiger and Longchamp, among numerous others.
(b) Medium premium brands like Lacoste, Furla and Lanvin, among several others.
(c) Low premium brands are brands like Zara, H&M and Gap, among others. This group can no longer be considered as merely fashion brands, in the same sphere as supermarket brands such as Wal-Mart and Tesco, as a result of the elevation of their offerings and strategies. The brands in this group are playing a key role in the 'trading-down' phenomenon of luxury consumers.

There are also several 'luxury' brands that have adopted strategies utilized by premium brands including licensing and end-of-season sales. However, this factor doesn't make them premium brands as their overall corporate strategies reflect luxury and prestige status. At the same time, implementing mass-focused strategies without effective control could lead to the eventual loss of the brand cachet.

The premium fashion brands segment has arguably witnessed the greatest changes in the consumer market. They are also facing aggressive competition from the higher-priced luxury and prestige brands and the lower priced mass-fashion brands.

Mass-fashion brands on the other hand are those that dress the masses. A recent evolution brought about by competition has also created a significant change in the way this category is viewed. Although brands in this group include supermarket ranges such as Wal Mart, Carrefour, Tesco and Asda; and other brands like the U.K.'s Primark and France's Tati, these brands are effectively implementing differentiation and are currently developing strategies to elevate their offerings.

The difference between luxury brands and fashion brands is not only in the marketing mix aspects of product quality and pricing. It also applies to availability and exclusivity of the products. Fashion brands are for the mass market, whether the products are of high quality or not. Luxury brands remain for a distinct market although this market has broadened. They are defined by high quality, differentiation and precision in product design and manufacture.

A brand is either a luxury brand or it is not. There is no in-between. If a brand does not set out to target the high-end market, then it would be difficult for it to become a luxury brand as a result of all the factors identified so far in this chapter.

So who are the true luxury brands?

The traditional view of luxury has been affected by the recent changes in the luxury market. Despite this, the true luxury and prestige brands remain, unwavering and uncompromising of their core values and continuously influence their consumers' thinking. These brands have also benefited from long histories, as heritage and tradition have always played a vital role in the luxury goods sector. New brands that have devised strategies that enable them act as old brands also fall within this group.

Luxury brands that desire to succeed in the marketplace must develop strategies that address the difficult paradox of the combination of exclusivity and availability and an appeal to many while appearing to be right for only a special few. They must remain relevant to the consumer population even as the market continues to change.

While I am not going to provide you with the easy solution of listing the true luxury brands, I can suggest a simple test that can be applied to ascertain whether a brand is a true luxury and prestige brand or not:

If you move the Louis Vuitton boutique 30km away from its flagship store on Avenue des Champs Elysées, will the consumer be ready to follow the brand to the new location? If you also move the H&M boutique on rue de Rivoli 30km away, will the consumer go an extra 30km for a pair of H&M trousers or will they find an alternative?

The answers you give to these two questions will help you define luxury and non-luxury brands.

How the future looks

In as little time as the next decade, the luxury marketplace will definitely be different from what it currently is. The causes and effects of the changes that have been evaluated so far are proof of the changing environment.

The current luxury environment requires a shift away from the product-focus strategy to the adoption of the consumer-focus strategy. This means making consumer needs the central point of brand strategy development. It also means that the future will be difficult for brands that are relaxed about innovation and understanding consumer needs. The future will also be less about tradition and sameness; and more about substance, originality and relevance, through continuous innovation. Consumers will expect to be taken through a seamless experience of everything that encompasses a luxury brand and not just its products and services. There will also be a level of brand attachment that will go beyond the current lifestyle scope, to a cultural phenomenon that will separate itself from commerce and lavishness. Therefore less will mean more and consumer emotion will replace product quantity and cost. Consumers will also continue to seek abstract forms of freedom and expression in fashion and will reject brands that seem apparently wealth and profit-driven and lacking in substance. This means that only the brands that show deeper meanings and foster simplicity in creativity will thrive.

Chris Sanderson, Creative Director of The Future Laboratory sums it up in his statement in an interview granted to *Luxury Briefing*:

> Nu-luxury invests much of its values and worth in brand intangibles – the magic of its offers, the experience of its brands, the uniqueness of its narrative and the emotional and psychological impact all these have on our senses. (*Luxury Briefing*, October 2005)

In the near future, the consumer society will place more value on ethical and moral issues including environmental protection concerns. They will respect the luxury brands that 'give back' to the society and support ethical production. This outlook will also be directly transferred to the feelings that consumers will have regarding their expenditure towards luxury purchases. Consumers will seek an honest justification for the lavish purchases of luxury goods. The recognition of moral and ethical values will affect all high net-worth consumers including those that still need to assess their affordability of luxury goods. This means that in addition to a brand's offerings, consumers will need a concrete and morally right 'background story' to endorse a brand.

In addition to the consumer outlook towards luxury goods, the way consumers will shop in the future will be different. Internet and communications technology will enhance online shopping, trading and borrowing of luxury goods. Mobile shopping, which is already a high growth retail business in Japan, will also see significant growth in other parts of the world, notably the US. This will result in an increased pace of retail and commerce, leading consumers to expect and demand more from luxury brands.

Personal service and attention to consumer needs will become a key success factor for brands that pay attention to consumers. Also consumers will want to see real value and essence in the luxury brands that they endorse and will desire products that have enduring value. Consumers will not have the patience to decode unclear brand messages and will move on to the next choice if confused. This will make them seek the brands that hold true meaning in terms of luxury and prestige. The brands that will feel the impact most are those that are 'stuck in the middle' without appropriate positioning as neither luxury nor premium brands. Luxury, premium and mass fashion brands need to work harder to maintain their competitive position.

The list below provides a quick overview of what to expect from the fashion market in the near future:

1   Second-hand luxury goods will become more fashionable and more purchased.
2   Specialist stores with rare products will become more successful.
3   Online retailing and trading between luxury brands and consumers and among consumers themselves will thrive.
4   Consumers will recognize and patronize indigenous designers especially in Britain, China and Japan.
5   Consumers will demand more of personal shopping and a total immersion experience with luxury brands.
6   Customized and bespoke goods will become the order of the day.
7   Uniquely handcrafted products will continue to remain popular among consumers.
8   Environmental awareness will drive consumers to seek knowledge of the materials used for their products and to support brands with visible ethical practices.
9   The fusion of luxury fashion with art, travel and lifestyle will be more attractive to consumers.
10 Luxury brands that ignore the intangible needs of consumers will lose loyalty.
11 The Chinese market will have a great positive impact on the sales of goods from Western luxury brands in the short term, but in the long term

China will promote and support native creative talent both acquired locally and abroad like Barney Cheng and Jimmy Lam. The country's size and vigorous nature are ingredients for the success of local talent.

12 Mobile shopping will grow in different parts of the world.

13 Innovative brands will advance marketing and Customer Relations techniques through technology such as Neuromarketing.

The strategic challenge luxury brands face in the light of these factors is that it is time to get rid of the old strategy where the product was king that drove the company forward. New luxury is less about the brand's tangible attributes such as the product design and packaging and store location. Instead, the New Luxe embodies intangible brand associations like the complete magic of each consumer's experience and the unique impact of the brand on the consumer's emotions and subconscious.

Finally, luxury brands also ought to recognize that mass fashion brands have created an escalated portfolio of offerings that sometimes represent a more justifiable value to consumers than those of luxury brands. Mass brands have also fine-tuned their strategies, which sometimes surpass the standards that were previously set by luxury brands. In order to maintain their luxury status however, luxury brands must sustain a distance from mass fashion brands to avoid becoming commonplace. At the same time, luxury brands should visibly embrace the mass fashion brands as both partners and collaborators because mass products now complement luxury products creating a co-existence between the two product categories.

Chapter 8
Customize me!

'The one word definition of true luxury in the 21st century will be
"bespoke".'
> Daniele de Winter, CEO, Daniele de Winter Cosmetics, Monaco

Henry Ford, the man who founded the Ford Motors Group and brought auto-
mobile ownership to the masses, famously made a statement in the early
twentieth century about the colour and design choices that his customers
could have of the Ford Model T car. He said:

'The customer can have any colour as long as it is black.'

His unenthusiastic comment about providing customers with multiple colour
choices of the Ford Model T (all the cars were black) was made mainly from
a technical and manufacturing viewpoint. This is because, at the time, production flexibility in terms of multiple colours, designs, styles and other forms of
customization had very high time and monetary costs that would have
increased the prices of the cars substantially. However, Ford's competitor,
General Motors, came along and by the middle of the 1920s was able to offer
customers multiple colours and annual model changes at no additional cost.
Through this method of product variety, they encroached on the market share
of Ford and soon surpassed Ford in popularity and sales.

Fast forward 90 years to 2006 and, quite startlingly, several business practitioners still think like Henry Ford did in the 1910s, despite the enormous
advancement in technology. It is not uncommon to find executives in the
luxury goods sector that still believe that standardized goods are manufactured at low cost while customized goods are manufactured at high cost. The
same perception is widespread in other sectors.

Now, fast forward again to 2050 and think of what the consumer society
would feel like if we were all treated like the character Tom Cruise played in
the futuristic American movie *Minority Report*. When he visited a shopping
centre, he was greeted with his first name by digital screens. Computerized
customer services teams were also at his constant service, and while he
strolled around the stores, he was asked if he would like the same product as
the ones he had previously purchased? This implies that a record of his
personal tastes, preferences and shopping habits was kept and consulted for
his benefit. It also shows that the stores understood his needs and applied

them in their offerings to him. He was recognized, respected and appreciated as a customer. This scenario would be a consumer's dream world and should be the luxury brand manager's ideal world.

The reality we currently live in is perhaps decades or even centuries away from the techno-savvy world portrayed in *Minority Report*. However, the global marketplace has evolved from the production-based Henry Ford era to that which utilizes advanced technology in several facets of commerce, especially in streamlining products and services according to individual tastes. This includes the customization of products and services on a broad level for an extensive consumer base.

The concept of customization currently exists in several business sectors on different levels. For example, several companies in the computer sector such as Dell provide customized products to consumers through the internet. This type of customization is on a broad level because it addresses a mass consumer base. In the luxury goods industry, customized products are currently provided on a narrow level to a small and select segment of consumers. The industry is yet to adopt customization on a broad base.

Customization of products and services is one of the key requirements of current luxury consumers. The previous chapters of this book have repeatedly emphasized the importance of understating the luxury customer and designing products and services to exceed their expectations. This is because luxury consumers are the biggest opportunity luxury brands have to gain competitive edge. This cannot be said often enough. The luxury consumer desires an exceptional and exclusive total experience with luxury brands and this can be achieved through products and services customization. Luxury consumers are also becoming more individual in their fashion tastes and increasingly seeking customization as an outlet to their fashion creativity.

Customization ensures that consumers are ushered into an exclusive experience area where their individual preferences are addressed on a broad and equal level. It provides them with the empowerment to apply their imagination and desire to be in control of their choices. It also enhances their satisfaction and creates a deeper relationship with the brands, paving the way for brand loyalty. Customization also provides luxury brands with the opportunity to tap into the intellectual capital of their consumers and to understand their design expectations better.

The luxury fashion goods sector is yet to make customization a core aspect of the corporate strategy. Currently, several luxury brands offer bespoke products and services but this service is often reserved to a narrow client base of very important personalities (VIPs) or very important clients (VICs). The reality is that every luxury fashion consumer has become a VIP and desires to be treated as one. Consumers perceive the offerings of luxury brands to be exceptional, and they desire to be treated as exceptional people by luxury brands. One of the ways of treating all customers as exceptional and endearing them to a brand is through offering an exceptional experience through customization. Also customized products can now be manufactured en masse as advanced technology has made their production cheaper. Although this strategy is now feasible for luxury goods, several luxury brands seem reluctant to adopt mass customization and determined to remain in Henry Ford's world of mass production. It is now past the time to rethink this stance.

The history of the luxury goods sector shows a strong link to customization, although mass production later overtook this. It is interesting to note that the majority of the successful luxury brands of today were started by skilled artisans and craftsmen who produced made-to-fit goods mainly by hand, with the assistance of a limited number of machines. This process was rewarding but also time-consuming, expensive and labour intensive. As time progressed and innovative manufacturing techniques were developed, luxury brands adopted the use of machines that produced more goods at less costs without compromising the product qualities and style. This however led to the standardization and uniformity of goods. Several brands, however, retained a limited range of products that continued to be manufactured by hand. These products are currently classified as 'bespoke' or 'made-to-order'. They usually have a high price cost (approximately €5,000 for a Hermès bespoke Birkin bag); and high time cost (six to eighteen months waiting period for a Hermès bespoke Birkin bag and approximately four months for a Gucci made-to-order men's shoe).

However, the current provisions of technology have made it possible to produce more personalized goods using mass production techniques without substantial additional costs. Companies that manufacture goods in other categories, including mass fashion brands, effectively utilize these techniques to optimize production and sales. Luxury brands are, however, yet to apply advanced systems in the production of customized goods for a mass client base.

The view of some luxury practitioners regarding mass customization is that it is at odds with the need to retain the 'exclusivity' attribute of luxury brands. It has been argued that if customers are provided with the tools to customize their products, the products might lose their 'superiority' appeal. This rationale is however negligible as luxury goods are currently purchased by a mass group of consumers globally and luxury brands have increased their production capacities to welcome this 'mass' consumer base. It is, however, purely logical to streamline the operations approaches of mass production to include one of the major needs of this mass consumer group, which is customization. Satisfying the needs of consumers has nothing to do with diminishing a brand's attributes but everything to do with enhancing the image and equity of the brand.

Previously, the product design and manufacturing process of luxury brands was driven by standardized products and services, parallel markets and long product lifecycles. Today, the situation is the reverse and the consumer has become the strongest market force in the luxury market. These consumers exhibit several strong attributes including the need for personal attention through the products and services they're offered. Luxury brands have to wake up to the real consumer world. The rules of the game have changed.

The consumer market has evolved from a mass-production based one to a market where products and services need to be streamlined according to individual consumer needs. To assume that the luxury marketplace is still a global homogeneous scene will be to live in bygone fiction. The days of uniformity and sameness are over. Individual consumer tastes have risen above semblance. These consumer tastes are also no longer predictable. A European City Mayor has the same likelihood of riding around the city on a bicycle or in the public underground train as a blue-collar worker has of using his/her earnings to shop at Chanel. Customers must be thought of as individuals with varying needs and not continuously grouped together as a bunch of 'luxury brand loyalists'. Today, the key to success in the luxury business is to understand the consumer and the market. This however is easier said than done.

What is customization?

Customization is simply the adaptation of goods and services according to individual consumer needs. It is the tailoring of the offerings of a company to provide multiple choices and variety in such a way that every consumer finds exactly what they are looking for. Customization is not the same as product variety, neither is it the same as personalization. Creating customized goods from the existing product portfolio is different from launching multiple or seasonal product designs. Also, customization is different from personalization. While personalization involves the adaptation of either existing or yet-to-be-produced goods to particular individual demands, such as name inscription on products or bespoke goods commission; customization involves goods adaptation that can be done en masse. Personalization is, however, a part of the customization process.

Mass customization is the production and sale of highly individual products and services on a bulk scale, to a mass market. In other words, it is the provision of customized products and services to every consumer who desires so. It involves using mass production techniques and economies of scale processes to manufacture a larger variety of products at lower costs and capture more personal style needs of customers. Writer and notable proponent of mass customization, B. Joseph Pine calls this 'Economies of Scope' in his book, *Mass Customization: The New Frontier in Business Competition*. Economies of scope involve companies saving money on a wide range of possibilities in products and services offerings, in the same way that mass production saves costs through economies of scale.

Although it might seem that customization cannot be applied to a mass market and at a similar low cost level as mass production, it is possible for companies, including luxury brands, to achieve the benefits associated with mass production through applying mass customization techniques. This can be done through resource sharing and allocation on standard components, which can further be utilized to create variety in the end product.

Customization works on three levels. First, a wide variety of product designs, styles, colours and materials that appeal to a broad taste level should be available to the consumer public. Secondly, this range of goods should be easily modified and adapted according to specific consumer requirements such as providing multiple leather and hardware choices for a particular leather goods range. Thirdly, customers should also be able to add personalized features to their chosen products such as their names or short messages on specific product parts. These services or features could be provided at either no cost or with an additional small fee. This is one of the ways to guarantee that the customer receives the optimum satisfaction, which should be the target of luxury brands.

A simple illustration of customized versus standardized service is the customer services letter that often accompanies the delivery of ordered luxury products. I once made an order from a major luxury brand which arrived two weeks late, accompanied by a letter of appreciation from the Customer Services Manager. The letter was obviously a standard letter that is sent to all customers addressing them as 'Dear Customer', instead of with the customer's name as would be expected from a luxury brand. Had this letter addressed me as 'Dear Uche', instead of 'Dear Customer', it could have been elevated from the status of 'toneless' and 'drab' to appreciation for recognizing me as a valuable customer. This simple action would have incurred the brand no additional costs in terms of time, paper and ink. This attitude of customer generalization is prevalent among several luxury brands, despite the availability of advanced business systems that aid customization.

Who wants to be customized?

If you ask a randomly selected manager from a luxury brand to name one of the most prominent traits shown by the current luxury consumers, they're likely to tell you that it is individualism and independence of choice. It is absurd that several luxury brands are aware of this need and yet continuously ignore it. It seems like something that is read in journals and newspapers and discarded, only to be dug out of the brain when required to give smart answers to delicate questions.

Customization and personalization of products, services and also web pages rank highest among the yearnings of the current luxury consumer. Consumers seem to be going around screaming, '*I want personal attention!*' and luxury brands seem not to be listening. Although some luxury brands offer bespoke services (even though much of these need to be seriously upgraded and updated!) but they either forget to tell their consumers about this service or they guard it like a treasure reserved for two clients in a year. Consumers want to be treated as important through the provision of choices in product and service offerings. They want to feel special. They want to be provided with the opportunity to show their high knowledge level and *savoir-faire* in fashion. They want to be given the power to request and choose what appeals precisely to their individual tastes. They want courtesy and uncompromised product and service quality. These are all achievable through product customization and majority of luxury consumers are not getting this service from luxury brands. It is also important to note that the same group of consumers are getting customized services in other product categories such as in information technology (with Dell and Apple), sportswear (with Levi's and Nike), fast food (with Subway), cars (BMW) and services like telecommunications and banking. These benefits have increased their expectation of customized goods from luxury brands.

The current strongly defined customer tastes have been aided by the digital revolution, which has exposed consumers to style options and propelled their thinking and expectations to a fast lane. This is more apparent with the steady growth of the size of the online luxury consumer market. This factor has made customization an important strategic tool for competitive leverage and a key feature in product and brand development.

The luxury consumer need for recognition and appreciation, which has become more apparent in the last decade, has been recognized by independent companies who have created parallel services. A notable example is the French company, Soirée de Star, which offers consumers a package of customized celebrity 'frills' such as limousine rides to staged 'red carpet' events, complete with photographers and fans. Although these customized offerings are illusive in nature and expensive in cost, they provide evidence of the consumer need to be courted and treated as special collaborators. Luxury consumers have evolved from using luxury goods as a platform of defining themselves, to accommodating luxury products in their independent styles. This emphasizes the need for customization.

An example of a fashion brand that has responded to the consumer need of customization in an efficient manner, which luxury brands ought to emulate, is demin brand Levi's. The brand provides customers with an option to customize denim trousers before purchase on its website, through the 'Jeanfinder' feature (Figure 8.1). The tools that aid this service include colour selection, size, style, fit preference, cut preference and leg style options. Levi's also encourages customers to be creative in styling their jeans and sharing their creativity ideas with other consumers on the website. The innovation of Levi's in product customization is an excellent strategy that enhances brand affiliation with consumers.

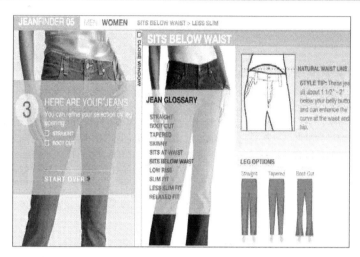

Figure 8.1 *Denim brand Levi's provides mass customized product services through its innovative 'Jeanfinder' feature on its website (May 2006)*

What are the benefits of customization?

Mass customization brings multiple benefits to companies and to consumers. The most prominent of these are increased customer satisfaction and lower total production costs and time. Increased customer satisfaction is achieved through empowering customers with the tools to choose their products and services the way they precisely want them. This is one of the quickest routes to brand loyalty, repeat purchases and increased sales. Customization also reduces the risks of comparative shopping with competing brands; and paves the way for production flexibility and quick responsiveness for companies. Mass customization focuses on customer satisfaction at low costs, while mass production focuses on lowering operations costs and increasing efficiency and volume. They both guarantee the same results: increased sales!

Other benefits of customization are shown in the following list:

1 Closer relationships with consumers.
2 Reduced waste or complete waste elimination of materials.
3 Production of optimum quality goods.
4 Increased labour productivity.
5 Higher labour flexibility.
6 Improved production processes.
7 Lower overhead costs.
8 Integration of innovation and production.
9 Shorter product cycles.
10 Higher sales turnover.

11 Greater profitability.

12 Higher success potential of New Product Development projects.

How can luxury brands customize goods and services?

The luxury industry has several misconceptions regarding mass customization of goods and services. The most prominent of these misleading ideas is that mass customization increases operations costs. Another misapprehension is that the 'supposed' high costs incurred through customization will automatically be transferred to the price tags of the end products, making the products more expensive for consumers. There is also the doubt that luxury consumers will be willing to pay more for customized goods.

The first assumption, which is that customization equals higher operations expenditure, is wrong. This is because advanced interactive technologies such as the internet can be used to identify specific product requirements and to manufacture them using automated systems. This system applies similar economies of scale advantage of mass production. So instead of higher costs, mass customization actually lowers production costs in the long run!

The second assumption, which is that the 'supposed' higher operations expenditure incurred through customization will automatically mean an increase in the price of the end products, is also wrong. This is because the same systems that are used in mass production can be adjusted to produce the standard or basic components that are required for mass customization. The question of higher product prices does not arise.

The final assumption, which is that consumers might not be willing to pay more for customized luxury goods, is wrong as well. This is because customization is highly dependent on choice and selection and not an option imposed on consumers like standardized goods. A consumer who opts for customization knows exactly what appeals to them. This means that choice would rank above cost for the consumer, making customization a strong selling factor. When consumers choose customized products, their level of expectation is higher than that of the consumer that chooses mass-produced goods. This higher expectation is also accompanied by an envisaged higher price. The price difference between customized and standardized goods should however be minimal.

The mass customization formula can be applied to luxury goods at little cost difference from the current cost of mass production. This naturally should not affect the prices that consumers would pay for the goods, although luxury consumers are willing to pay more for mass customized goods, if required. For example if a consumer can purchase a handbag for $2,000, they will likely be willing to pay an additional $50 to have their component choices or personalized message embossed on the bag!

As previously highlighted, advanced computer-aided technologies currently provide companies with the opportunity to customize virtually any product. Technology also creates the possibility of producing higher quality goods; therefore luxury brands will not compromise their quality standards by adopting mass customization techniques. In addition, mass customization allows the manufacture of products in smaller batches without substantial cost difference. This is an advantage for luxury brands as they can maintain a fast design turnover while customizing goods.

The model of mass customization of luxury goods has also been recognized by several consumer and business analysts, academics and practitioners. Amsterdam-based Trends and Consumer Research company, Trendwatching.com termed the concept 'Massclusivity' which is a combination of the words 'Mass' and 'Exclusivity'. London-based Trend Information and Consumer Insight company, The Future Laboratory, calls it 'Masstige', which combines the words 'Mass' and 'Prestige'. These two companies recognize two underlying factors, which are the existence of a mass consumer base and the need to feed these mass consumers with special goods and services; that is exclusive and prestigious offerings through customization.

According to Trendwatchers, *massclusivity* simply means 'exclusivity for the masses'. This is mainly achieved through understanding the driving force behind the mass consumer need for exclusive products. As earlier indicated, the major factor driving this need is the immense consumer desire for respect, privilege and choices. This partly arises from the increased access that luxury consumers have to customized products and enhanced customer services in other categories of goods. Since the same consumers are already exposed to customization, they transfer the same expectation to the luxury goods category.

The Future Laboratory defines *Masstige* as offering prestigious goods and services to a mass consumer base. One of the ways of providing this is through bespoke services in the form of personalized and customized goods, without compromising the design and quality features. Consumers desire recognition and evidence that their needs are important to luxury brands. They increasingly look for these qualities in the offerings of luxury brands.

Several luxury brands currently offer customized product services to a select clientele but, often, customers are required to wait for several weeks or months for delivery of the goods. More importantly, a large proportion of the mass consumer population who are yearning for this service are unaware of its existence at luxury brands. This is because the concept of mass customization has not been fully introduced by luxury brands. The majority of the luxury brands that offer customization services continue to adopt the outdated bespoke made-to-order approach for a limited client group rather than the mass customization model for a mass client base. It's no wonder that the mass luxury consumer population feels that the qualities of recognition and respect are scarce among luxury brands.

The need that consumers have expressed for customization is also being exploited and addressed by companies in the new extended segments of luxury goods and services such as hotels and spas. A noteworthy example is the customized package offered by two London hotels, The Metropolitan and The Halkin, which provides guests with in-house appointments to order bespoke goods from a host of luxury brands, including Mulberry and Philip Treacy. Also luxury brand Ermenegildo Zegna is reputed to be obsessed with tracking customer preferences through CRM technology and providing products and services to suit their needs. This has led to a reinforced emphasis on customized and bespoke services to a broad consumer base as a part of the brand's core offering. Also, new luxury brand André Ross was launched on the core concept of bringing bespoke quality goods to a broad consumer base. Ralph Lauren and Tommy Hilfiger also provide all consumers with tools to customize a range of their products through their websites. The features include the inscription of customer-chosen monograms on the polo shirts for men, women, children and babies.

There are different ways that luxury products can be customized by luxury brands. As previously mentioned, several luxury brands currently provide bespoke products and services of varying scales to a select clientele. These services, however, come at very high time and monetary costs, which are often out of reach or unavailable to all the luxury consumers that desire them. Luxury brands can make product customization accessible to a broader client base through adapting the product development, manufacturing, marketing and delivery systems. A few recommended methods of customization are provided in the following sections.

Method 1   customizing standardized products

The product portfolio of luxury brands features goods found in the permanent or seasonal collections. These products, although differing in colour, style and design, form a part of the standardized goods that luxury brands provide to their mass consumers. They are purchased off the counter and the choices that consumers have regarding these products are restricted to colour, size and sometimes cost.

Customizing standardized products could be exploited in two ways. The first approach is to develop products that can be easily customized. In this case, products are manufactured with the intention of making component adjustments or modifications possible in a short time space. The second technique is to provide customization for already existing products. As an illustration, we will use the Louis Vuitton 'Passy' ladies bag (Figure 8.2). As at the time of writing, the bag existed in one leather type (the Epi), two size choices (large and small), two colour choices (red and black) and two price points (€800 and €950). This provides the consumer with three choice options of the bag (size, colour and price). The choice variety could however be made

luxury fashion branding

Figure 8.2 *The Louis Vuitton Passy bag exists in one material and two-colour, size and price choices, limiting consumers to a standardized product. Some of the alternative material choices that could be used by consumers to customize and modify whole or parts of the bag include the monogram canvas and other materials used by Louis Vuitton. This strategy could also be applied to other products.*

multiple if consumers are provided with the opportunity to modify this bag using other materials existing in the product range, such as the Monogram Multicolore, the Suhali leather, the Monogram canvas, the Damier canvas and so on. There could also be the possibility of combining several materials and components to customize this bag. This might compose of using different body materials, hardware materials and attachments such as logo-ed hardware parts. The possibilities for customization are endless.

The processes of customizing standardized products and developing customizable products are not limited to design, production and sales. This process affects the complete value chain of a luxury brand, from product development and manufacture to marketing, retailing and delivery. The value chain is a business analytical framework, developed by notable business expert Michael Porter. It aids in the evaluation of specific aspects of a

Development	Production	Retailing	Delivery
Standardized products and services	Standardized products and services	Customized products and services produced with standardized methods	Both customized and standardized products and services

Figure 8.3 *The changes that occur in the value chain during the customization of standardized products and services*

Source: Adapted from B. Joseph Pine II (1997) *Mass Customization: The New Frontier for Business Competition.*

Note: Coloured areas indicate changes.

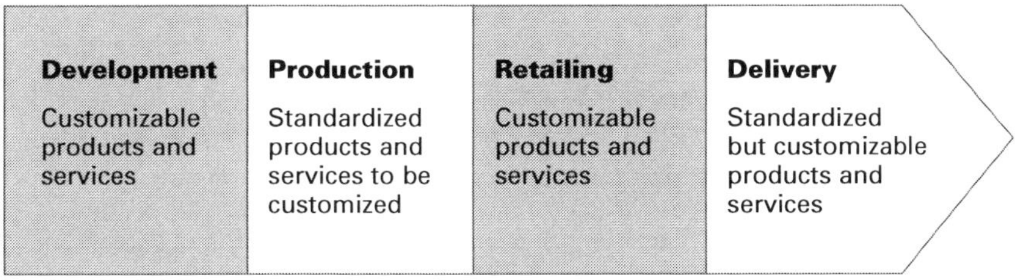

Development	Production	Retailing	Delivery
Customizable products and services	Standardized products and services to be customized	Customizable products and services	Standardized but customizable products and services

Figure 8.4   *The changes that occur in the value chain during the creation of customizable products and services*
Source: As Figure 8.3.
Note: Coloured areas indicate changes.

company's internal processes and activities that contribute to the creation of value to customers and competitive advantage to the company.

The impact of the method of customizing standardized products and producing customizable products on the value chain of the average luxury brand is illustrated in Figures 8.3 and 8.4.

Method 2   point of delivery customization

Products and services can also be customized at the point of sale or delivery. This can be done in the physical retail store or through the online boutique. This method is most efficient through rapid and quick modification of products and services. Examples include personalized packaging choices, printing and delivery of personalized 'thank-you' notes to customers at the payment point and the already cited Customer Relations letter, which could be personalized instead of the classical mistake of addressing consumers as 'Dear Customer'.

On the product level, goods can be modified according to individual tastes at the time of ordering, the point of payment and the point of delivery. In this case, the products are manufactured with the view of possible alteration during the 'fast' customization process. These products would normally have a feature that can easily be modified to turn them into customized finished products. The feature could be an aspect of apparel such as attachments like buttons, sequins, pockets and message prints; an accessory such as eyeglasses lenses; external attachments to leather goods such as straps and logo-ed hardware; timepiece straps; charms for bracelets and pendants (Figure 8.6) and earring attachments, among many others.

A noteworthy example of the effective application of point-of-delivery customization is not surprisingly outside the luxury fashion sector. Computer technology software company Apple provides online customers with the possibility of customizing their Apple iPod with a short message at no additional cost (Figure 8.5). After selecting the desired product in the e-store, the customer is given a choice of customizing their iPod before payment. If this option is selected, the customer is provided with a tool to provide a personalized message of up to 54 characters over two lines on the reverse of their chosen iPod. A preview tool is also provided to the customer to glimpse the customized end-product. This customization service is made possible through the application of laser embossing inscription technology on the standardized iPod. Although opting for this feature increases the delivery time from 24 hours to 1–2 business days, the short time cost becomes almost irrelevant for consumers because the option of personalization compensates for this. Apple might not be a luxury fashion brand, but the level of customized service offered to its customers is worthy of emulation by luxury brands.

The Apple online store provides the online shopper with the tools to customize their iPod with personal messages. There are also ideas and suggested topics and phrases for the personalized messages, categorized according to subject and occasion.

Point-of-delivery customization affects a company's value chain on the levels of product

Figure 8.5 *Apple provides point-of-sale customization through an online tool to personalize the iPod before purchase from its website, www.apple.com (June 2006). Image courtesy of Apple Source www.apple.com*

Figure 8.6 *The individual charms on certain products such as Louis Vuitton jewellery are easily customizable by consumers at the point of sale or delivery to add a special touch to customer experience.*

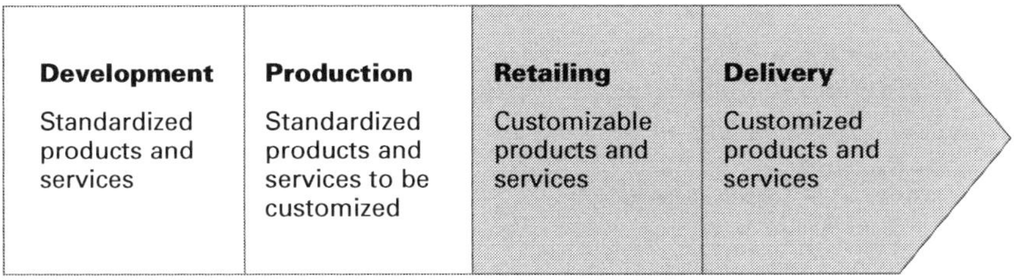

Development	Production	Retailing	Delivery
Standardized products and services	Standardized products and services to be customized	Customizable products and services	Customized products and services

Figure 8.7   *The value chain changes in the point-of-sale customization of products and services*

Source: Adapted from B. Joseph Pine II (1997) *Mass Customization: The New Frontier for Business Competition.*

Note: Coloured areas indicate changes.

retailing and delivery. The customized service can be provided within the hour of purchase or within a few days after the purchase, in which case the product should be delivered straight to the consumer to maintain the seamless luxury experience. The impact of point-of-sale customization on the value chain is shown in Figure 8.7.

Method 3   customizing the retail shopping experience

Retail shopping forms an intricate part of the luxury consumer's total experience with the brand, and the shopping experience can be customized according to customer preferences. Consumers have become increasingly individual in their tastes and inclinations and have differing and changing needs during shopping. These needs are now too varied and unpredictable. The apparent common consumer indicators such as age or gender are no longer adequate for grouping or measuring consumer retail needs. For example, logic might tell a sales representative in a luxury store that a 70-year-old consumer would require shopping assistance and a 27-year-old might not. However, the reality could easily be that the 70-year-old might have a crisply clear idea of her taste as a result of years of experience in luxury shopping. She could also have preferences for her shopping style such as a penchant for trunk shows. On the other hand, the 27-year-old consumer might prefer style advice from a shopping assistant in the store. It is risky to assume that shopping styles can be predetermined.

The most effective manner of discovering consumer preferences is to question them directly or to provide an opportunity for customers to indicate them. One method of implementing this is to provide a wide range of shopping options for a broad customer base including trunk shows, pre-collection previews, exclusive customer events and home shopping. The second method is to ask customers their preferences for shopping and to allow them to

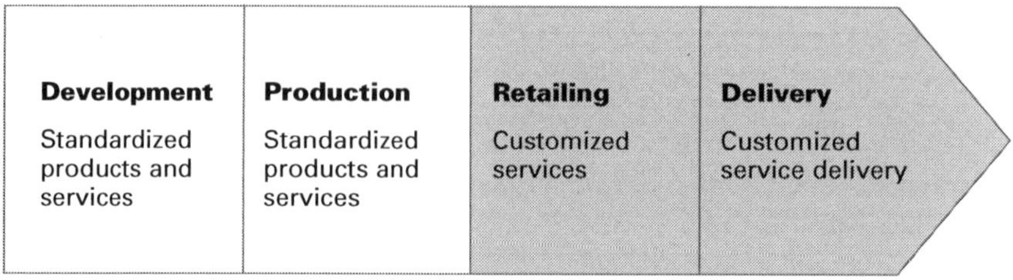

Development	Production	Retailing	Delivery
Standardized products and services	Standardized products and services	Customized services	Customized service delivery

Figure 8.8 *Changes in the value chain during the creation of customizable products and services*

Source: Adapted from B. Joseph Pine II (1997) *Mass Customization: The New Frontier for Business Competition.*

Note: Coloured areas indicate changes.

customize their shopping style according to these preferences. This information could be registered in a customer database and retrieved when necessary. Innovative airlines have utilized this system for decades in streamlining their services to customers. Airline passengers are often asked to select their in-flight meal and seat preferences during flight reservations or registration for frequent flier programmes. This information is stored in the customer database and each time the customer purchases a ticket from the airline, their customized preferences are automatically recognized and applied in the services that are offered to them. Some luxury brands such as Burberry provide a variety of shopping choices including trunk shows for a broad customer base although this feature is yet to be applied in customized shopping.

Customizing the shopping experience has an impact on a company's value chain, as shown in Figure 8.8.

Method 4   producing bespoke goods

French luxury cosmetics and fragrance brand Guerlain has been creating exclusive bespoke fragrances for more than two centuries and continues to do so at the Maison Guerlain on Paris' Avenue des Champs Elysées. The process of creating personalized fragrance involves close collaboration with the client to identify their personality, scent preferences and scent memories. This information is used to create the final product, packaged and presented in a Baccarat bottle. The process takes approximately three months and costs an average of €15,000. Needless to say, it is out of the reach of numerous luxury consumers. Guerlain also provides its fragrance made-to-order services to the masses through its mass customization service called the '*Speed Perfumery*' service. In this case, customers choose customized perfumes from six already made scents, which are packaged for them. This is a typical example of the stage of bespoke product provision at most luxury brands.

customize me!

Bespoke services are also provided by other luxury brands. Gucci has a renowned custom-built service for its leather goods collection, available to both male and female customers; Ermenegildo Zegna provides excellent made-to-measure product services to a wide clientele; and the list goes on to include Louis Vuitton, Prada and Armani, among many others. At the same time, several other luxury brands have shunned bespoke services as a result of the inkling that it is a declining retail service that is on the verge of disappearance. This wrong view could have a negative impact on luxury brands that intend to erase bespoke services from their offerings.

Made-to-measure goods have been a core aspect of luxury branding for a long time. However, as previously highlighted, the current level of bespoke services available from the majority of luxury brands is exclusive and restricted. While exclusivity is important in maintaining the prestige aura of the brand, retaining a limited bespoke service without providing a parallel service to a broader consumer base spells of old-fashioned aristocracy. This element is contrary to the attributes that modern luxury consumers seek to identify with.

A luxury brand that has struck a balance between providing exclusive bespoke services and taking customization to the masses, is British leather goods brand, Anya Hindmarch (Figure 8.9). The brand provides a package that addresses the customization yearning of the new luxury consumer and at the same time appeals to the bespoke nostalgia of the old luxury consumer. The brand, which was launched in 1993, offers customized services through two main categories in its product portfolio. The first is the bespoke range called '*Be a Bag*', which provides customers with the opportunity to transpose their personal photographs onto a bag, made of different materials. This

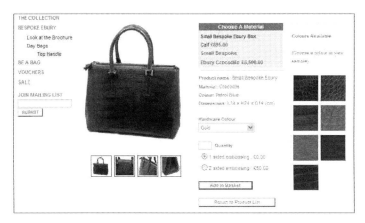

Figure 8.9 *Anya Hindmarch provides one of the most efficient bespoke services in the luxury sector, through the Bespoke Ebury (above) and the Be A Bag (not shown) collections. The brand has effectively combined the innovation of product customization and personalization provided through its website, to enhance customer satisfaction (May 2006).*

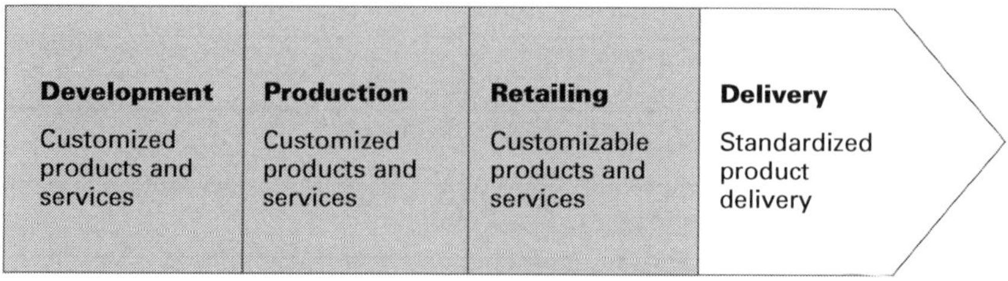

Development	Production	Retailing	Delivery
Customized products and services	Customized products and services	Customizable products and services	Standardized product delivery

Figure 8.10 *The changes in the value chain during the provision of bespoke products and services*

Source: Adapted from B. Joseph Pine II (1997) *Mass Customization: The New Frontier for Business Competition.*

Note: Coloured areas indicate changes.

product costs an average of £200 with a waiting period of approximately three working days. This bespoke service is targeted at a broad consumer group.

The second bespoke range is the more exclusive '*Bespoke Ebury*'. It offers customers the opportunity to provide a message that is discreetly embossed onto the leather of a bag, in silver or gold, in the buyer's own handwriting. If the bag is intended as a gift, the name of the person it has been made for is also embossed on the bag. A wide variety of materials, colours and hardware choices are provided for this. Each bag has a unique number with a record of the maker and the batch of skin it was made from. This bespoke collection is premium-priced, ranging from £800 to above £6,000, depending on the materials used. There is also a waiting time of four months for delivery of the Bespoke Ebury. Although the high cost of the Bespoke Ebury narrows its market, the bespoke services of the brand are available to all consumers and can be ordered through a few clicks of the mouse on the brand's website.

The provision of bespoke services affects the company's value chain on the levels of product development, manufacturing and retailing (Figure 8.10). This is sometimes extended to the delivery of the products, but since bespoke products already utilize a complete customized process they are often delivered using standardized methods.

Method 5   customizing the online experience

One of the most efficient and cost-effective ways of providing customized products and services to customers and creating a special relationship in the process is through the web. The internet is a medium that provides endless opportunities in product development, production streamlining and online retailing. It is also an excellent means of tracking consumer preferences and storing information that could be used for the future development of products and services.

The online experience that a customer has with a brand is significantly different from the offline experience mainly as a result of the lack of human presence and other sensory elements online. The lack of human contact gives an impression of a more negative rather than positive experience. However, several tools can be used to compensate for this and enhance the web experience as well as improve shopping interactivity. The same tools can also be applied in the online customization of different aspects of the brand's package.

Online customization can be done in different ways. The first is through providing customers with tools to personalize or customize whole or parts of a product. The example of the Apple iPod shown earlier in this chapter highlights this point. Another method is through providing tools for online consumers to manipulate product components such as pendants and charms of jewellery and straps of wristwatches. Other online customization means could be related to the web experience such as the choice of music type, web page background and web contents according to preferences. Currently, the online customization offerings of luxury brands are limited, mainly because the internet and e-business strategy of the luxury fashion sector is still in the introductory phase.

One of the few luxury brands that exhibit an understanding of experience customization through the internet is Italian luxury fashion brand, Roberto Cavalli. Online visitors to robertocavalli.com are ushered into a virtual space where they can choose the pages that they view according to their mood. Choices are also provided for customizable screen backgrounds and background music. Although the variety is limited to less than five choices for each category, the impact on the total web experience is high. This is a first example of how luxury brands can extend the customization of experiences online.

On the value chain, the online customization of products and services is significantly experienced in the development and retailing levels as shown in Figure 8.11.

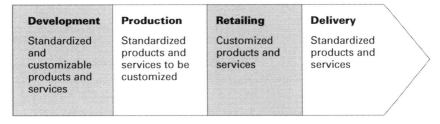

Development	Production	Retailing	Delivery
Standardized and customizable products and services	Standardized products and services to be customized	Customized products and services	Standardized products and services

Figure 8.11   *The changes in the value chain during the online experience customization of products and services*

Source: Adapted from B. Joseph Pine II (1997) *Mass Customization: The New Frontier for Business Competition.*

Note: Coloured areas indicate changes.

Method 6   allowing the consumer to customize the process

This method of customization involves close collaboration with consumers both during the product development and final assemblage stages and the retailing and delivery stages. Allowing the customer to participate in the customization process provides a total experience on every facet of the offerings of a brand. The consumer is invited to be a co-creator and an in-house collaborator and adviser in the process of designing and providing their desired products and services. This gives the customer control in the customization process and is crucial in optimizing customer satisfaction. This method also provides a deeper insight into the exact likes and dislikes of customers.

Consumer customization can be approached through providing customers with the components with which to create their end products or through proposing a choice of materials from which the product components will be created from scratch. For example, a product design could be created by the in-house design team and presented to customers through the company's website with a variety of suggested materials for whole or component parts of the products. Customers can then be allowed to 'build' the product based on the materials they have at hand. This process can be aided by interactive tools that allow customers to view the progress and eventual end product.

The shift of the product development and manufacturing process to the customer is a challenge that requires careful management. This is because it is easier to manage customers in the customization process of services than in the production process. However, the major advantage of this method is that customers that choose a total customization process have a high satisfaction rate, are likely to be loyal to the brand and contribute positively to the profitability potential of the brand.

On the service level, customers can also be allowed to make suggestions regarding how they will like to be served by luxury brands throughout their interaction with the brands. For example, sales assistants in a retail store could be trained to question customers regarding particular preferences of services that could potentially be customized.

Consumer customization requires innovation within the company as it affects every aspect of the value chain. This means a total integration of the different process aspects of the value chain, to provide a seamless customization experience. This integration could involve maintaining a high inventory of raw materials or the standardized components that would be used by customers in the customization process. It could also involve centralizing the customization process for products, services or both. The impact of consumer customization on the value chain is illustrated in Figure 8.12.

Customization must have a high quick response and production rate in order to be successful. Providing customization to the luxury mass market without making it an efficient, flawless and high-impact experience for every

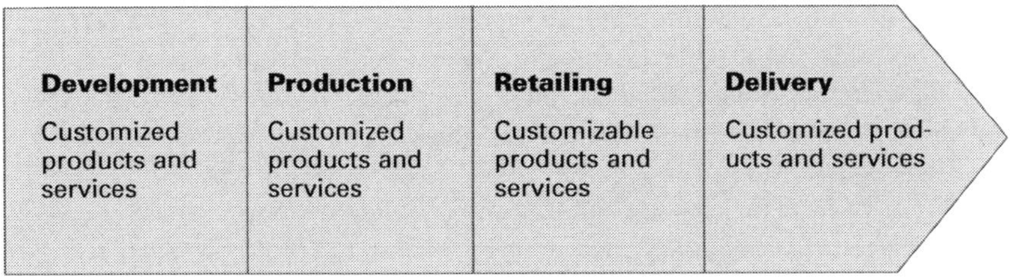

Development	Production	Retailing	Delivery
Customized products and services	Customized products and services	Customizable products and services	Customized products and services

Figure 8.12   *The changes in the value chain during the consumer customization of products and services*

Source: Adapted from B. Joseph Pine II (1997) *Mass Customization: The New Frontier for Business Competition.*

customer would be defeating the purpose of customization. Dell's customized personal computers are delivered within three days of ordering and Apple delivers the personalized iPod within two days of ordering. Luxury brands should however strive to exceed the pace of customization of these consumer goods because their consumers have high expectations. Customization is, however, not restricted to products as is mistakenly supposed by several brands, but can also be extended to services. Therefore quick response should also form a part of the service aspect of customization.

What are the challenges of customization?

The prospect of customizing products and services to a wide audience constituting of millions of global consumers is a task that holds several challenges for luxury brands.

The first major challenge of mass customization is the transformation and integration of the complete internal organization for mass customization. This is a challenging task as it involves a complete change of operations systems and processes as well as the reorientation of the employees to be receptive to customization. It also involves the absorption of the different functional units involved in the customization process and the separation of specialized resources and dynamic boundaries. The luxury brands that seek to implement a successful mass customization strategy must first launch an internal change process that involves every employee, department, unit, function and process being attuned towards a relentless focus on the individual customer and their personal needs. This is no easy task.

The second major challenge that luxury brands could encounter in the process of mass customization is the issue of ethics in retail marketing. This is related to customer data collection methods and use. Mass customization involves interaction with consumers on an individual level, with an implication of the exchange of vital personal information such as name, age, contact details, marital status and other key personal data. The information is often stored in a database with the aim of being retrieved when required, to track the customer's shopping habits and preferences. It can further be used to tailor products and services to the customer.

The key ethical issues related to sensitive personal data are the methods of collection and the methods of execution. Several luxury brands wrongly collect and store consumer data without informing or obtaining permission from the consumer. There are numerous cited cases when customers have been surprised to find their personal details being retrieved from the database at a luxury store's counter. Although luxury brands recognize and respect the personal data protection act, this does not justify the storage of the personal data of consumers in an internal database without permission. It is both unethical and goes against the laws of permission marketing. Consumers should choose to have their personal information stored in a company's system and not have it imposed on them. Also the relationship with the brand is strengthened when consumers willingly make their personal data available to luxury brands.

Ethical marketing also extends to the ways that consumer personal data are used. In most cases, the information is retained in-house and used to design products and services that would appeal to customers. In some other cases, the information is passed onto third parties that often partner with luxury brands in consumer data exchange and tracking. In this case, the luxury consumer sometimes receives unsolicited marketing messages from different companies. This is both tacky and a complete consumer turn-off. It also diminishes the image of the luxury brand.

The strategic objective of customization, whether offered to a narrow luxury market or to a mass luxury consumer base, is to increase customer satisfaction, improve brand loyalty, foster stronger customer relations and increase sales and profitability. Therefore mass customization and bespoke services should form an important part of every luxury brand's strategy, package and communications. If offered in a timely and uncomplicated way, customization has the potential of being an asset to luxury brands.

Chapter 9
The luxury fashion business strategy model

'A stand can be made against invasion by an army; no stand can be made against invasion by an idea.'

Victor Hugo, French writer and poet (1802–85)

It is perplexing to find out that when several practitioners in the luxury goods management are questioned about their business strategies or business models, they often look puzzled. The majority of these managers perceive business models and strategy plans as documents drafted by consultants to be filed away and reproduced during the annual reporting exercise. A senior executive of a luxury brand once told me that if I were interested in evaluating their business strategy plan, he would not hesitate to send a copy of the 'Strategy' to me. When I asked him the main features of the strategy plan, he replied, 'How could I know? I am occupied everyday with managing the company, I don't have enough time to read the Strategy Report.' It was my turn to be puzzled. For this manager, the company's strategy, (which by the way is its lifeline), was represented by a pile of papers stored in a drawer to be retrieved when a Consultant visited. This is part of the reality of the state of luxury fashion management.

Despite the luxury industry's aversion to business strategy development and business modelling, the sector direly needs these tools to aid its strategic direction.

The prospect of developing a business strategy model is often perceived as daunting and intellectually tasking. For this reason business modelling seems to be reserved for eyeglasses-wearing nerds who spend their lives behind a computer in smart business consultancy firms. The task of crafting a business model for the fashion industry is even more difficult to envision. This is because of the wide credence that the creative and business development aspects of fashion are incompatible.

This chapter aims to provide a simple view of business strategy development as a complement to fashion designing. The business modelling process is presented in an easy-to-understand format, even for the most creative minds. If you've enjoyed reading this book so far, you will discover that this chapter will be no less interesting than the rest of the book.

What is a business strategy model?

A Business Strategy Model in simple terms is a graphical representation of the elements, processes, plans, tactics and all the features that make up the direction that a company follows in executing its activities. It comprises features that are identified after the assessment of several factors. These features are also some of the elements that would normally be found in a Business Plan of a start-up company. However, the factors are designed to be useful to both old and new companies. These factors include **external environmental** characteristics such as the consumer and competitive markets, the economic and political climate and the socio-cultural economy among several others.

Additional features shown in the business strategy model could be related to the **microenvironment** of the business. The microenvironment normally addresses issues that affect investors and shareholders, customers and employees as well as alliances, associations, suppliers and distributors. This level also comprises a competitor analysis and an evaluation of the overall sector trends.

An additional analysis required in developing business models is related to the **internal environment.** At this level, a company evaluates its in-house competences and capabilities. This evaluation also involves the assessment of the company's human resource capabilities, its internal business processes, its financial shape and its overall strengths and weaknesses. These factors determine the potential execution viability of the chosen strategies.

Other aspects that are considered in developing business strategy models are the tools and techniques used in the implementation and control of the strategies; and the indicators that will be used to measure the company's performance, post-implementation.

The analysis stage of the business strategy model development forms the first part of the exercise. This is followed by the identification of the strategic issues and challenges bordering on the operations of the business. These issues include problems that the company and/or sector currently face or are likely to face in the future. They could also include sector-wide influences or issues related specifically to the company in question.

Since every company is unique and every sector is different, it is not possible to find two identical business models. The levels of business environments analysed in business strategy modelling are shown in Figure 9.1.

Business models act as guides in the planning and development stages of

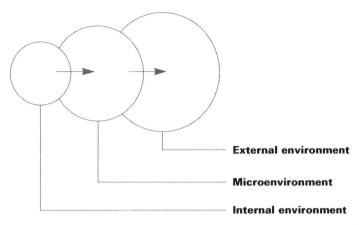

External environment

Microenvironment

Internal environment

Figure 9.1   *The environmental analysis levels of business modelling*

any business venture, irrespective of sector. They are also useful for companies that intend to expand, restructure or re-align their business approaches to suit changing market needs. A business strategy model can be compared to a road map. When a driver embarks on a new journey, he needs a map to guide him. In some cases, the driver might have travelled down that road in the past but there might also have been several changes and even new routes since his previous trip. This calls for the road map. Without a map, the driver would be likely to get lost or arrive at his destination later than he would have done with the assistance of a map. This scenario is applicable to every business including luxury fashion brands. Without the map, which in this case is the business strategy model, luxury brands would find it tough to advance in the marketplace.

The business strategy modelling process

As indicated earlier, business models are brand-specific because every luxury brand has features that make it unique and different from others. This means that the process of developing a business model for luxury brands and companies in other sectors ought to be flexible in order to accommodate company-specific features and market changes. As a result, the process of crafting a business strategy model for the luxury industry shown in this chapter is not a strict and inflexible magical tool but is aimed at providing a general direction. The identified features in the business model presented are aspects of the luxury goods industry that affect the majority of luxury brands to varying degrees. The business modelling exercise can be applied by both old and new luxury brands.

The recommended procedure for business modelling is as follows:

1 Evaluate and understand the current situation of the brand and the company.
2 Identify and define existing and/or potential problems the company is facing or could face. This is summed up as the Strategic Challenge.
3 Formulate a set of alternative business strategies that could solve the strategic challenge and analyse them. This will lead to the recognition of one of the strategies as a viable alternative.
4 Create a Plan for the implementation of the recommended strategy(ies). This involves checking internal competences and resources.
5 Identify performance measurement indicators to check the progress of the implemented business strategies.

Each of the six identified steps will now be tackled. A unique graphical shape will represent each step.

Level 1: evaluate and understand the current situation

The current situation of a company is the complete overview of the Internal, Micro and External aspects of the business. This includes the features of the **internal organization** such as:

- The company's core competences. They are the distinctive features that only the company possesses, which make it unique and dynamic and create competitive advantage in the long run. These inherent and specific attributes could also include a combination of integrated and applied knowledge, skills and attitudes, which competitors cannot easily copy.
- The company's competitive leverage, i.e. the factors that give the company an edge in the marketplace. This could include size, financial position and market position.
- The company's Key Success Factors (KSF), that is those actions that the company has taken so far that has earned it success and advancement in the market.
- The company's strengths and weaknesses.
- The company's manpower and core capabilities.
- The company's organizational structure, culture and management style.

The current situation leads to an assessment of the **micro environment** of the company. This evaluation should normally include the following features:

- A thorough consumer market analysis, i.e. understanding who the consumers are, what their key characteristics and demographics are, where they are, what factors influence their buying decisions, what their expectations are and what their future evolution is likely to be.

- An exhaustive analysis of the competitive market, i.e. identifying the company's competitors, where the company stands relative to the competitors, what the strategies of the competitors are and what changes are likely to affect the competitive environment.
- An evaluation of the connected facets of the company such as its manufacturers and suppliers, alliances, partners, associations, trade relations and investors. The factors connected with these groups that will likely affect the business should be identified.

The final assessment aspect of the current situation involves the **external environment**, whose features include the following:

- A comprehensive analysis of the socio-cultural environment and how it currently affects or is likely to affect the business. This involves tracking societal trends and evolutionary factors such as the influence of culture, globalization, advanced technology and international travel on the global consumer society.
- An evaluation of the economies of the markets where the company operates and how the economic performance affects consumer responses to the company's products. The key connecting issues here would be related to the average disposable income of consumers, the gross domestic product (GDP) of the economy, the rate of inflation and deflation and the level of consumer credit, borrowing and expenditure. These features often affect the buoyancy and spending attitudes of consumers towards luxury goods.
- A thorough analysis of the political and legislative climates of the markets where the business operates. This includes the stability of the governmental structure and their influence on consumers and retail activities, through legislation regarding commerce. This factor affects consumer confidence and attitude towards luxury goods.
- An exhaustive analysis of the technological factors, which are likely to affect the company and its business. This includes advanced technology systems of commerce and new communications media such as the internet and digital television.

The identification of the environmental features above ought to be followed by a re-evaluation exercise, which often spots further distinctive elements that affect the business significantly. These are the elements that will be represented on the business strategy model.

Since the business strategy model is represented graphically, a shape has been chosen for each feature of the level of the current situation analysis.

Level 1: current situation

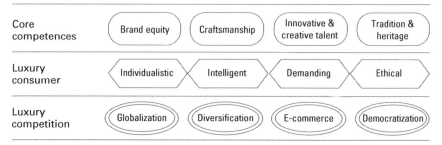

| Core competences | Brand equity | Craftsmanship | Innovative & creative talent | Tradition & heritage |

| Luxury consumer | Individualistic | Intelligent | Demanding | Ethical |

| Luxury competition | Globalization | Diversification | E-commerce | Democratization |

Figure 9.2 *The current situation analysis level of the luxury fashion business model*

Figure 9.2 shows some of the identified features that could appear on this level of the business strategy model of a luxury brand.

Level 2: identify the strategic challenge

This level of analysis features the existing and/or potential problems the company is facing or is likely to face in the future. A luxury company should normally have a set of current business problems or potential problems that act as a challenge. Some of these problems would have been uncovered during the current situation analysis in Level 1. Others might be spotted through identifying what competitors have missed in their strategy development.

In order to spot a luxury company's major strategic challenge, it is wise to list all the identified problems or potential problems and analyse them singularly. This exercise will usually provide an insight into other hidden problems, however minor. It might also lead to the identification of a new set of problems. In this case, the set of problems should be prioritized according to their impact on the business. It usually reveals a major strategic problem with connected features to other minor problems. The major problem is summed up as the Strategic Challenge. For example, a luxury brand might discover that it is losing its market share, while not necessarily declining in sales or profitability. The reason for the loss of market share might be that the brand's competitors have adopted new channels of distribution like e-retail, thereby tapping a new extended market of luxury consumers. In this case, the strategic challenge of the brand would be the adoption of e-commerce.

Figure 9.3 provides a graphical representation of some features of the strategic challenge.

Level 2: strategic challenge

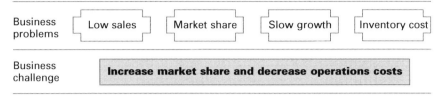

Business problems | Low sales | Market share | Slow growth | Inventory cost

Business challenge | **Increase market share and decrease operations costs**

Figure 9.3   *The strategic challenge level of the luxury fashion business model*

Level 3: formulate and analyse the strategy alternatives

The third level of the business modelling process involves identifying the tools to address the already spotted business problems and major business challenge. At this level, a set of realistic options of alternatives should be identified to solve the major business challenge and also address the minor problems. These options should be evaluated, using the pros and cons criteria. The strategy alternatives should also tackle the competitive market factors and provide the luxury company adequate leverage above its competitors. The strategies should also be aligned to provide the best output to fit with the characteristics and expectations of the consumers already identified on Level One. The analysis of the strategic business alternatives will often lead to the recognition of one of the alternatives as the most viable option. The proposed alternative must be justified with a clear statement of reasons for its choice.

Figure 9.4 provides an indication of some of the features that could be found at this level of the business strategy model of luxury brands.

Level 3: formulate and analyse the strategy alternatives

Strategy alternatives | E-commerce | CRM & ECRM* | Expansion | CSR**

Proposed strategy | **E-commerce adoption**

*   Customer relationship management and electronic customer relationship management
**   Corporate social responsibility

Figure 9.4   *The strategy formulation level of the luxury fashion business model*

Level 4: implementation plan

Level 4: implementation plan

Implementation criteria		Risk	Cost	Time	Total
	Strategy one	XX	XX	X	XXXXX
	Strategy two	XXX	XXX	XX	XXXXXXX

Figure 9.5   *The implementation planning level of the luxury fashion business model*

The fourth level (Figure 9.5) of the business strategy modelling process involves the development of an implementation plan for the chosen strategy option. The plan features connected factors such as a risk assessment, the cost of the strategy plan, the required execution time-frame, the potential success or failure rate and a contingency plan. The implementation plan also includes a thorough assessment of the internal resources and competences for implementing the recommended strategy. The criteria for the implementation plan is not rigid but can be aligned to a luxury company's specific requirements. The chosen criteria must, however, be justified in order to be effective.

Level 5: performance measurement indicators

The final step in the business strategy modelling process is the identification of suitable performance measurement indicators that will be used to check the progress of the implemented business strategies. These indicators are often applied in the weeks and months following the adoption of the business strategy model. Their main objective is to track the progress of the business model and to identify areas of improvement.

The following are three performance measurement frameworks that address the needs of the luxury fashion goods industry (see also Figure 9.6):

1 The Balanced Scorecard
2 The 7-S Framework
3 The Brand Asset Evaluator

The balanced scorecard developed by Kaplan Norton is one of the most efficient tools in clarifying and communicating vision and strategy into action. It works from four perspectives:

(a) The financial perspective, which places an emphasis on the need for financial data as an indicator of the effectiveness of the business strategy. It also provides a means of incorporating risk assessments and cost-benefit data in the strategy implementation process.

Level 5: performance measurement indicators

Figure 9.6   *The performance measurement level of the luxury fashion business model*

(b) The customer perspective, which emphasizes the importance of adopting a customer focus and constant customer profile analysis.

(c) The business process perspective, which places emphasis on the efficient running of the internal business process and the development of appropriate metrics for competence.

(d) The learning and growth perspective indicates the importance of employee training and development as well as staff empowerment and the development of a favourable working culture.

The 7-S framework is a model developed by Value Based Management that describes how an organization can effectively manage a change process. It recognizes seven inter-connected factors that often lead to an efficient strategic change process. The factors are the following:

(a) Structure
(b) Systems
(c) Style
(d) Staff
(e) Strategy
(f) Skills
(g) Shared Values

The brand asset evaluator developed by advertising firm, Young & Rubicam is a performance measurement indicator that can be used to gauge brand value through the application of four broad factors; Differentiation, Relevance, Esteem and Knowledge. Since the brand value is a key aspect of the luxury industry, a constant check of the brand vitality and stature through this model is essential.

Connecting loops

The business strategy model provides a clear picture of a luxury brand's complete business direction. This includes an analysis of the internal and external environmental factors as well as strategic challenges and alternative proposals and their implementation tactics. The features highlighted in the

luxury fashion branding

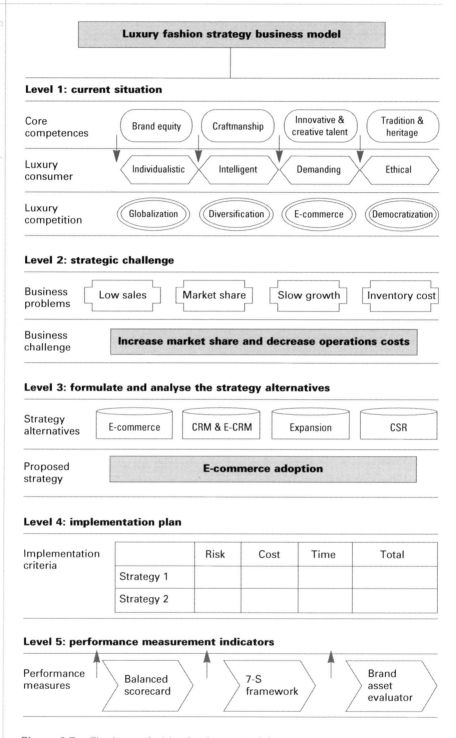

Luxury fashion strategy business model

Level 1: current situation

Core competences — Brand equity · Craftmanship · Innovative & creative talent · Tradition & heritage

Luxury consumer — Individualistic · Intelligent · Demanding · Ethical

Luxury competition — Globalization · Diversification · E-commerce · Democratization

Level 2: strategic challenge

Business problems — Low sales · Market share · Slow growth · Inventory cost

Business challenge — **Increase market share and decrease operations costs**

Level 3: formulate and analyse the strategy alternatives

Strategy alternatives — E-commerce · CRM & E-CRM · Expansion · CSR

Proposed strategy — **E-commerce adoption**

Level 4: implementation plan

Implementation criteria

	Risk	Cost	Time	Total
Strategy 1				
Strategy 2				

Level 5: performance measurement indicators

Performance measures — Balanced scorecard · 7-S framework · Brand asset evaluator

Figure 9.7   *The luxury fashion business model*

business model are not mutually exclusive but are inter-connected and have an organization-wide impact. For example, the proposed strategies should be incorporated with consideration of the current strategies of the company and its competitors as well as the environmental factors. Another crucial element in the strategy modelling process is the relationship between the proposed strategies and the core competences. The core competences directly address the needs of the consumers and are considered the root of the strategy formulation process. Therefore the business strategies should be in congruence with the core competences to ensure feasibility. This guarantees that the proposed strategies are implemented without sacrificing the real values and strengths of the company.

The complete business strategy model for the luxury fashion sector is presented in Figure 9.7. It indicates the inter-relations and inter-connectivity of the different levels and features.

End notes

This chapter has highlighted the steps required in business modelling for the luxury fashion sector. As previously indicated, however, the model is not a magic tool for everlasting business success, but rather a guide that facilitates strategic direction. Its huge potential and positive impact will be most appreciated if it is applied effectively and revised frequently. This includes identifying and applying the features that are intricate to each luxury brand.

The principles of the business strategy model can be applied not only in the luxury fashion sector, but also across several industries.

Chapter 10
Case illustrations

'Tell me your story and I'll tell you your future.'

African proverb

The purpose of this chapter is not to repeat the brand stories that have been written about extensively, like the famous tale of Burberry's brand repositioning or the redefinition of mass premium fashion by Zara. This chapter rather aims to raise questions related to the main issues of luxury fashion management, using relevant brands as illustrations. So, in the following pages, you will not find the interesting history of Louis Vuitton or the great turnaround story of Gucci. You will rather find brand stories that will prod your mind, arouse your creative thinking and appeal to your business aptitude.

The brands presented in this chapter have been carefully selected, not because of their popularity or extraordinary positions but as a result of the strategic business examples they embody and the messages they offer. The analyses are purely external and independent of the brands. The case illustrations presented are the following:

1 The Armani brand extension success story.
2 The boom and bust of boo.com.
3 The effect of licencing on Pierre Cardin's brand equity.
4 Is André Ross the first twenty first century luxury brand?
5 What does Britishness mean in luxury fashion?

Case illustration 1: the Armani brand extension success story

The brand Giorgio Armani is considered to be Italy's most glamorous luxury brand. The founder and designer of the brand, Giorgio Armani, is also widely viewed as one of the most talented fashion designers in the world. He is the source of much of the brand's allure and intrigue. His personality and disposition in addition to his creative talent and business acumen have contributed to establishing the Armani brand as a global fashion empire and one of the most valuable brands in the world. Giorgio Armani is also one of only a handful of fashion designers with full control of their companies. This is

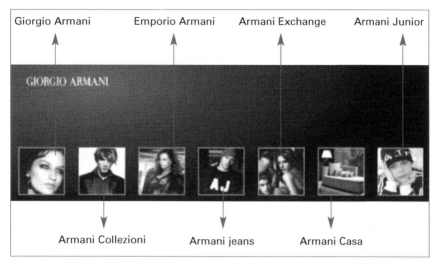

Figure 10.1   *The Armani brand portfolio*

mainly as a result of his successful blending of the delicate combination of creativity and commercial know-how. As a fashion designer and businessman, Giorgio Armani has earned a pristine reputation worldwide. He has been heralded as 'The Indispensable', 'The King of the Catwalk', 'The Fashion Maestro' and 'The Most Fabulous Italian Miracle', by the international press.

The Giorgio Armani brand (Figure 10.1) has retained unparalleled profitable status in the 32 years of its existence. In the first half of 2004, the group sales turnover was €644m, a year-on-year increase of 8 per cent. Its pre-tax profits for the same period was €89m, a year-on-year increase of 23 per cent. Recent financial records of the company shows that it has zero debts. Also, at the end of 2000, which was a boom year for the luxury sector, the company had $300 million in its cash reserves. The brand also made its debut on the annual Interbrand/*Businessweek* Top 100 Global Brands Scoreboard in 2004 with a brand value of US$2.613 billion. This value increased by 2 per cent in 2005, to US$2.677 billion and again by 4 per cent to US$2.783 billion in 2006. The brand value represents the intangible asset worth that the company accrues as a result of its brand. The brand value figure is an intangible asset that is represented minus other company assets. The company operates 300 boutiques worldwide and employs a staff of 4,800 people.

The achievements of the brand are remarkable particularly as it is fully owned by one man, Giorgio Armani. In an industry that has gravitated towards acquisitions and conglomerates, the Armani brand is an exception in leadership and brand style.

History

Giorgio Armani was born in Piacenza, Italy, in 1935. While growing up in this small town he was highly influenced by his mother's great sense of style, which would eventually lure him towards fashion and business.

As a child and student, Giorgio Armani was curious and read widely. After reading the book *The Citadel*, by A.J. Cronin, which was an account of a young doctor's work during the depression years, he decided to study medicine. He lasted three years in medical school before he grew restless. His love for creativity and fashion, which he could no longer suppress, prompted him to leave medical school to pursue a career in fashion.

His first fashion job was as a men's wear designer at Nino Cerrutti. He worked with the house of Cerrutti for eight years before establishing his own design house with his business partner, Sergio Galeotti. Their first collection was presented at a fashion show in 1974 and had an audience of only six people. Today, the brand that was humbly begun by these two men has been translated into a + €3.5 billion business and one of the best success stories in the fashion industry.

Branding strategy

The Giorgio Armani branding strategy is one of the most extensive and yet one of the most meticulously managed in the luxury fashion sector. The brand has skillfully crafted a single umbrella identity, personality and image from which other sub-brands have been developed. This is a delicate and risky venture for a luxury brand but the success that Giorgio Armani has achieved in managing a portfolio of sub-brands under the platform of a single brand is both remarkable and worth emulating.

The Armani branding strategy functions on three different levels, that have been used to craft the brand's identity and personality. It is also the tool that is applied in the projection of the brand's image to its public. The three levels are:

1 The man, Giorgio Armani
2 The parent brand, Armani
3 The sub-brands of Armani

Giorgio Armani has redefined the concept of using the power in a brand name to extend its product and brand categories. When consumers hear the name 'Armani', an image of the designer is likely to pop into their heads, followed by certain linked attributes of the brand. For those that haven't been exposed to an image of Armani (and this is rare), a collection of abstract brand associations forms in their minds. In both cases, perceptions of what the Armani brand represents is immediately developed in the mind. These perceptions are likely to be influenced by descriptive words like glamour, style, sexiness, expertise, talent, sophistication, trend and precision. These can be described as some of the elements of the Armani brand personality, which the public understands through the brand image.

These elements can also be used to describe the personality of the man Giorgio Armani because the Armani brand personality is an extension of the personality of Giorgio Armani himself. This personality comprises the overall image that consumers associate with the brand or any product or service that has 'Armani' attached to it. This means that Giorgio Armani is the brand and the brand is he. The man Giorgio Armani and everything he represents has been stretched to form the parent brand of Armani, making up the first and second levels of the Armani brand strategy previously listed. The third level of function of the Armani brand, which comprises the sub-brands, is the main essence of the Armani branding strategy.

Armani offers a luxury fashion product portfolio comprising *haute couture*, *prêt-à-porter* and children's apparel, leather goods such as bags and shoes, underwear, jewellery, fragrance, cosmetics and eyewear. The brand has also diversified into non-fashion product ranges such as cafés, restaurants, hotels, nightclubs, flowers and even sweets and chocolates. In addition, the company has varied its offering in different ways. For example, in 2003 Giorgio Armani worked in collaboration with luxury carmaker Mercedes to design a limited edition CLK Mercedes-Benz car.

The Armani brand has been stretched into seven sub-brand categories ranging from high-end to medium priced men's and women's fashion goods, children's fashion and home products. These sub-brands are aptly named the following:

1 Giorgio Armani
2 Armani Collezioni
3 Emporio Armani
4 Armani Jeans
5 Armani Exchange
6 Armani Casa
7 Armani Junior

A look at this list indicates that each of the sub-brands has 'Armani' linked to it. This means that the brand power lies in the name 'Armani' with all its associating attributes already described.

The seven main brand categories have different functions in the overall Armani branding mix. They range from women's and men's wear collections to diffusion lines that target different segments of the luxury market. The first is Giorgio Armani, which represents the most exclusive and highest priced products of the brand. It features goods showcased on the brand's runway fashion shows such as apparel for men and women, accessories, eyewear, cosmetics and perfumes. The Giorgio Armani brand is the ambassador of the Armani empire and represents its image, heritage, personality, product precision and high quality. It also generates great publicity for the entire Armani group of brands.

Armani Collezioni is the diffusion sub-brand of the Giorgio Armani range. It features products like fine tailored clothing, sportswear and male and female accessories. The product group also includes home furnishings. The Emporio Armani sub-brand is targeted at young modern-minded and fashion oriented consumers. It includes clothing, accessories, eyewear and jewellery. Armani Jeans is the denim sub-brand offering a jeans-based product category. Armani Exchange is the sub-brand for casual wear and accessories with a lower premium-pricing strategy. Armani Casa is the home furnishings and decorations sub-brand, while Armani Junior is the children's products sub-brand.

Although the sub-brands have different products targeting different segments of the luxury consumer market, the product groups however share a common feature of the Armani touch and style, seen through the signature characteristics such as the fit and finish of the clothing, the exquisite materials used for the accessories and the exceptional attention to detail given to each product. The offerings of the brand have also successfully transcended beyond fashion and propelled Armani to a lifestyle brand.

The key to the effective brand extension strategy of Armani is that the brand had an early recognition of the important role of the luxury consumer in a brand's success. While several luxury brands focused on the product as the key selling factor of their brands, Armani concentrated on the consumer and on crafting its brand based on consumer needs and characteristics. This was achieved by identifying the different luxury consumer segments that exist and designing products that would appeal to them. Through understanding the consumer segment structures and their driving needs, Armani adopted the brand extension strategy of sub-brands; and the brand diversification strategy of non-fashion categories. As a result, Armani has successfully created a high-clout brand that has revolutionalized the branding strategy of the luxury goods industry.

Although Armani has been criticised for extending its product category to include ranges that are too mass-market focused to be considered as luxury goods, for example jeans, the Armani brand-extension strategy has been successful. This is because the brand has effectively managed to maintain its superiority and high quality standards across the offerings of all the sub-brands. It has also implemented a uniform marketing mix strategy for all the sub-brands and the same level of expertise and skill to products across every range.

Another factor of the success of the Armani brand is the genius of the brand founder Giorgio Armani, both as a designer and as a businessman. He is one of the few luxury fashion designers that have successfully combined creativity with astute business sense and commercial *savoir-faire*.

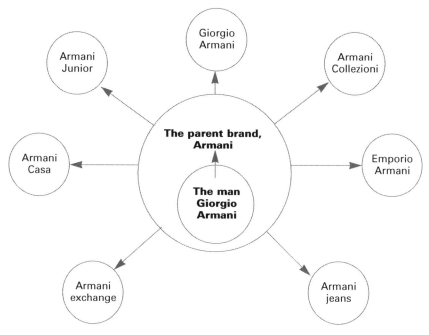

Figure 10.2   *The Armani brand extension model*

The Armani brand extension strategy has also been emulated by other brands. Louis Vuitton and Dior for example have introduced demin and sports accessories collections, although these are not sold under a sub-brand name. Burberry has also extended its brand, *à la* Armani.

The Armani brand-extension model is represented in Figure 10.2.

Marketing strategy

The Armani fashion empire currently employs 4,800 people worldwide, owns 13 factories and has 300 outlets in several countries. This feat was not achieved by accident but through carefully developed business strategies and models that have been effectively implemented. The following is a summary of the main elements of the Armani marketing strategy:

- **Product**   The Armani product range is developed under different sub-brand categories to fit with the market requirements and to address different segments of the luxury consumer market. The products however have a single unifying factor in the elements of its development. The same high level of skill, precision, craftsmanship and quality materials is applied in the development of each product, whether it is denim-based, a lamp or a pair of shoes.

- **Pricing** Armani's pricing strategy is the premium-pricing strategy. Some of the sub-brands have products in lower priced categories such as denim but the brand applies the same premium-pricing principle to all product categories in varying degrees.
- **Distribution** Armani goods are retailed through directly owned stores and selected distributors. The company's online boutique also retails selected products in the US market only. Armani also has stores at outlet shopping centers such as the company's own outlet shopping center located in Vertemate, near Como in Italy and Gucci Group-owned 'The Mall' located in Florence, Italy. In addition, Armani products can also be found at several of the Value Retail Outlet Villages such as La Vallée Village, Paris and Wertheim Village, Frankfurt. The brand might need to tighten up its product distribution to generate a higher level of brand equity.
- **Promotion** Giorgio Armani had an early recognition of the relationship between the cinema and luxury goods. He was the pioneer designer to skillfully use film to promote luxury products. The international recognition and subsequent global expansion of Armani began after the brand 'dressed' movie stars in several films. The most notable of these are the characters played by Richard Gere and Lauren Hutton in the famous Hollywood movie *American Gigolo*. This has been cited as the movie that propelled Armani to 'star' status in the fashion world. Armani has also designed clothes for more than 100 films, including *The Untouchables, Goodfellas, Father of the Bride* and *Arriverdeci Grazia.*

  Another entertainment related strategy of Armani is his use of celebrities and movie stars as artists and ambassadors of the brand. Armani hardly features paid celebrities in its print or other mass media advertisements but the brand's creations are often worn by the most talented and notable celebrities at important ceremonies such as the American Oscar Awards. Giorgio Armani also frequently collaborates with celebrities in the creation of special pieces such as apparel and leathergoods. An example is his cooperation with the actress Ziyi Zang, to create a dress for her for the 2006 Academy Awards ceremony.

  Armani's relationship with celebrities and the cinema has resulted in a wonderful chemistry with international stars and has also contributed to creating a fashion empire and turning the designer into an icon. As a pointer, in 2002 and 2003, the New York Guggenheim and the British Royal Academy of Arts put up retrospectives of Armani's work, recognizing him not only as a fashion designer and businessman, but also as an artist.

However, the long-term strategic challenge of the company is the possibility of retaining its profitable status as a one-man business in a sector that is propelled by acquisition and consolidation. Armani is one of a few luxury brands that is neither owned by a larger group nor traded publicly. This is an enormous achievement but at the same time a challenge. The brand also has the challenge of finding the right successor(s) to the 72-year-old Giorgio Armani, when he eventually retires. Giorgio Armani is a master of his craft and has created both a brand power-name and a power persona. His successor(s) will require not only an equal level of talent but also a double dose of personality to sustain the Armani aura.

Business lessons from Armani

1 It is imperative for a luxury brand that wants to remain competitive in the market to understand everything about its consumers.
2 It is possible to successfully extend a luxury brand into several sub-categories without diluting the brand equity. This strategy however requires meticulous crafting, implementation and management.
3 Brand and product stretching beyond 'traditional' luxury goods categories is a viable strategy but needs effective management and an alignment of all the brand elements across all the offerings.
4 Movie and celebrity endorsement is an effective brand communications and marketing promotions strategy.
5 The Brand Value of a luxury brand is directly linked to the total offerings of the brand and not through the accessibility of the products.

Case illustration 2: the boom and bust of boo.com

The story of boo.com, the largest global e-commerce company to collapse during the 2000 dotcom crash, is very often told in business circles, especially to highlight a significant investment error. Boo.com was a major mistake; there is no doubt about it. History has also shown that the failure of the company was more than a case of being a casualty of the emerging internet commercial sector.

Boo.com failed as a result of the adoption of several external unfeasible strategies and internal management missteps. These errors led to the misuse of US$130 million of capital investment within the two years of the company's existence. The story of boo.com is sensational, engaging, intriguing and somewhat entertaining. It is also a story that provides invaluable and relevant business lessons.

Boo.com was a pure virtual e-retail company established to retail fashion and sports goods online with an aim to eventually extend beyond an e-retailer to a lifestyle brand. The company was founded by three Swedes, who were thought to be dynamic and innovative. Their professional backgrounds ranged across information technology, poetry criticism and modelling. These are hardly the standard qualifications required in establishing a pioneer company in an emerging business sector. However, these young entrepreneurs obtained investment backing of more than £80m (approximately US$130m at the time) in cash from investors that included investment banks JP Morgan and Goldman Sachs, LVMH chairman Bernard Arnault, the Benetton family and several Middle Eastern investors.

With strong financial backing, envisaged global operations and a business concept that seemed to be eagerly anticipated by both shareholders and consumers, the three entrepreneurs went about setting up the business that was at the time aiming to be the world's premier e-retailer of high-end fashion goods and an online global brand.

Boo.com was expected to lead a market revolution and to conquer the new business channel provided by the internet. The company was launched during the period of the emergence of several start-up pure-play e-retailers also known as the dotcom companies. Consequently, the sector needed strong influential companies as a blueprint for the business channel. Boo.com aspired to fit the bill. The business community and beyond were enthusiastic about the company which was seen as the next major e-retailer after amazon.com. Prior to the company's launch, boo.com was declared to be one of Europe's coolest companies by American business magazine, *Fortune*. As a result, its stock market worth soared and boosted investor confidence. The aspiration of boo.com was, however, doomed to have a short history.

Boo.com was launched in November 1999 amidst fanfare and anticipated success. The company was headquartered in London but began with simultaneous operations in 18 countries including offices in Paris, New York, Stockholm, Munich and several other locations. Remarkably, six months later, in May 2000, these offices closed down as the story of boo.com ended as dramatically as it started. Boo.com therefore became the first major casualty of the internet era and made the number one spot on the list of the '100 Dumbest Moments in e-Business History'.

It is worth asking how such a company could fail. It is also important to establish whether Boo.com failed as a company or as a result of its activities in e-commerce.

Business concept and strategy

At the time of boo.com's launch, its founders stated the following:

> We believe very strongly that in Boo.com there is a formula for a successful business, and fervently hope that those who are now responsible for dealing with the company will recognize this.

In retrospect, it is evident that boo.com had no clearly defined business concept or strategic plan except the over ambitious plan to make the company both the largest and most sophisticated e-retailer of fashion goods in the world. Its business formula focused on developing internal expertise in Information Systems as a key success factor. The company strived to develop a complicated system that would support global trade in different currencies through multiple distribution centres from its onset. Boo.com's focal point was also to create an extraordinary web space for customers and usher them through an online shopping experience they had never witnessed. While these objectives were sound, they had no supporting strategies to back up their implementation. The business formula of boo.com was based on shallow assessments and vague strategies.

Boo.com was one of the start-ups in an emerging industry founded on innovation and advanced technology. Therefore at the time of its launch the company had no real competitors or points of reference. However, future competition was anticipated for this sector in the form of local and global e-retailers, but boo.com made no provisions to counter potential competition. There was no evident competitive edge to make the company unique and able to withstand future competition.

The company also lacked a clearly defined consumer market segment as a target. The products were aimed at consumers in the 18–30 year age group, which is a broad consumer group. This meant that the products were designed and priced to appeal to this age group. However, this target consumer segment exhibits differing characteristics in terms of tastes, choices, income and expectations. For example, the disposable income and fashion expecta-tions of 18-year-olds were hardly the same as those of 30-year-olds. Also, the company wasn't clear if its target market was the high net-worth luxury consumers or mass fashion consumers. Boo.com aspired to sell high-end fashion goods and sportswear at premium prices but its shallow business assessment and lack of market definition made this difficult.

The business concept of boo.com and its strategic plan is also not clear in the aspect of e-retail. The e-retail strategic option adopted was that of 'pure-play' e-retail only with no physical store presence. This meant a completely virtual relationship with customers. However, boo.com did not evaluate the interactive needs that selling fashion goods online required. The company designed its online selling strategies like those of consumer products and ended up merchandizing fashion goods like books.

Boo.com had a business concept that was superficial, imprecise and largely focused on marginal aspects of business development and ignored the major facets of business planning. The company was driven by its ambition for short-term gains and ended up starting a business without being ready.

What went wrong?

Boo.com was beset by problems from the start. Its launch date was postponed several times as a result of unready operational systems, and this had mone-tary and time-cost consequences. When the company eventually commenced operations, the anticlimax that followed the months of anticipation was inevitable. However, within weeks the business was already being overwhelmed with problems leading to restructuring plans that included frantic efforts at cost-cutting that led to employee dismissals.

The business mistakes that led to the demise of boo.com are discussed in the following sections.

Error no. 1: poor business planning   At its time of launching, boo.com was the largest e-retail funded company in Europe, yet the company had a poor business plan and an ill-defined business model. The company also lacked strategic direction and made its future earnings projections based on assumptions that e-retailing was a gold mine with strong growth potentials.

Boo.com was started as an e-retailer that sold fashion goods online. However, as a company it had an unclear corporate image. For example, the company spent millions of dollars on advertisements and promotions in a bid to create market awareness. However it was not clear if the advertising message was to project boo.com as a fashion brand, or boo.com as an online sales channel, or boo.com as a corporate brand or all of the above.

Also, the company had no identified competitive leverage that would have given it an edge in its market. It was unclear whether boo.com was positioned as a niche player with highly differentiated products and services, or whether its competitive strategy would focus on cost advantage, thereby providing 'value for money' goods. The competitive strategy of boo.com seemed to be stuck in the middle between high-end differentiation and low-end cost efficiency. The company failed to realize that operating in a virtual environment meant creating a distinct advantage for customers that was better than what could be obtained offline. Boo.com also did not recognize that the internet required more than appealing products and service parity. Online retailing entailed an exceptional positioning and boo.com lacked this element.

In addition, the business model of boo.com featured a poor marketing plan with unfeasible strategies. Aspects of the marketing planning such as consumer segmentation and targeting were ill-defined. The targeted consumer group was identified as young fashion consumers between the ages of 18 and 30. However, no further apparent efforts were made to determine the key characteristics of this group; the influencing factors of their consumption patterns; and their attitudes towards online shopping. The company assumed that since the consumers were young, they would shop online because the internet was a new medium that had a strong appeal to young consumers. Business investment decisions are however not made by assumption but by concrete and viable market indicators.

In addition, boo.com aimed to reach a global consumer market but the lack of the definition of the competitive positioning of boo.com made it difficult to determine if the target market was the global high-end fashion consumers or the mass-market consumers of fashion goods. These two groups of consumers have starkly different attitudes and characteristics in different global markets.

Also, the products were designed to appeal to young consumers but also lacked distinct product development features. The core differentiated features of the products were neither the type and quality of the materials they were made of nor the style and craftsmanship of their designs and finishing. There were no identified features that would have made the products unique and different from the fashion goods that existed on the high street.

The pricing strategy was also unclear as the fashion goods of boo.com were neither premium-priced nor low-priced. Boo.com aimed at selling high-end fashion goods that would be priced higher than the average high-street fashion brand but within weeks of its operations, the prices of the products were reduced through price discounting in a bid to generate additional revenue.

The business plan of boo.com featured a huge advertising budget that was intended to create market awareness and generate online shopping traffic to its website. However, the promotional tactics of the company backfired as a result of a lack of substance in other aspects of the company's overall offerings. The advertisements represented a beautifully wrapped but empty gift box.

Boo.com also placed a strong emphasis on its distribution channel, an aspect where the company aimed to develop expertise and core efficiency. However, a heightened focus on creating expert internet operational systems led to the neglect of other crucial aspects of e-retail like e-merchandizing and e-CRM and also the overall business strategy.

The company's sales forecast and future earning projections as well as the payback time for its investments were handled almost dismissively. These were all based on the assumption that e-business was the future growth area of global trade and that the return on the invested capital was assured.

Boo.com was unable to develop feasible corporate strategies to ensure the efficient alignment of technological and business development. The company also ignored the importance of using commercial reality and several attributes of physical businesses to check the viability of its business concept and development.

Error no. 2: lack of branding strategy   In order to sell fashion goods, a company needs to create a brand. It is unrealistic to try to sell fashion products to savvy consumers at premium prices without first being a fashion brand with a brand message. In order to become a brand, a company needs a clearly defined branding strategy. When fashion goods are sold exclusively online, the efforts of developing a clear brand message ought to be doubled. This is because of the lack of human interface on the internet, which makes achieving high impact and lasting impressions more challenging. Boo.com failed in creating and defining its brand.

It was unclear whether boo.com was a fashion brand or an e-retail distributor selling fashion goods on the Internet. Consumers had no set of brand attributes to allocate to boo.com. The company lacked a brand concept, brand identity, brand personality and brand image. As a result, consumers were left confused and guessing about where to place boo.com and above all what to expect from the company in terms of brand promises. There was no reference point to aid in the brand positioning of boo.com in the minds of the consumers.

Boo.com had the intention of creating a global fashion brand but it was unclear what type of global fashion brand it intended to become. Was it striving for a luxury fashion status, or a high-end premium (but not luxury) fashion brand position or a mass-market brand stance? Which brands did it intend to compete with or view as its associated reference points? What type of qualities and characteristics did boo.com expect its consumers to associate its brand with? Was it a sophisticated and glamorous brand or a cool and classy brand? Or was it not a brand at all but a company that focused on selling fashion, similar to a supermarket? Where did boo.com aim to be positioned in the mind of the consumer?

There were several unanswered questions regarding the branding of boo.com. This was a major oversight because a company that intended to succeed in the fashion manufacturing and retailing business must be a brand.

Error no. 3: weak market assessment   Boo.com showed a profound lack of understanding of its consumer and competitive markets. It failed to make an appropriate assessment of its market environment and to determine the factors that could affect its business. In this regard, boo.com made several unfounded assumptions.

The first wrong supposition was that there was a ready online consumer market waiting to shop until they drop. The company also assumed that this supposedly ready online market had continuous internet access and were prepared and sophisticated enough to purchase fashion goods online. The reality was that at the time of the company's launch, the UK, which had the highest internet penetration in Europe, had only 20 per cent of its population with Internet access. Also a large percentage of this population was still using slow dial-up connections that were incompatible with the heavy interactive features on boo.com. The case was the same in the rest of Europe, which was boo.com's principal market. The features on boo.com such as an animated style adviser, Miss Boo, were incompatible with the computer systems of consumers.

In addition, e-retail was still in its introductory phase and consumers were concerned with issues related to online transactions such as credit card security and personal data exchange. Other concerns were connected to intricate sensory aspects of shopping for fashion goods online such as the sensory requirements of touch, feel, look and fit. There were also concerns related to shipping, returns, refunds and exchanges. Since boo.com was purely a virtual company, consumers were not clear about how customer relations issues could be resolved. The bottom line is that online customers were not as savvy with technology as boo.com presumed. They were also not patient enough to wait for hours for boo.com's interactive features to load or to restart their computers when the features of the website ground their systems to a halt. The consumer market was unready for boo.com.

The second wrong assumption of boo.com was in relation to the competitive environment. Boo.com had huge capital investment backing which gave the company a lot of confidence in its leverage over competitors. However, the company wrongly identified 'supposed' competitors as book retailer amazon.com and travel and tourism business lastminute.com. These companies were channel competitors because they were virtual companies like boo.com. They were however not sector competitors because they did not sell fashion goods. Their selling strategies were different because they sold low-involvement consumer goods and services that didn't require extended evaluations by consumers. Although these companies had an online market, they were able to compete on price and service levels because of their specific sector characteristics. Boo.com measured itself against companies such as these and therefore failed to understand its competitive market.

In addition, the socio-cultural environment at the time of boo.com's launch had specific attributes that the company seemingly ignored. During the period of e-retail emergence, the consumer society was still at the stage where it was being transformed by information technology (info-tech). There were therefore several uncertainties regarding info-tech, which could not be clarified as info-tech itself was in its infancy. Unlike today, consumers of that period were not mentally and behaviorally influenced by info-tech. The market therefore needed companies that offered concrete solutions online in an easy and understandable format. Boo.com was unable to fit this requirement.

Error no. 4: over-estimated forecasts   Another major mistake made by boo.com is related to unrealistically escalated sales and consumer traffic forecasts. In this regard, boo.com made yet more assumptions that resulted in over-ambitious sales projections.

The main assumption was based on the idea that the trendy products and the savvy technology offered were good enough to attract and retain customers and also boost sales. Although the website attracted an ample number of visitors, the online traffic figures were significantly below the projections of the company. Also, only a small percentage of those that visited the website actually completed their shopping. Boo.com failed to recognize that building online consumer traffic and loyalty required time but could also be destroyed in very little time. Online consumers also exhibit certain attributes that are significantly different from offline consumers and boo.com ignored this apparent fact. For example, online consumers need a high-impact experience to retain the memory of a website in their subconscious, which would aid future recall and visits to the website. Also they are unlikely to return to a website that they were unsatisfied with and are likely to share unsatisfactory web experiences with others. The technical hitches of boo.com contributed to a more negative than positive online experience for most visitors and eventually led to the decline of consumer traffic.

Boo.com also expected a high sales turnover from inception. This did not happen for several reasons. The first is a lack of a concrete marketing strategy plan and strategic business direction. The second is basing the company's projected profitability on the 'first-mover-advantage' and ignoring other crucial aspects of the business. This unrealistic optimism was however inadequate to generate enough revenues to offset high set-up costs and make profits.

In order to increase its customer base and boost sales revenue, boo.com relied heavily on advertising, promotions and price discounting. This led to higher expenditure, lower profit margin and higher debts. The end result was that the ambitious sales forecasts were never met but led the company to its demise.

Error no. 5: managerial incompetence   Boo.com was founded by three young entrepreneurs who were dynamic in their various fields, but showed a lack of strong business skills and understanding. Their backgrounds in information technology, poetry and modelling were hardly the experience fields required to develop a global business in an emerging sector. They lacked a clear understanding of business fundamentals in strategy, marketing, finance, retailing, distribution and operations management, and as a result were unable to develop and implement a sound business strategy, required for the type and scale of operations of boo.com. This was a major problem for a company that aimed to be an avant-garde leader in a new business sector.

The managerial incompetence of the company founders was evident from the lack of focus on key strategic issues related to business planning and execution. The company's management were inexperienced in developing and implementing sound business strategies and managing funds effectively. As a result, they failed to design a business model that would assure a sustainable long-term operation. Their lack of proper business skills is also evident from the way that the initial investment capital and cash flow was handled. The company's expenditure was channelled towards several wrong undertakings, resulting in excessive spending and poor financial management.

The poor management system also permeated to several aspects of the company, leading to a profligate corporate culture that was characterized by excessive spending. Eventually, cost-cutting measures were put in place and the staff was downsized, but by this time boo.com was already on its way down.

Error no. 6: poor budgetary and cost control   During the conception stage of Boo.com, the founders estimated start-up costs to be approximately £20 million; the staff strength to comprise approximately 30 people and the operations set-up to be completed within three months. The company ended up exceeding its initial budget by spending more than four times its start-up budget by its launch date. It had also employed 400 people in its eight global offices, against the estimated 30 people. This is a typical example of a project that grew beyond proportion, indicating that the senior management lost control of the situation.

In addition to the loss of size and budget control, the senior management of boo.com also ignored the cost-control mantra that most start-up businesses adopt as a precaution against uncertain terrain. The strong investment back-up seemed to give boo.com's executives an excuse to ignore business common sense and adopt a lavish corporate lifestyle that did not discourage waste and excess. In addition, a huge budget was allocated to promotional methods such as advertising, in an attempt for quick returns and growth. This backfired on the company, as adequate budgetary allocation was not provided for the supporting business aspects of the complete value-chain system.

The lack of cost-consciousness and control by the management of boo.com coupled with the absence of a steady income stream through the projected high sales revenue contributed significantly to the failure of the business. Prior to its final closure, the company executives tried fruitlessly to raise additional funds to keep the business running. They estimated that an additional $30 million would propel the company into a clear path but their efforts were met by an uncooperative investment climate that had realized that the success potential of companies like boo.com were grim.

Boo.com's poor financial management and unrealistic extravagant spending pattern also contributed to an inefficient management of its sales revenue. In the final two months of the company's operations, its sales turnover was a mere £200,000, paltry for a company that was running operations in 18 countries. At the time of its liquidation in May 2000, boo.com had managed to spend £178 million without turning in any profit.

Error no. 7: global size operations   Boo.com launched with an ambitious plan to become the world's first and largest e-retailer of fashion goods. As a result, the company started operations simultaneously in 18 countries including its London headquarters, New York, Paris, Stockholm and Munich and several other cities. Its global operational focus meant that it had to develop and implement an international infrastructure that could handle sales in all the different currencies, secure orders and deliver clothes across the world. The company underestimated the potential complications that could arise from multi-country retail operations such as customer relations and logistics problems, taxation issues, legal implications and several other unforeseen daily problems.

The development of the back-end operations system with a platform to handle multiple currencies, different languages, country-specific tax calculation and logistics issues was no easy task. Boo.com was also the first e-retail company to launch in multiple countries from its first day of business operations; therefore it lacked a benchmark in the industry to learn from. Its size, which was intended to be an advantage, ended up being one of the factors that led to the downfall of the company.

Boo.com was in a hurry to create a market leadership position and exploit its 'first mover advantage' status and in the process ignored the important strategic and operational issues that arise from managing a global business.

Error no. 8: technical problems   The online boutique sections and indeed complete website of boo.com were full of technical missteps that turned online consumers off. The company employed graphics designers and technical experts to develop the website and these experts created and implemented a highly sophisticated website with the most advanced technology. This unfortunately is not the only requirement for e-retail. The lack of proper strategic e-business planning meant that several crucial aspects such as functionality, usability, navigation and ease of use and interactivity were almost completely compromised in favour of high-tech advanced systems.

On the features level, the website used heavy graphics and flash animations in an avatar-based style. This system required high-speed internet connection, which a large proportion of consumers with internet access at the time lacked. High bandwidth internet connections were largely unavailable at the time, and boo.com's system was too advanced for most computer systems. As a result, several of the website's pages took a long time to load and some of the pages were too heavy, leading to system crash in some cases. Also, the flash-based graphics were not pre-installed in most computers and online shoppers had to download and install the software before gaining access to the web pages. Consumers were indisposed to this as a result of the time cost and also security concerns associated with software downloads. The website would have been more effective had boo.com applied technologies that were widely used and didn't require additional software.

In addition, the website could not be viewed by online consumers using the Macintosh platform. A large proportion of boo.com's supposed consumer group constituted young people that worked in the media, design, art and graphics sectors that were fond of the Mac system. This meant that boo.com lost this consumer group because they couldn't access the website and online boutique.

On the level of functionality and navigation, the website used several pop-up windows and 3-D images that were too many for browsers to maintain track of. Shoppers literally got lost on the website with no clear way to return back to the previous pages or their starting point except closing and restarting the browsers. With new windows popping up at nearly every click, online shoppers couldn't keep track of their movement on the website and therefore felt out of control. This led to the opposite effect of one of the most important advantages of e-retail, which is to empower consumers.

The apparent confusion created by the directionless website and array of new windows was even magnified by the appearance of a window with Miss Boo, the animated online style adviser and shopping assistant. While Miss Boo commented on the clothes choices being made, four other windows were popping up showing the range of clothes being chosen from, detailed image of an item example with tools to spin and magnify the product, a Boo shopping bag with the current selection and a mannequin dressed in the clothes currently selected. In all of this, the shopper had no apparent control of what was going on. It was too much and left shoppers bewildered and confused, with no obvious direction of how to proceed with the rest of the shopping (that is, if the pages managed to load).

After a few weeks of operations, boo.com identified these problems and redesigned its website, replacing Miss Boo with a printable catalogue and provisions for offline shopping. Other modifications included a simplification of the bandwidth requirement for easy access and navigation and a no-graphics version of the website. However, the majority of the damage had been done by this time and the shoppers that previously had a negative experience with the brand were gone for good and were spreading the bad news in the process.

Although the fashionable range of boo.com's sports-oriented designer clothing was initially appealing to consumers, the difficulty of purchasing them online led consumers to seek other alternatives. The website's failure comes from the fact that the online store was incompatible with both Internet users and their computers.

What could have saved boo.com?

The story of boo.com indicates that the company largely left its performance to fate because of the high confidence and assumption of automatic success in the new e-business sector. This is a major error that indicates a lack of understanding of fundamental business issues.

Boo.com could have supported its business goals with identifying and implementing feasible strategies and including these in a solid business model. The company could also have put in place effective planning, monitoring and control of its budgeting and financial systems and assets. Other supporting aspects of the business such as the internal organizational planning as well as the front-office and back-office systems could have been better integrated and managed.

The e-business plan of boo.com was also poor and unrealistic with a focus on design and advanced technology while ignoring usability and experience enhancing features like e-CRM.

A look at Chapter 6 of this book will provide more insight into the e-retail strategies boo.com should have implemented. Boo.com would probably still be in existence if it had a strong alignment between technology, business strategy, sound management and an understanding of consumer needs and market key drivers. Its strategies and technologies were in disparity with reality.

Boo.com did not fail as an e-retail company but failed as a company which happened to be in the e-retail business. The classical mistakes made by boo.com would probably also have led to the demise of the company had it been in another business sector.

There have been several reports regarding the relaunch of boo.com. At the time of writing, a short message on the company's homepage indicates that a new website will be launched shortly. Let's keep our fingers crossed for the new boo.com.

Business lessons from boo.com

1 Launching a new business requires a solid business plan and business model. No matter how conversant the business founders are with the sector, the business plan is inevitable.
2 It is important to thoroughly understand the market environment before launching a new business, especially in an emerging sector such as the Internet.
3 Any company that desires to sell fashion goods must first create a BRAND with well-defined dimensions of Brand Concept, Brand Identity, Brand Personality and Brand Image. If a fashion company fails to do this, then they might as well be ready to become a supermarket brand.
4 Selling fashion online requires intricate strategic elements that must be implemented to compensate for the lack of human, sensory and atmospheric features found in offline stores. Chapter 6 of this book provides more insight into this.
5 The management style and leadership of a company makes or breaks the company.

Case illustration 3: the effect of licensing on Pierre Cardin's brand equity

Pierre Cardin, whose name and business has one of the highest global recognition levels in the luxury fashion sector, is not only a fashion design icon, but has also become an institution. At his current age of 85 years, Pierre Cardin has a career in fashion spanning more than 65 years. He continues to preside over a fashion empire that he built from nothing and still owns 100 per cent. He has been described as the godfather of the fashion industry and as an unparalleled revolutionary.

The Pierre Cardin fashion empire currently has 840 factories and employs more than 200,000 people in over 100 countries. It incorporates diversified fields ranging from fashion and accessories, to cosmetics, fragrance, jewellery and timepieces, restaurants, hotels and museums. Other product divisions include champagne, wines and spirits, sweets and chocolates and other consumer goods such as confectionaries and canned food.

Pierre Cardin was propelled to the global stage of fashion as a result of his high artistic talent and his innovative and often radical nature. He is a visionary who paved the way for several aspects of modern fashion business practices. He was also one of the first designers to take fashion beyond creativity, into the business sphere, through licensing agreements and diversification beyond the range of traditional luxury fashion goods. He also paved the way for the current Premium Fashion revolution led by brands like Zara and H&M, through his early quest to take high fashion to the masses.

The artistic talent and cultural innovation of the man, Pierre Cardin, has been recognized and honoured in fashion and beyond. The French government gave him several awards including the '*Legion d'Honneur*' and membership into the prestigious '*Academie Francaise*', which safeguards the French history, culture and art. Pierre Cardin is also an ambassador of UNESCO and a friend to several presidents, great leaders and innovators of the past and present century. It has famously been said that Pierre Cardin, whose company headquarters is opposite the Palais Elysées, where the French President lives, often exchanges morning greeting waves with the President from his office balcony. His influence stretches from Paris to Tokyo, Las Vegas, Moscow and beyond.

However, the mention of the name Pierre Cardin in fashion circles today conjures up several images and ideas in people. This is mainly as a result of the brand's multiple licensing strategy. The current perception of the brand Pierre Cardin has been greatly affected by the rampant licensing agreements and excessive diversification of the brand, which are viewed as a compromise to the qualities of a luxury brand. In a period when luxury brands are buying back licensing agreements in a quest to protect the brand's equity and increase its value, Pierre Cardin's licensing endorsements continue to grow beyond 900 products ranging from fashion goods to champagne, olive oil, tableware, floor tiles, toilet seats and even hospital mattresses.

These raise several questions about the extent and dimensions that licensing can be adopted by luxury brands and their potential impact on the brand's long-term equity.

History

Pierre Cardin was born near Venice in Italy in 1922, as Pietro Cardin. He was the youngest of 11 children and his father was a wine merchant who provided a comfortable life for his family. However, during the First World War, the family was forced to migrate to the south of France to escape poverty.

Pierre Cardin was only two years old. Pierre grew up in France and had dreams of becoming an actor and dancer. The Second World War however ended this dream but also brought another opportunity for him to join the Red Cross and help the military effort. There he studied Accounting, which contributed to sharpening the business skills that would guide him throughout his career in fashion.

His interest in arts and fashion led him to become an apprentice tailor in the French towns of Vichy and Saint Etienne. His apprenticeship years heightened his creative sensitivity and fashion taste and he decided to pursue a full career in fashion design. In 1945, he moved to Paris and joined the famous house of Jeanne Paquin, founded in 1891. He later worked for Elsa Schiaparelli and was also one of the first models of artist Jean Cocteau.

The talent of Pierre Cardin got him employment as the Master Tailor at the house of Christian Dior in 1946. He was in charge of producing the famous Christian Dior's 1947 New Look collection. Pierre Cardin, however, left the house of Christian Dior shortly afterwards; his departure prompted by a police investigation into a leak of Christian Dior's designs. Cardin was called in and questioned and, feeling insulted and humiliated, he left to set up his own design label. He was only 28 years old. The success of his design house was immediate. He showed his first *haute-couture* collection in 1953 and his first *prêt-à-porter* collection in 1959. Within a short time, he had a staff of 200 people and his client list included international celebrities such as Rita Hayworth and Argentina's then first lady, Eva Peron. At the height of his fame, he also dressed the famous English music band, The Beatles. He also gained global fame in the 1950s for his 'bubble dress', which led to a style revolution.

Although he trained under Christian Dior who was the couturier of the aristocratic class, Pierre Cardin preferred to lead a world of social and sexual revolutions fuelled by industrial growth and advancement. During the 1960s, Pierre Cardin's work was influenced by an outlook on the future, seen in the materials he used such as jersey, perspex and vinyl; and the styles he adopted such as graphic and geometric shapes and sharp line cuts. His style gained him a prominent leadership position among the French fashion Futurists that included Paco Rabanne and André Courreges. This style also sparked the fashion revival of the 1960s, which continue to influence today's fashion designers.

Pierre Cardin built his fashion business with his personal savings and is one of a handful of fashion designers that never borrowed from banks or investors to develop their businesses. He is known for his strong business principles and financial discipline. These characteristics were also extended to other aspects of his creative work especially the artistic rigour and meticulous attention he paid to his creations. Unlike other fashion designers of the time, Pierre Cardin was not carried away by the fame and fortune that he made in the 1950s and 1960s, when he earned one million French francs (approximately US$180,000) per fashion show. He reinvested a large proportion of his earnings into his growing business. This financial control led to the rapid growth and expansion of the Pierre Cardin fashion empire.

Today, Pierre Cardin is a multi-millionaire and one of the wealthiest fashion designers and entrepreneurs of all time. He is also one of the wealthiest men in France. He owns several homes including in Paris and Cannes, where he built a Palace with a swimming pool on every level. His riches were largely accumulated from his fashion business dealings and licensing agreements.

Corporate and brand strategy

The Pierre Cardin brand and the man Pierre Cardin have one personality and identity. There have been minimal significant conscious efforts made to separate the personality of the brand Pierre Cardin from the man himself, Pierre Cardin. Although Pierre Cardin is the owner and ambassador of the brand Pierre Cardin, the brand entity has been entwined with the personality of Pierre Cardin, his beliefs, business practices and evolution. It is quite impossible to think about the brand without conjuring up several aspects of Pierre Cardin, the man, such as his multiple licensing deals and other drastic fashion practices. As a result, the brand Pierre Cardin has no separate personality and image. The numerous products in multiple categories, which are produced by both Pierre Cardin and several licensees, also contribute to a confusing perception of the brand and what it stands for. A part of the consumer public perceives the brand as a 'high-end fashion brand', while others see it as 'a low-quality and cheap brand' as a result of the licensed products, even though the brand's own products are well-crafted and premium-priced. These unclear factors make the task of assessing the branding strategy of Pierre Cardin a challenge.

The corporate strategy of Pierre Cardin has been related to innovation and creativity both in fashion design and business approach. Pierre Cardin is a highly talented fashion designer and an astute businessman. He is an innovator who adopted several aspects of the current fashion management early in his career when they were considered as near taboos. His vision and innovative (sometimes radical) approach to fashion has led to numerous fashion revolutions such as the emergence of the premium fashion sector and other fashion retail practices like licensing, global expansion, brand extension and diversification. He was the first fashion designer to adopt several practices discussed in the following points:

- He was the first *haute couture* fashion designer to launch a ready-to-wear collection in 1959, at Au Printemps in Paris. Until then, high fashion had been exclusively for the privileged wealthy few and Pierre Cardin's attempt to take high fashion to the masses had never been heard of in the fashion world. The uproar his ready-to-wear collection created and the perceived dishonour that it brought to the luxury fashion world, led to his expulsion from the strict French governing body of *haute couturiers*, the '*Chambre Syndicale*'. Today, high fashion for the masses has been adopted by several luxury brands through diffusion lines and also by premium fashion brands like H&M, Zara and Top Shop.

- Pierre Cardin was the first to license his name to products ranging from fashion apparel and accessories to food and furniture. His democratic vision of fashion led to his first licensing agreement for men's shirts and ties. He later extended this outlook outside the fashion category in 1968 with other licences. This launched a new era of luxury fashion brand extension and designer lifestyle goods that have been adopted by luxury brands today. His licensing deals have also extended to consumer goods such as stationery and luggage. However, the licensing partnerships became too rampant and seemingly uncontrolled, leading to a loss of the brand's core equity and value.

- Pierre Cardin was the first luxury fashion designer to embark on global expansion by opening stores all over the world, including Japan, China and Russia. His fashion shows in China in the 1970s was the first by a Western fashion designer. This paved the way for the luxury fashion romance currently existing between luxury brands and the Asian market.

- He was also one of the first designers to adopt expensive and rare materials in product manufacture. For example, he was the first designer to use crocodile skin instead of leather in his accessories creation and also fur in graphic patterns. These practices have since been adopted by several luxury brands.

Licensing methods and results

The major retail strategy adopted by Pierre Cardin is licensing of the brand name to third parties in multiple product categories. The company currently has more than 900 licensing agreements in several product groups like fashion and accessories, wines and spirits, confectionary, toiletries, home decorations, furniture, restaurants and hotels, among several others. These licensing agreements span more than 140 countries. In addition to these, there are several Pierre Cardin stores which retail the designer's own fashion creations at premium prices, in different fashion cities, including his Paris home base. Pierre Cardin also owns a publishing business and the Maxim's sub-brand, which includes a restaurant and hotel chain, boat services and other goods such as champagne, confectionaries, sweets, chocolates, cigars, fruits and florists. He also has a US$20 million private museum 'Espace Cardin', in Paris. These ventures paint an unclear picture of the complete product and services portfolio of the brand and what Pierre Cardin owns and controls and what he doesn't. It also makes it difficult to position the brand and its offerings.

The products of Pierre Cardin are retailed at different price points from low pricing, discount pricing to premium pricing. They can also be found at different retail channels, ranging from exclusive stores to supermarkets, online stores and auction websites like amazon.com. These broad pricing and retailing strategies contribute to an unclear image and positioning of the brand, which has led to the depreciation of the brand's equity.

Pierre Cardin's venture into licensing deals arose from his vision of 'dressing the man and woman on the street with creative and affordable fashion goods'. He has famously said that he wants to work for ordinary people and not only for wealthy people. He also had the vision of creating a mass global luxury fashion market and influencing the lifestyle of this market through his offerings. He could also have embarked on licensing agreements as a result of dissatisfaction with the aristocratic nature of the luxury goods sector. Pierre Cardin justified the rampant licensing of his name with statements relating to his interest in bringing high fashion into the sphere of consumer goods. He also indicated that he would continue to license his name to different products, including toilet paper, because he could dress himself and his house and his lifestyle all in Pierre Cardin-branded goods. This implies that the level of consumer adoption of the brand would follow the path of the following scenario:

> A consumer wakes up in a Pierre Cardin branded bed, takes a shower with Pierre Cardin toiletries, shaves with Pierre Cardin razors, uses Pierre Cardin aftershave or perfume, dresses in Pierre Cardin from the tie to the shirt and trousers or from a dress to shoes, handbags, jewellery and wrist watches. Then he/she has breakfast of Pierre Cardin branded tea and coffee with confectionary served in Pierre Cardin tableware, while also drinking the Pierre Cardin branded bottled water. For lunch, he/she could go to the Pierre Cardin restaurant, Maxim's de Paris, and the evening could be ended with a concert at the Pierre Cardin theatre or a visit to the Pierre Cardin museum.

The reality, however, is that the luxury consumers of the twenty-first century are neither inclined to nor interested in this level of interactivity with one single luxury brand. This disposition is even heightened when it involves a brand that has ill-defined brand characteristics and parameters. Consumers are moving beyond the supposed obsession with logo-embossed products and services towards the accommodation of suitable luxury brands that have substance, to be a part of their lifestyles.

The Pierre Cardin brand image is currently more negative than positive among the luxury consumer population. The extensive licensing, brand extension and product diversification have contributed significantly to the devaluation of the brand's image. These have overshadowed the creative work of Pierre Cardin in *haute couture* and *prêt-à-porter* and relegated his innovative fashion revolutions to the background.

Among the several disadvantages that have impacted the brand image and perception of the Pierre Cardin brand are the following:

1 Loss of brand positioning. This is as a result of an unclear brand identity, increased by a lack of brand control.
2 Loss of quality control of the products, leading to low product quality, which has diminished the brand's image.
3 Multiple and uncontrolled product and services range, which has led to an unclear market positioning and confused consumer expectation of the brand.
4 Undefined pricing strategy from premium pricing for certain products to low-cost pricing and discounting for others. This has led to an unclear brand positioning.
5 Loss of retail channel control. The licensing agreements of Pierre Cardin gave way to multiple retail channels ranging from exclusive stores to supermarkets, airports, newsstands and departmental stores. This has led to the loss of the 'exclusivity' and 'prestigious' attributes that form a part of the core competences of a luxury brand.

Pierre Cardin has focused more on licensing and less on developing the brand and maintaining its luxury aura. Brand building is a long-term investment while licensing provides short-term benefits. The brand seems to have chosen the short-term option. Pierre Cardin earns approximately €6 million annually from licences, but this figure is paltry compared to the financial intangible brand asset value the brand would have accrued had it protected its brand equity in the market.

Although the brand paved the way for several modern business practices of the luxury goods sector, it has exhibited a lack of control of its penchant for licensing, which has badly damaged the intangible asset aspect of the brand. Other brands that have been through periods of rampant licensing, which destroyed their luxury image and positioning, include Gucci and Burberry. These brands, however, regained their 'luxury' status through a carefully managed process of licence buy-backs and brand re-positioning. Pierre Cardin still stands a chance to recover its once glorious 'luxury and prestige' status.

Conclusion

Pierre Cardin has indicated his intention to sell his luxury fashion empire with a price tag of approximately US$500 million. The Maxims brand is also on the market for an undisclosed amount, while other connected product lines totalling about 800 will also be sold for another US$500 million. Not surprisingly, potential buyers are sceptical about the real value of the company in terms of both tangible and intangible assets.

While the debate of the sale of Pierre Cardin continues in the fashion sector, the brand maintains its expansion focus with a recent opening of a seven-storey store in Moscow.

1 In luxury fashion, brand image is imperative and cannot be compromised.
2 A brand that aspires to attain or maintain a luxury status must have a clear Brand Concept and Brand Identity in order to create the appropriate Brand Positioning in the mind of consumers. Without these, a brand is going nowhere.
3 Licensing is always bad news for luxury brands. In a case where it is inevitable such as expansion in strictly governed markets, it should be kept to a minimum and all aspects of its agreement such as production, distribution and pricing should be tightly controlled.
4 Brand extension and product diversification are important tools in the elevation of luxury brands into lifestyle brands. However, these strategies require meticulous monitoring and careful management in order to retain and enhance the equity of the brand.

Case illustration 4: is André Ross the first twenty-first century luxury brand?

There is a general perception in the luxury goods sector that it is difficult to develop a luxury brand in the current luxury business context. Several industry insiders have also acceded that a luxury brand needs a minimum of thirty years to assume luxury status. There are numerous reasons for these assumptions. The first is the notion that history and heritage makes a brand prestigious. A second reason is the massive initial capital investment required to introduce a new luxury brand in a global market. An additional reason is that the luxury goods sector is a closed sector that doesn't easily admit newcomers.

Some of these reasons are realistic while others are unfounded. For example, a brand's history is undisputedly important and also amplifies its communication power through providing a background story that consumers are particularly attracted to. As a communications tool, history and heritage also reinforces a brand's identity and appeal. Examples of a recent emphasis on history by luxury brands include Bally's inclusion of the tag-line '*Since 1851*', to its print advertisements and products, and Lacoste's use of a picture of its founder Renée Lacoste taken in 1927, in its print advertisements. Also words like 'timeless', 'classic', 'craftsmanship' and 'genius' evoke the notion of a long history. However crucial history and heritage are in enhancing luxury brands, they are not the sole ingredients in the development of a modern luxury fashion brand.

Although history and heritage are critical in developing a luxury brand, it is time to ask if these elements are still imperative in launching a luxury brand. In other words, can history be substituted in the current luxury market?

Do consumers really care to know when Louis Vuitton was born or if Chanel died in 1991 instead of in 1971? The answer to the first question is yes, history does matter in crafting a luxury brand although in a continuously decreasing degree. The answer to the second question is no, the current consumers' interest in the launch dates and milestones of a luxury brand is declining. Consumers are more interested in a brand's relevance to them. At the same time, they appreciate other 'background stories' of the brand which increases the brand's appeal level. These stories could include a brand's association with the environment, arts, culture and entertainment. The current luxury consumer is also interested in brand stories related to ethics, morality, corporate social responsibility and other ways that the brand provides substance. These stories are however most effective when complemented with those related to skill, craft and history.

The second reason for the credence that it is nearly impossible to develop a luxury brand in the twenty-first century is the need for a high level of initial capital investment, which might be a constraint to several designers. This factor previously contributed to the existence of a high entry barrier in the sector although this has been lowered. Other reasons are the increasingly high failure rate of new brand launches, which currently surpasses 60 per cent, and the saturation of the fashion market with products found in both the luxury goods and mass fashion categories.

However, the luxury goods market has undergone several changes that dispel these traditional beliefs related to the development of new luxury brands. The most notable is the lowering of the previously high entry barrier into luxury fashion, which existed for centuries. Although high capital investment is still required to set up a luxury brand, notably in product development, manufacture and retailing, several communications and technological breakthroughs such as the Internet have contributed to decreasing the costs of entry and distribution. The Internet and other communications tools have also shortened the time requirement for a new brand to gain market awareness through providing instant and uniform information to a global market. Also, advanced operations system techniques and product manufacturing outsourcing have immense impact on cost reduction.

As a result, several luxury brands have emerged in the last decade among the multitudes of fashion brands that are launched annually. However only a small percentage of them make it as recognized luxury brands. Among the successful new luxury brands launched in the last fifteen years are British brands Jimmy Choo and Stella McCartney and French brand Paul & Joe. This decade has also witnessed the launch of several luxury brands and the subsequent failures and disappearances of a large portion of them. The difficulties these new brands face include a high level of competition and miscomprehension of the evolving luxury consumer and modern market structure. In addition, the emergence of large conglomerates with growing power, influence and independence in the sector poses a problem for independent brands.

Other factors are high media advertising costs and the application of feasible business strategies. Also new product failure rates are dramatically rising and product life cycles have become shorter, making operations management more challenging.

In the face of all these factors, it might seem that new luxury brands are doomed to fail. However, new luxury brands have a high success potential if they apply suitable business strategies. The most important tool a new luxury brand currently requires is a crisp clear Brand Concept and a well-defined Brand Positioning as the platform for developing the other aspects of its business strategy. A new brand which possesses these qualities and stands out from the rest is French brand André Ross. The brand has a potentially successful future as a result of its relentless focus on integrating high creativity and advanced business techniques.

History

André Ross is a French luxury fashion accessories brand that produces and retails highly crafted luxury leather goods. It is considered to be the first truly French luxury brand of the twenty-first century and is also one of only two true luxury brands that have emerged from France in the last ten years. The brand's origin is France and its foundation is built on the specialized fashion savoir-faire of the artisans on Paris' Rue Saint Honoré, where the company is based.

The brand was formed to design, produce and retail exclusive luxury fashion accessories made by skilled artisans with a distinction in rigorous high standards, contemporary designs and exquisite craftsmanship. The brand name is taken from that of its Founder and Creative Director and is a mixture of the French forename (André) and American surname (Ross).

Figure 10.3 *Andre Ross spring/summer 2005 product collection and autumn/winter 2005/2006 advertisements*
Photography by Sara White Wilson

The idea of creating luxury and prestige fashion accessories for a broad consumer group, which André Ross provides today, was sowed in 1998 when Ross recognized the growing market potential and need for fine bespoke luxury accessories. He teamed up with a business partner and set up an atelier in Paris manufacturing only made-to-order goods for a highly select clientele. As their orders and waiting lists grew, their business inevitably expanded. This prompted the skilled craftsmen to review their business practices and strategies and the result was the expansion of their bespoke luxury accessories business to accommodate a larger proportion of the luxury consumer market. They launched this new business as André Ross in 2004.

Brand concept

The André Ross brand has its foundation in designing and producing highly-crafted bespoke products for a highly sophisticated clientele. This bespoke heritage base has been transferred to the production of a range of accessories for a broader luxury consumer group. This simple proposition that bespoke luxury accessories can be made available to a wider luxury market forms the essence of the brand.

This brand core was developed from the recognition that the world's fashionable women invest in stylish accessories that combine fine materials with intricately crafted hardware. For this reason, André Ross' products are made using luxurious leather and fine materials, accompanied by hardware coated in high-quality solid 23-carat gold.

André Ross has also made its brand synonymous with product customization through providing bespoke goods for a broad customer base. This brand strategy is highly relevant in the current global luxury market as it is an effective means to addressing the luxury consumers' increased demand for individualism and recognition.

Despite its relatively young existence, the products of André Ross are sought-after and collected by luxury connoisseurs and an elite consumer group. The brand's consumers are also known for their devotion and loyalty. These results are from a well-defined brand concept and positioning; and an effectively managed brand strategy. André Ross recognizes branding as one of its core competences and therefore makes branding the springboard of all its strategies.

Products and retail

André Ross also places great emphasis on its product development as one of its key success factors. The products are designed through internal creative talent and external consultants and designers with outstanding experience. In some aspects, such as hardware production, the brand also partners with ateliers and matelliers with proven *savoir-faire*. This production flexibility provides the brand with the ability to easily adapt to changing consumer needs.

The workmanship reflects handcrafted traditional know-how as each André Ross product is assembled by hand. Several products in the range have also remained under the bespoke collection. For example, the Luxury Fur bag collection of autumn/winter 2005 was a limited edition of 40 pieces.

The brand uses materials that possess the greatest possible strength and reflect a perfect fusion of traditional leather-making and technical triumph. Each of the products is made with hand-selected materials and completed with lavish fittings. The products also feature the distinctive André Ross logo with the signature 23-carat gold plated hardware on the exterior and butter soft lambskin lining on the interior. The individualized bespoke bags often come in solid 18-carat yellow or white gold hardware.

Other product features of the *prêt-à-porter* range indicate distinctive qualities such as a soft suede lining that can be pulled out for cleaning, a turn lock for extra security, screwed down buckles for longer wear, individual serial numbers and a lifetime guarantee. The brand is also the pioneer of the Haute Couture Index Item code (HDII) which is a mark of quality and authenticity for each product.

The retail strategy of André Ross is both innovative and revolutionary. The brand adopted the Reverse Positioning strategy in its retail development, as a result of its understanding of the nature of the global luxury market. This strategy features an implementation of strategies that are often contrary to the structural techniques of an industrial sector. Luxury brands have traditionally followed the technique of opening up stores in the major fashion capitals like Paris, Milan, New York and London and then expanding the retail network afterwards. André Ross, however, adopted a strategy contrary to this by launching its first retail store in the lucrative Asian market, Hong Kong, and then expanding its global retail network from there. Although the brand maintains its bespoke ateliers and overall product development in France, it used the Asian market as a launch-pad for its extended global retail network. This strategy is highly feasible in the current luxury market context as the Asian market has the potential of becoming the world's largest luxury market.

Companies often adopt the reverse positioning strategy in markets that are either currently undergoing an evolution or those that require new practices. The strategy is often a challenging and sometimes risky venture. The key to the success of the strategy is timing, as this strategy only works if implemented at the right time to a ready consumer market. In the case of André Ross, the strategic implication of this tactic is the use French *savoir-faire* and heritage to tap into the high-yielding Asian market.

An additional viable retail strategy that André Ross has adopted is e-retail through its website, andreross.com. The brand is one of only a few luxury brands that have effectively implemented e-retailing for a global luxury market. Unlike several luxury brands that currently feature limited products that are distributed to a few markets, André Ross retails its complete product range to a global market. The brand maintains and protects its brand aura online through a website that is highly functional, aesthetically pleasing and exudes a luxurious atmosphere. The products are also retailed through exclusive boutiques in Paris and New York, with planned expansion in other key markets.

Conclusion

André Ross is one of the few new luxury brands that is neither owned nor funded by a large conglomerate or other corporate investors. It is also one of a handful of luxury brands that is completely and privately owned by a single person. The brand's founder and owner, André Ross Blencowe, is both a visionary businessman and a talented craftsman. This combination of skills is one of the core potential success factors of André Ross.

Although the brand has set off on the right footing and headed in the direction of success, its longevity will depend on its continued adoption of viable strategies that can sail it through the rife luxury business environment. Only time will tell if André Ross will maintain its position as the first true luxury brand of the twenty-first century.

Business lessons from André Ross

1 It is possible to launch a new and successful luxury brand in the twenty-first century, without a long history and despite the high failure rate of new brands. This is as a result of several factors including the lowering of the high entry barrier into the luxury sector and info-tech. The cost of success, however, comes high, as the brand not only needs exquisite products but also a solid business and branding management system.

2 New luxury brands must highlight their brand core and use this as their key selling points and success factors. André Ross' brand core is its *savoir-faire* in designing and manufacturing bespoke goods, which is featured in every product and every communications about the brand.

3 New luxury brands must have extremely high quality, well-crafted and desirable products with differentiating factors that should set them apart from the old brands.

4 The key to a successful new luxury brand is to act like an old and new brand at the same time. This means implementing all the strategies used by old luxury brands such as tightly controlled distribution and directly owned stores; and at the same time, adopting modern business techniques like e-retail and brand equity management.

Case illustration 5: what does 'Britishness' mean in luxury fashion?

There has always been a silent credence that the traditional luxury fashion arena belongs to France and Italy. This is perhaps because of the special affinity these two countries have had with fashion as an intricate part of their cultures for centuries. This fact is apparent from the host of the current major global luxury fashion brands originating from France such as Louis Vuitton, Chanel, Yves Saint Laurent, Christian Dior, Chloé, Hermès and so on; and from Italy such as Prada, Gucci, Armani, Versace, Dolce & Gabbana, Bvlgari, Valentino and so on. In the same way, the major influential global fashion capitals have often been regarded to be Paris, Milan, New York, London (in this order) and recently Tokyo, once again indicating the prominent positions of the French and Italian cities. As a fashion city, London has been viewed for a long time more as an important luxury retailing centre, than as a city that influences fashion. However, the current luxury market context challenges these preconceptions as Britain is continuously playing a significant role in the development of the modern luxury fashion goods industry.

Historically, designers from France and Italy ruled the global luxury fashion scene for a long time, while the rest of the world silently obeyed their creative outputs and have also been in awe of the products of their highly artistic machinations. The art of 'high-fashion' branding belonged to these two countries, just as Switzerland has been the home of the craft of watchmaking for centuries. However, the American fashion branding uprising from the 1960s to the 1980s brought a change to the luxury fashion scene with the emergence of brands like Donna Karan, Ralph Lauren and Calvin Klein. Although several American brands have yet to attain the 'luxury' landmark according to European definitions, a distinct place has been created for the Americans in the global luxury fashion arena. Just as the American brands strive to make a mark in the global fashion scene, several British brands have also embarked on a luxury fashion branding revolution.

The British traditional fashion style is characterized as conservative and ceremonial while from a modern perspective, it can be described as quintessential and elegant. Somehow, the rest of the world does not naturally ascribe the attributes of fashion creativity, sophistication, chic and *art de vivre* to Britain. This perception could perhaps be historically justified (or not) but the current global luxury fashion-branding scene indicates the high influence of Britain in defining luxury fashion style, design and business direction.

Britain has always used fashion as a platform to express different aspects of its society through the styles and attitudes of its consumer public. This was exemplified by Mary Quant, Biba and Ossie Clark during the pop culture revolution in the 1960s and the punk uprising of the 1980s. The current sophisticated consumer culture also amplifies this fact. Today, the popular street culture and several aspects of art, literature, history and entertainment including music, blend to result in a style that can only be described as quintessentially British. This style has been given several names including 'Boho', 'Bohemia' and 'Vintage' and all point to the existence of a fashion manner that originates in Britain.

In addition to the consumer style, Britain also has an enormous amount of creative fashion design talent. Several of these designers wield unmistakable high influence on the global luxury fashion scene. They include the talented men's tailors of London's Saville Row, who established a fashion tradition at the beginning of the twentieth century; and the highly prominent designers of major global luxury brands. Notable among these are John Galliano at Christian Dior, Ozwald Boateng at Givenchy, Matthew Williamson at Pucci, Christopher Bailey at Burberry and Phoebe Philo who was the Creative Director of Chloé until 2006. The influence of the British fashion talent has never been more apparent in the history of luxury fashion as now. This is hardly a surprise, after all, the first inventor of *haute couture* and first fashion entrepreneur, Charles Frederick Worth, was an Englishman.

The British fashion influence has been propelled by globalization and convergence of consumer lifestyles through increased mobility and communications. This has blended the tastes of fashion consumers worldwide, leading to the creation of channels of inspiration for fashion designers and entrepreneurs. This evolution has resulted in the emergence of new British luxury fashion brands such as Alice Temperley, Stella McCartney and Anya Hindmarch; the re-emergence of old luxury brands like Burberry and Mulberry; the reinforcement of established brands like Vivienne Westwood and Nicole Farhi; and more interestingly, the appearance of luxury-fashion entrepreneurs such as Tamara Mellon, the founder of Jimmy Choo. Just as America did, Britain has also embarked on a luxury fashion branding revolution.

British luxury brands have shaped a unique place for themselves in global luxury fashion, through an understanding of the requirement of both high imagination and creativity in product design and a solid entrepreneurial flair in retail and brand management. This is one of the keys to their successful re-entrance into the luxury-fashion arena of the twenty-first century.

As a country with a deep root in education, Britain has some of the best fashion schools in the world. Notable among these are Central Saint Martin School of Fashion, London, which has produced talented designers, including John Galliano, Alexander McQueen, Stella McCartney and Zac Posen. In the past however, the talented graduates of the British fashion schools were often forced to find their fortune abroad, notably in France and the United States, as a result of minimal funding and support at home. Examples of these designers are Norman Hartnell who was the dressmaker to the Queen of England, and Zandra Rhodes who dressed the English royal family and the stars of the 1970s and 1980s. These designers were tremendously talented yet they never made any real money in Britain. This is because at their time, the British culture did not promote fashion as serious business, despite its great textiles companies, which supplied apparel to the major global fashion brands.

Today, however, the story is changing and bountiful examples attest to this; Stella McCartney left Chloé Paris to launch her very own successful brand; Alexander McQueen has a flourishing luxury brand; Ozwald Boateng's brand was already thriving before he joined Givenchy as the head of the men's wear design team. Also, Matthew Williamson's own design label is prosperous, while John Galliano's *haute couture* designs continue to be sought after by celebrities and the world's wealthy. Jimmy Choo is another notable British brand that has achieved a global cult following in a decade of existence. Other notable British designers include Alice Temperley, Hussein Chalayan, L.K. Bennett, Philip Treacy and Stephen Jones. Among the rising British designers are Osman Yousefzada, Clare Tough, Christopher Kane, Richard Nicoll and Roksanda Ilincic, Marios Schwab, among many others. Several of these emerging designers are now able to receive financial support and funding to launch their fashion brands from institutions like The British Luxury Council. This shows a change of attitude towards fashion. Consequently Britain is today known as not only a country of history, tradition, literature and education but also one that nurtures fashion talent.

These talented individuals represent a revolution that is taking place in the luxury fashion scene, which has its underlying strength in understanding the current consumer market needs and aggressively striving to fulfill them. The majority of the designers also have a rare combination of creativity and entrepreneurship, which is lacking in high doses in the fashion business. The rise of the British fashion designers has also significantly contributed to the lowering of the previously high entry barrier of the luxury goods sector. Also, British brands represent more than 70 per cent of the new luxury brands launched in the last fifteen years. Through this, the British luxury brands have defied the popular belief held by several luxury practitioners that it takes a minimum of thirty years to build a successful global luxury brand. The achievements of British luxury fashion brands lead to the following question:

Are there branding lessons to be learnt from the British fashion brands?

The following brand fundamentals form a part of the key success factors of the British fashion brands and should serve as directional tools for both young and new luxury fashion brands.

1 Innovative brand development strategies in product design and communications. For example, Jimmy Choo adopted celebrity endorsement as a core brand-awareness and appeal-development tool.
2 Product and services personalization and customization, which contributes to customer empowerment and satisfaction, brand loyalty and enhanced

relationships. For example, Anya Hindmarch used product customization as a launch pad for the luxury accessories brand.

3 First-Mover-Advantage through recognizing a gap in the luxury fashion sector and moving swiftly to fill it. For example, net-a-porter.com launched one of the first successful luxury fashion e-retailing businesses.

4 Luxury Fashion Intelligence through the provision of market information and sector analysis. For example, the pioneer industry Journal Publication dedicated to the practitioners in the luxury sector is British-owned '*Luxury Briefing*', which major luxury brands subscribe to. The journal, which was created by James Ogilvy in 1996, when the management aspect of the luxury goods sector was directionless, serves as the background brain of the industry. *Luxury Briefing* also organizes several events where management ideas are exchanged and these events are among the most important in the luxury goods sector.

5 A vibrant, ever-growing and highly creative luxury-retailing arena. For example, luxury departmental store Harvey Nichols has expanded beyond the shores of Britain; Harrod's remains a luxury retail institution; and several other luxury retail departmental stores like Selfridges and House of Fraser continue to exercise great innovation in their retail and selling strategies.

6 Personal branding of talented fashion designers and entrepreneurs as a tool to elevate the fashion label. For example, the name and personality of Tamara Mellon has become synonymous with Jimmy Choo in the same way that Alexander McQueen, John Galliano and Stella McCartney have been with their brands.

Other key success factors have also contributed to the rise of Britain as an important associate of the luxury fashion arena. The first factor is the British luxury consumer, who can be described as trendy, affluent and has a deep appreciation for luxury goods. As a result, brand consciousness is a part of the consumer society. The fashion consumer market is also larger than most European luxury consumer markets. There are 2.4 million individuals in the United Kingdom that make up the 'affluent' target market for luxury retailers and suppliers. These consumers have annual family incomes in excess of £60,000 and live in properties valued on average at over £220,000.

Also, the UK's economy is the most vibrant and stable in Europe, resulting in high consumer confidence. The positive economic climate has also created a buoyancy of consumer credit. In addition to this, immigrants from India, Pakistan, Africa and the Caribbean have contributed to shaping the British national culture and identity. Their influences have affected the styles, tastes and product preferences of the entire country. This setting has created a prolific atmosphere for old brands to flourish and for new luxury brands to emerge. Several of the newly emerged luxury brands have prospered because they deliver a sense of exoticness to luxury consumers.

Figure 10.4   *Some of the key factors of the British luxury fashion revolution*

The British luxury market is also thriving as a high retail revenue genera-tor of famous brands from other countries. As a result, the country lives up to its reputation as 'a nation of shopkeepers' and has emerged as the European leaders in fashion retail. Luxury retailers like Harrod's, Selfridge's, Harvey Nichols, John Lewis, Debenham's and House of Fraser hold a large share of the European luxury retail market.

Another key success factor of the British fashion revolution is the utiliza-tion of the power of marketing intelligence and intellect in branding. Anyone who is conversant with branding knows that branding is a powerful concept that resides in the mind of the consumer and not on a piece of company docu-ment. The leading luxury goods industry journal, *Luxury Briefing*, which originates from Britain, provides relevant and highly specialized market information and analysis on key issues in the sector. Another notable publi-cation is the *High Net-Worth* magazine produced by Ledbury Research, London. The business approach of these companies provides an innovative contribution to luxury fashion branding and intelligence.

Figure 10.4 indicates the key factors that British luxury fashion brands utilize as a strategic guide and leverage to outperform competitors.

Conclusion

While the French brands have maintained an outlook on fashion as an art form that must be guarded and treasured, British brands view fashion as a business venture that is sustained by artistic talent and business innovation. The British brands therefore develop and apply their corporate strategies accordingly, while recognizing the core competences of the sector such as creativity, skill and brand development. These varying approaches raise an important question.

What is the current luxury consumer and competitor market requirement?

The current extremely competitive luxury marketplace calls for the highest form of innovation in brand management strategies and in product creation and development. This implies aggressive effective business strategies, a relentless focus on satisfying consumers and an unparalleled level of creativity in product design. A balanced combination of these factors contributed to the immense success of the world's first fashion entrepreneur, Charles Frederick Worth, who was British. There are several business lessons to be learnt from his story, detailed in Chapter 2 of this book.

Although British brands may lack the long history of luxury brands like Hermès and Prada, and fashion may not be a part of the British heritage, and the British government may not support the fashion industry as the French and Italians do, a definite place has been carved for Britain in the modern luxury fashion scene. As a pointer, the Metropolitan Museum of Art, New York, recognized this and organized an exhibition devoted to the creative contributions of Britain to the world of fashion in 2006.

Business lessons from the Brits

1 The previously high entry barrier of the luxury sector has been lowered and it is now possible to launch a successful global luxury brand within a short time period.
2 A new brand doesn't need a long history of fashion and cultural assimilation to conquer the twenty-first century fashion market.
3 The role of country of origin in the luxury fashion is declining.
4 Modern fashion management requires constant innovation in product design and business management systems.
5 There is power in sector knowledge and this power can be used as a core aspect of the strategy formulation process and competitive leverage.

References

Chapter 1

Clifton, R. *et al.* (2003) *Brands and Branding*, London: Profile Books.
Doyle, P. (2002) *Marketing Management and Strategy*, Harlow, Essex: Pearson Education Ltd.
Kapferer, J. (2004) *The New Strategic Brand Management*, London: Kogan Page.
Burberry.com
Gucci.com
Vuitton.com
Ninaricci.com
Givenchy.com
Hm.com
Dior.com

Chapter 2

Arogundade, B. (2000) *Black Beauty*, London: Pavilion Books Ltd.
Ball, J. D. and Torem, D. H. (1993) *The Art of Fashion Accessories*, Panama: Schiffer Publishing.
Cawthorne, N. *et al.* (1998) *Les Grands Moments de la Mode: Evolution du Style*, Courbevoie: Editions Soline.
Clifton, R. *et al.* (2003) *Brands and Branding*, London: Profile Books.
Cosgrave, B. (2000) *Histoire de la Mode*, Paris: Carlton Books.
De Marly, D. (1990) *Worth; Father of Haute Couture*, New York: Holmes & Meier Publishers.
Edition Taschen, *Fashion, Une Histoire de la Mode du XVIII au XX siècle, Volume II: XX siècle*, Paris.
Ewing, E. (1992) *History of 20th Century Fashion*, London: B. T. Batsford Ltd.
Jimminez, J. B. (2002) *Picturing, French Style, Three Hundred Years of Art and Fashion*, Alabama: Mobile Museum of Art.
Kirke, B. (1998) *Madeleine Vionnet*, San Francisco: Chronicle Books.
McDowell, C. (1997) *Histoire de la Mode Masculine*, London: Thames & Hudson Ltd.
Milbank, C. R. (1989) *New York Fashion, The Evolution of American Style*, New York: Harry N. Abrams Incorporated.
Mulvagh J. (1988) *Vogue: History of 20th Century Fashion*, London: Penguin Group.
Mulvey, K. Richard, M (1998) *Decades of Beauty, The Changing Image of Women, 1890s–1990s*, London: Reed Consumer Books Ltd.

Ribeiro, A. (2002) *Dress in Eigtheenth Century Europe*, New Haven and London: Yale University Press.

Ribeiro, A. (1995) *The Art of Dress: Fashion in England and France, 1750–1820*, New Have and London: Yale University Press.

Steele, V. (2003) *Fashion, Italian Style*, New Haven and London: Yale University Press.

Wikipedia.com

Historyofashion.com

Made-in-italy.com

Trendwatching.com

Eu.art.com

Artpictures.co.uk

Courtworth.com

Kipar.org

Art.com

Metmuseum.com

Chapter 3

Keller, K. (2003) *Building, Measuring and Managing Brand Equity*, New Jersey: Pearson Education.

Schiffman, L. and Kanuk, L. (2004) *Consumer Behaviour*, New Jersey: Pearson Education.

Tungate, M. (2005) *Fashion Brands: Branding Style from Armani to Zara*, London: Kogan Page.

Businessweek, 24 October 2005. Time Style & Design supplement, Spring 2004, 2005, 2006.

Luxury Briefing, February 2006.

Luxury Briefing, November 2005.

Luxury Briefing, July/August 2005.

Luxury Briefing, June 2005.

Newsweek, 15–22 May 2006.

Time Style & Design, Summer 2005, 2006.

Time, 8 May 2006.

The Economist, 4 March 2004.

The Economist, 24 May 2003.

World Wealth Report by Merrill Lynch and Capgemini.

Euromonitor, Global Market Information Database.

Harpersandqueen.com

Style.com/vogue

Vogue.co.uk

Chapter 4

Dennis, C. and Harris, L. (2002) *Marketing e-Business*, London: Routledge.

McGoldrick, P. (2002) *Retail Marketing*, London: Mayfield Books.

Luxury Briefing, February 2006
Luxury Briefing, November 2005
Luxury Briefing, October 2005
Luxury Briefing, July/August 2005
Harperandqueen.co.uk
Style.com/vogue
Vogue.co.uk

Chapter 5

Aaker, D. (1991) *Managing Brand Equity*, New York: The Free Press.
Allérès, D. (2003) *Luxe: Métiers et Management Atypiques*, Paris: Economica.
Brassington, F. and Pettitt, S. (2003) *Principles of Marketing*, Harlow, Essex: Pearson Education Ltd.
Clifton, R. *et al.* (2003) *Brands and Branding*, London: Profile Books.
Dennis, C. and Harris, L. (2002) *Marketing e-Business*, London: Routledge.
Doyle, P. (2002) *Marketing Management and Strategy*, Harlow, Essex: Pearson Education Ltd.
Kapferer, J.-N. (2004) *The New Strategic Brand Management*, London UK and Sterling Virginia: Kogan Page.
Keller, K. (2003) *Strategic Brand Management: Building, Measuring and Managing Brand Equity*, New Jersey: Pearson Education Ltd.
Sicard, M.-C. (2003) *Luxe, Mensonges & Marketing*, Paris: Pearson Education Ltd.
Solomon, M., Marshall, G. and Stuart, E. (2006) *Marketing, Real People, Real Choices*, New Jersey: Pearson Education Ltd.
Tungate, M. (2005) *Fashion Brands: Branding Style from Armani to Zara*, London: Kogan Page.
Time, Style & Design, Spring 2004, 2005, 2006.
Time, Style & Design, Summer 2006.
Luxury Briefing, October 2004.
Luxury Briefing, April 2005.
Luxury Briefing, June 2005.
Luxury Briefing, July/August 2005.
Luxury Briefing, October 2005.
Luxury Briefing, November 2005.
Luxury Briefing, February 2006.
The Guardian, 17 Feb 2006.
Business.guardian.co.uk
Chloe.com
Coty.com
Diesel.com
Dior.com
Furla.com
Gucci.com
Guccigroup.com
Hermes.com

Hm.com
Interbrand.com
Jimmychoo.com
lvmh.com
richemont.com
luxury-briefing.com
News.independent.com
Prada.com
Samantha.co.jp
Style.com/vogue
Valuebasedmanagement.net
Versace.com
Vuitton.com
Ww2.wpp.com

Chapter 6

Chaffey, D. (2002) *e-Business & e-Commerce Management*, London: Prentice-Hall/Financial Times.

Chaston, I. (2001) *e-Marketing Strategy*, London: McGraw-Hill.

Chicksand, L. and Knowles, R. (2002) 'Selling "Look and Feel Goods" Online', IBM E-Business Conference, Birmingham University, UK.

Dennis, C., Fenech, T. and Merryllis, B. (2004) *E-Retailing*, London: Routledge.

Dennis, C., Harris, L. (2002) *Marketing the e-Business*, London: Routledge.

De Kare Silver, M. (2001) *E-Shock: The New Rules*, London: Palgrave Macmillan.

Engel, J., Blackwell, R. and Miniard, P. (2005) *Consumer Behaviour*, Belmont: South-Western College.

Lauterborn, R. (1990) 'New Marketing Litany: 4Ps Passé; 4Cs Take Over', *Advertising Age*, 1 October New York.

Mohammed, R. Cahill, A., Fisher, R. and Jaworski, B. (2002) *Internet Marketing: Building Advantage in a Networked Economy*, New York: McGraw-Hill/Irwin.

Nielsen, J. (1999) *Designing Web Usability: The Practice of Simplicity*, Berkeley: New Riders Press.

About.com
Alexandermcqueen.com
Andreross.com
Anyahindmarch.com
Armani.com
Bluefly.com
Chanel.com
Coach.com
Designerimports.com
Dior.com
Elizabethhurley.com
Eluxury.com
Fendi.com

Fiorezi.com
Forbes.com
Glam.com
Gucci.com
Hermès.com
Imrg.org
Jimmychoo.com
Johngalliano.com
Landsend.com
Lying-awake.com
Neimanmarcus.com
Netaporter.com
Prada.com
Rafellonetworks.com
Robertocavalli.com
Royalelastics.com
Trendwatching.com
Valentino.com
Versace.com
Vuitton.com
Yoox.com

Chapter 7

Silverstein, M., Fiske, N. and Butman, J. (2004) *Trading Up: Why Consumers Want New Luxury and How Companies Create Them*, New York: Portfolio Books.

Tungate, M. (2005) *Fashion Brands: Branding Style from Armani to Zara*, London: Kogan Page.

Time, Style & Design, Spring 2004, 2005, 2006.

Time, Style & Design, Summer 2006.

Luxury Briefing, July/August 2004.

Luxury Briefing, June 2005.

Luxury Briefing, July/August 2005.

Luxury Briefing, September 2005.

Luxury Briefing, October 2005.

Luxury Briefing, November 2005.

Financial Times, How to Spend It, May 2006.

Chapter 8

Gilmore, J. and Pine II, J. (2000) *Markets of One*, Boston: Harvard Business Publishing.

Pine II, J. (1997) *Mass Customisation*, Boston: Harvard Business School Press.

Tungate, M. (2005) *Fashion Brands: Branding Style from Armani to Zara*, London: Kogan Page.

Luxury Briefing, February 2005.
Luxury Briefing, July/August 2005.
Apple.com
Anyahindmarch.com
Chanel.com
Ermenegildozegna.com
Levi.com
Polo.com
Robertocavalli.com
Vuitton.com

Chapter 9

Balmer, J. and Greyser, S. (2003) *Revealing the Corporation*, New York: Routledge.
Hamel, G. and Prahalad, C. (1994) *Competing for the Future*, New York: Wiley.
Harding, S. and Long, T. (2003) *MBA Management Models*, Hampshire: Gower.
Joyce, P. and Woods, A. (2001) *Strategic Management, A Fresh Approach to Developing Skills, Knowledge and Creativity*, London: Kogan Page.
Kapferer, J.-N. (2004) *The New Strategic Brand Management*, London: Kogan Page.
De Wit, B. and Meyer, R. (2004) *Strategy, Process, Context, Content: An International Perspective*, London: Thomson Learning.
Valuebasedmanagement.net

Chapter 10

Luxury Briefing, February 2006.
Luxury Briefing, April 2006.
Luxury Briefing, September 2005.
Luxury Briefing, June 2005.
Challenges magazine 7–20 July 2005.
Emerald Group Publishing Limited
Lexis Nexis Database
Andreross.com
Amazon.com
Armani.com
Boo.com
Emeraldinsight.com
Financialtimes.com
Newsweek.com
Pierrecardin.com
Vogue.co.uk

Index